AN ETHICS FOR THE AFFLUENT

Peter L. Danner

UNIVERSITY
PRESS OF
AMERICA

University Press of America, Inc.

P.O. Box 19101, Washington, D.C. 20036

Printed in the United States of America

Library of Congress Cataloging in Publication Data

Danner, Peter L
An ethics for the affluent.

Includes bibliographical references and index.
1. Social ethics. 2. Wealth, Ethics of. 3. Middle classes--United States. I. Title.
HM216.D26 174 80-5528
ISBN 0-8191-1163-5
ISBN 0-8191-1164-3 (pbk.)

Acknowledgment

No man is an island and no thought is exclusively one's own. To acknowledge my indebtedness to all whose insights have inspired my own would be impossible. Yet clearly there are some who deserve special expressions of gratitude: to the Society for Values in Education whose post-doctoral grant gave me the time to initiate this project; to Marquette for financial aid and more importantly leave time to continue it; to many colleagues at Marquette and in the Association for Social Economics whose brains I shamelessly picked; to the students in my courses whose questioning forced me to seek better answers. Among so many I must thank a few by name: Audrey Lemanske and especially Sue Hambel for their competent typing and their tolerating my many rewrites; Robert Ashmore, Jonathan Boswell, Brian Brush, Lowell Dunlap, Theodore Marburg, Richard Roberts and George Rohrlich for their constructive and encouraging criticism.

Finally I wish to thank *Thought* for permission to use my article, "Moral Dimension in Modern Credit", Winter, 1973 which became substantially Chapter Eight, and Sheed & Ward for permission to quote lengthily from Karl Rahner's *Christian in the Market Place*.

TABLE OF CONTENTS

AN ETHICS FOR THE AFFLUENT

INTRODUCTION

An Ethics for the Affluent is intended for undergraduates who accept in a general way Judaeo-Christian ethical values. Its subject is ethics as applied in economic relations, and its orientation is personalist. The book is offered in the hope of helping students lay a foundation of ethical principles as they prepare to take fully adult roles in the economy, not only as managers and employees but also as householders and citizens.

Unlike most business ethics texts, the moral problems and issues encountered in business will be treated here as auxiliary and illustrative to the central concern of personal moral formation. Even less so is the text directed toward analysis of corporate social responsibility, albeit such considerations loom importantly in the thinking of those who are concerned to square their corporate duties with their moral convictions. Least of all, is the text a blue-print for social and institutional reform or revolution. Rather it addresses the element prerequisite to the viability of social and institutional reformation -- formation of one's own attitudes, practices and principles.

The student will immediately recognize how this approach differs from typical discussions of ethical issues in business journals, newspapers, and even in other courses. There the emphasis usually is on how to make "them" act morally -- them usually being corporate entities -- and what laws or reforms in practice are needed to make "them" behave responsibly. In such commentaries it is almost taboo to suggest that personal morality and personal responsibility are factors in society's malfunctioning. Yet students -- and the public generally -- are not so naive as to believe that the millions, who find themselves in reformatories and prisons, before divorce courts and in abortion clinics, in asylums, and in drug- and alcohol-induced accidents, had no choice and responsibility in their difficulties. However "society" may be at fault, people recognize the personal element in all such tragedies.

Students today, more so than students of my generation, have not been isolated from moral evil or moral tragedies. Often, they can cite their own or the experiences of people close to them. In summer and part-time jobs they have been exposed to injustices and other conduct offensive to their ethical sense. Their problem is seldom lack of awareness of evil, but the opposite, a vague foreboding that the world beyond commencement expects conduct quite at variance with principles taught in college.

It is for them this book is written. But it promises no tidy solutions to future moral problems, for the simple reason that such answers are seldom made to order. There is no moral dilemma in which two persons, equally of good will, will choose exactly the same course of action. Rather and more modestly, the book proffers some economic, business, and ethical insights as aids in the student's developing his or her own moral attitudes and patterns of decent human behavior. Having thus set an overall tone and tenor to one's life, it is hoped, a person would be more alert to knotty moral issues when they arise, better disposed to seek counsel, and better prepared to work out reasonable resolutions.

More basic than justifying a personalist ethics is answering why the need for an economic ethics. For the title imports that there are ethical problems which arise from being affluent and are, therefore, peculiar to the affluent. Most students at this stage in their lives would be inclined to say that sex, drugs, and alcohol pose more serious moral problems. They will concede, however, that they feel great and sometimes unmanageable pressure to maintain grades, to finance their education, to be accepted into professional or graduate school, and to find that first job. Yet this pressure, in a broad sense economic, is only a foretaste of a greater and more varied economic pressure to come.

The justification for an economist writing ethics, therefore, rests on the premise that the economic aspect has, justifiably or not, a more prominent place in contemporary living, and economic issues are more urgent than in times past. The anomaly, of course, is that this urgency results not from industrialized economies' failure to feed, clothe, and house people but from their very success in doing so abundantly. A theme running through this work is that for the affluent their economic abundance may impoverish their lives.

That this statement will recall for most readers scary headlines about the limits to growth, energy shortages, unemployment, job alienation, costs of pollution, and the like highlights the prominence of economic worries in our lives, despite the fact that, even with no growth, industrialized economies would provide a plane of living the highest in the history of mankind. Quite to the contrary, the impoverishment referred to is more ontological, the danger, because of excessive concern for material well-being, of losing sight of our well-being as total persons.

When this ontological poverty is addressed by social critics, their criticism too frequently is directed against affluence itself, often following this disjointed logic. "We really do not possess as much economic well-being as economic statistics imply. Even if we did, free-enterprise economics, because of the dynamics of freedom and growth, will inevitably self-destruct. In any case, since freedom and material well-being are incompatible, they do not bring happiness and people will only abuse them." In short, the fashion in secular wisdom is that economic abundance is illusionary, not particularly desirable, and can not be entrusted to people.

Counteracting both the popular and the critical pessimism requires delicate balancing. Agreeing with popular convictions against the social critics, the book maintains that economic abundance is good, that having it is better than not having it. Indeed, it is optimistic that, barring cataclysm, the present generation of students will continue to enjoy increasing abundance. At the same time it acknowledges the truths in current social criticism that economic abundance has not lived up to people's expectations of it, that it has not brought happiness or allayed strife among men, but rather increased dissatisfaction, envy, and contention. Whereas contemporary secular wisdom will fault economic abundance and the greater freedom it grants, the book seeks the failure of affluence in our unreasonable expectations and misuse of economic abundance.

This approach is not likely to set well with contemporary secular wisdom. For it provides cold comfort to that attitude which excuses personal self-seeking, greed, and sensuality on the basis that society and its institutions are out of joint and need reform. Indeed the book tends to be somewhat tolerant of social and institutional dysfunctioning. It is inclined to locate such dysfunctioning in the excessive demands of people upon institutions. Even structurally inadequate institutions can function, given their constituents' good will. Finally, the moral tone of institutions and society reflect the moral tone of people. In short, our institutions are largely what we make them. If institutions need reform, we need reform.

This frankly personalist emphasis goes further in insisting that dysfunctional and even unhealthy institutions do not alleviate us of our moral responsibility. Even in, indeed especially in, such situations hard moral decisions must be made, and a personalist ethic is necessary. In this very general sense, the life of modern man differs little from that of his forebears. Life has always been a pilgrimage between the unknown before birth and the unknowable after death. It is a time of trial and error, punctuated by our biases, mistakes, miscalculations, inadvertencies, and inadequacies. Reforming the institutional context of life will not remove all life's contingency, ambiguity and unpredictability.

MAN AND ACTION

Obviously, a personalist ethic implies a philosophy of man, a view of man as a particular kind of being existing under particular conditions. It would be pretentious to choose any one philosophy of man among all the differing explanations of man's nature and ultimate destiny. We need only consider the facts of common experience from which all philosophizing about man begin. Man is one, yet both material and immaterial; he is self-conscious and purposive; he is related to other people.

Man is a material system, an individual vortex of matter, drawing in and emitting the air, water and minerals in which he is immersed and by which he is sustained. Man is rooted in the here and now in the deeper sense that all knowledge and sensation have their origin somehow from contact with his material environment. Yet man is not fully explained by his materiality, for he is aware that his beginning and ending are distinct from his material surroundings. Knowing himself as distinct, a person also knows himself as related, to material things for sustenance and knowledge and to other persons like himself for love, understanding, mutuality of feeling and purpose.

Man is purposeful, that is, he is creative. Not only can he imagine what does not exist, but he can order material things to bring his dreams into being. Though dependent upon his physical and social circumstances, he can transcend them in ordering his experiences toward goals only hoped for. This is at the heart of the human paradox: man is tensed between what he is and what he would be. The intimate bonding of the physical self to man's self-aware and purposeful self is manifested in his emotional and neurological make-up. It is a two-way link. The person can marshal physical forces to effect an action. More frequently the body's spontaneous responses to stimuli condition, and sometimes dictate, a person's actions.

Thus the human being is a marvelous and marvelously complex being, coming in all shapes and sizes, varied alike in physical appearances and capabilities, in interest and purposes, and subject to a variety of ills and failures. Each is a world onto himself and yet each is an authentic expression of human nature and is potentially open to all humaneness. Just as the person is many-faceted, so his action is a blend of many elements, each reflecting an aspect of the human condition and each adding its accent to the action. Every act has a material and biological aspect because the human person is a physical organism. Every act is social, directly or indirectly, because every human being exists related to others. Every act is political at least in this minimal sense that it is lawful or unlawful, and economic in that it involves the use of scarce material goods, time, and energy. Every act is psychological, relating to what the 'I' is, ethical in relating to what the 'I' should be, and religious, in the broad sense of affirming or denying a meaning which transcends the present. In the same sense every act can be viewed as healthful, aesthetic and the like. Indeed, the simplest act like eating is a multi-faceted blend of many elements.

Each element adds its necessary note to the whole, yet each is distinct in impact and origin. Some are instinctive like physical and biological responses; some require careful cultivation like moral and intellectual habits; some are evocations of ontological yearnings like the hope for a better life. They constitute, consequently, a hierarchy, some relating to man's higher purposes, some to animal survival. While they are so blended that none can be omitted without impairing the whole, nevertheless, one or the other element may predominate. Buying a new automobile, for example, is material, biological, political, social, moral and so forth but it is called an economic act because that aspect predominates. Indeed, one aspect may completely overwhelm the others: the animal fear of fire for instance, may cause one to jump to his death.

This notion of action as a blend of many elements is key to the argument of the book. But for that we need a word with a more dynamic connotation. The better term is 'principles of action', used in its root sense of origin, source, or spring of action, and not in its more usual secondary meaning as a general formulation about the nature of a subject of study such as in 'principles of economics'. The idea wanted is more like the Aristotlean formal and material cause, the effective components of a thing, what makes a thing what it is. For our interest in the principles of action lies in their dynamic blending together in the human act and more precisely in how a change in one principle modifies others and thus changes the action.

An example may help. An opera is a blend of many elements, libretto, music, acting, staging, financing and the like, each with its own skills and effects on the whole. Suppose the director changes the staging from a simple, intimate setting to an elaborate one. That change will modify how the arias are sung, how the acting projected and, most certainly, how the financing is achieved. In effect, there emerges an entirely new presentation of the opera. In the same sense our actions change when their principles change.

ARGUMENT AND FORMAT

The argument of _An Ethics for the Affluent_ begins with the anomaly mentioned earlier that, despite the material bounty enjoyed by affluent people, economics looms as a very worrisome element in their life. Further examination of the anomaly suggests that affluent people have experienced a slight but decisive change from _wanting_ more material goods and income to _expecting_ more. This heightened expectation is called, lacking a better name, the _affluent attitude_ and signalizes a change in the economic principle of action. Since tracing the effect of this intensified economic concern upon all the principles of human action would balloon the book monstrously, it focuses more narrowly on the impact of the affluent attitude on those principles central to man's moral development. In short, the book argues that possessing economic abundance makes a difference in the way people act and, therefore, affluence differentiates the moral context of the affluent from that of the non-affluent.

Two comments are apropos to this examination. The

study involves little economic analysis as ordinarily understood and does little to push back its frontiers. Rather the emphasis will be on using the common fund of economic analysis as descriptive of general behavioral tendencies -- as principles of action. This will entail some reorientation from viewing economics as just an analytic tool kit for problem solving to seeing it as a valid insight into one aspect of human conduct. As such, the student is warned, economics comes with its own particular -- many say, peculiar -- meaning to words, sharply differentiated from their use in common parlance. Care in using words like scarcity, cost, value and the like with their precise economic meanings will avoid much needless semantic confusion.

The second comment relates to the conviction that economists and moralists of the past, even though they had little experience with affluence and none as a mass phenomenon, nevertheless, have much to say which is relevant today. Scholars over thousands of years have hammered out some understanding of the principles of human conduct, and it is senseless to jettison this heritage without testing its applicability to contemporary living. The book will regularly summarize the development in the history of human thought of key analytic concepts.

The format of *An Ethics for the Affluent*, therefore, is determined by this one factual conclusion, that the affluent attitude is real and makes a difference, and the one conviction, that the past has much to tell us about ourselves today. The agenda for Part I begins by examining affluence and the affluent attitude and their effects on contemporary living, drawing out first their implications for economic relations. It then pursues this change in its effects on Value-espousal and personality development; on the moral principles of moderation and justice as they apply to wanting and using wealth; and, finally, on the religious significance of wealth as means to an ultimate human destiny. Concurrently, these chapters attempt the more important task of showing how these principles can direct the affluent attitude away from self-destructive excesses to purposes enhancing and enriching our humanity. The value of the book may arise solely from its reaffirming that material well-being is a means not the end of the good life.

Then in Part II we will apply this complex of principles to those issues arising from the distinguishing features of an abundant economy; the moral legitimacy of the corporate aggregate as a new form of social property; the moral implications of modern credit; the need to find new and more flexible links between labor income and labor productivity; the question whether personal freedom and responsibility can survive amid vast power structures; and the new relations between the economic and political orders. A last chapter will summarize by laying the ground rules for blending ethical and economic principles in daily decisions.

In summary, An Ethics for the Affluent is written with the conviction, that whatsoever the problems, to be affluent is better than not to be affluent. It is almost quixotically optimistic that with the help of the wisdom of the past, we have the wit and the patience to find sense and meaning in affluence, and that, however difficult the attaining, the very effort forms the substance of a good life.

It will not provide a blue-print for remaking the world, but at best a survival kit in a moral wilderness. More hopefully it will examine those principles by which we can act reasonably in our economic relations and live decently with others. Thus it aims at a middle ground between stoical passivity and revolutionary zealotry.

The work starts from the obvious fact that the world is as it is and that people are as they are. There is no way of stopping the dynamics of history or remaking the human race before one can do anything. One must act and bear the consequences of acting in today's world and not in some figment of a social planner's imagination. And today's world is constantly changing, its social values are in flux, and ambiguity is the context for much of contemporary living. Thus this book affirms that in examining the principles of human behavior, one can see their inter-relations and from this fashion a more and more integrated set of attitudes and convictions by which to achieve meaning from the flux of events. Furthermore, it affirms the personalist philisophy that this is the only human and effective way to achieve institutional and social reform.

At the very outset, however, the student is warned that this is no pollyannish enterprise. Ethics is not simply a matter of good will. Its issues and inter-relationships are complex and demand intellectual effort. It requires a humble recognition that many issues have no definitive answers. It requires courage, not heroism but the more difficult daily decision-making which determines a life pattern. For following principles makes one vulnerable to the self-centered and selfish, and appears wishy-washy to the bigot or zealot. Principled persons are seldom aware of their strength, nor do others acknowledge it except by an imperceptibly increasing reliance on them.

Given the problem, purpose for tackling it, and a format, let us get on with it.

CHAPTER ONE

AFFLUENCE AND ECONOMIC ABUNDANCE

Whatever ills the U.S. economy suffers -- inflation, recessions, environmental degradation, income maldistribution -- it provides for our material wants abundantly. We enjoy plenty of food, commodious housing, easy travel and communication. It supports a large part of the total population, children, students, the retired and those receiving welfare who make little material contribution to its productivity. Students, for example, will spend more than a fourth of their allotted years of life before they contribute to as much as they draw from the economy. This in conrete is the meaning of economic abundance: we possess material well-being well beyond a meager survival. It may not be much to celebrate, but celebrate it we can.

People who are reasonably secure in their enjoyment of economic abundance are called affluent. Affluence, considered only as possessing economic abundance, is not analytically noteworthy. Being affluent becomes significant only if it makes a difference in how people think and behave. The contention in this first chapter is that being affluent, especially in a society which is affluent, causes a slight but significant shift in one's economic attitude. Instead of simply <u>wanting</u> more material goods and income, the affluent <u>expect</u> more, that is, they want with some degree of confidence and aggressiveness.

It is not a difference which is quantitatively measurable. Nor does it entail a psychological change such that a person could say, "Yesterday or last year, I simply wanted but now I expect." Indeed most students today would have no way of comparing. Since they have experienced economic abundance from infancy, they may have never felt anything but confident that their growing wants would be fulfilled. Nor finally should any one read into this affluent attitude some moral defect. Like the changes of puberty the affluent attitude is a normal development. As such it is morally neutral: it is good or bad depending upon what is desired and how.

Since this psychic difference is unmeasurable, how to demonstrate it poses a problem. We will attempt this by first contrasting an abundant with a survival economy, by then analyzing the constituent elements of abundance, and finally by examining its affects on all phases of contemporary living. Our examination will then encounter the paradox that affluent economies seem to labor under greater scarcities and more complex difficulties and that the affluent seem almost to anguish in their affluence. From this paradox we will infer that the heightened wanting of the affluent is a factor in the state of the economy and, more to our concern, is a significant element in their moral life.

Affluence, however, is nothing new. History offers many examples of individuals and classes who were affluent, the kings and warrior leaders, the nobles and priestly classes, and more rarely princely businessmen like the Roman Cassius. It records epochs in which nations enjoyed relative material abundance: Mesopotamia around the time of Hammurabi (2130 - 2075 B.C.), imperial Egypt (1500 - 1200 B.C.) and the Ch'in and Han dynasties in China during the two centuries before and after Christ; the Mediterranean litoral in the first century or so of the Roman Empire; the City-States of Northern Italy and the heartlands of France and England during the 12th and 13th Centuries. Indeed every civilization recalls a golden age, or even several, of relative economic plenty.

But a *people* cannot be called truly affluent unless economic abundance is 1) *broadly shared by a large majority* and unless 2) they can recover from both minor and major economic set-backs so that 3) they *experience a certain hope in the permanence of economic abundance*. By these criteria no people before modern times could be called affluent.

For economic abundance in the past always stopped short of ameliorating the lot of the masses, the slaves, the serfs, the peasants, or the urban poor. All these civilizations rested on the inherent contradiction that those who supplied most of the toil for the great public works and provided the food for rulers, priests, and artisans, themselves enjoyed little more than a precarious subsistence. Even after a century of rapid economic growth Adam Smith in 1776 felt it necessary to make this obvious point:

> "No society can surely be flourishing and happy, of which the far greater number are poor and miserable. It is only just that those who do the work of feeding, clothing and lodging people should have such a share of the produce of their own labor as to be themselves tolerably well-fed, clothed and lodged."[1]

Consider the second criterion. The affluent may well fear that their own excesses or a nuclear holocaust could destroy their economies. But aside from ultimate cataclysm economic abundance provides means to recover from ordinary vicissitudes and to rebuild after major catastrophes. Pompei was simply obliterated; Chicago and San Francisco were rebuilt within a decade. The Mayan civilization disappeared; Germany and Japan were reconstructed at higher levels of productivity. Modern economies can and do recover from recessions and depressions. This ability to renew economic production gives people of industrialized economies a confidence which people of other epochs did not have.

This confidence is confirmed by our greater ability to control energy, to discover raw materials, and to regenerate the fertility of the soil. For ultimately every civilization survives on its resources of energy, food, and raw materials. When the main source of power was manpower, when finding raw materials a matter of luck, and agricultural production dependent on the soil's ability to rejuvenate itself, decimation of the population by war or plagues, petering out of mines, and soil depletion often spelt the end of economic growth. When Rome's silver and tin mines gave out and its supply of slaves dwindled, she found it increasingly difficult to defend the frontier agricultural lands needed to feed its population. When the Black Death in the 14th and 15th Centuries devastated the peasantry and urban workers, European economic progress was set back several centuries.

While food, energy and raw materials are critical today, the problem we face is not declining output but the inability of increasing output to keep pace with world-wide demand. Our continued, and often profligate, use of resources underscores our almost blind trust that better scientific knowledge and developing technology will preserve and increase economic abundance. Since this is the point of the chapter, we can begin our agenda by a closer look at economic abundance.

ECONOMIC ABUNDANCE

Economic abundance is best seen in contrast to economic survival. Comparing the United States with India needs little defense or detailing, since the differences have been so sharply etched by newspaper and television. The United

States is an abundant economy; India is a survival economy.

India: A Survival Economy

While a survival economy, India is far from being culturally primitive. Unlike the pockets of stone-age peoples found along the Amazon, in Africa, in the Phillipines and elsewhere, whose cultures seem to wilt from contact with technological civilization, India boasts a long history graced with literature, philosophy, religious thought and ceremonial, architecture, commerce and trade. Far from wilting, India's culture has been exported to the Western World.

Since independence India has undergone a vast social, political and economic revolution as she tries to meld a continent of peoples into one. Yet despite these changes, India is still unable to produce enough to house, clothe, and feed her people adequately. For the masses, education is minimal, their homes hovels and, even after the "Green Revolution" the threat of famine is still a fact of life. Hundreds of millions live on the edge of destitution. Any natural disaster, an untimely illness or death, a drought, or war can plunge a family into poverty from which the children and, even, grandchildren cannot emerge. World recognition was given to Mother Theresa for the very basic charity of gathering the dead and dying from the streets of Calcutta. Despite the ferment of economic change, 80% of India's 600 millions wear out their lives in unrequited agricultural toil. Despite India's culture, schools, traditions and religion, most Indians live out their lives in economic hopelessness.

The United States: An Abundant Economy

The face of affluent United States is totally different. A shop or office worker takes for granted amenities in living, eating, and travel which Louis XIV in his great palace at Versailles did not enjoy. Yet only the smaller part of U.S. productivity is required to house, clothe and feed people at high levels of adequacy. The larger and increasing part goes to purchase luxuries and comforts and toward increasing production through investment in facilities and training. In the twenty-five years since 1946, the 50% of personal disposable income needed to buy essentials declined to 45%, adding $40 billions to non-essential spending. By the early 1970s, 55% of all family units had discretionary income, that is, income which was not committed to habitual consumption, to contracted spending, or to saving.[2]

Poverty does exist in the midst of this affluence. Some twenty-five million people live in poverty, as defined by income guide-lines of $6000 per family. Yet the guidelines are higher than the incomes of 90% of families throughout the world. (Braceros for example, earn enough from their meager wages as migrant workers to live in style in their villages the rest of the year.) Family income is also protected from the worst disasters: 90% are covered by Social Security, 80% of families have some life insurance and over 50% private pension funds. Unemployment insurance protects 86% of all payrolls and workmen's compensation 82%. Almost all families have some form of medical insurance.

America is still a land of opportunity. Its economy has absorbed millions of Spanish-speaking people and three waves of political refugees since World War II with scarcely a pinch of Americans' well-being. Its greatest challenge is still the racial -- the black -- problem. Yet millions of blacks have left their rural ghettoes over the last thirty years and, despite cultural shock, poor education, and prejudice, entered the economic mainstream. The progress is agonizingly slow and nothing to be proud of, but it is real. More to the point, children can break the poverty which shackles their parents. Welfare is supportive, better education is available, the economy's thirst for skills insatiable. That the achievement is less than what could be is due as much to the unwillingness of the poor to grasp opportunities as to the indifference of the majority to offer them.

Other Characteristics of Abundance

Economic abundance has ameliorated the lot of the masses of workers. A century and a half ago, the masses could look forward to a life of working sixty to seventy hours a week, starting at twelve or fourteen and ending with their deaths. Today work-life begins six to eight years later and retirement ten to fifteen years before death. Workers' standard work-week is forty hours, liberally laced with holidays, sick leave, and vacation. Industrialization and automation have freed men and women from much of the brute labor of heaving and hauling. More and more industrial work involves planning, setting up, and controlling the use of vast inputs of energy. A larger and growing percent of the labor force is involved in teaching, government, professional and personal service, sales and finance, all demanding a personal touch and responsibility.

Tremendous incomes and wealth have been generated. More remarkable is their wide-spread sharing, which the longer picture demonstrates. Since 1890 the U.S. labor force has more than tripled and today is a larger percentage of a larger population. Yet labor's share of national output, as opposed to the return going to the owners of property, has remained constant around 75%. Those who contribute human effort and skill have shared equally in rising national income with those who contribute productive capital. Most college graduates and skilled workers can anticipate earning over a million dollars during their working lives. Economic growth, in short, requires both a larger input of human skill and effort, and their increased compensation.

Finally, an abundant economy has the ability to get out of its own difficulties. As every student of macro-economics knows, a dynamic and growing economy by that very fact is subject to cyclical upswings and downswings. Thus an abundant economy may be suffering a recession while a survival economy may be enjoying a boom. The important distinction is that the abundant society can pull out of a recession by using its own resources; the boom of a survival economy is dependent on outside help: favorable harvests, increased foreign trade, or increased foreign assistance. When that help fails, the economy falters.

In summary, the characteristics of economic abundance are: 1) an increase in material means beyond the requirements of adequate physical living; 2) the assurance of a certain permanency of that high level of material well-being; 3) the real possibility of breaking the chains of poverty; 4) widespread sharing in abundance, and 5) economic self-reliance.

The Abundance Revolution

Economic abundance is not just an American phenomenon. In fact, the change, which has revolutionized the living conditions of people in abundant economies over the last 200 years, is better seen by contrasting a more settled and mature community like London than a city like New York which then existed on the frontier of raw wilderness. Were Socrates brought back to George III's London, he might puzzle at the dress, political interests, religious feeling and cultural patterns, but he would perceive a continuity in the economic life with what he remembered of Athens 2000 years earlier. The small shops, the flow of produce from farms to city, the crowded homes of the many, the wealth of the few, the pace of travel and news, even the far-flung commerce and colonization would hardly strain his credence.

Were Dr. Samuel Johnson transported to London today, he might well comprehend how present cultural and political patterns developed from those of his own day. But he would have no understanding of the economic changes: the miles of dwellings sprawling out from London, the daily surge of people leaving for the returning to work, the instantaneous communication with other continents, the easy travel to all parts of the world, the flow of goods from farms across oceans, the daily spew of goods from factories, and what transpired in the huge office complexes. The crusty philosopher might not be happy but he would admit that the last two centuries produced a greater change in what people possessed and their style and pace of living than the preceding twenty centuries. Above all he would find it difficult to believe that these vast changes were indeed in embryo in his own life-time.

For from its bleak, grimy beginnings as a gaggle of stone hovels about a cotton mill in Huddersfield in the Yorkshire hill near modern Leeds, industrial society, in two centuries, spread across the world. It touched here and there on the continent in France, in the Lowlands and in Germany. Its best and most successful missionaries were British colonials emigrating to the American colonies, to Canada, to Australia and New Zealand, and to South Africa. Political and social revolution fostered it in European Russia and Japan. Its spores were carried by the winds of trade and more recently by international assistance to commercial centers throughout the world, spreading from there to the hinterlands. Even Christian missionaries carried the arts of western civilization and planted the seeds of economic growth. Today economic abundance like a hardy verdure girdles the globe.

The quarter century since 1950 has seen the most spectacular growth in economic abundance. The Cold War, the string of nationalistic explosions around the globe and the opening of the space frontier have overshadowed this unprecedented economic growth. But the fact emerges clearly from world per capita income statistics.

If we should take, assuming that the U.S. economy in 1950 was generously abundant, a per capita income equivalent of $1000 as the measure of abundance, then in 1950 only some 190m. people, or about 7½% of the world's 2.5b., could be said to possess economic abundance and enjoy relative assurance in its permanence and growth. These rich nations would include the United States, whose almost $1800 of per capita income would top the list, Canada, Australia, New Zealand, Sweden, Switzerland and Iceland, in other words, industrialized nations spared the worst ravages of the War. Not included in the count would be people in industrialized centers, like Johannesburg or Rio de Janiero, in otherwise undeveloped economies.

By 1977 that list would include all the above plus every European country (except Portugal), Japan, Venezuela, Kuwait, Saudi Arabia, Israeli, and European Russia, all told over 900m. people, or 20% of world population. Typically throughout Europe per capita national income, again in terms of the 1950 dollar, increased 300-400%, the exception being the United Kingdom which only increased 70%. Biggest gainers were West Germany with 900% and Japan almost 1000%, while Kuwait's astronomical increase made its over $6000 per capita income the highest in the world. Indeed the United States also slipped behind Switzerland and Sweden in the world ranking.

A lower tier of nations, which have per capita incomes approaching those in Europe in 1950, add another 12% to the above. These include Portugal, East Germany, Poland, Hungary, Yugoslavia and Czechoslavakia in Europe; Brazil, Mexico, and Argentina; Taiwan and Korea; South Africa, Iraq and Iran. Thus almost a third of the world enjoys high economic hopes. While the absolute number of the world's poor and destitute has increased from 2.5b. to 3.0b., nevertheless, the second half of the 20th Century has seen over a billion people pass from simple survival to abundance or near-abundance.

Whatever the travails of world hunger and desperate want, this unprecedented economic growth makes it possible to envisage realistically all peoples' being delivered from the spectre of destitution. Whether rich nations have the will to help the poor or whether poor nations will explode in frustration before then are sobering considerations of another dimension.

THE ANATOMY OF ABUNDANCE

Abundance as a total physical transformation is no simple affair. The abundance revolution is a complex of many revolutions: industrial, commercial, financial and managerial. All of these have received detailed treatment elsewhere of which the student of business is familiar. The point here is that they are constituents of a more comprehensive revolution, the Revolution in Abundance.

Put simply, the generation of economic abundance requires a motivation, greater sources of energy and raw materials, enhanced technology, more sophisticated organization of production and sales, and an enlarged economic role of government. All abundant economies possess these features, howevermuch they may differ in national style and ideologies. By contrast, non-abundant economies will be deficient in some or all of these basic elements. The fleshing out of these ideas which follows will rely mainly on our experience of the U.S. economy.

The Dream of Abundance

Prior to the generation of abundance is the dream of its possibility. But that dream must become a conscious conviction, shared by a significant segment of a population, that a nation's wealth can be increased markedly by improved production and trade. Such occurred in England in the Seventeenth and Eighteenth Centuries. It was not entirely new. It had occurred earlier in Northern Italy and Holland. Indeed the motive of <u>individual</u> gain-seeking must be present whenever economic growth occurs. But earlier movements of economic growth tended to break on the rocks of technical limitations or to be limited by commercial opportunity. In the Middle Ages, moreover, they were dampened by a moral queasiness about gain- and profit-seeking.

In other words, for the hope for gain to become a broad motivating force, to become a critical mass changing a nation, it needs scope for its exercise, the technical means to achieve success, and a moral sanction for social acceptance. This conjuncture was realized in England in the Seventeenth Century. Despite Spain and Portugal's priority,

Englishmen saw two new continents open up to their adventurousness and appetite for gain. They had at hand the most advanced agricultural, industrial and commercial technology in the world. Finally, instead of the disdain or, at least, uneasiness of Medieval morality, gain-seeking received moral approval. A softened Calvinism was disposed to see diligence, frugality, and thrift, all ingredients of economic success, as signs and symbols of predestination. Sir Josiah Child expressed the more universal sentiment that England "is wonderfully fitted by the bounty of God Almighty for a great progression in wealth and power."[3]

This theme, increasingly secularized, was the assumption, often unconsciously, behind hundreds of pamphlets and monographs debating policies how England could increase her national wealth. This discussion over two centuries was progressively synthesized, culminating in the work whose very title expressed the abiding concern of the age, Adam Smith's An Inquiry into the Nature and Causes of the Wealth of Nations.

The Technology Revolution

Technology is the second critical factor. The modern spirit of gain-seeking fortuitously found a new intellectual thrust, an empirical curiosity into the forces of nature. Thus, gain-seeking was able to direct this scientific impulse toward improved techniques for finding new sources of metals and minerals, and for improving the renewable productivity of fields, forests and fisheries. Above all, science opened up new sources of energy, and technology developed new ways of using it to advantage.

Men from the beginning had used animal, wind, and water power to supplement human effort. Since the Eighteenth Century man has tapped vast new sources of energy: the expansion of gas, electrical and magnetic force, light waves, atomic fission and, on the horizon, geothermal, atomic fusion and, the most plentiful of all, solar energy. New and more efficient fuels were developed -- wood, charcoal, coal, coke, gas, oil, oxygen, uranium and hydrogen -- and more sophisticated ways of generating, controlling, and delivering energy for production of goods.

Even more importantly than increasing output, the energy revolution accelerated the pace of technological change by freeing men of much of the burden of providing energy.

Thus intellectual curiosity could range over the entire spectrum of physical phenomena and probe deeper into the hidden resources of nature. Moreover, since each new discovery found applications to what was previously known, technology tends to increase exponentially. Even though major technological break-throughs are chancy, nevertheless, every new discovery finds, not as in the past hundreds of applications, but literally thousands. Men through centuries slowly developed the use of cutting instruments, the knife, the spade, the saw and the blowtorch. A laser's immediate application ranges over all these uses from delicate brain-surgery to crude excavation. In addition, its application to optics and communication is just as extensive.

The Work Revolution

The discovery of an abundant source of man-made energy centralizes machines in the factory. The energy and technical revolution initiated a social revolution. For the first time in man's history, people on a massive scale must leave the household to work. Dwellings now concentrate near the factory. Mechanization in farms and mines and forests replace workers who drift toward factories for work. Others congregate to service the commercial, financial, political and cultural needs of the worker. Thus industrialization begets new kinds of urbanization, not political, religious or cultural in origin, but economic.

These megalopolies are largely devoid of both the parochialism and distinctive character of ancient and Medieval cities. Factories and offices, producing massive quantities of goods and services must sell nationally and internationally, and the workers in turn must buy the mass-produced items produced elsewhere. The city has become a place where people make their living, and has ceased to be the *patria*, the focus of their allegiance. Even where some cities attract by their distinctive charm, like Paris, the inhabitant who most proudly calls himself Parisian may not be native.

Mass production, besides changing man's external environment, has radically changed industrial craftsmanship. Workers no longer produce for individual and personalized sale. Rather they service the flow of product through machines, both in the office and shop. They consequently must pace themselves to the machine, starting and stopping it, removing its waste and finished product, overseeing its care. Yet tremendous responsibilities ride on their shoulders, for a moment's carelessness can ruin thousands of items, close down an assembly line and can maim or kill the worker besides. Mass production means standardized production, goods sold in mass markets, appealing to a common-denominator taste. What individualization is possible, is within an overall standardization.

Labor consequently is socialized. Men and women are fitted into an integrated chain of production, each performing a small part of the total work, passing it on to another, and never seeing the completed product. All the more so is this true of the office worker, who merely presides over the flow of the paper work which parallels the production and sale of real goods, and could not visualize the product or how it is produced. Thus the real, basic, and new distinction between workers is not in terms of working conditions -- blue collar vs. white collar -- but whether they oversee a whole or part of production. Only the former can make decisions affecting the whole.

The Corporate Aggregate

The socialization of production in turn generated revolutions in management, marketing and finance. Large amounts of money must be laid out to begin even a modest business. Consequently, every source of saving must be tapped and pooled for borrowing. Products which are mass-produced must be sold massively, so that what people want must be constantly studied and the means of physically distributing goods constantly improved. Most importantly management itself has become a profession, for which a person can prepare through all the educational levels up to the doctorate. It has become almost a scientific art in itself, permitting the manager to move from steel-making to agri-business with hardly a change in stride.

These revolutions are concretized in the large corporate aggregates of interrelated plant, equipment, transportation facilities and warehouses, employing hundreds of thousands of workers and marketing billions of dollars of goods annually throughout the world. While the one-man or family operation of an earlier age has not disappeared, the corporate aggregate is the distinctive institution of abundant economies. Ownership is collective, thousands pooling their resources and holding a variety of claims against the corporation. Management and full knowledge of what the corporation is doing and how it is fairing is lodged in a small team of professionals. Legally "hired" by stockholders, corporate managers succeed to power by a largely internal and anonymous process of cooption by the current managers. Their ownership in the corporation, though often a substantial part of their personal wealth, is usually a miniscule part of total ownership. In practice, since they alone have a comprehensive view of the corporate aggregate, they make the significant management decisions. They are the industrial elite.

Beneath them is an ever-widening ladder of subordinates, including talents as diverse as those of a research chemist and a janitor. Most of these belong to another workers' organization, a professional society or a union, whose principal function is to represent workers in negotiating for compensation and working conditions. Locals of these organizations follow policy set by national organizations who in turn study the gains gotten by other national groups. Thus most workers find that they are microcosmic parts of two large collectivities.

The corporate aggregate, in turn, is set in its own web, hundreds of corporations, large and small, some satellites and some independent, who supply materials, subcontract parts, or sell its product. Super-corporations also face other giant rivals which it must outpace or, at minimum, keep pace with in order to survive. Where that rivalry is keen, the corporation is under constant pressure to improve product or, at least, make it different; to push sales and advertising; to add to its product line; to change waste into product and to sharpen management methods. Not to submit to this discipline spells corporate stagnation and eventual demise. For vast sums of money and credit are on the ready to buy into or to buy out the management of a faltering firm.

The Role of Government

While watching each other super-corporations must watch the economy. A downturn in one industry soon affects all others, because the giants depend greatly on their sales to other giants and to their workers. Thus the economic health of each is importantly fraught with the economic health of the economy. Despite the rhetoric of business, the large corporate aggregates are the biggest supporters of Federal government efforts to maintain stable economic growth and a steady level of prices. Modern democracies in contrast to the most economically involved Renaissance monarchy is more central to the economic process and their fiscal impact is greater.

Indeed industrial urbanization necessarily means more government. On the local level inner city decay and suburban sprawl demand more public services: more effort against crime; more policing the movement of peoples and traffic; greater costs in removing waste and maintaining the purity of water and air. Education becomes burdened with more remedial and recreational functions. These, together with the demands for higher technical training, have ballooned the cost of public education. The flight from cities, made possible by affluence, is the inevitable response to these mounting problems and taxes. With the consequence that many areas in the urban center are hardly habitable, wastelands of ugliness, decay, dirt, and pollution. Welfare rolls become bloated, and the cities periodically paralyzed by strikes, the weather, or technical malfunctioning.

Just as big business has evoked more government it has fathered bigger government, a greater government role in monitoring, regulating, and stimulating the economy. This blend of private and public effort is called the "mixed economy". It characterizes all modern industrial economics over the entire ideological spectrum from the United States to Red China. What differentiates free enterprise capitalism from centrally controlled capitalism is not economic or technological, but ideological.

In the United States the control functions of the Federal Government are numerous and varied. An alphabet soup of agencies has been established to maintain competition within industries; to preserve industrial peace; to regulate the flow of commerce and communications, the exchange of securities and the creation of money and credit. Yet, the United States' direct economic impact, its income and spending of over $500 billions, is the single most important fact in the economy today. It is the largest employer in the world; its purchases are the principal support of whole industries -- agriculture, electronics, aerospace, airlines, maritime construction and low-cost housing. It supplies most of the funds for urban renewal, for renovating railroads, for constructing highways, and for scientific research. It is the largest insurer against unemployment, operates the largest pension plan and provides the most extensive medical insurance. Finally, its credit is the practical guarantee that the economy will operate at full tilt most of the time. There is no area of national economic life which is not touched by the economic power of the Federal government, and the most immediate beneficiaries of these government functions, most of which began in this generation, are the giant corporate complexes.

This is the anatomy of abundance: the incentive for economic growth and personal gains, the exploitation of science and technology; industrial urbanization, socialized production, big business and big government. These features are inherent to the dynamics of abundance. They are so woven into its institutional fabric that one cannot be destroyed or changed without destroying or modifying the whole. They mutually interact and mutually complement. Therefore, the process is irreversible, barring cataclysm. Therefore, too the environment they have created -- highly technical, ceaselessly changing, urbanized, socialized, standardized and centrally monitored -- is also irreversible. This generation, and future generations, as far as we can see, if we want abundance, must live in an industrialized world.

THE MEANING OF AFFLUENCE

We turn then to the second, more intriguing idea, affluence which here is taken to mean the condition of possessing and using economic abundance. From this we will argue that affluent people develop a new attitude of _expecting_ more material goods and income which is significant both for the economy and for their moral life. But now we examine affluence itself, the life and behavioral patterns of peoples who are endowed with the economic plenty industrialized economies bestow. The preceding sections should have helped free the student from historical parochialism, convincing him or her that our way of life is vastly different from our ancestors and most of the world today.

What we are seeking is how people behave differently as the result of cultural and social changes produced by economic abundance. There are three principal characteristics of affluence. 1) Affluent people enjoy increasing income and they purchase more economic goods. 2) They enjoy a wider range of economic opportunities and are not locked into the economic life style of their parents. 3) Their life is fraught with change in income, jobs, and habitat in contrast to the more static living of pre-industrialized economies. Consequently, their life is more uncertain, less predictable and less stable. Environmentally, an affluent people is serviced and faced with an immense technology and removed in many respects from direct confrontation with the forces of nature. A word about each.

Increased Income and Spending

The affluent not only get more income but they spend more. This after all is what economic abundance means. Industrial output in the U.S. economy has since the turn of the century doubled every quarter century. Whether the rate of change is accelerating or not -- and it can be argued either way -- the fact is that the absolute amount of real income and output is constantly increasing. Real per capita income, despite a rising population, over the forty years from 1880 to 1920 increased from $450 to $900. In the thirty years from 1920 to 1950, despite the Great Depression, it doubled to $1800. In 1976 it stood at $3500.

These are real not inflated figures. They mean that every generation over the last three has doubled the income and the spending of the previous. Since the War the present generation has experienced few years, despite six recessions and a nagging inflation, in which real per capita income has fallen. This is the single most obvious fact of the U.S. economy: we receive more income and we spend more. Households, governments, firms, non-profit organizations not only have larger incomes but they seek more. Governments say they need more revenue to meet rising costs and increasing citizens' demands; firms scratch for more sales revenue; unions demand higher compensation; schools, hospitals, the arts are probing for additional funds; even welfare recipients are demonstrating for larger assistance.

To ascribe this to mass greediness is simplistic. For we would all be guilty, the poor no less than the wealthy, governments no less than private individuals, charitable organizations no less than profit-maximizing corporations. Even those moral leaders and social critics, most vocal in castigating the "greed" which motivates the economy, find themselves scrambling to increase their own salaries, honoraria, and royalties. To call all this greediness is in effect to empty the word of meaning. A more prudent course would be to withhold judgment until all aspects are considered.

Rather than a kind of greedy self-seeking, wanting a larger income and wanting to spend that income seems entirely normal responses to abundance. For, after all, economic growth does not occur in a vacuum. It really means the production of more economic goods whose production generates more income. This increased income must go somewhere and to someone. The ordinary person knows instinctively that a larger national output means larger shares for all. Moreover, unless each seeks larger portion, the lion's share will go to the few or to government. Greediness in this case is not in seeking a larger share but in seeking too large a share. But that is another matter.

As to spending, every student of economics knows the remarkable long-run constancy of household consumption to disposable income and governments' penchant to spend up to, and beyond, their income. These are fundamental principles of national income analysis. They express in aggregate the instinctive behavioral tendency of individuals to spend whatever income at their disposal.

All of this is so obvious that little more than citing convinces. More output means more income; more income means more spending; more spending, as we shall see, means more production. This relation is as old as human consciousness and expresses the most fundamental rationality that the fruits of labor are for the purposes of life. Certainly one can criticize how this spending is done: on trivialities or for show, by careless cost over-runs or high living under guise of necessary expenses. But criticizing how spending is done is quite different from indicting wanting more income and more spending.

The Range of Opportunity

The first consequence of increased income is expansion of the range of economic opportunity. No one, except those suffering from total and irreparable brain damage, is locked into a life predetermined by birth. Schools, technical colleges, universities, special education and rehabilitation programs are available for those who would use them. Billions of dollars go into the humane effort to ferret out physical and learning disabilities in children and to improve the employability of the paraplegic, the blind, and other handicapped. The phenomenal achievements in athletics, in entertainment and the arts, in science and scholarship, in the professions and business of those who had to overcome physical or family disadvantages bear witness, more so than the success of the normal, to how affluence has expanded economic opportunities.

The paths of opportunity are more varied. False starts into a vocation can be corrected without disaster. The very complexity of modern living yields many more niches into which the individual can fit more suitably to his aspirations and abilities. That same complexity means that the ambitious and the bold can achieve fortune in many different ways. At the same time, every life style can be accommodated. Though the financial predominates as the criterion of success, most can gain a comfortable living in doing well their own thing.

But increased opportunity also magnifies uncertainty. The very range of possibilities make it difficult for young people to commit themselves to one. Other fields are always alluring. This is particularly so when a person sees others grasp success seemingly without effort, while recognition to them, despite years of patient attention to detail and quiet sacrifice in mastering a craft or profession, comes only late or never. Success, measured in power or money, is elusive in a complex society and may seem less dependent on hard and intelligent work than on luck, privilege and favor. While a radical vocational change is possible, the uncertainties of a new field or a fresh start still demand real courage.

Change and Uncertainty

With enhanced opportunity comes greater mobility. Change is built into affluent living, not merely increased travel and visiting but radical uprooting of families socially and geographically. Some is self-induced, like a mother, once the children are in school, returning to her profession or business, or like an executive resigning his career to fulfill his dream of a chicken farm in Vermont. Some results from the break-up of families. Some from seeking a better opportunity in a field whose market is national or international in scope. Some change is as simple as taking a new job; some as radical as moving an entire family. Some change is forced upon us: an executive returned to the home office; the closing down of a division, the phasing out of jobs, lay-offs and firings. More people see the inside of prisons today. More are institutionalized because increasingly mobile families cannot give personal care to the mentally or physically sick, or to the aged.

Change breeds uncertainty. The affluent, unlike their grandparents, cannot predict their lives. The village smith, if he stuck to his forge, was assured a decent living in his community till his death. People today have no assurance that they will die in the towns of their birth, or retire from their first jobs. A person may want to remain in a particular employment, only to find the job disappear. A family may want to send out roots in a community, only to find the neighborhood decay or town change its character. Even the largest corporations are subject to radical changes: an economic downturn, a management become lax, a merger, sale or take-over. All affects employment especially of the unskilled, the inexperienced, or the discriminated against. But they are not alone. A person may train for a field only to find hiring has declined. A capable executive may be swept out in a general corporate house cleaning.

The life-style of the affluent changes before our eyes. In a single generation a new product may permeate an entire culture. Television, for example, from the home spread to schools, hospitals, assembly lines, stores and banks. We are inundated by the cult of the new and different. Product obsolescence is not only built into goods but guaranteed by changes in fashion. Fads sweep across the country and die out. The litany could go on. It would only strengthen the point that an affluent people are subjected to a kaleidoscope of change, inconceivable several generations ago.

It is not true that the affluent have no moorings and cannot sink roots in a vocation or in a community. But most do so only after much moving about. What is true is that the stability of affluent life rests less than before on one's physical or social environment, familiar scenes, and familiar faces, and more on one's inner resources and convictions.

The Technological Environment

Finally, the heightened expectations, the enhanced opportunities, the pace of change and uncertainty of life all point to one common cause, the technological character of abundance. An affluent people has been removed to a large extent from contact with and dependence on natural forces. Instead they are much more dependent on man-made forces, the flow of non-human energy and impersonal management.

Awareness of growing things and freely-flowing things does not occur spontaneously in ordinary living but must be consciously sought and planned for.

The deeper question whether machines diminish man may be answered at different levels. Recent psychological studies conclude to what we would expect, that individuals vary greatly in their ability to absorb sense impressions and information.[4] Consequently, the performance or even breakdown of individuals depends greatly upon whether their sensory and informational capacities are being overloaded. Undoubtedly stress arises from the fact that people cannot run by their own inner time and rhythm but must run according to the time and rhythm set by machines, dead-lines, calendars and schedules. These are the hard facts of man's relations to his technological environment.

The more romantic question is whether man is dominated by machines. This question is asked of every technological advance. One can easily reconstruct discussions around Stone-age campfires about how the bow and arrow was eroding hunting skill and courage. Every tool enhances human abilities and extends the range of possibilities and the computer and the automated assembly line do no less, and no more. But the person remains the vital microcosm -- the planner, programmer, controller -- within the technologic macrocosm. The real issue is not man versus the machine, but the men who man the machines versus the men who command the machine. Is the knowledge and skill of technocrats so exotic that there is no practicable way to control their programming machines when, how, what, and how much they will produce? The real question is, "By manipulating machines, can they manipulate other men?" The real question is a question about power, not about productivity and must be postponed to a later chapter.

This sketch of abundance, as a mammoth technology which feeds increasing material wants and enlarges human possibilities in an ever changing, albeit more precarious, existence, is real enough, though somewhat roseate. In contrast to that affluent man faces the paradox which, more than his larger income, enhanced opportunities, and more fluid and technological environment, differentiates him psychically from non-affluent man, that <u>economic abundance generates more scarcity</u>.

SCARCITY: THE ESSENCE OF ABUNDANCE

For most people that statement is not a paradox but a contradiction, because in ordinary conversation scarcity means 'dearth', just the opposite of abundance. But in economics scarcity has a somewhat different scientific meaning. It is not used in an absolute sense as 'few', 'little', or 'not much' but in a relative sense. A scarce good is one whose quantity available is less than what is wanted or desired. Abundance, on the other hand, is used absolutely, meaning 'much' or 'many' or 'a lot'. Thus there is no contradiction in saying that wheat production in the U.S. is abundant but that wheat is scarce. That is, while there is much wheat, there is less than what is wanted. Just the opposite, a little of something may not be scarce. For example, there may be only one stack belching smoke over a city, but that may be one too many because no one wants any of the noxious stuff.

Economists have not always been careful in the use of scarcity. Sometimes they slip into the common parlance usage. Sometimes they mean limited. But while all scarce goods are necessarily limited, not all limited goods are scarce. Ordinary air is limited -- the atmosphere extends only five miles around the earth -- but it is not scarce: everyone can breath as much as he wants. Purified or compressed air is scarce because more is wanted than available. All this the student heard in his first lecture on economics. Its repetition should emphasize that scarcity is used throughout in its strict scientific sense. Since, therefore, scarcity refers to relative amounts and abundance to absolute amounts, the statement, "Abundance creates scarcity", while paradoxical, is not contradictory.

A second point which can be made, as well here as elsewhere, is to warn against a too materialistic concept of scarcity. Material things are scarce but in fact the non-material is scarcer. Human time is scarcest of all -- "Alas, alas, how time flees" we lament with Horace. Human energy, knowledge, wisdom, friendship, love are all in short-supply relative to our needs and wants. In this very real sense the human person is an infinite appetite which can never be satiated. What is important for scarcity, in the more material sense, is that none of these wants can be fulfilled without some material goods. The full story of this is saved for a later chapter. We now address the paradox which is at the heart of the affluent psyche.

The Scarcity in Abundance

Economic analysis begins with the problem of scarcity. While conceding that an individual may have more than he wants of a particular good, economics starts with the basic assumption and universal experience that all human wants exceed the means available to satisfy them, so that increased satisfaction of one set of wants is at the expense of satisfying less of another. Economics assumes that this condition is as inevitable in human affairs as gravitation is in human motion. Scarcity, like gravitation, can be counteracted but it must always be taken into account.

Here is where the relativity of scarcity is important. As a ratio between what is wanted and what is available, scarcity can be decreased by either increasing means or by diminishing wants. An abundant economy, therefore, can overcome general scarcity if, while production increases, wants are maintained at previous levels. This is the rub: increased production increases wants.

Production is always limited. Economists call this limit the production possibility frontier. While theoretically the frontier can always be pushed back, at any one moment it is a limit, because there are available only so much energy, natural resources, labor and labor skills, and because technology and managerial organization have reached a particular level of sophistication. Wanting, on the other hand, is limited only by the imagination's ability to conceive new ways of satisfying wants. Its only effective restraint, therefore, is self-restraint.

To push back the production frontier or even to reach it with available means, more resources and talent must be used and paid a higher income. But the very generation of income increases the possibility of spending. Larger incomes increase wanting and enhance the hope of people for a higher plane of living by taking advantage of expanded opportunities, by responding to new circumstances and by protecting themselves against greater risks. At minimum, we can expect that increased production will generate proportionately increased spending. More likely, larger incomes will tend to free the wanting imagination so that a wider and wider spectrum of desirable goods spreads out before people. Like a person climbing a little hill, whose horizon expands many times the height climbed, so desiring tends to expand more than the ability to buy. Moreover, there is a feed-back effect. Just as increased production stimulates increased spending, so increased spending stimulates more production, and on and on.

The resolution of the scarcity-abundance paradox can be highlighted by once again contrasting survival with abundant economies. In survival economies, for whatever reason -- the niggarliness of nature, the lack of knowledge and skills, or simply indifference -- wanting tends to be traditional, static, and in an arrested state. Consequently, production and wanting are normally in near balance. Scarcity exists but it is ordinarily not much of a problem except when disaster strikes. In an affluent economy, scarcity is largely want-produced because abundance itself generates the expansion of wants. Scarcity, therefore, is an ever-present and insistent problem. Scarcity in survival economies is due to meager production; in an affluent economy to abundant wanting. Affluent scarcity, therefore, is qualitatively different from survival scarcity.

The Affluent Sixties

The U.S. economy during the sixties (now that we can acquire some perspective on that turbulent period), exemplifies well affluent scarcity. For whatever else the sixties were, economically they were soaring -- the "American Economic Miracle". The sharp shift in its growth rate from 3% annually to well over 4% by this most productive economy in history capsules in one figure the unprecedented nine years of continuous growth from 1961 to the first quarter of 1970. In the decade GNP in real terms (inflation eliminated) increased better than 50% largely because of the 60% increase in industrial production. Not only were 13 million new jobs created but output per man-hour increased 35%. Weekly paychecks, consequently, were fatter by almost 50% and profits soared by almost 80%.

These figures translated into an additional $3500 of real income for the average family. They increased their purchase of new homes from 1.3 millions to over 2.0 millions annually and of new automobiles from 6.7 millions to over 10 million annually. But everyone had more income, government, business and households, and they spent lavishly on more missiles, more public buildings, more education, more furnishings, more travel, more recreation and more liquor.

All that increased income created more problems, however, than it solved. Mayor Lindsay's promise that doubling New York's income would solve all the problems of Fun City dissolved into the nightmare of civic bankruptcy. Yet New York is not alone; governments at all levels are down to bare-bones budgets (usually 15-20% higher than the preceding year's). School districts, though educational costs are doubling, lose more bond issues than they win. Property owners demand a tax freeze while welfare mothers are picketing city hall for larger allowances. Central cities desperately need rehabilitation and the environment sanitation. Every day reveals new pockets of destitution while congressmen cannot make ends meet on their salaries. Education and research funds are drying up. NASA has been decimated, capital investment is lagging, medical services and housing priced beyond the middle-income family. Farmers are still going out of business, though crops are record and prices high. Unions strike for astronomical wage-increases and firms scramble for sales, jacking prices up to whatever the market will bear. If housing starts to fall to 1.5 millions, construction is in chaos. If automobile sales slip to 7.5 millions Detroit is in panic.

The contrast shocks like a hot shower turned cold. Yet both pictures are real: the increased abundance is real, the desperate struggle to survive is real. What is happening to the nation is happening to individuals. A householder in 1960 with needs considered normal for his status might think, and probably did, that half again his current income would solve his financial problems. By 1970 with an increased income more than the 50% hoped for, he could compile a list of needs, all lawful and worthwhile, which an income twice what he had would not buy. If typical, the intractable inflation of the seventies slowed considerably the increase in his real income, thus widening the gap between expectations and reality.

This is increased scarcity. A scarcity increasingly aggravated by abundance. It is, though troubling like the stirrings of puberty, entirely normal. It is part of the human condition, that the more we have the more we see we can get. Columbus' world-changing expedition to the New World was financed by a few of Queen Isabella's baubles. To put a man on the moon cost the equivalent of several years' output of General Motors. Greed is present but not overwhelmingly. For more is spent now in one year on feeding the hungry, curing the sick and educating the ignorant of the world than in all the centuries before 1900.

These intensified economic expectations affect action at all levels, even the most exalted, and permeate all social relations, among nations, social classes, and family members. Scarcity, heightened by abundance, colors all of life and constitutes what we call the anguish of affluence.

Internationally, the super-powers have seen the costs of defense rise astronomically and realize more clearly that they cannot afford the luxury of mutual annihilation. Since the Cuban missile crisis, they have avoided eye-ball to eye-ball confrontation despite their many areas of conflict. The need for increased trade between the Free and Communist worlds has added some realism to the rhetoric of peace. The desire of emerging nations to share in world prosperity -- what Pere Lebret calls the "Last Revolution"[5]-- while sharpening nationalistic sensibilities, also provides a hedge against reckless adventuring. At the same time rich nations have accepted in principle, even if only reluctantly in deed, their obligation and the wisdom of assisting poorer nations to achieve economic viability.

Affluence and Society

Domestically, in the struggle of minority peoples, especially blacks, to achieve first class citizenship, which is the great social catharsis of our time, it is now apparent that economic equality is the necessary means for gaining social and political equality. The massive flood of funds, from all levels of government as well as from private sources, into education, welfare and health services have certainly helped. But at the same time, these have proliferated programs and spawned middle-class bureaucracies which have absorbed fifty cents out of every dollar intended for the needy. Norman Macrae's comment is to the point: "If you create wealth in America, it fructifies; if you create power groups, they go corrupt."[6]

Politics has become largely the politics of affluence. Economic pressure groups flock to Washington and to every state capital, grasping for privilege or handouts. Farm groups, labor unions, industry lobbyists, energy proponents, conservationists, consumer leagues, educators, medical researchers, artists and humanists, mayors and governors all are seeking a cut from the tax pie. Whole industries survive on the basis of government contracts or are geared to government agencies regulating for their benefit. The alliance between big business interest and the military is a worrisome fact. Business as a whole depends on federal economic policy. Corporations which are important for the national economy expect to be bailed out by the government if they get into trouble.

Consequently, a new art of government has emerged, arbitrating the excessive and conflicting demands put upon federal, state and local budgets by pressure groups. The success of such efforts is seldom measured by how well they advance the social good they espouse, but by how much advantage they wrest from government. Given the enormous resources of government, economic pressure politics is inevitable and maybe healthier than a closed bureaucratic disposition of revenues. While economic lobbying is not new to the political process, its extent and pervasiveness has radically changed the process itself.

Affluence and the Family

Affluence has affected the family circle. Greater wealth permits and encourages more social and geographic mobility. Home can become for parents and children only the place to hang their hats between jaunts in pursuit of their own interests. Family values, where they exist, are preserved only by an unequal struggle of parental amateurs against professionals in the art of persuasion. The seepage of TV violence and distorted sexuality, canned to sell goods in mass markets, is a constantly corrosive threat to family values.

Affluence has helped erode authority. For a family in straightened circumstances, "We can't afford it" means that and ends the discussion. For affluent families, it means the good desired is not worth the sacrifice of other goods, pitting the value-perceptions of the parents against those of their children. Thus affluence fires the pressure to spend on what seems luxuries to parents but normal and necessary to children. A youth counter-culture, radically different from their parents' in sound, rhythm, living style, aspirations and thrills, can survive because young people have the money to maintain it. Yet the delinquency of affluence continues to mount: shop-lifting, auto-theft, senseless vandalism, sexual assault, alcoholism, and drug-addiction are as much a part of suburbia as the ghetto. Many young people are afraid to face the adult world. Affluence coddles the fear, thus adding to the wall of incomprehension and tension between parents and children.

Family tensions, as divorces and wife- and child-battering testify, has increased. Affluence has contributed by affecting the relationship between husband and wife. The boredom of a wife and mother, the feeling of being locked in by her family, is heightened by her sense of economic dependence in a society, where worth is often measured monetarily. On the other hand, affluence does pressure women to take a job, from the side of her family, in order to supplement or be the principal source of family income; from the side of the economy, to respond to the increasing demand for labor. The danger lies in the irritations caused by two outside careers or jobs. A husband and wife can easily lose their sense of mutual commitment and shrivel their relationship to career convenience, or worse, to money.

Affluence and the Intellectual Life

Nothing illustrates better the impact of affluence on institutions than the change in higher education since World War II. The myth of a four year intellectual retreat, blending study and hy-jinks, was shaken by the flood of GIs who proved that many more than the upper ten percent of high school graduates could profit from college. It got lost in the surge of the sixties which turned quiet campuses into educational mills. It was condemned by the social activists rebelling against the impersonal processing of students into impersonal technological bureaucracies. It is ignored by contemporary students, who are pressured by the costs of education to earn part or all of their tuition and living expenses and who are driven by the difference in economic reward to get into college and once there to get good grades and to go to professional school.

Only an affluent economy could provide the amount and range of educational opportunity. College is a possibility for a young person from every social class, it offers a bewildering variety of programs, and it may be begun at almost any age. Necessarily it is low-geared and mass produced. Authority, arbitrarily administered, is seen as oppressive. The atmosphere is business-like. The desire to recapture the joy and challenge of the college experience still survives but it is considered somewhat odd-ball in both students and professors.

The influx of money has distorted the role of the scholar. The great educator is not the brilliant lecturer, but the administrator who can wheedle funds from legislatures, the clever dean who can expand his programs, the director of a research institute expanding his satrapy with foundation grants. In the wake of Sputnik, federal funds poured into universities. But research funds and honor have gone to those who respond to the needs of affluence, to prolong life, to improve productivity, and to develop military hardware.[7] The knowledge explosion since World War II has not only isolated professors from students but from each other. The days of the savant who would try to grasp all human knowledge are gone. His desire for a comprehensive wisdom is not appreciated. The humanist, the philosopher, the social scientist who tries to see the relationships among fields of knowledge gets a pittance of research support.

The artist, even more than the scholar, finds the milieu of affluence a cruel environment. Despite the impressive upgrading of the cultural level in the United States, the growth of dozens of civic into symphonic orchestras, the spread of community theaters, and the development of art galleries even in the provinces, art is still a hard and demanding mistress. Faced with a long apprenticeship in nurturing his vision and patiently developing his craft, the artist is violently tempted to the quick success of the bizarre, the startling, and the barbaric or to easily saleable sentimentalism. No artist starving in a garret has been recorded recently but there is reason for the artist's often cynical reaction against the bourgeois values of affluence.

CONCLUSION

The litany could go on but the point is made sufficiently. Economic abundance and affluence touch all institutions, modify all relationships, and affect every kind of acting. Our asserting that does not deny that other events and movements over the last two decades have caused perhaps greater social ferment: an unpopular war, a power struggle between Presidency and Congress, the agitation for minority civil rights, and above all a militant post-Christian secularism challenging some of our most deeply rooted moral values. But even in these one can find an economic, an affluent dimension. It is on this we are here focusing.

It goes almost without saying that in acquiring abundance we have not gained contentment. Glutted with goods, we are anxious for more. Wealth seems to make us more envious of some people's fortune and more indifferent to others' needs. We seem diminished as Christians. Part of the answer may be that we have demanded of abundance what it cannot give: peace in possessions, fulfillment of our innermost needs, and, in a word, happiness. Almost in revenge, it seems, abundance has yielded frustration, discontent, and a cloying surfeit, making us crabbed in our outlook, clutching of our properties, and paranoid about their diminution.

Granting some truth to this answer, the chapter reveals a deeper dimension. This more perceptive response points to the volatility, uncertainty, and stress produced by an abundant economy and, probing further, to a fundamental change in our hopes for economic well-being. From simply wanting more income, more goods, and a higher plane of living, we *expect* more. Wanting has become an active, aggressive and confident seeking after economic betterment. This entire complex of psychic changes is encompassed in what we call the *affluent attitude*.

Such expectation is not only a constant stimulus to the economy, even to overheating it, but as a force in our lives and as a principle of action it is particularly susceptible to injustice, greed and sensuality. Thus the affluent attitude becomes a more important consideration in developing personality and espousing Values, in controlling one's appetities, in treating others justly, and finally in finding some ultimate meaning to life.

After examining the economic effects of the affluent attitude, we will explore its moral implications.

CHAPTER TWO

AFFLUENCE AND ECONOMIC VALUE

The affluent attitude, as an intensified economic concern and heightened expectation, will obviously affect associations among people involving the exchange of economic goods. This is to say that it affects prices. For a price is nothing other than a ratio, the amount of money one must surrender for, or relative to, the amount of commodity or service one would obtain. Prices are central in relations between buyers and sellers, employers and employees, lenders and borrowers, tax-collectors and tax-payers, and other obviously economic relations. A perceptive student, however, can find prices lurking somewhere in relations not so obviously economic, the teacher-student relation, pastor-parishioner, artist-audience, and even in the husband-wife and parent-child relations.

PRICE AND VALUE CONCEPTS

Without going into all the nuances, we can say that wherever exchange of economic goods occurs and whatever the kind of exchange, there is usually a price, an exchange relation between money and goods. Further, these prices are related among themselves, the most obvious reason, among many, being that our money supply must be spent on many things. If the price of gasoline increases, there is less money available for movies and other things. That is, an individual price is part of a system of millions of changing prices. We will pick up this idea at the end of chapter but it should be kept in mind throughout.

"Why there should be a price at all?" is a question almost too trite to ask. Prices ration goods to buyers and money to sellers, when more goods and money are wanted than available, that is, when they are scarce. So our trite question provides the link between this chapter and first. That link is scarcity.

There we saw that scarcity was of the essence of abundance, so that a change in a thing's scarcity will change its price and, conversely, a change in price implies a change in scarcity. Here we examine the ways the affluent attitude affects scarcity and exchange relations. There we saw that our economic expectations affected all social relations. Here we examine their impact on the economic substratum of life and thereby on our actions and social intercourse. For our manner of living, the fulfillment of our aspirations, and even our relations to others are conditioned by the prices of goods and services we want and need.

More to the point, the logic of scarcity lays bare the paradox at the heart of economics: the more a good is desired, the less its desirability, since more must be surrendered to obtain it. In aggregate, the higher the standard of living, the steeper the cost of living. It cannot be otherwise. For were everything desired so plentiful that nothing need be sacrificed to get anything, there would be no room in the world to store all that would be available. This impossibility presses our noses to the hard fact of the human condition, that scarcity, even in the most productive economy, can never be eliminated. That is also to say, that every good must be rationed by what people are willing to surrender to get it, by the value they put on it. The affluent attitude, therefore, by increasing wanting for goods and income, changes the conditions for acquiring goods and income by changing their prices.

But this chapter will not be the usual excursion through price theory. For we want to get behind the abstractions of supply and demand, marginal revenue and marginal cost and the rest of that most useful theoretical structure to the attitudes and behavior of economic agents.

Signalizing this difference in emphasis is our preference for using economic or exchange value instead of price. They mean the same thing, the worth of a thing or service in exchange. They differ only in that for which a thing is exchanged. Price is worth in exchange in terms of a common medium of exchange, called money. Economic value is worth in exchange in terms of all possible things, in varying amounts, which could be exchanged for it. The price of a new automobile is $4500; its economic value is the down payment on a house, a year at college, 18,000 ice cream cones, or a whole variety of things in different amounts.

While substitutes, value and price have quite different connotations, which make them better adapted to different kinds of economic discussion. Price is simple and precise, objective, and quantitative. It slips easily into mathematical formulas and is convenient for empirical research. Consequently, it is preferred in explaining and using analytical tools, determining the market price, marginal revenue and marginal cost and the like.

Value, on the other hand, is more complex, more subjective, and more kaleidoscopic. Consequently, it is not amenable to mathematical formulation. But it is better adapted to explaining behavioral tendencies. For economic value gets to the heart of real life decisions: what makers of goods must surrender to produce a good; what users of goods must trade-off of the benefits from goods they forego for benefits from goods they choose. Because of our focus on behavior, value is the preferable term, price being used only to clarify or highlight a point.

There are other value-related terms which we will use, whose meanings can well be defined here. Besides price and value, they are: wealth, income and surplus value. They express concepts as old as trade itself. Suffice to say, the Romans had words for them: 'valor' for value; 'pretium' for price; 'reventum' for income; 'divitiae' for wealth; and 'lucrum' for surplus value. While Roman jurists expended considerable effort in defining these concepts for their implications for justice in exchange, they showed little interest in analyzing what is our interest, their affects on economic behavior.

The following definitions are offered as helps for later discussions:

Value is the ability of a thing, a service, a right or a claim to command amounts of things in exchange. The elements which go into that ability are the theme of the chapter.

Price is value expressed in money, the ability to command money in exchange. Introducing money into exchange adds its own complicating factors.

Income is one's share in the valuable things produced by an economy, and usually it is expressed as a sum of money, but not always and never totally.

Wealth is the sum of the value of things which have not been used up. Mostly it consists of capital goods, things used to produce other goods, or claims to income from lending capital. While wealth is usually measured as an amount of money, very little wealth is in the form of money.

Surplus value is best rendered by the notion of gain, an increase in value realized variously by consumers, laborers and owners of natural resources, investor and entrepreneurs.

In a sense, surplus value is the key concept. The attempts to explain the phenomenon of gain started economics on its modern way.

With these preliminaries, we are ready to dig into the concept of economic value itself. From a survey of the development of the concept of value, we will draw a few implications for daily living. These then will guide us in the main effort of the chapter, examining how the affluent attitude affects the formation of economic values.

THEORIES OF ECONOMIC VALUE

The real richness of the concept of value and related concepts is revealed only in the history of great minds' struggle with them. For like all the great themes of intellectual endeavor, being, life, sex, matter, and energy, which form the context of the human condition, economic value does not reveal its full meaning in one blinding insight. We must struggle with it, as great scholars have struggled with it, treasuring their partial insights but always open to new facets which contemporary experience reveal.

In this quick journey into the past, we must keep our sights on one important land-mark, the phenomenon of national economic growth. Prior to the 15th and 16th Centuries, writers on value had little experience of other than largely static economies. Consequently, the community estimate of value, as opposed to the individual's estimate of a thing's worth, changed so slowly that it was an adequate measure of justice in exchange, moral and not economic behavior being their main concern. But even this non-economic approach has important analytical interest.

Ethical Theories

Aristotle (384-22 B.C.) saw the difficulty value poses for justice in exchange. In insisting that justice required the exchange of equalities, he realized that these equalities could not be identities because exchange can only involve differing amounts of different goods. Therefore, equality in exchange must be in terms of a common denominator, the values of the goods exchanged. Values, therefore, for Aristotle are the prices of goods, insofar as they express the social "demand" or the social function of the goods (and consequently of their producers) in the common life of the city, e.g., the services of a doctor vs. the services of a carpenter. In this enunciation Aristotle laid down the fundamental principle that exchange or economic value expresses and is measured by community standards and needs.[1]

Christian moralists never really deviated from this. Among the many who wrestled with the problem of fitting a temporal, mutable, and human order into an eternal and Divine order, Augustine (354-430) recognized clearly that the value of a thing expressed the desires of people for it rather than its intrinsic worth.[2] Aquinas (1225-74) carried the analysis one step further. A just price in exchange demanded that goods be exchanged according to equal quantities of value. Value in turn derives from a certain common estimate of producers, consumers, and authorities regulating trade. Since a common estimate was never quantitatively precise Aquinas argued for a range within which the just price could fall. Secondly, he allowed that the just price could vary from time to time and from city to city.[3]

These hints engaged some of the greatest minds in a continuous debate over the next three centuries. Scholars like Scotus, Antoninus, Biehl and especially the Jesuits, Molina, Lessius, and de Lugo, in defining justice in exchange, brought value theory, lacking only marginal analysis but including a wealth of empirical observation, to a stage which the science did not again achieve until 1870.[4]

Physical Concepts of Value

Many reasons are advanced why this development did not become the foundation of the new science of economics. The religious revolution is one, though Protestant moralists were concerned with much the same problems of just price, usury, moderation in seeking gain and the like as their Catholic counterparts. The shift of international trade from the Catholic Mediterranean lands to the Protestant Atlantic countries, as an explanation, forgets that Catholic Lisbon was as important as Protestant Amsterdam in opening the new world.

The more likely explanation, really encompassing the two, was a shift of concern away from the ethics of exchange to fascination with economic growth itself. The realization, that a nation as a whole could increase its economic well-being, turned men to the entirely this-worldly problem of how and why economies grew. Practical men, public administrators mainly in Germany, France, Spain and Italy, business men more so in England, they wrote about how to build up the State economically and how to increase international trade. They were laymen not clerics, men of affairs not scholars, excited about national wealth not eternal salvation. Though believing Christians for the most part, their interest was strongly secular.

The great volume of this mercantilistic writing was based on the rather crude and obvious assumption that the wealth of a nation was dependent on a favorable balance of trade, selling more abroad than was purchased. The desire to increase this 'over-vent' formed the basis of typical mercantilistic policies of the emerging nation-states regarding trade, tariffs, colonial development, stimulation of domestic industry, and the flow of specie. Out of this *ad hoc*, and often self-serving, literature emerged the clear understanding that a national economy grew from within by the creation of 'surplus' value.

The 100 years preceding the publication of the *Wealth of Nations* in 1776 may be called the age of the political economist. For the varied contributions of thinkers like Petty, Cantillon, Quesnay, Turgot, Steuart, Hume, Smith and many lesser lights had as common denominator an holistic view of the national economy. That is, unlike contemporary micro- and macro-economics which views the economic process from two different perspectives, from the level of individual and corporate decision-making and from the over-all aggregate level, the political economists looked at the national economy as a whole, incorporating individual gain-seeking within a social framework. They thus addressed themselves not only to the question what caused economic growth, but what was economic value itself and how it was distributed by production and exchange through all strata of society.

Impetus to this first great wave of modern economic analysis came from the work of Sir William Petty (1623-87). A medical doctor, surveyor, then economist, he was given the very practical problem of what taxes could be raised from the Irish estates acquired by British subjects after Cromwell's conquest of Ireland. This was a perfect laboratory for analyzing economic growth, simple, agricultural and controlled. Despite his crude methodology, Petty concluded that economic value must, and consequently could, be expressed quantitatively, and, secondly, that the basic unit of value could be expressed either as the amount of land necessary to support a worker or as the amount of labor necessary to make land productive. Any value over this was a 'surplus' value and represented economic growth.

Richard Cantillon (1680-1734), an Irish expatriate who became a successful French banker, systematized Petty's work. He applied his ideas to France, the most advanced economy at the time, placing it in its sociological setting, working in the circulation of money, and relating France to other countries through trade. Francois Quesnay (1694-1774),[5] court physician to Madame du Pompadour and founder of the Physiocrats, further systematized Cantillon, depicting the economy in his rightly famous Tableau Economique as a set of quantitive relations of two countering flows of goods and of money. For the first time the economic order was seen as distinct from the political, following its own principles of economic enterprise and generating its unique good, surplus value.

What emerged from French thought was a materialistic concept of value as the stuff from which useful goods were made. Thus Quesnay, in particular, confined the generation of value to the primary industries, agriculture mainly but also to forestry, fishing and mining. All other crafts shared in economic growth, not by generating value, but by transforming it into useful shapes.

What clarity this French development lost, when imported into England, it gained from the British commonsense intuition that all production and exchange generated value. One of the more brilliant contributors to British thought was David Hume (1711-76)[6] who in a few essays, in a career otherwise devoted to philosophy and history, sketched in how man's natural liveliness as expressed in the desire for gain caused surplus value to percolate rhythmically through the economy. Beginning with a favorable balance of trade, Hume showed how this stimulated the flow of money, raised the level of domestic prices and profits, and thus increased production and employment. Hume may be called the first business-cycle theorist.

Spurred by these hints and his own concern to square individual self-seeking with public benefit, Hume's friend, Adam Smith (1723-1790), presented in his Wealth of Nations[7] the first comprehensive treatment of the national economy. However the Wealth may lack in analytic sharpness even in comparison with Smith's contemporaries, it was enriched by empirical studies, contained a moral justification of economic enterprise, and further delineated the economy's independence of and relations to the political order.

Smith extended the notion of value beyond the Physiocratic 'stuff' to include all exchangeable goods. Value, for Smith, was what a good could be exchanged for, ultimately command over the labor necessary to produce other goods. Thus he eliminated services, which, however useful, evaporated on performance as unproductive labor. The creation of exchangeable value, as described by Smith, was a complex process. Sparked by man's desire to better his lot, it was woven of increased productivity through division of labor and mechanization, of stimulation to expand markets and accumulate capital, and of effecting necessarily a wider sharing of output. Throughout, Smith optimistically perceived the formation of exchangeable value -- as naturally harmonizing private with public interest, labor's well-being with the capitalist's desire to accumulate, and industrial production with agricultural improvement. Though Smith still confused exchange value with the valuable thing, he expanded the scope of exchange value as a worth-while and justifiable object of human enterprise, essentially social and necessarily having social consequences.

Cost Theories of Value

The *Wealth of Nations* brings to a close the first great wave of economic analysis. It became the text-book for all students of economics in England and for many on the Continent for some fifty years, even though its career was curtailed by the French Revolution and the Napoleonic Wars. After the turmoil, when scholars returned to more usual pursuits, the Industrial Revolution was in full swing. Inexplicably almost, they worried about population outpacing productivity, and distribution -- How output is shared? -- became the urgent question. A retired stockbroker, David Ricardo (1772-1823),[8] unschooled but sharp, clever and mathematical, developed a concept of value which gave the most convincing, though entirely pessimistic, answer to the distribution problem.

Ricardo's theory of distribution was simultaneously a theory of value and a theory of growth. Consequently, ignoring unique goods like the *Mona Lisa*, he focuses on the production of reproducible goods. In this Ricardo discovered an inherent contradiction in that, while labor is the substance of a commodity's value, its price must be shared by all factors to insure continued production. Thus at minimum labor must be paid a survival wage, capital a profit adequate to maintain or increase production, and land a rent. Unfortunately, since land was fixed while population was growing, land-owners, who merely owned free natural resources, inevitably garnered the lion's share. Labor's share, on the other hand, could only be reduced to the level of survival, and, consequently, profits inevitably declined to a level discouraging further increase in production. Therefore, economic growth generated its own demise and Smith's optimism was transformed into the pessimism of economic stagnation.

Where Ricardo's concept of value foundered was on the fact of industrial experience, that labor and capital could be mixed variously in producing the same good selling at the same price. Thus the rate of profit would differ depending upon the technology used. Ricardo, unfortunately, died too young to start his analysis anew.

From the intense debate on the Ricardian schema, consensus settled on the obvious, that exchange value must cover the costs of production: a minimum wage, a return to owners of land and raw materials, and profits compensating the sacrifice of capitalists in tieing up their funds in production. Thus the laws of production determined the value of the product. John Stuart Mill (1806-1873)[9] in summarizing the classical achievement could face with equanimity the paradox of increasing output and declining values, because the State could intervene to effect a more equitable distribution of goods. It is no credit to economists that this rickety solution satisfied most of them for almost a quarter century.

But not all. Standing head and shoulder above the rest, Karl Marx (1818-1883)[10] returned a pure labor theory of value to the center of a new political economy, a revolutionary view of man and history. Man, according to Marx, is essentially homo laborans. For by his own efforts not only does he wrest a better living from nature, but fulfills himself as man in union with others. Thus the labor expanded on a commodity is its value. The concrete, historical labor of this man is its use value, while considered abstractly as labor power, it is its exchange value. Value does not arise in exchange but in production, and only from labor.

Techniques of production, therefore, determine the stage of human development and all other social institutions, capitalism being but one stage in the inevitable march to universal community and fellowship. In capitalism, however, the use value of labor is swallowed by its exchange value, for the capitalist cannot perceive labor as serving the needs of man but only as a means of generating the surplus value he can expropriate. In destroying the natural purpose of production, the capitalist turns it into a nonsense activity, alienating not only worker from worker and worker from consumer, but the capitalist from himself.

Driven by the quest to accumulate, the capitalist devotes his exploited surplus value to expanding production, to mechanization, and to buying up other capitalists. This essentially irrational process of working labor longer, reducing wages, lowering skills and hiring fewer, while increasing output and centralizing wealth inevitably results in producing more output than can be purchased. Periodic crises succeed in greater magnitude until the last exploiters are themselves exploited by a classless worker society.

History, even in communist countries, has proved Marx and his pure labor theory of value wrong. Nevertheless, what we owe Marx is his clear insight that exchange value and all the paraphenalia of economic analysis only describe the necessary technique by which human productive effort can service the needs and wants of people, that ultimately the production of goods and services must unite not divide people. The implication of this, rather than his dialectic of oppressor and oppressed, is our real legacy from Marxian thought.

Utility Theories of Value

While Marx himself would perceive no implication of use value for a free-enterprise system, as a matter of fact within a half-dozen years of the appearance of Capital I, the concept of utility as an explanation of exchange value surfaced from the economic underground where it had held on since the writings of the last Scholastics. Simultaneously almost, W. S. Jevons (1835-1882) in England, Leon Walras (1834-1910) in France and Karl Menger (1840-1921)[11] in Austria in the last quarter of the 19th Century asserted that value is ultimately determined by people's desire for a thing.

But, and this is the all-important difference from late Scholastic analysis, what people will surrender in order to have more of a good is determined not by the thing's total but by its *marginal utility*. That is, the exchange ratio of a good with other goods is determined by how much extra satisfaction more of this good adds in contrast to the satisfaction which must be surrendered by having less of another or other goods. This is that most fundamental economic idea of *opportunity cost* which had hovered in economic thought for hundreds of years but which was only now seen as applying to both the exchange of final product and to the hiring of productive resources. Utility is now *imputed* to labor, capital and resources, and their mix is determined by each one's contributions to the utility of the product.

Thus marginal utility completely reversed the explanation of value. The synthesizing genius of Alfred Marshall (1842-1924)[12] integrated classical into marginal utility analysis, forging not only the first complete and consistent view of the economy but a set of analytic tools for use in solving practical problems. Marshall's concept of economic value is thoroughly modern. For the first time he consistently explained the related phenomena of market price, wealth, income, and gain while integrating all the fragmentary insights of previous thinkers.

A summary of this two-thousand year effort could be as follows: Economic value is the worth of a commodity in exchange, not as a good in itself. Value expresses a community estimate, importantly determined by labor and ordinarily covering the costs of production. Value, therefore, is shared by those contributing to its production. Value is quantitative, even services resting on a material substratum; it is exchangeable; and finally, it is ultimately determined by people's desires. Reflecting all these aspects, as an exchange relation it constantly adjusts to changing relative desires of consumers, to changing perceptions by producers of greater efficiency and more profits, and to the changing costs of productive resources. This infinitely varied and varying relation bound all economic phenomena into an interdependent system. At the same time, though a uniquely economic relation, different from ethical, social, psychological, political and even the physical relations which arise in production for exchange, economic value was influenced by all of them.

Modern Price Theory

The 20th Century economic thrust carried the Marshallian achievement along three lines. First, by concentrating on the margin of indifference, that state where having a bit more of one thing and a bit less of anything else does not change one's total satisfaction, economists were able to bypass measuring the intensity of satisfaction and the comparison of utilities between persons. Since all exchange relations could be expressed in money terms, economic analysis for the first time fulfilled Petty's dream of a defensible unit of measurement, and price theory superceded value theory.

This opened up two lines of development. Economists were able to study, supported by empirical research, a whole new menagery of influences on value: changes in consumer preferences, changes in income and income certainty, the force of competition and business market power, the effect of government regulation, change in the desire for profits, the effects of labor union power and the uniqueness of resources. The other development explored the effect of money itself on price: how changes in its amount and flow through the economy changed individual prices and the general level of prices.

These two veritable knowledge explosions, besides assuring economists an unlimited agenda for inquiry, has seemed to turn price theory into a morass of conflicting opinion. It is true to this extent that no comprehensive schema has been developed as yet showing the relative influences of all the monetary, marketing, production and consumption determinants on the kaleidoscope of prices. It is not true if it means denying that exchange value and price have definable meaning.

THE VALUE OF VALUE THINKING

The distillation from this intellectual effort over many centuries may seem trivial. Yet assimilating its lessons will have important implications for daily living. We feature three ideas as particularly helpful in reading the rest of the chapter and in one's everyday conduct. 1) Value thinking is primarily important in penetrating the surface, or economic value, of things to get to the underlying reality, their usefulness. 2) Economic values and prices are less substantial than the goods themselves for they are not things but only relations among things. 3) Hence, economic values and prices are volatile, subject to many influences beyond the control of consumers. Nevertheless, consumers are neither impotently passive nor defenseless victims. We turn to a brief discussion of each.

Useful and Exchangeable

People relate to economic goods in two ways, perceiving them as use objects and as exchange objects simultaneously. As useful, commodities are seen as satisfying or not satisfying wants, as fulfilling or frustrating goals, as yielding pleasure or pain, as, in short, being good or bad, or as blending any combination of these subjective responses. As exchange or wealth objects, goods are seen as possessing value in exchange for money or other goods. Goods as wealth objects reflect, not so much our personal preferences, but a common or market estimate of their worth.

The perceptive student of economics recognizes this distinction as the source of the famous paradox of value, that diamonds whose use value is trivial command a high price while water which is vital for survival may be free. The paradox, upon which classical economists were hung, was resolved by marginal utility analysis which demonstrated that exchange value was ultimately determined by use value.

The neo-classicists unfortunately, in reducing all economic phenomena to a common denominator, tended to blur the essentially analogous nature of economic goods. For everyone relates uniquely to each of his economic possessions, variously blending value in use and value in exchange. Some treasured trinkets, pictures, and old toys have nothing but scrap, or even negative, exchange value -- someone must be paid to cart them away. Some wealth, like rights or claims to income, will have no use value beyond the comfort and confidence they give in meeting future vicissitudes. All economic goods blend the two, each in a particular manner.

This is not merely a philosophical nicety but bears important consequences for behavior. The degree to which use value predominates largely indicates the joy or pleasure one takes from economic possessions. The degree to which exchange value predominates measures the confidence one faces the future, which confidence is at the heart of the affluent attitude. Unlike our ancestors who drew their economic confidence from the very things which satisfied material wants, mainly their dwelling and its furnishing, we derive our confidence and measure our wealth in terms of exchange value, the earnings from a job, the market value of a home, the cash value of insurance policies, the expected income from pensions and social security. The awe that the affluent attitude has for exchange value can be counteracted by more insight into the usefulness of things, the pleasure which possessions can bestow, the joy of work well done.

This point is illuminated by resolving the distinction which people make between material things and human services. Things are not desired so much for their material content or the amount of labor expanded as for their form, arrangement, and, in general, what they can do for us. All this is a function of their human input, designing, engineering, fabricating, transporting and servicing the good. On the other hand, a service does not consist in just the immediate contact of person to person. A golf pro's instruction distills long years of practice and experience, and hopefully results in a permanent modification of the pupil's putting technique. Then too no instruction is possible without a putter, a ball, and a putting green. The difference between a golfing lesson and a new automobile is, from a production viewpoint, only in the mixture of human and material inputs. Consequently, we can look on both economic things and services as bundles of services, qualities perceived as useful in satisfying wants. These bundles are differentiated only regarding the manner and speed with which their usefulness is released to satisfy human wants.

Relation not Substance

The disposition to see beyond exchangeability to usefulness will further help to correct a common myopia that prices and values are inherent to the substance of things. Orthodox Marxists still maintain that a product's value is the labor incorporated in it. Most others assume the costs of the factors of production. It is true these are determinants but not the only, or even the most important, determinants of value. There is no proportion between a product's value and the aggregate of resources used. (Rationalization of production, the substitution of human ingenuity and knowledge for matter, is a hallmark of abundant economies.) Value is not an amount of some physical quantity, nor is it a substantial quality. It is an <u>estimation of a thing's worth</u> in terms of what must be surrendered for it. It is an exchange ratio, a relation between things.

The distinction between the useful and the exchangeable can also help keep perspective on one's wealth. For wealth, as values which are not used up, is determined by the market value of possessions. Wealth is objective, their consensus value or market price here and now. But a statement of one's wealth is not necessarily a statement of one's material well-being. Many major items like homes or automobiles can drastically lose their market value and most personal items, once bought, possess little, yet they continue to serve our material well-being. Stocks and bonds may even lose their market value but continue to pay the same dividends and interests. While there is a wealth effect, a feeling of well-being in possessing what others or society generally values highly, there is another criterion, one's subjective well-being. Value thinking will consider both the exchange and use sense of value, what a thing is worth on the market and what is it worth to me.

In the same vein one must be wary of reading Gross National Product and National Income too literally. Obviously inflationary increases must be eliminated for GNP figures to be comparable. A much more important consideration is that changes in real GNP do not measure exactly changes in economic well-being. For GNP does not take into consideration that many economic goods, particularly household services, now are purchased and enter GNP which previously were supplied within the household and did not enter GNP. It does not take into consideration that the production of goods and services entails harmful side-effects like over-crowding, pollution and the rest which require removal and alleviation. Much of GNP, increased police and fire protection expenditures, increased safety requirements add to GNP but may only reduce ill-fare and not add to well-fare. Thus GNP overstates economic well-being. But it also understates it. Goods produced more efficiently and in greater volume will tend to sell at lower prices. Thus they will add a measure to material well-being which is not matched by change in total sales. A washing-machine today is really cheaper than it was in 1950 but no less useful than before. Finally, GNP has no measure of the net benefit of leisure well-used versus the ill effects of its bad use, nor the net between the burden of and satisfaction from labor.[13]

Consequently, when we read that real Gross National Product in the U.S. increased from $387b. in 1950 to $906b. in 1975 and per capita from $2546 to $4254, both using 1967 as base, we can conclude with some justification that material well-being has increased, but we cannot conclude that it has increased 70%, even if that would mean anything.

Victims of Value Volatility

Value thinking can do much to unblock that most ingrained habit of consumers that they are passive victims of price changes. For the householder, especially, comes face to face with a price at the end of a long line of prices -- the prices of raw materials, the price of labor, the profit-mark-up of sellers and underlying these a series of price influences beyond their control, political privilege, market power, advertising, inflation and taxes. The only choice a householder has, it seems is to pay up or do without.

Take for example, the astronomical increase in the price of coffee a few years ago. In 1974 Brazil suffered a disastrous freeze of coffee trees, just at the time that OPEC announced a four-fold increase in the price of its oil imports. Consequently, Brazil adds a hefty export tax to the already higher price, resulting from the freeze. In the meantime, the Big Four in this country, smelling panicky stocking-up on coffee, slapped on thier own larger mark-up, and a cup of coffee rivaled a bottle of beer in price. Consumers howled, religious groups shouted moral outrage, Congress set up a committee to investigate.

In the scenario American consumers seem simply victimized by the weather, OPEC, Brazilian politicians, and greedy importers. Yet American coffee demand is still the important dynamic in the drama. For Brazil, needing to balance its imports, will hardly put an excise tax on casava roots but upon coffee beans, its big seller to the U.S. Coffee importers here in turn respond to consumer panic by increasing prices.

Yet however shocked, American consumers, as subsequent events prove, were hardly helpless. Twenty percent shift to tea and other drinks. Folgers drops the shelf price; coffee futures tumble; Colombia and Costa Rica gain a larger share of the market; as new trees start bearing, prices fall further, and Brazil is forced to balance its oil imports with increased exports of other goods. No doubt cynical self-interest accentuated price movements throughout the sequence, but the crucial determinant was still the American consumer's demand for coffee.

Even so, the individual consumer, assessing his individual against aggregate demand, is likely to be unconvinced. Indeed, no empirical study is sensitive enough to detect the effect of the individual's substituting one for another. A shopper may well question the cost in time and gasoline of shopping around against the savings realized. In rebuttal it may be pointed out that a total boycott is seldom necessary to bring suppliers to heel. Since profits usually swing on a 10-15% change in sales, buyer resistance need never be total to be effective. Intelligent buying with some willingness to make a sacrifice by a small minority generally suffices. To the private victory of buying at sale what one passed up at higher price is added the comfort of contributing to the consuming public's gain. A generally higher level of price consciousness will be that much more effective if only in establishing a climate of resistance which sellers must take into account.

Such resistance, furthermore, does not stop at the retail level. Since suppliers of goods can only pay prices for labor and materials in anticipation of their products' selling prices, decline of those sales do work backward to wholesalers, manufacturers, labor unions and suppliers of raw materials. What careful reading of value analysis will give the householder is that same confidence professional buyers have that they do influence prices and know that they do.

Value thinking finally provides the most important bonus in promoting the critical habit of contrasting a commodities worth-in-exchange to its worth-to-me. Such thinking is disastrous for impulse buying and frees one of the mindset that only a particular brand will satisfy. It goes further in stimulating substitution, finding another commodity altogether which at a lower price will do almost as well in satisfying one's want. Value thinking, because it is alert both to one's own market power and to personal considerations and subjective criteria, yields the conviction that no item on the super-market shelves is necessary, and thus frees us from the bogus tyranny, that prices are set by mysterious market forces beyond our control.

Persons, who are sensitive to the flux of values and to the complex of factors causing that flux, underpin their instinctive economic behavior with understanding. They are better prepared to see and accept that values reflect community estimates. They know that their economic decisions as householders, workers, businessmen or government officials influence with varied effects the price structure of goods. They are consequently no longer passive victims of value changes but learn to read economic signals in a way to enhance their material well-being.

The second half of this chapter will then discuss how affluent behavior generates economic values and thus modifies the economic conditions of life. Since the affluent attitude has two moments, wanting more goods and wanting more income, the discussion naturally divides into examining the demand determinants of value, consumer income and preference, and the supply determinants, production for sale and profit-seeking. It will do little to advance the theory of value. At best it will flesh out that theory with some of the contemporary influences on value dynamics. This review, therefore, is not intended to resolve value issues except in the general way that having seen the varied elements which engender values, the student is forearmed in dealing with them.

DEMAND DETERMINANTS

Demand as a willingness to buy implies not only the desire for goods but the ability to buy them. Hence, though wanting more income is the motive for supplying goods and services, possessing more income is a condition for wanting more goods.

Income

Income as a determinant of demand influences the price and value of goods. From the macro-point of view it is almost a tautology that the income generated in the production of economic goods will eventually clear the market of those goods. The corner stone of the economic structure is that governments inevitably spend all, even more than, their income and that households' spending is a predictable portion, within a narrow range, of their disposable income. Only business investment shows sizable deviations from income. Spending on the goods and services which are the stuff of our material living, as opposed to spending on the means to produce those goods always expands as income expands. Put another way, increased income increases the general demand for goods. An income of $3000 today would provide a miserably crabbed existence for a typical blue-collar family. Yet it would buy at today's prices the same amount of goods which provided a comfortable living for an unskilled worker and his family in New York in 1915.[14] This is the persistent push of income not only to have more goods but to have more of what is already had. Income elasticity, economists say, for most goods is positive.

This point can be made forcefully in applying it to a common complaint that services performed no more efficiently now than in the past command a higher price. Barbers and teachers are favorite examples. Barbering, not hair-styling, techniques have changed little, yet barbers get $3.50 for the same haircut which 25 years ago commanded a quarter. Most people immediately conclude that while the price of haircuts has increased astronomically, their value has not. The fact of the matter, however, is that the value of the haircut to the consumer undoubtedly has increased. The well-groomed appearance, necessary for a salesman to write $10,000 of sales thirty-five years ago is now necessary for him to write $100,000 today. The value of good grooming and periodic haircuts has increased with his income. The professor who drones on as he did decades ago is more valuable because students will pay higher tuitions. They in turn will pay higher tuition because the economic rewards are higher. The question, in these cases, is not whether barbers and teachers are more valuable -- they are and must be paid accordingly or we will not have their services -- but rather whether they are as useful as they claim to be or as they could be. To this question the market gives an answer but not the definitive one. Additional non-economic criteria must be used.

Wanting

Increasing income by itself will not increase values unless complemented by the proliferation of wants. For as common experience tells us more of the same thing eventually satiates. (This is the foundation of marginal utility analysis.) But the dynamics of wanting is not a one-dimensional relation of economic good to personal satisfaction. Just as life is multi-relational so want is multi-relational. Goods relate to each other as competing or substituting in satisfying wants, margerine substituting for butter, or as complementing or enhancing each other, as bread and butter mutually enhance their satisfying qualities. Substitution is the principle of shifting from one good to another as price and preference directs. Complementarity is the principle of fulfilling wants in new combinations. Like breathing in and breathing out they are elements in the same process, but complementarity is the more important in the growth of wants.

A helpful preliminary to what follows would be to unfreeze one's conception of material goods, and all the more so human services, as satisfying only one want at a time. The truer conception, applying even to the simplest thing, is to consider all economic goods as a bundle of useful qualities, as a number of possible ways of satisfying wants. Take one of the simplest substances, salt. Its production has not changed appreciably for as far back as we know. Its importance for daily living is revealed in that our word 'salary' originally meant salt-money, the amount given to Roman legions to buy salt. The possession of salt was a critical determinant of economic development. Yet the discovery of almost unlimited supplies encouraged studying more and more uses for salt. Today savoring food is its smallest use. More is used in preserving food and hides, as a refrigerant and de-icer, as a source of industrial sodium and chloride and their compounds. A grain of salt has many uses, it is a bundle of useful qualities.

Salt, however, is a natural compound. The range of its usefulness is extended by studying the properties found in it. For fabricated goods their quality features can be consciously built into them. Furthermore, every new one relates this good to other goods as a substitute or complement, thus revealing new uses in a proliferation which is conceptually limitless.

Want Accumulation

Wanting, however, is not just a passive response to new products but a drive to increase our want-satisfactions, to complicate them, and to derive a higher psychic benefit from them. The first principle of wanting is want accumulation: goods originally novelties, acquire daily usage. The automobile, once rare and a rich man's toy, is today a family necessity. Even in an abundant economy the accretion of wants takes place so gradually, even surreptiously, that we are not aware of it. The change shocks only when parents contrast their want-patterns as children with those of their own children. For children, for whom the history of the human race begins at their attaining consciousness, the wants their parents already have are given. There is no memory of a time when these wants were not satisfied and these goods not available. What disturbs parents is that children take for granted what their parents have struggled for and then demand more. But even parents look back at times and wonder how they survived without a favorite convenience. Wants for goods previously non-existant become part of our culture. Wants grow on us, and in so doing increase the scarcity and the value of the goods which satisfy those wants.

Want Combination

A far greater expansion of wants comes from the combining and fusion of wants into complementary packages. A family setting out from St. Louis for California in 1876 faced much the same kind of experience which families would have faced undertaking a similar journey since the beginnings of human history. It would be long, hard, dangerous and killingly tedious. It would call up immense reserves of courage to face the discomforts, the illnesses, the hard work, the heat and the cold, the wild animals and fierce peoples. Quite differently a family, setting out from St. Louis for California today in their Winnebago camper, carries the comforts of home with them, soft beds, good meals, climate control, radio and TV. They control an immense power-package which takes them quickly and smoothly across plains and through mountains. An adventure no less, but of pleasure not of courage.

The homes we live in, the meals we eat, the clothes we wear, even the ballgames we attend combine convenience, comforts, satisfactions with these goods' original and basic purposes which were undreamed of a generation ago. There is no reason to believe, no matter how ridiculous the combinations frequently are, that this dynamic of wanting will slow down. In fact, the opposite should be expected that we will attempt to combine complex packages of want satisfaction into more complex ones. And each more complex good is costlier than the previous.

Want Symbolization

Besides accumulating and complicating wants, we seek another dimension of satisfaction from the goods we desire. For example, Jeff is given a digital watch for his birthday. He likes it for two reasons, the obvious because it tells time accurately but also because in showing it off he becomes the envy of his friends. This is a very real satisfaction, over and above the usefulness of the good itself. While advertisers and manufacturers take advantage of it, it is largely owing to our own expectation that owning this particular thing will enhance our value in our own and in others' eyes. This dimension or principle of wanting we call want symbolization.

Moralists since Plato have ridiculed or inveighed against its more perverse manifestations. Adam Smith made such vanity an important element in economic self-seeking, insisting that half the world's business is motivated by the desire for place.[15] No one was more assiduous in ferreting out examples of conspicuous consumption in the daily lives of people than the American economist-sociologist, Thorstein Veblen (1857-1929).[16] Indeed he carried it to the point of caricature -- polished shoes, for example. (His own were always rather scruffy.) In a rather far-fetched way he traces it back to the predatory instincts of the nobility, now bowdlerized and democratized by a bourgeois middle-class. More accurately and sympathetically Smith founds it upon the normal hope to enjoy pre-eminence over others, no less manifested in conspicuous consumption by the well-to-do, by the esotericism of a technocrat elite, and by the personal use of government power by bureaucrats and public servants. In other words, wanting to lord it over others is a universal tendency.

No less universally but not as generally acknowledged, goods have a symbolic satisfaction in the more usually spiritual sense. Bread, for example, means more to people than simple survival. The breaking of bread becomes a symbol of friendship, of sharing in religious community and, in Christianity, of union with God. Meals, homes, clothes, public buildings, even factories, become means for expressing friendship, love, religious devotion, and concern for the public well-being.

This transcendent dimension of wanting cannot be emphasized too strongly both because it is often overlooked and because, when averted to, misinterpreted. Overlooking it cuts physical wanting off from the larger aspects of personality development and Value formation. Such oversight, therefore, misses the real dynamic of wanting which is to fulfill wants which have no fulfillment, to love and to be loved, to know and to be known, to have power and to be held in awe, to possess beauty and to be admired. When accorded consideration, this drive is too frequently misunderstood. Its more perverse aspects -- emulation, invidiousness, diletantism and tyranny -- are dramatically played up as the effects of affluence. But the more human impulses of the spirit -- generosity, commiseration, and social concern -- are also abetted by affluence and in turn influence the course of abundance. That is, they both increase economic values.

In summary, the insistent force of desiring more economic goods increases both their scarcity and their values. Given increased income as pre-condition, the affluent acquire an ever larger burden of goods and services, both satisfying more complex packages of wants and pressed to fulfill wants with limitless 'psychic' dimensions. While too frequently ignored or taken for granted, in contrast to income expectations, wanting goods is, like the Japanese and Gulf Streams for the weather, the one massive and constant factor generating economic growth and value formation.

SUPPLY DETERMINANTS

In shifting to the supply side of value formation we consider the second moment of the affluent attitude, income expectations. It is not unrelated to the first. For most income is wanted to buy present or future goods, for one's self or for others, to satisfy physical or psychic wants. Secondly, except when we steal or expect gifts, income expectations are fulfilled only by meeting in some way the wants of others.

Income wanting, however, is no less complex subject than wanting goods. It has two different, though related, aspects: 1) realizing income by supplying goods which are desired and 2) realizing profits by increasing efficiency or by exercising market power. Since profits depend upon, though not proportional to, production, we address the more fundamental principle first.

Bundles of Usefulness

The purpose of production is to sell commodities, which, it is hoped, demanders will perceive as useful and want-satisfying. Contemporary products do not satisfy different sets of human wants than did the products of the work-shops and farms of Imperial Rome. People still are hungry and thirsty and have sexual wants; they seek protection and shelter and adornment; and they want to travel, to communicate, to know and to love. But today's products do service wants differently, in greater doses, more swiftly, more conveniently, and in a more complicated pattern of satisfactions. A commodity does not satisfy a want, but many wants simultaneously. It is a bundle of want-satisfying qualities.

A natural thing like food is not simply nutrition. It must be appealing to finicky appetites. It must be presentable, have color, be sanitary, conveniently packaged and have the correct proportions of vitamins and calories. A fabricated item like an automobile must meet many more needs than the generic need for transportation. We want color, styling, beauty. We demand minimal safety and easy maintenance and above all comfort. An automobile ride is not simply a passage from here to there but a total human experience, swift as flying, comfortable as sitting at home, cool as the spring-time, made pleasurable with music and full views of the passing scenery -- or so advertisers would have us wish!

Such a complex product requires experts from many fields, mechanics and automotive engineers, safety experts, architects, designers, stylists, interior decorators, psychologists, even poets. Such a bundle of satisfactions comes with a bundle of maintenance worries, is subject to larger repair bills, and burdened with quicker obsolescence. For every gain in satisfaction there is an added cost in frustration.

Beyond these obviously useful features, commodities have others which are often taken for granted. Having products available at a time and place convenient to the customer are services which whole industries are devoted to providing. We do not travel to Detroit to buy an automobile but to a local showroom, where it had been delivered and stored against purchase. These are costly services and must be paid for. Without them mass production would be impossible. Sometimes the anomaly results that those who provide this service receive more than the original producer, the milk processor and delivery man, more than the dairy farmer. On the other hand, the demand for milk and the farmer's revenue would be considerably smaller if milk had to be picked up at the farm. So they are valuable and desired services. But they are also complicating links in the productive chain, creating the increased possibility of annoying break-downs and more frustration.

There are other productive services more strictly affluence phenomena. About them rages some of the burning issues of business ethics. Because they are not clearly delineated even by those who provide them they are attacked and defended with simplistic fervor. Neither their names nor number are standardized. We list three and call them knowledge, motivation and insurance services.

Knowledge and Motivation Service

Knowledge service is what its name implies. It is information about what a product is, what it can do, where it can be obtained and often its usual or current price. Good examples are the Yellow Pages of the telephone directory or a Sears-Roebuck Catalogue. To see how this is a distinct service which affluence demands, imagine how slender similar publications would be for London in 1760. Commodities proliferate at such a bewildering pace that experienced advice is needed just to read such catalogues successfully. Their convenience for long distance shopping is inestimable. The confused householder who has gone to the hardware looking for a "whatsis" is seeking information first of all. Real estate or used-car listings provide information both valuable to buyers and costly to produce.

Usually the costs of information are covered in the general costs of business. Sometimes expensive and specialized catalogues must be paid for, or are free only to large purchasers. In either case the buyer must rely on the good will, competence, and accurate descriptions of the seller. He really gains value when his ignorance or credulity are not taken advantage of, when he is supplied with exactly the right commodity to fill his want, neither needing to replace or to modify it. The wider the listing or more extensive the catalogue the more likely his needs will be matched and, hence, the more valuable the information.

Related to knowledge is motivational service -- in popular terms salesmanship and advertising. For motivational service goes beyond merely informing to helping the customer to make up his mind. Advertising must do this in a more general way; salesmanship in a more individualistic manner, tailored to customer and circumstances. The purpose of both is to persuade the customer that this product will satisfy a want and thus elicit the decision to buy it.

Whether this is a real service or an abuse is best approached from the side of the customer. Obviously, the customer must determine to buy if he would buy. When he knows what he wants, he needs only an order-taker. But where his wants are felt but unspecified like Milquetoast who has been told to get a new suit, or where what is wanted does not match desires like the sweet sixteen stack of blubber eyeing a mini-skirt, judicious guidance to decision clearly benefits the customer.

More typically, intelligent buyers who know their needs are still at a great disadvantage when faced with a variety of choices among highly complicated products whose engineering and scientific principles they cannot understand. Added apprehension comes from the customer's exposing his want to persons whose obvious self-interest is to sell as much and at as high a price as possible. The instinct of the experienced salesperson sets out to allay such fears by a friendly approach, a solicitude to ferret out the customer's precise needs, by demonstrating the proper use and cautioning against misuse of the product, and finally by assuring the product's serviceability, citing the manufacturer's guarantee and the selling company's reputability. Such adroit maneuvering by these practical psychologists is a real motivational service. They earn their commissions.

On the other hand, information and persuasion are very subtle goods, easily subject to abuse by the clever professional taking advantage of an inexperienced amateur, misinforming, selling for wrong reasons, doing violence to conscience and leading him by the nose. Overselling, hoodwinking, and outright fraud easily change the sale into a disservice. Unfortunately the pressure to move merchandise often earns high praise and reward for such tactics against the more conscientious servicing of customer wants. Only the firm, which values more highly the repeat business of satisfied customers over the quick sale and fast shuffle, rightly appreciates knowledge and motivational services and their significance in long-run value creation.

Advertising, except perhaps that pitched at small children, is probably more irritating than abusive of personal freedom. For all that advertising can do is to dispose people well toward a company, to motivate the customer to inquire about a product, or to give a brand name a memory edge when the buyer must choose among basically identical commodities. The deluge of TV and radio advertising has probably accentuated cigarette smoking, beer drinking, hair grooming, and our oral-armpit syndrome, one or all of which some will consider undesirable. But the phenomenal growth in sales of pornographic material, street drugs, liquor, contraceptives and abortion clinics, which many consider deplorable, owes little to these media.

Most mass media advertising probably does little more than keep a brand-name before a forgetful public. Some are among the cleverest productions of commercial television. Much of the blasting messages and weird vignettes does as much harm as good by blunting people's sensibility to advertising itself. The persistently frenetic tone of much advertising rather mirrors than dictates the kaleidoscopic shifting of consumer preferences. The most likely villain is our own affluence. For affluence has conditioned a sizable segment of the market, not just the young, to seek novelty for its own sake. Thus a slight advertising edge can produce significant sales leverage. Further, since intense advertising competition usually substitutes for price or quality competition, advertising exploits the reluctance of the affluent to engage in comparative shopping.

Insurance

Insurance is the last of the modern productive services we consider. It is, as a matter of fact, not very modern but as ancient as foreign trade itself. Wherever risk can be isolated as a distinct and predictable feature of business, insurance against such risk has arisen as a rational response. What is peculiar to abundant economies is the spread of insurance from foreign trade into every nook and cranny of economic life. Not only giant private firms but every modern government is in the insurance business. The mass popularity of insurance accurately reflects the changes, frustrations, uncertainties, the risks which affluence has generated because events beyond our control can turn comfortable living into bankruptcy.

Such insurance while called forth by affluence is also made possible by economic abundance. For only an economy which anticipates increasing abundance can provide out of current income against possible disaster. Secondly, only mass abundance permits mass insurance. Only when large numbers can afford insurance is it possible to take advantage of the statistical laws of large numbers where what is haphazard, occasional and accidental for the individual can be predicted with high probability for a large group.

Insurance against risk is itself a gamble but a gamble in which heads I win in one respect and tail I win in another. Take life insurance. The insured gambles that he will die before the predicted number of years. If he loses he enjoys the normal four score, more or less, man hopes for.

If he wins, his widow and family receive a hedge against the effects of his untimely demise. Since affluence has accentuated risk and worsened the adverse effects of accidents, it is entirely rational to make provision against responsibilities which carry on after death.

Insurance loses its hedge against risk when it subtly shifts from primarily restoring loss to guaranteeing reparation. When insurance premiums increase just to meet inflated hospital charges and doctors' fees, bloated settlements and mounting repair costs, insurance in effect benefits these recipients more than those who pay the premiums.

Less well understood and more frequently castigated is the insurance service and risk assumption called speculation. We all speculate whenever we buy more or less than ordinarily in anticipation of a price change. Thus American consumers stocked up on coffee, speculating coffee prices would rise higher. Speculation as a business, however, exists in the large, highly competitive markets such as in national currencies, in stocks and bonds of national and international corporations, in bonds of governments, and in basic raw materials. The risk inherent in these markets arises from either supply or demand changing drastically with little corresponding change in the other and thus causing wide swings in prices.

Such instability is attractive to the gambling instinct. But contrary to popular imagining, these markets are not made by professional speculators but by firms and individuals who want to invest their savings or whose business necessarily involves them in the market. They can be irreparably harmed if price swings generate widespread selling or feverish buying.

Thus the speculator in grains, in stocks and bonds, and in national currencies gambles against the swings of the market by buying when he thinks their prices will rise and selling when he thinks they will fall. Clear vision, decision, and luck are requisites for success. He can neither panic nor yield to greediness. For the successful speculator must be ahead of the market, but just ahead. He must deal with the future. He must assume risks. He realizes his profit -- and sometimes very handsomely -- on a very narrow margin of gain multiplied by a huge volume of buying and selling.

If he gambles successfully his action will tend to reverse price changes, thus stabilizing the market. If he gambles wrongly, he will accentuate the rise and fall of prices. But unsuccessful speculators do not last long. Hence, the overall effect of professional speculation is to counteract the violent ups and downs of these highly competitive, hence volatile markets. His profits are the wages of risk assumption.

Not all risk can be separated from the product and assumed by professional risk-takers. Most risk inheres in the production process itself. Where identified and localized in the enterprise itself, in what economists call the entrepreneurial function, it is a true insurance utility and gives title to a unique form of income called profit in the strict economic sense. But not all risks of production can be so localized. Much spills over unto employees and indeed unto the entire economy. For risk flows from the characteristic of affluence itself: its fluctuations, volatility, fluidity, its changeability.

o An abundant economy, in summary, is a changing economy and its products are both changing and increasingly complex. Modern commodities require not only sophisticated
o production but sophisticated marketing. They are more difficult to understand, require greater persuasion to sell, and are fraught with more risks at every stage.
o Consequently, economic values are also constantly changing, usually upward, and greater disparities between value-in-exchange and value-to-me can arise. The abun-
o dant economy is more bountiful, more costly, and more bothersome.

Profit-Seeking

While providing useful products is the means, profit-seeking is the motive of production. Classical economics generally treated profit-seeking with benign neglect, assuming that businessmen would seek to maximize it but that competition would reduce it to a modest, even minimum necessary, return on capital. Contemporary economics is more ambivalent, often embarrassed by the fact of profits yet justifying it analytically, just as Victorians thought sex a dirty business but continued to produce babies and to laud motherhood. Like sex, it means many things to different people. In this context it will not mean profit in the strict economic sense mentioned above but simply the gain resulting from an economic decision or business enterprise.

But the desire for profits is the only rationale for business. This dogmatism is more easily defended by approaching it negatively. An economic loss -- negative profits -- makes no sense either for society or for private business. For society, a loss means that a commodity is valued less than the other goods sacrificed to produce it. For private business, a loss spells a worse state of affairs after effort than before. If losses must happen, society and individuals are better off if minimized. And this criterion of economic performance is no less true for socialist as for private enterprise. In a free enterprise economy it applies no less to government agencies, to non-government, non-profit enterprises and to businesses for profit. Loss-minimization is a universal criterion of performance.

No less universal is the profit-maximization principle since the two are opposing sides of the same coin. Indeed, profit-maximization is but a particular aspect of the more universal principle of gain-maximization which applies under all conditions of scarcity. For scarcity imposes the rationale of not sacrificing more in order to have less, but always the less to have more. Applied to profits and losses it is called the marginal-revenue, marginal-cost principle. This simply states that a decision should be made if the expected benefit exceeds, even by a little, the cost or sacrifice the decision requires.

This logic being so irrefutable, whence the contemporary waffling about profits? It arises precisely because profit-maximization as used in economic analysis is only a logic and its particular meaning must be determined from the context of each economic decision or policy. That is, like the connection between subject and verb, profit and losses are manifested in a great variety of ways and each time must be interpreted within the particular situation. To take extreme examples it applies both to a thief contemplating another burglary and a philanthropist another benefaction. For the thief must assess the possible loot from another heist against the increased risk of being caught; the philanthropist must weigh the benefit to one donee as against that of another. To both profit-maximization applies.

Profit-maximization runs into difficulty when torn from the context of the act. We may well judge, to return to our examples, that the thief is acting more intelligently, economically speaking, than the philanthropist, but that does not absolve the immorality of his act or deny the morality of the other. That is, economic rationality must always apply within the context of all the principles, moral, political, social, aesthetic, etc. which govern action. Thus in no two situations will profit-maximization have the same concrete manifestation. One need but read the footnotes in quarterly or annual reports to confirm that the same business interprets the principle differently under different conditions of competition, economic prosperity, or stages of growth. All the more so, profit-seeking varies according to moral conscience, social customs and laws, and the purposes of the profit-seeker. The contemporary discomfiture with the profit principle comes from using an analgous concept univocally.

While profit-seeking follows many paths, most can be categorized under two general headings: profit-seeking by way of reducing costs and improving efficiency, and profit-seeking by way of exercising market, or monopoly, power. While most profit policies may be a blend of the two, it is best to examine them in isolation to determine their specific effect on value formation.

Profit-seeking of the first kind is generally considered benevolent. It combines factors of production in ever new ways to reduce costs, to improve product, to increase output and thereby sell more. It seeks new markets and deeper penetration into old. It capitalizes on the interdependence of product utilities to combine them in ever new ways to titillate consumers. Some of this results from important technological break-throughs or better management; some of this is shrewd and efficient business getting a jump on competitors and an edge in a market; some of this is grotesque product differentiations, trivial differences trumpeted in mammoth advertising campaigns. Some of this profit-seeking is perverted: products are produced which cannot be repaired, or styles are changed to make older, still useful models obsolete.

Profit-seeking, resulting in improved efficiency, has a mixed effect on product values. Under the spur of competition production efficiency will tend to lower unit costs and hence prices. But since at lower prices consumers tend to buy more, the actual values produced and sold may increase. This certainly, is an important element in the growth of the economy. Product differentiation, too, to the extent that it responds to real differences in consumer wants may result in both more output and higher prices, a differential which consumers are willing to pay because of the added features. The false or fakey kind of product differentiation may raise the values of things simply by taking advantage of the credulity of people.

This last shades into profit-seeking by gaining a market advantage. In itself a normal and to-be-expected human reaction to the risks and competitiveness of business, it, like pleasure-seeking in sex is healthy but difficult to control. Such profit-seeking is limber, fluid and protean, taking whatever shape and emphasis the situation calls for.

Some take advantage of the differing demands of consumers, charging a higher price to those willing to pay more and lower to those less willing or unable to pay as much. Much price discrimination is accepted practice, like children-student-adult admissions to theatres, or discounts for volume buying. At the other extreme, it may be a bald attempt to take advantage of ignorance and credulity of some buyers rather than others.

Some profit-seeking is the crude exercise of economic tyranny: destroying or buying out competitors to raise prices, monopolizing raw materials, taking advantage of labor, colluding with potential competitors to fix prices, seeking legal privileges under guise of fair competition, health, and safety regulations, or the well-being of the local economy. All are power attempts to increase the market price of product by restricting production. But the increase in value is exploited by the profiteer, and what he gains, the buyer loses. The whole subject of market power will be explored in detail in Chapter Ten.

o In summary, profit-seeking, as a principle of action, almost always creates more value. Some is real, a true net value because of efficiency or a more desired product
o which the innovator pockets and no one else has lost. Some profit-taking is a rip-off. What the profiteer has gained, someone else has lost. Some profit-seeking is
o short-run and some long-run. The profit motive of the con-artist who will make a quick buck and then disappear never to return again is quite different from the profit desires
o of the company which hopes for repeat business, will be at the same corner to hear complaints, and will stand behind their product in the hopes of selling more. Whatever form
o they take, production and the hope for gain are constantly influencing the exchange value of goods.

Finally, wanting goods and offering goods results in exchange. In this final act value is also created. For no exchange between different but equal goods could take place unless both parties would feel better off after the exchange than before. Unless the supermarket would prefer my money to their stock of goods, and I their meat to my money, there is no reason for trade at all. Thus value is created by exchange itself.

THE KALEIDOSCOPE OF VALUE

This is the kaleidoscope of values. Values constantly change. For they are susceptible to so many determinants, changes in the ability of demanders to buy, changes in their preferences and their perceptions of use values, changes in productive techniques and costs of production, and changes in sellers' desires for profit and gain. There is no such thing as <u>the</u> price of a good, except as a momentary phenomenon, that particular exchange ratio of good for money in which all these changing influences find expression. Even that is not quite correct, for the value of something to me, what I would be willing to sacrifice for it, may be and indeed is different from what it is worth to you, even though we pay the same price.

Secondly no value exists in isolation but each is determined within an interdependent system of values. Every value is determined by all others and in turn determines them, so that a change in one changes the entire web of values. Thus my reluctance to buy a new automobile will mean some dealer's revenue is smaller, his consignment from Detroit is fewer, General Motors' profit is lower, workers are worth less and may be laid off or their work time cut, government tax receipts are less, unemployment compensation is higher, automobile workers have to cut back on their buying, retailers suffer, and on and on in an endless chain. At the same time I may have put the funds not spent into a savings account and this may set off another sequence of events changing values in a different direction.

Multiply this decision a million times and one begins to get a feel for the infinite flux of economic values. Where affluence impells all to want more goods, to seek more income and to strive for larger profits this flux becomes a quiet seething, day and night, beneath the surface of daily life. Just as the animals, the insects, the plant parasites, the forces of air, water and growth are simultaneously destroying and renewing a forest, so too affluence is constantly destroying and renewing the economic context of our life. To trace out the infinite ramifications of any economic decision not only boggles the mind, but is senseless, making choice impossible.

Concluding from this should not be fear but freedom, not depression but buoyancy. Just as the fierce dynamics of the forest ecology do not destroy but enhance its pleasures, its vistas, its coolness, and its wonder, so too the dynamics of economic value do not diminish but increase human possibilities. These possibilities can be realized by keeping in mind the practical lessons learned from value theory: that the more basic reality of goods is their uses not their values; that economic values and prices are not substantial but relational and very volatile at that; that even, when faced by economic values determined by objective forces, we need not be tyrranized by them.

Fortified with this understanding, we can plunge into the economy, confident that contributing to it will be somehow rewarded, respectful of its laws, wary of its dangers, tolerant of its irritants, expecting its good, enjoying not raping it, giving in order to get. Such an attitude combines the two polarities of the business of life, a constant awareness of scarcity with an openness to aspirations and principles beyond economic analysis and managerial techniques. There are many more things in heaven and earth, Horatio, than are dreamed on in your Samuelson!

From this it takes but one small step to conclude that this very dynamic principle of affluence requires a new look at the other principles which relate most closely with it in generating human actions. The next few chapters, therefore, will address themselves to these three micro-moral questions. Does affluence destroy personality and personal growth? Is affluence compatible with the life of virtue? Is affluence compatible with the Spirit of Poverty? They are specifics of the general problem: Can affluent people live a truly human existence?

CHAPTER THREE

AFFLUENCE AND PERSONALITY

The affluent expectation of more income and more satisfactions drives the economy by ceaselessly creating and modifying values. In doing so it changes the panorama of goods available to us, the ways we produce them, and our rights to their enjoyment. In short, affluence changes our style of living. The question here is "Does affluence change us, not peripherally in the things about us, but in our consciousness and personality?"

An easy 'yes' is given if one considers the looting when civic order breaks down, the white-collar crime of the already well-to-do, the violence committed for gain. Dramatic though these be, such crime involves only a minority and most of these only occasionally. A more guarded 'yes' is given, when the question is asked about the majority. For here one must rely on impressions and intuitions. Granted that the majority experience no trauma from their affluence, they have not been untouched. Otherwise, why their uneasiness about the permanence of economic abundance, why the guilt feelings about profit and gain, why the sharp irritability about anything which threatens income and property, why, finally, do the affluent seem to savor so little the abundance they possess?

All of these questions provoke fascinating speculation about what is wrong with society. But keeping to our personalist view, we stick to the central question: "What has my affluent attitude done, is doing, or can do to me?" Translated into our general theme, this question becomes, "How does affluence as an economic principle of action affect the psychological principle of personality growth and character development?" Perhaps in a catchier way, "How does the pursuit of economic values affect the espousal of moral Values?"

(In this chapter especially but throughout the book, we will be distinguishing between economic values (prices) and moral and philosophic Values. Since constantly modifying them becomes tedious, we will distinguish them by capitalizing philosophic Values and using lower case for economic values.)

Besides defining the purpose of this chapter, these questions establish the agenda of its inquiry. 1) What is the human person? 2) How does personality and character grow? 3) What are Values, and how do they affect personality? 4) How do Value espousal and economic choice mutually affect each other? These questions are specific of the overriding question of this Part I: Is affluence inimical to espousal of higher Values? Keep in mind also that out of the broad and fascinating subject of character development we focus on the very fine but basic point, how our economic desires affect our higher aspirations.

PERSON AND PERSONALITY

"What is the human person" has been asked by theologians and philosophers since people first became aware of their differences from other forms of life. The answers, though infinitely diverse, have always responded to the common experience that man is both animal and spiritual, a duality in tension. No philosopher has gone so far as to say that the person is two distinct realities. No one affirms man's absolute simplicity. St. Paul's lament, "What I would do, I do not; what I do not want to do, I do", graphically expresses both the philosophical issue and man's moral dilemma.

Since the philosophical position about the nature of man espoused in this book was outlined in the Introduction, little more is needed here except to recall the salient points. As material, the person is rooted in his historical circumstances, yet the I, the conscious Ego, transcends these, remembering what is not and intending what he hopes will be. That is to say, the person is conscious that he is both distinct and purposive. Finally, the person knows himself as social, as related to material things but more especially to other persons. From this view of the person as material, social, transcendent, self-conscious and purposive, we develop the idea basic to the argument of this chapter that man can aspire to be what he is not but those aspirations must be rooted in his material and social circumstances.

This is simply to say that the human person is a complex of many systems, chemical, biological, neurological, emotional, and, over-all, intellectual-volitional. The emphasis here on man's purposive and conscious action should not lull the reader into forgetting the many layers of physical, instinctive, and sub-conscious reactions and responses which are integral to acting consciously. Indeed to neglect this is to miss the point.

The Ascent of Man

This view, that man is a complex woven of many strands yet having purpose and direction, is strongly supported by the perspective of human history.[1] The transformation of the species over hundreds of thousands of years from the pre-hominoid tool-maker to the cave-man hunter and domesticator of fire at least suggests purposeful change. Purpose is more at work in Cro-Magnon's great achievements in measuring time, in cultivating herds and crops, and in developing the arts of living together. When history begins it reveals a civilization in all its rudiments the same as ours -- agricultural and pastoral skills, crafts, art, records, government, and always religion.

Indeed history begins with a religious revolution. Elaborate burial ritual expressed the hope, at least for the rich and powerful, of a life after death. At the same time the primitive totemism and animism gave way to belief that a transcendent personal power or powers ruled over human affairs. The great epics always celebrated man in conflict with or guided by his gods. This religious impulse culminated in great world religions proclaiming a single personal God, Jahwe of Judaism, the Triune Father, Son, and Spirit of Christianity and Allah of Muslimism.

From his belief that life itself had ultimate meaning man became convinced that each thing had a meaning which the human mind could grasp. This philosophical urge spilled over into a curiosity about how all things ticked. From this vastly increased knowledge of the forces of nature man was able not only to exploit his environment but to change it in ways more suitable to his wishes. Thus began the modern, the technological age.

A sweep like this through man's pre-history and history forms the substance of such visions as that of Teilhard du Chardin, the Jesuit geologist and evolutionary philosopher. He conceives evolution as a cosmogenesis, a world coming into being through aeons, in which living forces, the biosphere, work on the basic material of earth, the geosphere, culminating in man, the noosphere, who both draws support from them and decisively directs the course of their development. Thus all things human, living and material converge in Omega, the Supreme Act of Love.[2] However far one may wish to go in accepting Teilhard's vision (or myth), it is a powerful expression of man's purposeful ascent from the cave.

Growth in Personality

Every person can replicate this macroscopic transformation in his or her own life, each according to his native endowment and particular circumstances. Physical and biological changes will occur inevitably. Other and more significant changes are purposive and intentional. This purposiveness, vague and inconstant for many individuals but clear and focused for others, to become what he or she would be is what is meant here by personality growth and character development. It is obviously a principle of action.

The Swedish psychologist, Eduard Spranger, pioneered this conception of character development as an organic process.[3] Just as a tree grows from seed, transcending it though contained in it, conditioned by its environment yet transforming it, so too the person grows in a complex, yet inter-dependent and systematic, way. The ego, according to Spranger, is a congery of many drives, simultaneously biologic, economic, aesthetic, intellectual, religious, political and affective. The ego is an organism which struggles to survive. It is an appetite for want satisfaction and fulfillment. It desires and desires to create beauty. The ego seeks for the meaning of things and aspires to ultimate reality. Even in its striving for self-fulfillment, the ego reaches out to other human beings, in various combinations of imposing its own good on others and lovingly receptive to the good of others. Thus personality growth can be viewed as a spiraling movement, thrusting upward, yet still rooted in its most elemental drives.

At any moment, therefore, the self is a specific "fusion and inter-fusion" of these elements. The particular blend of these principles determines the tone and texture of character and establishes the general tenor of conduct. At the same time this blend determines the ability of the person to apprehend the meaning of objects and to see them as valuable. For example, different people will experience the Sistine Chapel in vastly different ways: one marvels at Michelangelo's technique; another an old man's courage; a third calculates its replacement value in today's market; still another may be enthralled by the painter's vision of man or of his conception of man's relation to God.

o Personality and personal growth, therefore, in practice translates to what one judges to be the goodness of other people and other things, and what one considers o worth striving for. In brief, the level of personality o growth determines the Values one espouses and, conversely, the Values one espouses denominates one's character. Values, therefore, would seem to be the link between personality growth and economic choice, as both the above and the term 'exchange value' suggest.

VALUES AND PERSONALITY

The linkage between Values and character is always assumed by writers on Value. Rescher assigns both a critical and teleologic role to Values, that is, that a Value is not only a norm for judging the goodness of an object but is a purpose or goal for overt action.[4] Angell, looking at Values' social significance, sees Values "as continuing qualities of life we desire to see realized."[5] Allport locates a Value deep in the personality "as a belief upon which a man acts by preference." He calls it "a deeply propriate disposition" which reveals a person's intentionality or the central theme of his striving.[6]

While interest in a philosophy of Value, according to Rescher, has receded before the tide of Logical Positivism, the Value point of view is creating considerable stir in economics and the other social sciences.[7] Contemporaries are reworking the question whether economics is a positive science, dealing only with facts, or a normative science, dealing also with Values. The debate has generally generated more heat than light.

The questions, what are Values and how generated, center on whether Values inhere in objects like color or shape, a conclusion blatantly contrary to experience that the same thing may be good for one and bad for another, or whether Values inhere in the valuing person either as his own creation, in which case each Value is purely subjective and unique, or as innate from birth, which position denies that Values are personal and implies they should all be the same. The solution, of course, lies in relating the objective characteristics of a thing to the Valuing perception of the person. Only this dynamic explains Values as affecting behavior and having meaning for character.

Avoiding all the fine points in dispute, we will in pursuit of our purpose follow, as best we can, the explanation of Value of the German Phenomenologist, Max Scheler (1874-1928), whose work has just been made available to English-only readers.[8] We will derive an understanding of

Values from analysis of the Value experience, and then from Scheler's rules of preference show how Values affect action and character.

The Value Experience

We learn what a Value is from the experience of Value. Though few people consciously examine what their Values are or how they come to espouse them, we can begin with an event that is frequent enough to be almost universal, the experience of the Value 'friendship', that is, the realization that another person is a friend. What does it mean? What psychic operations were involved?

When I call someone friend, I mean that person is good in a special way, and I prefer him or her according to a ranking of higher or lower. In other words, I perceive that that person bears the Value 'friendship'. I experience the Value in the person. But this experience gives me no more knowledge of my friend's qualities. Nor do I mean that the person is friendly, or a friend to everybody, and certainly not that my friend is friendship. That is, I realize that the Value, though founded in the good of the other person, is quite independent of him or her. For even should the friend prove false or drift away, I will still have experienced the Value. I may now realize that others, even former enemies, are friends. The experience of the Value 'friendship' is, therefore, a realization of the good of another which causes me to rank him or her higher or lower in my preferences, but the experience says more about the intensity and clarity of my perception than about the nature of the person so preferred.

To start, therefore, we can define the Value experience as the perception of the good of another person or thing, which perception simultaneously expresses a preference. It is a complete experience, neither an act exclusively of the intellect nor of the will, but of both acting simultaneously.

Valuing is an act of cognition but not by way of a concept. Values cannot be defined, only described. To say that friendship is the state of being a friend simply begs the question, "What does it mean to be a friend?" When I now call John my friend, I have no more information about him. Indeed, a Value is perceived without knowing all the properties of the object or even those upon which the Value is founded. Falling in love, for example, resists detailing the qualities of the beloved. The reasons advanced are either trivial, the dimple on her knee, or ineffable, "I love her because I love her." Falling in love, even after years of marriage, is an immediate intuition into another as a special and preferred good.

Thus Valuing is an act of cognition, not through conceptualization, but like sensation immediate. Unlike sensation, however, the goodness of another, not the physical qualities, is intuited, and, in the intuition, preferred. The Value experience, therefore, is in the same movement an act of the will.

But this willing is not in the Kantian sense of an "ought", innate to the will, which is draped upon the object. Quite to the contrary, I prefer John as good not because I ought to, but I ought to prefer him because he is perceived as good. This difference seems slight but it is decisive. For it proceeds from an entirely different conception of reality than that which evoked Kant's moral imperative.

Kant accepted reality, as described by Hume, as a chaos of sense impressions, and imposed order on it by an innate sense of duty. Where, to the contrary, the world is perceived as a world of goods, what-ought-to-be-pursued is not imposed but rather flows from perception of that goodness. Thus an "ought" does not become a Value, but a Value becomes an "ought". For the same reason, the Value experience precedes purpose, for a purpose is good or bad, depending upon whether the goal proposed bears a higher or lower Value. Finally, we cite daily experience that Values are not determined by the will but rather determine the will. Super-bowl players, for example, will so smell the glory and the money that these Values overwhelm consideration of all others, even the soundness of their limbs and joints.

While the will does not precede, it is integral to the Value experience. Valuing is not simply a perception of a good but a preference. Value, therefore, is an immediate intuition into the essence of a good which intuition simultaneously evokes a feeling of placing above or below in a rank order of preference with other Values. When I realize that John really is my friend, whether I have known him for a long or short time, that perception flashes upon me. I see that John bears that Value 'friend' and in seeing I prefer John to others. If I have never before had a friend, then in that experience I experience the Value 'friend'. An experience powerful as this cannot but change my attitude and conduct toward my friend. It may change the course of my life.

The Phenomenology of Value

Once sensitive to the experience of Valuing, we begin to realize that we are making evaluations all the time, that indeed Values pervade our daily life. We ascribe Values to both persons and things. The individual person, both myself and others, may bear Values, or a group or class of people may bear a Value. In the realm of action, we differentiate among the Values of conscious acts like loving or thinking, vital or sense functions, unconscious responses and instinctive reactions. We value differently a person's basic moral tenor and his individual deeds, his intentions as opposed to his states of feeling. Regarding relations, we distinguish among the Value of the persons related, for example, married spouses, the form of the relationship, that is, a sexual friendship, and the given experience of that relation, that this marriage is good or bad. Things may also bear Values and are distinguished as spiritual, cultural, enjoyable and useful. Finally, Values can be perceived in and for themselves, like a person or a work of art, or as means to other Values, like tools, technical Values or symbolic Values.

Values, besides being differentiated according to the bearer of the Value, also differ according *to whom* they are valuable, individuals, groups, or an entire society, and *in the way* they are valuable, as physical, intellectual, aesthetic or religious goods. Finally, Values differ by *how* they are valuable, by making life more agreeable, by preserving or restoring health, by enlightening the mind or by moving the will.

Thus Values can brush against us at every turn of our life and whisper to us at every level of our being and personality. Granted that most of our wanting is instinctive, reflexive, and habitual, or the experience of trivial values, nevertheless, consciously or unconsciously we are evaluating things, persons, actions, and relations every day, judging them pleasant or unpleasant, useful or harmful, beautiful or ugly, good or bad. *All of life, perceived horizontally or vertically, is Value-laden.*

The Rules of Preference

The pervasiveness of the Value experience also suggests the rules of preferring. In differentiating among Values we imply that the <u>ways</u>, the <u>principles</u>, and the <u>modalities</u> of preferring also differ. In examining these differences, we establish the nexus between Value espousal and personality growth. Still following Scheler, we look first at the <u>ways</u> of preferring.

Preferring is expressed either as a 'placing before' or as a 'placing after', thus distinguishing the enthusiast from the ascetic. The former stresses the positive preferability of one Value over others; the latter, the negative, that a given Value is less preferable than another. The former exuberantly overwhelms vices with virtue; the latter realizes virtue by suppressing vice. Neither way can be pursued with singular relentlessness, though Western attitudes are more attuned to the positive, enthusiastic approach, while Eastern philosophies to the negative, ascetic approach.

There is only one ultimate <u>principle</u> of preferring: an absolute Value is preferable to a relative Value. For, as Scheler says,[9] the more absolute Value leaves the conviction that preferring another Value to it constitutes a falling-away from a higher state of value-existence. Since there is only one absolutely absolute Value, the essence of an infinite being, all other Values participate in absoluteness to the extent that they share the features of absoluteness. These are four. 1) The more <u>enduring</u> a Value, the higher the Value. Thus the longer-lasting is preferred to the transient, the good to the pleasurable. The lover who says "I love you" perceives a higher Value in the goodness of the beloved than the wooer who says, "I take pleasure in you". 2) The less divisible a Value, the more preferable. Spiritual Values, therefore, are preferred to material, and works of art, whose division would destroy them, are preferred to artifacts, whose parts are useful as such. 3) The more <u>basic</u> the Value, the more it is to be preferred. The Value 'health' is founded on the Value 'life' which is founded on the Value 'being'. Thus 'to be' is a higher Value than 'to be healthy'. 4) Values, yielding a <u>deeper</u> contentment, are preferable to Values which yield only a non-fulfilling pleasure.

The last aspect of preferring Scheler calls <u>Value-modalities.</u>[10] With this we get to the dynamics of Values and valuing in their effect on personality growth. Its understanding hinges on the conception of the good as a system, more precisely, a hierarchy of Values. While what we value is fortuitous to our circumstances, the depth of our penetration into the Values born by even the simplest good is determined by our own effort and perception. Value-modalities, therefore, are categories of Values ranked in order according to our perception of their goodness.

At the lowest level the Value qualities, given in sensation and perceived as yielding pleasure or pain, are ranked across a spectrum from agreeable to disagreeable. At a higher level, Values, perceived in their relation to life and well-being, are ranked from noble to base in the case of substances and, in the case of means, like tools or symbols, are ranked according to their usefulness for our wellbeing. Such Values arouse the feeling-states of liveliness or depression, gladness or sadness, and feeling healthy or ill. Most economic goods and services fall into this modality. At a still higher level, spiritual values are classed as aesthetic Values, beautiful to ugly; ethical Values, right to wrong; and cognitive Values, true to false. Each evokes its corresponding feeling-states of approval or disapproval.

The sacral is the last and highest modality, that of the holy and unholy. This modality, in a sense, encompasses the other three since it embraces all objects which are given in intention as absolute and all Values which symbolize absolute Values. Indeed this modality correlates with the religious concept of the sacramentality of all things. Above all the modality of the holy and unholy relates to the Values of the person and, preeminently, of an infinite person.

This analysis of Value, the experience itself, the classification of Values, and analysis of preference, therefore, reveals an hierarchial Value structure which corresponds to the hierarchy of goods which constitute every thing and every person. Though a Value is perceived immediately and intuitively, penetration to another's absolute goodness is not achieved without great effort, without many years of loving experience, and without penetrating through the surface of pleasing and unpleasing to the innermost core of goodness. Seeking higher Values is not for the fainthearted, nor without consequence for our life and personality. Such Values become, in Allport's phrase, "deeply propriate dispositions", central themes of one's striving.

Such central Values are dynamic, not static. About

them lesser Values, wants, and habits coalesce, as a person's every act or choice enhances or erodes his central Values. Consistency among predominant Values is neither necessary nor always possible. Indeed, a person or a society can for a long time espouse contrary, even contradictory Values which, however, once seen as conflicting, produce personality or social crisis.[11] Personal Value systems, in turn, experience pressure from others' Value espousals and especially from class or societal Values. Thus a Value system, like personality itself, is the offspring of both an inner dynamic and social pressures.

In short, the analysis of Value reveals another moral helix, matching the helix of personality growth. Even without detailed description of their mutual penetration, it is obvious they condition each other. What I would consciously strive to become, given my native endowment and life opportunities, is expressed in the Values I espouse, and the Values I espouse are determined by my level of personality growth. Thus the first link is established: *Values and Personality are organically and creatively inter-dependent and inter-acting*.

With this we turn to the second nexus, the link between philosophic Value and economic value.

VALUES AND ECONOMIC VALUES

Though the words hint at relationship, the suggested link between the two goes against the grain of contemporary economic thinking. At best, most economists would concede only that exchange ratios (economic values) accommodate given economic resources to a given pattern of wants which more or less reflect current personal and social Values. Most economists are trained to describe an economic process totally devoid of value judgments.

They are encouraged in this attitude by the sharp contrast between Values and economic values, a contrast we may accentuate by substituting price for economic value. For Value is *subjective*, *qualitative* and, hence, *free*, while price is *objective*, *quantitative* and, in some sense, *constraining*. Values are intensely personal. Even those Social Values, like patriotism or love of Beethoven which one shares with others, are unique in the manner and intensity of their espousal. And they are unique precisely because they are qualitative. Though Values cannot be weighed, measured, or numbered, they are ranked by preference according to one's perception of the qualities of objects. For both reasons Value-espousal is always free, not only that they are freely chosen but that one Value need not be sacrificed to another. In preferring Mary to Suzy, I do not downgrade her nor is my love diminished (I may actually love Suzy more because of my love for Mary), even though -- and this is the crunch -- I may devote more of my time and resources to express my love for Mary and less for Suzy.

By contrast, price is objective, established by market forces or at minimum by bargaining between buyer and seller. Price is quantitative. However fluctuating and ephemeral, at any moment a price is the exchange ratio between a quantity of a good and a quantity of money. Hence, price always involves an element of constraint. That one must sacrifice something of one good to obtain another is itself coercive. That buyers must bargain with sellers, even when advantage is overwhelmingly one-sided, implies some lack of freedom. To pay a price is to acknowledge a constraint, the power of the market to ration to me less than I want or desire.

This sharp contrast between the two encouraged economists throughout most of this century to aspire to a science of neat, quantifiable price relationships, antiseptically free of Values. But just as physicists and biologists have found that what goes on in the laboratory cannot be divorced from the real world, so contemporary economics is returning to the tradition of the founding fathers of giving greater consideration to social issues and Social Values. Indeed, they have found that some of the most controversial Social Values, like economic growth, free enterprise, rational social planning, full-employment, equitable distribution of income, environmental protection and many others, possess large economic elements to which people expect economists to address themselves. Thus how Values influence values and more importantly how the creation of economic values conditions the espousal of Social Values is thrust center-stage once again. In view of this we are justified in another go-around in examining the same interaction at the personal level.

Utility as Value

The key to the approach here consists in a sharper understanding of the concept of utility. The ambiguity with which utility has been treated throughout the history of economic thought leaves its residue in the two quite different meanings of the term in contemporary analysis. On the one hand we describe total and marginal utility as the sum of and the addition to satisfaction derived from using a commodity. On the other, we define a commodity as a bundle of utilities. In the first, utility implies a psychic effect; in the second, the useful qualities of the product. Neither, obviously, excludes the other and economists have managed to advance analysis by waffling between the two emphases.

As one would expect, thinkers inclined to a labor theory of value tended to locate utility in the object. Thus Locke: "The natural worth of anything consists in its fitness to supply the necessities, or serve the conveniences of human life."[12] Ricardo, criticizing Say's confusion, is more forthright: "If two sacks be of the value that one was before, he (the consumer) evidently obtains double the quantity of what Adam Smith calls value in use, but not double the quantity of value."[13] Marx surprisingly is more ambiguous, affirming: "A commodity ... is ... so far as it is a material thing, a use-value, something useful." But then immediately, "Use-values become a reality only by use or consumption."[14]

Economists in the utility tradition emphasize the psychic aspect of utility. Jevons, however, can be read either way: Utility is "the abstract quality whereby an object serves our purposes and becomes entitled to rank as a commodity", that is "any object, substance, action, or service which can afford pleasure or ward off pain".[15]

Wieser, taking pains not to be "inveigled" into "regarding values as a natural or indispensable quality of goods" quotes Menger for having advanced the definitive statement on economic value as "the importance attached to concrete goods or quantities of goods because of a conscious dependence upon them for the satisfaction of our needs".[16] Yet earlier Wieser defined the "theoretical concept of utility" as "every quality that is calculated to bring about the satisfaction of need".[17]

Marshall, as so frequently, formulated the contemporary understanding: "Utility is the correlative of Want or Desire" and more specifically, "the total utility of anything to any one ... is the total satisfaction or benefit it yields him".[18]

This very difficulty of economic thought to define utility as either useful properties or psychic satisfaction is corroborated by common-sense experience that utility is in its essence neither. It is not the useful properties the producer intends the commodities to have. A manufacturer, for example, may fabricate a steel container to be used to ship milk, but a suburbanite buys it for a flower pot. The same cassette may open a new world of sound to one listener, an hour's diversion to another, an irritation to a third. The essential risk of production consists in guessing what people will find useful, and the whole thrust of advertising is to convince people of the useful qualities they will find fabricated into the good.

On the other hand, utility is not the satisfaction realized from possessing the commodity, because it is an effect, not a cause of the purchase. No matter what satisfaction was experienced from previous purchases of like commodities, no consumer is assured that this item will yield the same satisfaction for the simple reason that, even if the product has not changed, the consumer has. The purpose, after all, of garage sales is to get rid of goods which never fulfilled their anticipated satisfaction. Nor can a demander predict what satisfactions a commodity may yield. The copy of A Shropshire Lad may be just right to balance the kitchen table. This is simply to say that wanting is dynamic, ever seeing new uses for things, uses which no inventor or manufacturer could possibly foresee.

Thus both the ambiguities of thought and the clarity of experience force us to a definition of utility which encompasses both the useful properties of commodities and the satisfaction they give, but is essentially neither. That definition is supplied from our analysis of Value. Utility is the perception by the customer of the commodity's usefulness and so perceived, the commodity is preferred to the extent of sacrificing other goods to get it. Utility, therefore, is the Value 'useful'.

All arguments, therefore, persuade us to locate utility in the hierarchy of Values, specifically in the second tier of Scheler's Value-modalities.[19] Further all things, objects, services, persons, groups and relations, can bear the Value 'useful' in its myriad manifestations. Finally, the Value 'useful' is by nature not a final Value, a Value-in-itself but a means to other Values, both sensual and secular, spiritual and sacral. It is a Value-in-use, a means-Value. With this firm foundation in the hierarchy of Values, utility bridges the gap between economics and axiology. "To adopt a value" writes Rescher, "is to espouse principles of policy in the expenditure of resources".[20] If you really espouse a Value, you are willing to make economic sacrifices for the means to achieve it.

Values in the Exchange Process

While this conception of Utility does little to advance economic analysis, it has profound implications for conduct and moral responsibility in economic actions. It affirms that causality flows fundamentally from Value espousal to market price and not the other way. It insists that prices reflect Values more so than Values are conditioned by prices. Bohm-Bawerk in demonstrating a century ago that, while scarcity indicates how high values _will_ rise, utility indicates how high values _may_ rise, concludes in the same vein since consumer preferences are a factor in scarcity and are the sole element in utility.[21]

The argument so far, therefore, makes what is now the obvious point that wanting and preference, not suppliers' intentions and ability to produce are the more active principles determining utility.

The marginal condition itself, that the intensity of desire is conditioned by the amount of the good available or already possessed, rather confirms than controverts this insight. For satiety, according to marginal analysis, is simply realizing that more of a good would benefit little. This is entirely subjective and implies no dilution of the good qualities of the commodity. On the same basis, when much of a good is available, it is possible to perceive many other uses besides those satisfying the most intense wants. Whatever influence does arise from the side of supply -- advertising, media pressure and social conformity, massive influences on demand which economists a hundred years ago could not imagine -- must be funnelled to influence utility perceptions. Indeed advertisers are blatant in suggesting how their products fulfill the Values they think we cherish.

Finally, the very root concept of opportunity cost argues in the same direction. For opportunity cost, in expressing what a demander must forego to obtain a good, implicitly measures the demanders estimation of the good he gains. What one is willing to forego tests the intensity of desire for the good preferred.

Affirming this, of course, does not allay all the difficulties. It does not say, for example, that the intensity of a Value experience is proportional to the price one pays for the means to the Value. A music major may be enraptured by records borrowed from the library while a banker with season symphony tickets may sleep through to the coda. But it does say that a genuine Value espousal increases the demand for the means and thus raises their prices. It also says that the ultimate test of a Value espousal is paying the price for the means, of accepting the Value's opportunity costs. Thus the increased demand for good opera and light opera in the provinces over the last decade and a half not only increased the fee of a quality tenor ten-fold but doubled ticket prices.

There may by other externalities to test a Value espousal from the supply side. A love of experimental theater may require one's going into a seedy neighborhood at night. Suppliers too in a rush to profit may offer shoddy goods, poorly engineered and high priced. Such happened to energy conservation. Not only were prices of insulating material driven sky-high but fly-by-nights sprang up to capitalize on demand and to prey upon an unwary public. Such test convictions with a subtler courage, holding to Values despite irritations and a sense of outrage.

A more common complaint is that debasing Values drive ennobling Values out of a free market. In indicting the market place, the complaint is misdirected. For while Values are free and personal, they do compete in the market place with other Values in this sense, that the means to Values compete with each other. In production geared to mass production, goods to fulfill the Values of the masses will be catered to over the Values of the few. What sells will be produced: pornography, sentimental entertainment, faddy clothing, chrome-covered hard goods, superficial news reporting, and cheap politicking, the whole gamut of the cheap, the shoddy and the tinselly. No one should be surprised, however grieved, that artistic talent, engineering skills, scholarly dedication, and political charisma are prostituted to serve such wants, and that advertising and the power of the mass media are marshalled to merchandize the tripe. The opportunity costs of art, virtue, and integrity have risen not because they are not valued as before but because their contraries are valued more.

Comfort, however, comes from two directions. First, from the resources and diversified production of our economy, almost all can find the means to achieve their Values, not without sacrifice certainly, but not beyond the pale of possibility either. Secondly, in the tide of the vulgar and venal genuine insights and artistic integrity find ways of surfacing. Jazz produced Gershwin, rock Godspell, and Watergate some needing airing of government. Even 'sit-coms' have moments of comedic greatness or touch chords of human pathos. Time, furthermore, has a way of winnowing the nuggets of good from the flood of trivial, popularly banal, and ephemeral. So in choosing to be selective one gains a double victory, in not supporting the trashy one incurs little risk of losing what is permanently valuable.

o All of the difficulties which Values meet in the market place may cloud but they do not controvert the fact that we eventually realize in some ways the Values we are
o willing to pay for. The conclusion that utility is a Value perception should effectively direct the finger of suspicion away from the market to ourselves. Put succinctly:
o we are not prurient because _Penthouse_ sells; _Penthouse_ sells because we are prurient.

If somehow affluence is destructive of higher Values, then the reason must be sought in something in our own nature which is itself erosive of higher Value aspirations. That something is implied in every ethical theory as, in a real sense, constituting the ethical problem.

In truth, each of us recognizes that our actions never live up to our aspirations because of the pull of our material nature. Medieval moralists called these pre-dispositions the _fomes peccati_, meaning by that our natural attraction to the prurient, to the sentimental, and to power over others. If affluence somehow endangers higher Value aspiration, the most likely way is by supporting and implementing these materialistic dispositions.

AFFLUENCE AND THE FOMES PECCATI

'Fomes peccati' translates literally as 'the tinder of sin', the material to start the fires of sin. It falls strangely on the ears of a generation which has largely lost a sense of sin. Yet it refers to a fact of the human condition of which we are all too familiar, indeed, the same St. Paul complained about, that our performance seldom lives up to intentions and often goes counter to them. While this conviction is central to the Christian economy of salvation, it is not unique to Christianity. All religious and most moral philosophies recognize that the human person is in some sense flawed, that we have pre-dispositions, even pre-dilections, which make living up to ideals difficult and generally require counter-acting.

Since this is not a theological treatise, we avoid how these predispositions lead to sin, to turning away from a Divine Will and Order. Rather we undertake the more mundane examination how affluence, if used to accentuate these psychological flaws, can erode higher Value aspirations and thus impede the growth of character.

The Stages to Materialism

Medieval commentators on the 'fomes peccati' took as their text First John, 2, 16, where the Eagle of Ephesus warns against the sensual body, the lustful eye and the pride of life. This is St. John's time-tested blue-print of how materialism coarsens and eventually corrodes character. Immediately we caution that resisting materialism is not to deny materiality. We will avoid both angelism, that man's material principle is somehow bad, and puritanism, that sensual pleasure is to be shunned. As said earlier, man is a duality in tension: both aspects of his nature are essential. His dis-integration happens when one aspect overcomes the other. For most people, however, the material bias is stronger than the spiritual and for them affluence poses a danger precisely at this point.

Reading John carefully reveals that materialism erodes higher Values at several distinct, though interrelated, stages. At the lowest, the sensual body, we are attracted to pleasure and resist disturbing our ease. Pleasure, of course, is good and integral to most physical acts, especially eating, drinking, sex, sheltering the body and the like essential for survival. To seek the pleasure of such acts, therefore, is entirely legitimate, provided that the higher good the act is designed to achieve is not precluded. For example, the seducer or rapist does not want to express his affection or to fulfill his partner emotionally or biologically but only his own gratification. Obviously, such a one perceives only the sensual Values his victim bears. The gross sensualist is thus barred from higher Value-modalities, even the useful, often seeking pleasure to his own destruction.

Though they may seem contrary, the love of ease is correlative to the love of pleasure. For the pleasure-seeker does not want to be disturbed in his pleasure, nor disturbed except by pleasure. Again, ease and quiet are good and necessary for the human animal. But a love of ease which prevents starting an enterprise worth doing, which procrastinates and rationalizes the futility of acting, no less than the passion for pleasure, prevents aspiring to more spiritual Values. At advanced stages of sensuality, the person is mired in his own pleasures and weary of anything else.

The *lustful eye* corrupts especially those Values which relate us to others, the useful, the vital and the spiritual. The *lustful eye* sees more than an object of pleasure, but stops short at its surface beauty and attractiveness. To be attracted to beauty is normal and healthy. For beauty lures us on to an object's inner meaning. Poets and artists convey insights more convincingly than theologians--and economists--who are tedious and dull. But the *lustful eye*, being superficial and sentimental, sees other things and people as enhancing one's self, as adornment. It is attracted to glitter, styling not engineering, *kitsch* not artistic insight, wit not truth, manners not morality. Consequently, it is restless, faddy, discontented with the old, on tenterhooks to try the new. The sentimentalist has no roots in things or in others, for he cannot rest long enough to savor the real goodness of another. In seeking to be admired, rather than to admire, the lusty person easily falls into sensuality.

The *pride of life*, the highest stage of materialism, almost seems to transcend materialism. For the self-glorification it implies is not incompatible with a spartan disdain for wealth, a negative conspicuous consumption sporting baggy clothes, a decrepit automobile and shunning the limelight. For the essense of such pride is not displaying wealth but possessing power and exercising domination over others. Even where accompanied by sensuality and greed and graced in gaudiness -- hallmarks of the noveaux riche -- pride of life sublimates them into a consuming love of power.

There is, of course, a legitimate pride, a recognition of one's worth and an appreciation of the good possessions and power can do. Even authority over others is justified as the ability to help others achieve their own fulfillment. A hero, after all, is one who inspires us to surpass ourselves. But the *pride of life*, the love of power and love of wealth, which glorifies only self and enhances one's own ego, stops short of regard for others. Like sensuality and superficiality, pride of life has self as its ultimate and only referrent. Thus, it denies in effect that anything or any other person but self bears an absolute value.

The gradations and intermingling of the ravages of materialism is the stuff of human biography and drama. But this fascinating subject must be put aside to return to the task of examining how affluence can accentuate our biases toward sensuality, superficiality, and love of power. The next three chapters on moderation, justice and spiritual poverty will flesh out this discussion. For the rest of this chapter we will explore how the general climate of abundance and affluence can feed the 'fomes peccati'.

Enriching, not Fulfilling

In earlier chapters we saw that an abundant economy pours out things and services which can sustain life better, make it more pleasant, and help people realize what to now they only aspired to. Abundance does enrich human existence. This is why the world's poor, having glimpsed the life of the affluent, hanker after it. Yet for the affluent themselves, life may be richer but less fulfilling. Too many seem to have more income and goods and to enjoy them less.

When expectations of more simply feed materialistic predilections, then affluence enriches without fulfilling. The conclusion needs but mentioning when applied to gross, and often tragic, sensuality. Addictions to alcohol, drugs, sexual pleasure, eating and the like are both costly in money, time, and energy and yield a diminishing return of satisfaction. Let us look instead at two milder but more prevalent forms of addiction. We accumulate things beyond their usefulness to us. Most rummage sales testify that people have gathered things, still useful and maybe originally expensive, whose value is now less than that of the space to store them. Secondly, affluence permits our becoming 'hooked' on any kind of pleasure, most of which are good and desirable in themselves. The couple which must have a weekly night on the town or of tavern hopping, the man whose bowling night is sacrosant, the person with season tickets who must attend every game all display mild and relatively innoxious symptoms of addiction. They are hooked precisely because they do not question whether more of the same is worth sacrificing for something else. Such addictions go far toward explaining the profitability of bars and restaurants, the value of franchises, the salaries of athletes and entertainers, and the profits in tobacco and liquor.

For many, if not most, of us, routine accumulation and mild addictions are abetted by the more active force of the lustful eye, in this context, the allure of the trivial and of glamor. The trivial is, of course, relative to want. A beer and brandy, after a hard day of work, may be a much desired relaxation and a pledge of camaraderie. It is trivial after a night of tavern hopping. Routine spending is almost always trivial -- another steak dinner if we always order steak.

The lure of the trivial is no trivial matter. Shopping centers, those most characteristic institutions of abundant economies, are founded on impulse buying. The supermarket principle is to display acres of goods temptingly within reach of thousands of shoppers needing only a credit card to possess them. Hosts of retailers, from diners to bookstores, emulate the same principle. This is not to say that all of these attractive goods do not meet real desires sometime and for someone, but at any particular moment all but a few are trivial to my particular wants. Some spending is for fun and does no particular harm. But for the affluent, who expect the next paycheck to recoup overspending today, the allure of the trivial can prove very compelling and, in cases, disastrous.

The pursuit of glamor, in person and vicariously, is perhaps the most insidiously trivial. The pursuit of glamor ranges from the relatively innoxious lure of "Avon calling!" to the siren-songs of Hollywood, Las Vegas, and the Washington cocktail circuit. Though their glitter, which masks bitter struggles for money, fame, and power, has been tarnished over the last decade, their activities still titillate the general public. Most popular reading and the largest expenditures on advertising celebrate the theme of glamor. Glamor is big and widely popular business in an abundant economy.

The Power Game

Affluence, finally nourishes the desire to lord it over and dominate others. The passion of the person who must have the first of everything new is often triggered by the hope of demonstrating superiority. Veblen's biting commentary on conspicuous consumption is still the wittiest description of this wide-spread human failing. Read with a little compassion, The Theory of the Leisure Class[22] details all the foibles of spending to impress. Advertising, as expected, capitalizes on this passion and further stimulates the carcinoma of consumption, the almost purposeless proliferation of buying from routine, from product enticement, and from desire to enhance our sense of superiority over others.

Affluence, while abetting household spending to impress, dangles tremendous temptations to self-glorification before government and business decision-makers. Bearing responsibility for millions, even billions, of dollars of spending, these men and women need the space, the personal help, and time-saving equipment to perform their roles efficiently. Being human, however, they can easily rationalize their love of ease and vanity under this rubric. Perquisites become prerequisites: the limousine, the luxurious office, first-class travel and entertainment, a staff catering to their wants. These amenities usually emerge unscathed from budget cut-backs, their escape being rationalized as serving little in view of the total budget, but really because those who enjoy them are the budget-cutters. The first item in cleaning up the federal income tax mess was to raise legislators' allowable deductions for living expenses from $3000 to $7000 a year!

Consequently, the corporate and government elite enjoy an insulation from physical discomfort which significantly differentiates their style of living from that of the majority. It may differentiate their style of living "at the office" from what they experience "at home". The desire for courtly elegance is universal with wielders of power, regardless of political ideology and their economy's ability to afford it. Carried to excess such spending becomes a drag on the economy, just as Trevor-Roper fingers the excesses of the Renaissance Court as the cause of the demise of monarchy.[23] Even in moderation, however, the tendency saps the vitality of authority, making calls for restraint and sacrifice sound hollow and hypocritical.

The perquisites of office only symbolize power. The reality lies in disposing of millions and billions of corporate and government funds. And this power in varying amounts is possessed by men and women deep within the bureaucratic structure. Like Roman politicians, dispensing coins and favors at their morning levies, they dispense funds to implement programs, to hire, to contract, to make grants, to further causes and charities. Power is maintained by courting constituents, wealthy contributors, big buyers, organized power blocs. The temptation to power is greater the more money is involved.

Power lies also in control, dominating a key committee or getting one's ideology ingrained in company policy or agency regulations. In government this may evade the public eye. In business it is often more blatant. There is, of course, the quiet chess-like moves through the power structure into executive suites, which however lust for power may sully motives and action, nevertheless, implements the inevitable passage of power from current to would-be holders.

The more publicized power plays occur in corporate empire building, one management group buying into, taking over, and replacing another. The Lings, Cornfields, Vescoes and Geneens prowl the business community, leaving their spore in political parties and legislative committee rooms, usually skirting the law, sometimes making a killing, but often only wounding their prey. Undoubtedly their stalking performs a social function in weeding out the weak and shaping up the inefficient. Its evil lies in that it is a power game played like Monopoly, but played with other peoples' money and other peoples' jobs, making them pawns in a game of ego-glorification. Economic abundance both provides the means and makes the ante worth the adventure.

These sketchy paragraphs are sufficient to establish the configuration: Affluence can feed the *fomes peccati*. It enables not only gross sensuality, crass superficiality, and blatant love of power, but permits a climate in which we, the vast majority of the affluent, can more easily pamper our desire for pleasure and comfort, feed our predilections for the specious and glamorous, and wet our thirst to lord it over others.

At the same time, it must be conceded that these tendencies in absorbing enormous amounts of economic values, goods, money, income, time and energy stimulate economic growth. Thus we face again a modern version of Mandeville's paradox that private vices are public virtues. Beneath the reluctance to develop a personalist ethics for economic abundance lies the vague fear that a virtuous people, who rein their materialistic tendencies, would impair economic growth. This argument is already advanced in cheering a birth rate which has fallen in Western societies below the replacement level. From this there is but one step to affirming that affluence not only makes people materialistic but requires it.

Thus the moral issue is joined. We seem faced with a choice between enjoying economic abundance, which is not conducive to virtuous living, and foregoing abundance for the sake of a healthier moral climate. That the vast majority of affluent people live generally decent lives, display real compassion for others less fortunate than themselves, and espouse the traditional Values of family, children, education, religion, and fairness in dealing with others is often drowned in the statistics of social tragedies, of broken marriages, abandoned and abused children, sexual promiscuity, drug and alcohol abuse, crime, poverty and social disaffection. Such data, viewed en masse, is disturbing: society itself may be crumbling. Indeed every family has experienced or knows first-hand another which has felt the trauma of one or several of these social tragedies. But the more disturbing fact of affluent living is the pervasive feeling of unease, a vague fear when conversation turns serious that national character has deteriorated because we are affluent, and a sense among scholars of the problem that squaring affluence and virtuous living is an enormously complicated business. This sense of unease, almost dis-ease, bears a somewhat closer look.

Frustrations of Affluence

Predominant in this unease is a hydra-headed sense of frustration. An element of this flows from the differing abilities of people to cope with technological society, the crowding in urban centers, the level of noise, work loads, and sensory stimulation, including here the flood of new products and the advertising touting them. Depending on their capacity to filter out undesired sensual stimulation people can suffer psychic disorganization from the mild to acute schizophrenia. (Counterbalancing and yet adding its own tensions is the progress achieved in assisting those disadvantaged by birth, by accident, or by their own bad habits to re-enter the main stream of productivity and social intercourse.)

Affluence itself, as we have seen, provokes its own frustration. By generating wants faster than the means to satisfy them, affluence heightens scarcity. Because the affluent have more available to them and perceive more which is possible, they must forego absolutely more than the destitute who can realistically aspire only to their simple survival needs.

This frustration has many faces. Basic is a continuing sense of poverty. No matter what amenities we enjoy, we can always see others possessing what we cannot afford. Thus we are touchier about any lessening of our income flow, and a recession is viewed with national alarm. Teenage unemployment has become a national issue where twenty years ago it would be accepted as a normal condition for an age-group whose main concern was their own education. This poverty syndrome is, of course, more intense among families and individuals falling below the poverty guide-lines, and by that very fact. Their problem is not that of destitution for most enjoy a plane of living higher than most people in the world, but in view of the majority their expectations are more frustrated, since they see themselves falling further and further behind. This frustration of expectations is the key. Thus a factory worker with a growing family and $12,000 a year income may feel a greater sense of frustrated expectations than a graduate student struggling on his $4000 stipend.

To this feeling of poverty is added the treadmill syndrome, a running faster and faster yet advancing little. Inflation or spending more for less, mounting taxes matched by poorer public service, higher prices for shoddier goods, greater demands on our time and more urgent calls for our concern all combine in a mounting pressure to work harder and to worry more just to keep up in business or to survive at home.

In many people these feelings of poverty and being on a treadmill are capped by a sense of barreness, that all the good things abundance provides do not add up to satisfaction. The suburban housewife, bored with house and bridge, and turning to alcohol, is a classic example. Her children, restless in school and dulled by drugs and alcohol, or worse, by crime and prostitution, and her husband, experiencing a sense of hollowness in a seemingly successful career, illustrate a like sense of frustration, a feeling of ontological poverty in their affluence.

These personal frustrations are heightened by the cosmic frustrations, that the promises made in the name of affluence to resolve international strife, to allay domestic discord, and to mitigate interpersonal tensions have proved false. We take an almost masochistic delight in national self-criticism. From international savior we have become, despite generally good intentions, an international bully. We are demoralized at the discovery of fraud and chicanery in government and business. We become nearly paranoid that a booming economy can turn sour, or when booming it generates shortages in vital goods and services. These frustrations are further fed by the pollution, the chaos of urban living, the competitive rat-race, the dysfunctioning of institutions, the disproportionate gain by the cunning and rapacious.

The Decline of National Character

That national character has deteriorated is impossible to document empirically. The usual citations of mounting crime, drug-related stealing, murder, mugging and rape reflect fearsome conditions in inner cities and worsening ones in suburbs and rural towns. White collar crimes, shoplifting, fraud, embezzling, income-tax evasion, forgery and bribery are estimated to cost the nation $40 to $200 billions annually. The profitability of illegal drugs, gambling, and prostitution points to wide-spread economic support. While these facts indict perhaps a large minority of the populace, that minority, however, includes many so-called "pillars of society". While these citations do not prove a decline in public morality, they certainly point up a problem.

More subtle evidence may actually be more telling. The coarsening of language, the highway carnage due to drunken and irresponsible driving, the popularity of violence in entertainment, the cheapening of sex and life, the neglect of the old, the resentment, even hatred, for children, the undiscriminating hue and cry against the costs of welfare point to increasingly tense interpersonal relations and a decreasing concern for others. If affluence has not caused the decline in national character, it seems to have contributed to a set of circumstances which are a singularly difficult matrix for true personality growth.

Responses to this social malaise are as varied as the social and moral scientists who have struggled with it. Most can be grouped under three broad classifications: the rugged individualism of someone like Ayn Rand, the social paternalism of which B.F. Skinner is representative; and the social dropping-out preached by Herbert Marcuse.[24] Though each view is myopic in some important respects, each has important insights into the condition of contemporary society. A student who is predisposed to one or the other is well advised to read opposing views. The following sketches may help in ascertaining one's leanings.

Rugged Individualism

As a social philosophy rugged individualism has the least respectability, though it has deep roots in the Social Darwinism of a century ago and a taproot drawing from the old laissez-faire liberalism of the eighteenth century and earlier. As an amorphous attitude from which people act, it probably comes closest to expressing the American practical wisdom: the conviction that you make it on your own. Two current aberrations are the modern Law of the West that the Saturday night special close at hand gives protection and makes one strong, and the more widespread conviction that the Law is primarily to protect my rights and, consequently, I can trim the law to suit my convenience or break it to meet my needs. Rugged individualism is the foundation of those two most glaring contradictions in American public morality, that all have the right to personal and political freedom, provided they are strong enough to wrest it for themselves, and that all welfarism is bad unless I am a beneficiary. These contradictions reveal the radical weakness of rugged individualism against the socializing forces and institutions in American society. The inexorable growth of corporations, unions, public education, and government bureaucracy means that rugged individualism, despite the current revival of libertarianism, is an ebbing force.

Social Paternalism

As it loses, social paternalism gains. In particular, this philosophy has gained academic respectability. The romancing of Chinese Communism is but the latest crest of the wave. It is founded on the radical equality of all individuals with respect to those differences which can be defined and classified by law and consequently can be conditioned. Population can be controlled; incomes can be redistributed; deviant (not immoral) behavior can be socially conditioned; inferior intellectual ability and other handicaps can be compensated for. Such a vision requires an overall social plan, including a monitored economic growth and a set of imposed Social Values which are defined by the social planners and techniques to implement the plan. Thus social engineers, viewing the overall resources and the desired social goals, will use conditioning techniques to effect the highest achievement of those goals by disposing of materials, people and incomes in the most "efficient" way.

Within these Social Values, be they economic growth or no-growth, population expansion or population control, this ideology or that, within these Values, the individual is free to do as he wills. So Social paternalism is a bastard of absolute individualism, in which the individual has no moral responsibility other than to society, and social authoritarianism in which "moral" values are defined by the State. Conflict will inevitably arise over defining the private sphere of absolute freedom and the public area of control. Nor will perfect egalitarianism be achieved. The Social Planners will be an elite, insulated from the masses, whose power to define and to implement make them in effect above the law. Consequently, the ambitious, especially the unscrupulous in getting more than others will develop the power to change social plans to their advantage. As Orwell predicted, all animals will be equal, but the pigs will be more equal than the rest.

The Great Refusal

The most radical solution is proposed by the guru of the hippies and flower children, Herbert Marcuse.[25] Drawing much of his inspiration from Marx, as does social paternalism, Marcuse is, however, to Marx, as a castrati is to a basso profundo. Where Marx thunders for social justice, Marcuse bleats for dropping out of society. His criticism of society holds no promise and shows no success in bridging the gap between the present and future. It remains negative, and without hope, suggests nothing but the "Great Refusal". For Marcuse sees industrial society as "underneath its obvious dynamics, ... a thoroughly static system of life: self-propelling, in its oppressive productivity and in its beneficial coordination." It is built on the contradiction, that its technology by achieving the more effective domination of man and nature and the more efficient utilization of resources opens new dimensions of human realization, but at the same time the institutions of industrial society contain human aspirations within the status quo of economic growth for its own sake, and for the sake of the "warfare and welfare state".

Thus, however comfortable, however endowed with gadgets and labor-saving devices, however the speciousness of liberty and free choice is maintained, the individual is nevertheless a slave, his thought and behavior is one-dimensional, his soul is found in his automobile, split-level home and the rest. For slavery, Marcuse concludes, is not determined by the hardness of labor, or by the need to obey, but by the reduction of the individual to the role of an instrument and to the state of a thing.

The Personalist Approach

The Marcusan Great Refusal stands squarely against a personalist philosophy of man. For, if the individual person can espouse Values which transcend the status quo and exercise free-choice among the goods which an affluent economy produces, then the Marcusan vision evaporates. Industrial society is no longer contained within "inherently necessary goals", it ceases to be a dynamic which is essentially static -- squirrels running faster in a revolving cage -- and the individual now has a purpose beyond his producing and consuming role.

On this point, a personalist philosophy is corroborated by rugged individualism, that the person is ultimately responsible for his own life and his own actions. Where personalism differs from both rugged individualism and Marcuse is in reducing the person to just an individual solely on his own. (It should be noted that Marcusan dropping-out is also radically individualistic. But, whereas laissez-faire individualism is aggressive and ascendent, Marcusan individualism is pacifist and defeatist.) Hence personalism also sees the good contained in social paternalism, that a person is essentially social. A person draws sustenance from society with others, must interact with others, and draws support from the institutions of society. Social Values are real personal Values provided they arise from the blending of many personal Values and are not imposed *a priori*. Personalism, therefore, preserves the ancient idea of a common good, as a good for many individually and hence a personal good of each. It denies, that a collective good, which is imposed on all in the collectivity, irrespective of personal preferences, is a true common good.

Thus personalism maintains the delicate balance between the individual as both self-determining and socially determined, and in terms of this chapter, as able to formulate and espouse Values and personal goals, which however they might be subsumed into the goals and Values of society, are the person's own. Since the Values one espouses are both sign and substance of personality development, a person's Values reveal his intentionality, the direction his life is taking and the level upon which he acts. Since, furthermore, what one wants reveals not only what Values he espouses but, more critically, those Values which have power to orient wanting away from and beyond what Allport calls, the "clamorous immediacy of the body and ego-centeredness", a personalist approach best counteracts the effect affluence can have in fostering materialism. Personalism thus concedes that perhaps it is harder to be both fully human and affluent but it holds out the promise that it is both possible and more rewarding. Indeed it says the very reward is in the striving.

Wanting More and Wanting Better

The question whether raising one's Value sights as opposed to sopping up all the alluring and enticing things, which an abundant economy turns out, fosters or impedes economic growth cannot be answered with mathematical certainty. A personalist philosophy takes as absolute: one's first obligation is to one's self, to become that which one can become. If that should harm General Motors, then so be it. General Motors will have to take care of itself.

But wanting better does not necessarily mean wanting less. It does mean wanting differently. Arguments that certain social Values like clean-air or privacy will harm business income and destroy jobs stop short of the full truth: some businesses will be harmed and some jobs destroyed, but other businesses will gain and other jobs created. This shifting of resources is paralleled by changes in personal Values: Detroit may lose a job as another living is gained in the arts; an income from providing luxuries for the rich may be lost to an income providing housing for the poor. No one can trace out the effects of a change in personal or social Values. It takes faith to believe that an economy geared to satisfying conscious and convinced Values, although more spiritual, is more stable and healthier than an economy which produces to fulfill trivial, ephemeral materialistic Values. Such a faith matches the Christian paradoxical imperative: "Seek first the kingdom of God, and all things will be added to you."

Deeper conviction, perhaps, comes from examining one example, cast on the heroic mold. No one would deny that Mother Theresa of Calcutta was more committed to the principles of poverty and of helping the most disadvantaged of people today, than when she was a teaching nun of the Sisters of Loretto or a peasant girl in Yugoslavia. Yet she wants and uses far more material goods -- buildings, trucks, jet planes, hotel rooms, food and medicines -- today than as a high school teacher or as a peasant wife and mother. She realizes (in her zeal for the most destitute), a larger income and manages greater expenditure than all but the richest people in the world.

More than this her zeal, her "deeply propriate disposition", to help the poor, creates new wants in the poor, hopes in orphans for schooling, clothes, jobs and a family, hopes in the sick for medicine and health care, hope in the dying for a shelter and the last loving service of a fellow human being. These are wants which now influence the creation of values which before were, at best, impossible dreams. She creates these wants by changing others' Values. The wealthy matron's desire for a bottle of fine perfume is changed into a desire to help Mother Theresa's efforts. A poor man may forego a meal to help those more destitute than he. The Indian government may devote a largely empty building for a hospital for the dying. Her Values which consume her and ignite others has not only changed people's wanting but increased it.

Looked at another way, only in an economy can resources beyond the survival of people be marshalled for such enterprises. The possibility of doing good deeds on the heroic mold, what the medievalists and Aristotle called 'magnificent', is increased the more affluent an economy. It takes Value aspirations to set them in motion. Only a moral pessimism looks askance at such efforts and calls them dreaming and futile.

Conclusion

The conflict in personality growth which affluence poses is not in wanting more but in wanting better. It is, therefore, a Value crisis. Without a goal or purpose beyond immediate sense satisfaction -- a person, an ambition, social ideal, a religious or intellectual conviction, or some blending of these into a Value pattern -- the increasing wanting generated by affluence will be dissipated in self-gratifications, increasingly repetitive, trivial, and cloying. Just as affluence is a dynamic so too it imposes a dynamic on one's Value formation. One either responds to the higher

Value aspirations which affluence makes possible, thus refining and elevating character, or one's character is coarsened and dulled and materialized by want satisfactions which are empty of purpose beyond themselves.

Once assured that affluence can be used to enhance character development and, in turn, that affluence is not destroyed by higher Value aspirations, we must go into some detail in showing how the virtues related to wealth and wealth-seeking must be re-formulated to fit the dynamics of affluence. These virtues are moderation which relates to our use and enjoyment of economic goods, justice which relates to our relation to other people by means of economic goods, and spiritual poverty which defines our attitude as to their ultimate meaning and goodness. The next three chapters will take each in turn.

CHAPTER FOUR

AFFLUENCE AND MODERATION

Despite the widespread concern about this generation's almost orgiastic indulgence in sex, drugs, alcohol and the rest, it is all but taboo even to mention the morality of self-control, temperance and moderation. Polls measuring the incidence of alcoholism, drug addiction, and sexual indulgence and scientific probings into their causes, deleterious effects, and probabilities of cure have explored all dimensions of the problems except the moral reasons for controlling sensual appetites. This evasiveness will inevitably generate a puritannical back-lash which will only make sane discussion of the moral issues that much more difficult.

It is important, therefore, that students face honestly and frankly the need for self-control and moderation in their lives, seeing this virtue not so much as a repression of and a brake on their activity but more as a guide and directive to healthier and saner living. Students should, in the course of reading this chapter, examine their own attitudes to the sensual appetites and wants. But the main emphasis will be on exploring the effect of affluent income expectations on living within the bounds of moderation. For affluence obviously is an element in the problem, in that excessive indulgence of any want is more possible when income provides a living beyond necessity or bare sufficiency. At the same time affluence has increased the costs and raised the economic penalties of over-indulgence.

This relation suggests the two dimensions of moderation, as self-control over the sensual appetites and over the appetite for gain. These two aspects, the student recognizes, correspond to the two moments of the affluent attitude: the expectation of more economic goods and the expectation of more income. Analysis of the interplay between these two distinct but related aspects of moderation, therefore, is a task particularly appropriate for an economic ethics. That task divides into three problems: 1) to distinguish between moderation as related to the sense appetites and to the appetite for gain, and to show their interrelationship; 2) to justify gain-seeking as a healthy appetite considered in itself; and 3) to outline a moderation of the affluent psyche which is not repressive of affluence's natural dynamics but an inner control producing higher Value espousal.

SENSE AND GAIN APPETITES

In making a sharper distinction between the sense appetites and the appetite for economic gain, our discussion will assume that controlling our proneness to sensuality is just as necessary as ever. The rules governing the sense appetites have not been changed by affluence, except in their wider applicability. They are part of the wisdom of mankind and have been spelled out on all levels of moral conviction, from their use as guides to good health to their ascetic Value in moral and religious aspirations. Even the disinclination to treat addictions as anything but illnesses has not obliterated the common-sense conviction that addictions are basically moral disorders. One becomes addicted only after repeated abuse of a material good and overcomes or neutralizes the addiction only after a painful moral effort of self-denial. The brief discussion of the sense appetites here, therefore, will only be by way of showing their differences from the appetite for gain.

A second preliminary remark is apropos also. Satisfying wants and seeking income does not occur in a social vacuum: others are affected in their efforts to satisfy their own wants and to seek income. That is, moderation has a justice dimension. Even though justice will be more formally treated in the next chapter, this justice dimension should be kept in mind as we turn to our tasks, the first of which is to differentiate the sense appetites from the wealth appetite.

Distinct but Related

Social philosophers have always realized that satisfying wants and seeking wealth, though related, present different moral issues. In the Classical and Medieval periods they were lumped together for two reasons: 1) a person's style of living was largely a function of his wealth, the destitute poor having less overt problems about moderation than the affluent rich; and 2) in static economies extravagent living habits as well as profit-seeking almost always involved depriving the poor of some means of livelihood.

Wealth seeking is still played within this context, touching upon justice in economic dealings with others, on the one side, and offering temptations to sensuality, on the other. Nevertheless, because of the universal possibility of economic gain, seeking a larger economic return for one's self will not necessarily deprive others of their fair share, and because wealth can be acquired and held in non-tangible form, increasing wealth may not imply more extravagent living. But this weakening of the linkage between the sense and gain appetites does not argue that their nexus has been broken, rather it does argue that their distinctiveness is more prominent.

The appetite for gain differs from the sensual appetites in two ways: 1) the appetite for wealth is a generic appetite and its object a generic good, while sense appetites are specific and their objects are specific; and 2) the brakes on wealth seeking are more general, less identifiable, and extrinsic while the brakes on the desires we share with animals are more specific, clearer in their control message, and intrinsic to the appetite.

An appetite is taken here in its generally accepted sense as a natural desire or propensity for some material good. Our sense of smell naturally desires odors. Given an odor, whether pleasant or not, it will smell it. Appetites, of course, vary with individuals and can be improved by training and use, or blunted by disuse. Avoiding the finer philosophic points, the nature of sensation, the locus of appetites, and the psychology and physiology of satisfaction, we assume that appetites are good, natural, and necessary for survival. Indeed those appetites most necessary for survival, the appetite for sex, for food (including drugs), for drink, for warmth and comfort, all somehow related to the sense of touch, are the obvious sources of moral difficulties.

These appetites are specific and have specific objects. I am thirsty for a glass of beer, any one but specifically for this one before me. My hunger is not satisfied by food, but by this plate of beans. Therefore, the control command is specific, "Don't smoke this joint, or pass up each and every drink containing alcohol."

The wealth appetite, by contrast, is general and its object, money, is generic. While money can be wanted for a specific reason -- the addict craving a "fix" -- the money itself is a universal good which could be exchanged for any other good. Because it is generic, as Aquinas points out, the gain appetite is stronger than the sense appetites.[1] The paradox of a good which has little sensual appeal evoking a stronger desire is explainable precisely because of money's universality. It is confirmed in action by the common experience that any human motivation, e.g. a doctor's aspiration to cure the sick, can be changed into and corrupted by the desire for money. So too people who have lost most desires for sensual goods may still retain a keen desire for more money.

What is true of money is true of the more generic good, wealth. For just as money yields purchasing power now and in the future, so wealth is a hedge against the insecurity, risks, and uncertainties of the future. In none of this is there the suggestion that the desire for money and wealth is anything but rational and good. In a money economy, one must have and desire money to survive. In an economy subject to rapid change one must have and desire wealth to tide one over shifts in fortune. Money and wealth may be the root of evil; they are in a material sense a necessity for all good.

The second difference between the animal and wealth appetites is the braking power inherent in the appetite itself. Sensual desires have several; wealth seeking has none. The first brake on sense desire is a sense of justice, that unrestrained appetites harm or are offensive to others. This is particularly true of the sex appetite. Indeed, the injustice of wreaking one's will in rape, seduction, or "kinky" sex on an unwilling partner may be a more potent spice than the sexual gratification itself. Self-respect is a second restraint. The shame of making a spectacle of one's self, of being lowered in others' esteem, and especially of surrendering one's humanness, even temporarily, to acting like an animal is often sufficient to brake an unruly desire. Finally, these failing, satiety provides the most effective constraint. For excessive indulgence produces physical revulsion and usually shortens life. This fact is foundation for the economist's concept of diminishing marginal utility.

While these brakes are morally necessitous, not physically, like gravitation, they do warn, often loudly and clearly, in a physical way. Only those, who have so lost control over their animal appetites as to stifle these signals of abuse, feel no mental discomfiture at continued indulgence.

There are no such brakes on the appetite for wealth. That is, there is nothing in the wealth seeking process which says "Enough". For money as general purchasing power, potentially satisfying all appetites and a means to all other kinds of power, and wealth, as a means to achieve esteem and importance in our own and others' eyes, really feed an ontological appetite, one coextensive with one's being, and like that potentially unlimited. That appetite is at root a propensity for power: as purchasing power obviously; as esteem, for the ultimate esteem is the sense of worth, of being able to work our will; and as security, for security is power to overcome the uncertainties of fickle fortune. To the extent that wealth or the command over wealth yields such power, there is no *a priori* limit to the wealth appetite. Aristotle recognized this[2] and medieval philosophers coined the phrase describing it, *appetitus divitiarum infinitus*, the infinite appetite for wealth.

In the affluent this is enhanced by the change in the way wealth can be held. This is so for two reasons. Where wealth must be held in visible form, as in estates, palatial mansions and gold plate it inevitably leads to a more ostentatious style of living, more retainers, finer clothes, more beautiful furnishings. In fact, such expenditures were in part investment for the sake of security: retainers who will do one's will, a fine coat with which to reward a servant, gold plate sold to raise funds. Wealth in financial assets, stocks, bonds, mortgages, and bank accounts, on the other hand, do not require a change in one's living style. The story is told of the mathematics professor, generally looking so seedy that his students periodically bought him a suit, who left to his university over a million dollars from his stock-market speculations. It is not an isolated example of a living style belying a person's wealth. In fact we see the phenomenon of *inconspicuous* consumption as a mark of wealth. Contrariwise, the modestly well-to-do may spend lavishly and beyond their income simply to impress others.

Secondly, wealth in the form of financial assets, unlike that in large estates, art objects, and jewelry, needs no great care and concern to protect. Its accumulation can be as quiet as a January snow-fall. One can, almost with little effort and much luck, wake up to find oneself wealthy. This is the will-of-the-wisp which make state lotteries so successful. This is the hidden dream which ignites the hysterics, the jumping, hugging, and kissing, on give-away TV programs.

If there is a brake on the appetite for wealth it is

subtle, and psychological. Wealth accumulation is not subject to diminishing returns in the same sense that satisfaction of the animal appetites are. A vague feeling of the irrationality of wealth accumulation for its own sake may suggest the futility of struggling further for what yields little enjoyment for one's self and little good for others.

This too has been documented time and again in the generous grants which the wealthy have made to education, scientific research, medical care and the arts. A variety of motives may inspire such bequests: the ancient idea of the stewardship of wealth, that one cannot take it with him, that he has, consequently, a responsibility that the wealth be used beneficially for others. The generosity may be inspired by no more than disgust that one's wealth has narrowed his range of human interests and purposes, that money is being accumulated for its own sake and not as a means. Satiety of the appetite for wealth may come with the realization that the struggle to accumulate is not worth further effort, that too much of humanness is surrendered in the effort and that a Vermont chicken farm provides a more human climate for living. Whatever the motive, the brake on the appetite for accumulation is not inherent in the appetite itself but demands an intervention from a higher Value, a higher purpose or goal in life.

Enough has already been said to demonstrate that the wealth appetite is a healthy and human drive and a powerful one. What needs to be done is to show its necessary role in the dynamics of affluence. What wealth and gain-seeking needs is the same kind of frank discussion and scientific analysis which is going on for the sex instinct. It must be taken out of the underworld of our thinking, recognized for what it is, frankly discussed and analyzed not just as a means for human survival but as a powerful force binding people to people. The analysis of sex has passed beyond the sniggers stage to frank discussion of both its wholesomeness and its vicious aberrations. But for the gain motive a Marxian prudery has thus far inhibited open and balanced analysis. Another jaunt through the history of thought will reveal the dimensions of the problem and demonstrate how inadequate current understanding is.

The Ethics of Gain-Seeking

While philosophers have discovered new depths to and

new applications of moderation over two millenia, the thorny issue continues to be the ethics of gain-seeking. Even a sketchy review like this captures the persistent difficulty social philosophers have had in relating the desire for economic gain with the desire for sense satisfaction while including both under the umbrella of moderation.

As in much of economic thought, the history of this effort breaks into three periods: the pre-economic when gain-seeking was suspect or, at best, tolerated; the age of political economy, starting about the middle of the 16th Century when gain-seeking obtained an almost a-moral independence; and the contemporary period when economic growth and gain-seeking again come under suspicion but now for economic, not moral reasons. Again, the student is warned, our interest is not antiquarian: thinkers of the past had insights which are valid today, each from the perspective of his time and the issues of his age adding another tile to the mosaic of understanding.

Plato, living in the period of Athenian defeat and defeatism, thought of moderation as the harmony arising from the mastery of reason over unruly sensual passions. Just as social harmony is realized by the willingness of citizens to obey civil authority, so a person achieves harmony by self-control in sensual matters.[3] As to gain-seeking, Plato consistently viewed it as morally dangerous. When he describes his ideal state in the Laws, he constitutes it as in effect a zero-growth economy and one in which the ordinary citizen is isolated from foreign trade.[4]

Aristotle further develops the notion of harmony, moderation being a balance or mean between self-indulgence and insensibility. Thus he concedes the good of pleasure, though acknowledging the need to lean against the attractions of sense delights.[5] More realistic than Plato about the ordinary business of life, Aristotle, nevertheless, legitimizes only trade undertaken to satisfy normal wants. Exchange to satisfy disordered wants, or what is worse, for its own sake, was unnatural, and accumulating wealth for its own sake led to pride and willful self-indulgence.[6] Thus Aristotle accords a certain autonomy to economic activity, requiring a special virtue of Liberality which maintains the mean both in the manner of earning income as well as in its spending. Liberality, therefore, establishes a balance between stinginess and prodigality and disposes a person to share his surplus wealth with those in greater need.

The two practical ethics spun from Platonic and Aristotlean thought were Stoicism and Epicureanism. In practice they differed little as in the case of a man of affairs like Cicero (106-43 B.C.) who both loved the good life and had a penchant for philosophizing. Stoicism in the extreme form preached by Epictetus (c.100 A.D.) would sacrifice every sensual good to preserve the integrity of the will. Its most conscientious practicioners were Christian hermits, both men and women, who fled the cities' turmoil for the desert, there to contemplate God and their eternal destiny.

One of the strongest influences on Western thought during the Middle Ages was Augustine, a pagan humanist who converted to Christianity and later became Bishop of Hippo in Africa. In wrestling with the problem how a Christian could live in a secular society, Augustine sees the Christian as on pilgrimage to his Eternal City, cautioning him not to set his heart on the distracting pleasures of the Secular City, using but not enjoying the goods it offers.[7] His warning that the merchant immersed in trade for profit could seldom be pleasing to God confirmed a suspicion of trade which persisted throughout the Middle Ages.

Aquinas was no less forthright than Augustine in condemning covetousness. The inordinate desire for riches, is a root moral evil not only because the appetite for a more universal good is stronger than the appetite for any particular good but because riches, especially money, are means for procuring the satisfaction of all other appetites.[8] He consequently agreed with Aristotle and Augustine that profit-seeking for its own sake arose from a disordered concupiscence, which, having no limits, sinned against both moderation and justice. On the other hand, being aware of the tremendous growth in trade, Aquinas did not condemn gain as such. The merchant was justified in his desire for profits if he intended to subserve the ends of man, e.g. by providing desired goods, and if he acted justly in economic dealings.[9]

Aquinas' concessions to profits and the profit-motive (see also p. 45 above), slight though they were, were an opening wedge as theologians and moralists during the commercial transformation of the later Middle Ages grudgingly conceded the universal possibility of economic gain. This struggle is best exemplified in the usury debate which exercised moralists for five centuries. For usury was the commercial evil and in the popular mind encompassed not just taking interest unjustly but every form of commercial exploitation. (A somewhat fuller description of this debate will be given in Chapter Eight.) The commercial classes, despite their increasing influence as bankers to both monarchy and papacy and their essential role in provisioning cities, were still generally suspect, in Protestant as in Catholic lands, of avariciousness, sensuality, and pride.

The one crack in the dike was provided by John Calvin (1509-1564). Calvin was no less medieval than his Catholic and Protestant contemporaries in his condemnation of usury, of violations of justice in exchange, and of exploitation of the poor, but he preached his reforms in Geneva, an important commercial center, and took for granted the moral respectability of his hearers' commercial and industrial careers. His basic theme was salvation by divine election only, that a person could not be saved unless God so predestined. Nevertheless, while man could not be saved by his good works, he could not be saved without good works.[10] In effect this meant accepting one's lot in life, sticking to one's vocation, living industriously, frugally and soberly, using and enjoying the good things in moderation.[11] In the community of saints, each person's calling, whether as a rich merchant or a poor tradesman, had essentially the same features. Upon this simple proposition the Puritan Ethic was erected.

For the virtues fundamental to the Christian's calling are the very ingredients of personal economic success and national growth. Secularized during a period of exhilerating commercial expansion by political economists like Child, Mun, North, Petty, Cantillon and the like, these virtues effectively unleash the spirit of gain-seeking because they themselves are hedge against the vices of sensuality. Montesquieu (1689-1755), who was only periperally influenced by Calvinism and a Frenchman, nevertheless, enunciated this comforting British conscience on wealth:

> "When a democracy is founded on commerce, private people may acquire vast riches without corruption of morals. This is because the spirit of commerce is naturally attended with that of frugality, economy, moderation, labour, patience, tranquility, order and rule. So long as this spirit subsists, the riches produced have no bad effect."[12]

This comfortable conscience, however, was already being cut to the quick by the 'pot-house' philosopher, Bernard Mandeville (1670-1733). In his Fable of the Bees[13] Mandeville argued that puritan frugality and sobriety did not stimulate but depressed the economy while, to the contrary, the libertine's sensuality and the selfishness of the ambitious were the true causes of economic growth. Thus private vices are public virtues. That these cynical sophistries, derived from the radical individualism of Descartes and Locke and immediately from Hobbes, should touch such a tender nerve is evidenced by the half-century debate on the altruism-egoism issue. All the great moralists of the period, Bishop Butler, Francis Hutcheson, David Hume, and Adam Smith among others, engaged in the effort to translate egoism and self-interest into socially considerate and beneficial results. This issue is central to the three most widely held ethical theories of the 19th Century: Kant's moral imperative, Reid's common sense, and Bentham's utilitarian calculus. The issue is with us today.

In economics and business, however, it was practically resolved by the work of three men, David Hume, Francois Quesnay, and Adam Smith, all with significant ethical and economic credentials and mutual friends. Hume's notion of "liveliness" which in business becomes an instinctive urge to compete for the elusive prize of profits,[14] actually formalizes Quesnay's description of the entrepeneur-farmer busy with investment and production plans to increase his net product. This spirit then is emancipated from moral intentions by Smith's Invisible Hand. For economic self-seeking, according to Smith, so required mutuality, reciprocity and harmonizing of economic interests, that private gain-seeking became the very instrument of social economic well-being. While -- to do justice to Smith -- it was never his intention to absolve economic actions of moral implications, in effect the morality of gain-seeking became a strictly private matter and ceased to be a public issue.[15]

Thus liberated from its ethical shackles, the appetite for gain, one would suppose, would enjoy an uncheckered career. Almost perversely, however, the Classical Economists -- Ricardo, Malthus, J.S. Mill -- saw in the profit motive the very key which turned economic growth into economic stagnation. Karl Marx went further. He reconstituted the medieval infinite appetite for wealth as the irrational desire of capitalists to accumulate which impelled capitalism into communism. For the blind need to accumulate capital by exploiting the workers' surplus value generated periodic crises of over-production, accelerated the centralization of capital, produced the reserve army of the unemployed, and intensified the immizeration of the proletariate. Capital accumulation was at the root of personal alienation and social irrationality. Its inevitable logic was the final exploitation of the last exploiter and, thus, communism. Marx, therefore, could both denounce with prophetic fervor the appetite for wealth as capitalistic greediness and coolly analyze it as an inevitable condition in the dialectic of historical materialism. Capitalistic greed carried to its logical conclusion destroys the system which fostered it, and in that destruction tolls its own knell.

Marginal Utility analysis rescued gain-seeking from this Marxian limbo but at the cost of emasculating all moral content. Profit-maximization and more generally gain-maximization become simply amoral principles of rational behavior under conditions of scarcity, premises of a logic of choice among alternatives. They simply begin rational economic discourse, a technique which is Value-free, positive and quantitative. This is the position of the overwhelming majority of contemporary economists.

But the ghost of the ethics of gain-seeking could not be put to rest. While discussion of the morality of the appetite for wealth dropped out of even textbooks on moderation, the gain and especially the profit motive, as social principles, were attacked and defended with simplistic fervor.

Their most vigorous defense was launched a hundred years ago by Herbert Spencer, Charles Sumner and the Social Darwinists. Spencer in particular hardened laissez faire into dogma: absolute freedom to gain, absolute private property, and untrammeled competition were necessary conditions for both economic progress and the enlargement of human liberty. Economic freedom, which for Adam Smith was revolutionary and salutary, but never absolute, for Spencer became conservative, necessary, and dogmatic.[16] Social Darwinism survives in its original dogmatism in the essays of Ayn Rand but only in greatly modified form in contemporary Libertarianism.

The attack on the profit-motive as a social principle achieved respectability with the Fabian Socialism of Sidney and Beatrice Webb (1858-1947) who argued for wider sharing in private property, unionization of labor and democratization of industry -- revolutionary doctrine in the period before and after World War I but hardly startling today. Their most telling attack on the profit-motive was R. H. Tawney's The Acquisitive Society in which he detailed its evil effects, attacked its moral sanction, and argued for its control.[17] The more dogmatic Marxian attacks came later, as well as a host of social criticism of capitalism. All tend to be hung upon this dilemma: fostering economic growth by state means endangers the private incentive essential for growth.

More recently economic growth itself has come under attack by economists themselves. Beginning with Keynes's 'euthanasia of the rentier', Schumpeter's decline of investment innovation, Hansen's secular stagnation, Meadows' limits to growth, Boulding's spaceship earth and Georgscu-Roegen's entropic degradation, economists, during a period of unprecedented and world-wide economic development, have sought, in a remarkable reversion to the dismal predilections of Classical Economists, for reasons why and when the economic clock would run down. Around these have flocked a host of environmentalists, conservationists, ecologists and populationists, each with a valid but limited vision of conditions threatening economic catastrophe.

While seemingly staying clear of the morality of personal gain-seeking and moderation of the sense appetites, attacks on the gain-directed free enterprise system both from the side of social philosophy and from the view of its economic viability inevitably pose threats of enforced restraints on private actions. Hegel (1770-1831) may be more expressive of the Germanic mind:

> "...society has the right and duty of acting as trustee to those whose extravagence destroys the security of their own subsistence or their families. It must substitute for extravagence the pursuit of the ends of society and the individuals concerned." (emphasis added)[18]

But even J. S. Mill's forthright dictum that the state must not legislate on matters of private morality unless they infringe on another's rights[19] is written more in sand than in granite. For where is the line drawn between public and private, between my rights and yours? There is little I do, even in dreams, which does not affect another.

> Thus the long effort to free the appetite for gain from moral and self-restraint has worked its revenge by increasing the danger of legal and social restraints. That inevitability could be predicted from the nature of gain-seeking itself. As the appetite for a universal good having the strongest pull yet possessing no internal braking mechanism, gain-seeking naturally tends to get out of hand, at the risk of both endangering the gain-seeker himself -- Howard Hughes? -- and/or the viability of the economy.
>
> Thus there are two possibilities, which can be applied separately or in some combination, self-control or social control. Social controls, while absolutely necessary to establish minimum traffic rules for the economic process, and probably necessary to protect the public good and to harmonize private with social goals, pose the danger of stifling the very incentives which make the economic system go. Self-control, on the other hand, works on low voltage signals arising from progressive disharmony between the sense appetites and reason, and from increasing imbalance between stinginess and prodigality in spending money. These signals may be further muted in that a rational gain-seeking is not grossly greedy but acknowledges economic mutality, that one gains by allowing others to gain. Finally, the signals may be rationalized away by the argument that self-indulgent spending -- a high consumption function -- is requisite for economic growth.
>
> That leaves but one effective option, a self-control which imposes restraint on gain-seeking in terms of a person's own goals, purposes, and Values. All other reasons are auxiliary. This is essential.

Economics for all its heady advance in understanding the economic process and in developing techniques for its analysis has done little to resolve the moral questions attending its basic principles of gain-seeking. Euphoria turned to gloom as it became more apparent that this uncertainty itself undermined the assumption of the beneficent operation of a free-market economy. The moral sciences, for their part, seemed reluctant to meddle in matters so esoteric. Since nature abhors a vacuum, economists themselves have stretched their economic principles to fashion an ersatz economic ethics, often disastrously for both economics and ethics.

Granting that the above indicts this effort, yet painfully conscious that students must shortly try to live and make a living in this ambiguous climate, we continue to offer suggestions how they may cope with their affluence. With respect to moderation there are two tasks: 1) to justify gain-seeking both as an analytic device and as a motive for action, and 2) to suggest how the principle of moderation can be recast to balance increasing income, increasing wants, and changing Values.

A JUSTIFICATION OF GAIN-SEEKING

This section was originally titled, "A Justification of Self-Interest". The change is more cosmetic than substantial. For gain-seeking is necessarily self-interested. If I bargain for a higher salary, I am seeking that gain for myself, whatever other purposes or reasons I may have. Consequently, a more descriptive title would be "A Justification of Self-Interested Gain-Seeking". In subsequent discussion we will use self-interest and gain-seeking almost interchangeably and sometimes compress the two into self-seeking. It is the self-seeking in gain-seeking which causes the problem.

Certainly, this is verified in popular understanding. Albert Einstein, no economist but a keen critic of contemporary society, articulated the subconscious opinion of most people about the free enterprise system. He described it as "a huge community of producers the members of which are unceasingly striving to deprive each other of the fruits of their collective labor -- not by force, but on the whole in faithful compliance with legally established rules."[20]

This sentiment is echoed time after time in popular polls which generally rate business and business men low in moral sensitivity. This opinion prevails through a wide spectrum of society even though most people are involved in some way in business, even though business leaders are the first to be called upon to head and to staff charitable campaigns, and finally even though business leaders' dereLections are headlined as falls from grace to a much greater extent than that of politicians or union leaders. All point to a fundamental ambivalence about morality in business: we expect business to be rotten but not the people in it.

Indeed moralists, economists, business commentators and businessmen themselves have contributed to this confusion about self-interest and gain-seeking. As we saw above, earlier philosophers and theologians, writing against a backdrop of mass destitution, were little able to view economic self-seeking other than as taking advantage of the general public, as an unbridled lust for gain, and as a sin against the Providence of God. Later economists, light-headed with the wine of economic progress, side-stepped this issue and accepted without discrimination all forms of self-seeking whether greedy or not, as that self-interest which analysis of the free-market requires. Both failed in specifying their understanding of self-interest, moralists generally as a personal motive, and economists generally as an element in the logic of choice. Neither quite understands what the other is talking about.

The Semantic Confusion

At no time has the need to peel away the layers of confusion in which economic self-interest lies imbedded been more urgent. For this generation, floundering in its search for order and purpose in the flood-tide of abundance, needs as no previous generation to learn the distinction between a self- interest required for condition of abundance and a self-interest which becomes a witless accumulation of gain or a desperate fury to spend.

This confusion is largely semantic and unnecessary. It is unnecessary because economists can and should avoid any and all ethical implications in the terms they use. Unfortunately, such disengagement is contrary to the tradition of the science. For Economics, as we saw, was born from moral philosophy at the time this issue of self-interest, altruism and selfishness was hotly debated. Since the early economists were either moral philosophers or aware of the issue, the topic remained in the literature of the science. Contemporary economists, who wish to say something relevant about basic issues, are prone to hare-brained statements equating self-interest and selfishness, confusing their methodology for philosophy. Any one, as a consequence, can debunk the free-enterprise system by taking these statements seriously.

The semantic confusion has several layers. The first, a trivial but deeply rooted confusion, is that an altruistic motive is morally nobler than a self-interested motive. While often, this is not necessarily the case. For self-interest and altruism are distinguished by the term of the action: self-interest is for my good and altruism is for the good of another. Neither specifies the morality of the intent and purpose of the act. Thus a person wanting to rid a woman of her brutish husband by murdering him, would be acting altruistically but neither nobly nor morally. On the other hand, the desire to overcome drunkenness is self-interested and its aspiration both most noble and moral.

Digging deeper, we find that, while altruism and self-interest may be conceptually distinguished, in concrete actions they are inseparable. No act is exclusively self-interested or altruistic. For every moral act must consider the good of others. Every immoral act, by the very fact of our social nature, directly or remotely harms others. For the same reason, to act for another's good enhances in some fundamental way our own, and to harm another, harms ourself. This is most clearly illustrated in the mystery -- but daily experience -- of love and hate. For the lover in loving the beloved loves himself. The hater in hating others hates himself. In short, however self-interest and altruism are distinguishable in analysis, they cannot be divorced in reality.

The deepest layer of confusion, which was mentioned earlier but bears repeating, arises from the very use of economic terms. The confusion is almost inevitable because, unlike other sciences, Economics did not create a scientific vocabulary out of new Greek or Latin words, but used words from ordinary discourse and progressively gave them precise, scientific meaning. Words like supply, demand, and costs have different, though related, meaning in economic analysis from their perfectly good usage in daily speech. Unless their scientific meanings are clearly kept in mind, such terms tend to intrude their popular connotations and their moral overtones into economic reasoning.

The Semantics of Competition

A good example is the term competition. Unravelling the confusion in its use will have the further benefit of advancing our understanding of economic self-interest because economic self-interest is always competitive. This condition is inherent in the fact of scarcity. For when many seek a good, of which more is desired than is available, they must compete for that good. Competition, therefore, is a universal condition of economic activity: consumers compete with consumers; workers with workers; firms with firms; governments with their citizens, and all with each.

Economic reasoning highlights the mathematical element in the term competition. A large number of buyers and sellers relative to the size of the market so that no one has a significant influence on the market price denotes a highly competitive market. A small number relative to the market so that each has some influence on the market price means little competition. In business usage, competition implies rivalry. Ford and General Motors are considered keen competitors in the business sense, though economists would rate the automobile industry as low in competition. Farmers, on the other hand, experience little sense of rivalry with each other, but agriculture is ranked as highly competitive.

Neither meaning is wrong, nor unrelated to the other. Economic competition implies rivalry, a striving after a limited good. Rivalry obviously implies competition. But the latter stresses besting the opposition, while the former emphasizes the need to be more efficient. The economic concept of competition is best illustrated in the striving for the Olympic gold in the individual events. Thousands throughout the world begin the competition which only one can win. Yet each hopefully gains by bettering his or her previous performance. Implicit is the assumption that good sportsmanship and mutual support will prevail. Rivalry is exemplified in team sports where one wins and the other loses. The rivalry may be healthy and mutually beneficial, but in an all or nothing context, winning becomes the only thing.

Economic competition expresses the inherent necessities of scarcity; rivalry stresses the element of motive and the means to achieve the goal. Confusing the two has dangerous practical implications. For it is easy to rationalize that any means used to best the opposition is justified in the name of competition. Stealing corporate information, using advantage unfairly to force another business to the wall, an unconcern about tax evasion, disregard for the public costs of waste and pollution, and a general indifference about financial and commercial practices which take advantage of the poor and most exploitable, all can be and have been rationalized under the rubric of competition. Such rationalization makes a travesty of the classical concept of competition and renders suspect the very principle of economic efficiency.

o As a result of all this confusion, businessmen, most of whom by far strive to be honest and fair in their dealings, are stuck in a moral morass in which no differentiation is made between selfishness and justifiable self-interest. In such doubt normal moral responses lose their crispness, further attentuating ethical influences in business. As always young people mirror adult ambivalence with disconcerting clarity. They either reject all ethical considerations with the off-the-cuff remark that one either has ethics or he does not, or they so stringently hedge business about so as to make acting impossible.

The Semantic Resolution

Sorting out the strands of this confusion comes down to distinguishing between gain-seeking as used in economic analysis and as a principle of concrete human actions. Gain, as we said in Chapter Two, is simply the difference, which inevitably arises under conditions of scarcity, between a person's perception of the value of the good obtained in exchange against the value of the good, or goods, foregone. Thus in every act of exchange, whether of commodities, of human services, of rights to income or of property, gain is realized by both buyer and seller, otherwise neither would exchange. Further buyers and sellers will prefer -- and again because of scarcity -- that exchange which *optimizes returns*, that is, yields the highest value obtained, and also prefer that exchange which *minimizes costs*, that exchange which requires the least sacrifice of value. That is to say, every buyer and seller acts rationally by *maximizing gain*, whether this gain is called a profit, a consumer surplus, or an economic rent.

Such is the necessary logic of economic choice. Further it occurs in a social context: it is competitive, buyers bidding against buyers and sellers against sellers, and each set negotiating with the other. Finally, choice takes place in time: buyers and sellers make decisions on information on what was, and, more difficult, on expectations on what will be. Given all this, when the individual buyer or seller has achieved *maximum gain*, he has acted *economically efficiently*. When all buyers and sellers achieve collective efficiency, the economy is in equilibrium.

Every student is immediately aware how abstract these relations are. But they are real, not imaginary. However such relations have been taken out of the context of complete and full reality by assuming 1) that people have reasons for choosing; 2) that they have an understanding of their own good; 3) that they act on the basis of the information available to them, whether that is adequate or not for decisions; and 4) that the competitive process proceeds smoothly, an informed, orderly and passionless process like a game of chess. Obviously, none of this holds in real life as it is assumed in analysis. No one, consequently, ever maximizes gain in an absolute sense, and the economy, and no segment of it, is ever at equilibrium.

What good is it is a good question! Analysis is only a logic. It provides a format for making and evaluating choice under conditions of scarcity. It is much like grammar, the logic of sentence structure. One might complain that grammatical analysis of Hamlet's Soliloquies destroys the meaning which Shakespeare intended to convey. Not so, a keen understanding of what is subject and verb and what modifies what, when joined to understanding of the words, both enhances comprehension of the text and appreciation of its artistry. So too economic analysis does tell us how people tend to act under conditions of scarcity and expresses, with a precision other social and moral sciences can not achieve, the relations which exist between people. Like grammar, however, it can kill understanding of such actions and relations, if not put back into the real life context of acting.

We can, therefore, talk about gain-seeking as a principle of action. People do seek gain. But such seeking is only one of many principles influencing action, and gain as a motive is only one of many reasons for acting. Moreover and this is the significant point, the economic motive is utilitarian: it is with respect to the means by which one acts, and not with respect to the final end or purpose. Economic analysis always starts with givens: given available resources and given purposes, Values and the like, one would, and should, choose in this manner. Gain-seeking, therefore, becomes disorientated when it loses purpose and, in effect, becomes an end in and for itself. Further, since its object is money, income, wealth which are universally useful and universally desired, it becomes an infinite appetite, an appetite out of control.

It is within this philosophic context that we examine gain-seeking as a principle of action and gain as a human motive.

The Gain Principle

Private economic self-seeking has deep social and cultural roots in Western history. Its seeds were planted by the peddlers wandering pack-aback from fief to fief selling their wares. They started a process which eventually destroyed feudalism and revolutionized society. Largely channelled away from land ownership and money lending, self-interest moved into investment first in commercial and then manufacturing enterprise. It carried European ships and people throughout the world. Whatever plunder and exploitation was committed in its name, and whatever human misery it has caused, gain-seeking has in balance benefitted the world. It has largely shifted the grinding burden of hauling and heaving from men to machines; it has expanded the horizons of man and increased his mobility; and has lifted from the people the cold hand of debt and economic stagnation by a wider sharing in material well-being. The contrast is etched more sharply by comparing European-style economies with the developing economies where a self-reliant self-interest is at best a feeble spark and does little to fan their economies into self-fueling growth.

Gain also is a much more protean phenomenon than its appearances as profit. The housewife, who buys a ten-cent rather than a twenty-cent bar of soap giving the same satisfaction, is trying to gain. The professor who leaves one appointment for another comparable in duties but at higher pay, is trying to gain. The person, who carefully scrutinizes the possible recipients of his charity for that which will receive the most benefit, is trying to gain. In the act of choosing, such gain-maximization acts no differently than in the profit-seeking of the directors of General Motors.

The same principle on an economy-wide scale is called national economic progress. That we actually have more material things by which we can live a fuller life than the people in grandfather's day is because people, individually and as a whole, intended to gain and firms sought profits. Economic self-interest is the basic cause of using goods more effectively and of devising more ingenious, more economical and efficient ways of combining human skills and energy, raw materials, and machinery to produce more desirable products. Whether resulting from collective decisions as in socialism or from the billions of decisions in a free market, the real output of economies have increased.

In this sense economic self-interest has found a more favorable climate in free-enterprise economies than in socialist ones, and the results are better. Ironically the most bitter critics cite this as criticism, that the free enterprise economies have gained a lion's share of the world's wealth. Even while criticizing, they enjoy the economic abundance self-interest has generated. We live longer; we support a larger population which works less and enjoys more leisure, goes to school more years and lives longer in retirement. We devote a greater proportion of national wealth to the ends of the good life -- to support scholars, moral and religious leaders, public administrators, artists and entertainers. The critics of free-enterprise seldom choose the drabber existence in collectivized economies or the fewer amenities in developing economies.

A free-market economy not only welcomes self-seeking but requires it. For where the output of the economy is increasing, that increase must be distributed, must be shared. Unless there is widespread effort on the part of all in the economy, each to get his share, the greater part will go to the few who control production, or, what would be worse, to government.

Given the above, little in addition needs be done to draw the conclusion that self-interest, gain- and profit-maximization are essential to the free-market economy. For the market mechanism can operate only on the two bases of what is wanted and what is available. Income can be earned only by making available what the public in some way desires and will pay for. Product can be taken from the market only by paying the price to make it available. That is to say that the market compensates self-interest. Those who best consult their own interests to supply the goods and services most desired are the most liberally rewarded. Those who find better ways of lowering costs receive more profits. Those who seek the better paying employment, get more pay. Those who seek the lower-price items, can enjoy a better living.

Conversely, it means that those who set their sites on higher goods, more socially desirable though not so well remunerated by the market, must be content with a lesser share. Indeed, some of the most socially useful goods do not and often cannot go through the market. This is the nature of the free market: it is a process of coordinating self-interests. Without self-interest there can be no free market.

To blame the market for not recognizing need or social worth is simply quixotic. The market is not geared to help causes or people who can not or will not sell their services in the market. Should people hold these in sufficient regard to pay for them the market will accommodate. More usually, though, the alleviation of personal need or the reward of social worth must take place outside the market.

A more serious charge is that the free market is geared to immediate satisfactions, often at the expense of the general public and to the harm of future well-being. These are valid reasons for governmental policy which would guide the market toward more socially desirable goals. But caution is necessary. Frequently enough there is some hysteria and loss of nerve in charges that the market is destroying the economy, and the trade-off in loss of other goods is not carefully thought out. Frequently, too, short sighted policy is adopted out of misguided hopes to spare people the somewhat harsh effects of the market. In almost all cases there is an effective way of using self-interest in the market to achieve the desired results. More of this will be explored in later chapters.

To trammell the market, forcing it to alleviate need and to reward worth presents its own difficulties. First, it will encourage the unscrupulously self-interested to seek to gain under these new titles. Thus closer scrutiny and more controls are necessitated. A second difficulty is more philosophical and involves a more fundamental contradiction. Those who are most suspicious of the gain-motive and self-interest tend to favor a pricing system structured and regimented by some extra-market authority, usually government. In doing so they are caught on the horns of dilemma. For the moral value of any act depends on voluntary choice. A forced act is neither a moral, nor strictly speaking a human act. But buying and selling is an aspect of practically all human acts. So to restrict human freedom and individual responsibility in market transactions is to restrict human freedom itself. To achieve freedom they would restrict it.

o Sufficient now to conclude that the free market system is based on and indeed processes economic self-interest. This is the principal justification of self-interest. But not the only one. The world has, on balance, greatly benefited by the search for economic gain in more output, in more efficient production, in calling into play the immensely varied resources of the earth, and in stimulating new ideas, new techniques and new wants. Given increasing material abundance, self-interest is a protean force which will realize itself whatever the circumstances or restraint. The gain-maximization motive which the economist assumes at the beginning of his analysis, consequently, can in real life be variously colored by egoism or altriusm, by base sensual desires or noble aspiration, by evil intentions or good, by short-sighted and immediate gratification or by longer-run concern for the quality of life. Moderating it will succeed not by hedging it about, suppressing it, or by putting extraneous limits to it. Moderating the spirit of wealth-seeking is achieved by keeping it in balance with the other goals of life.

A MODERATION FOR MODERNS

As from afar we reach the real moral problem of moderating the affluent attitude. Our approach is somewhat tentative because our analysis will not yield the same kind of definitive criteria which traditional concepts of moderation of the sense appetites yield. For though, as we have seen, the appetite for wealth and the sense appetites are related, they are distinct. 1) The appetite for wealth is generic, the sense appetites are specific. 2) The control mechanisms on the latter are relatively clear-cut, on the former, vague and imprecise. 3) The sense and wealth appetites are not so linked that the wealthy may not be modest in their sensual wants and the not-so wealthy self-indulgent. 4) Since gain-seeking in a free-market economy is essential for economic growth and for distribution of increased output, it would appear to be an important mainstay of economic freedom. All of these reasons combine to cast doubt on the facile conclusion that the desire for gain manifestly leads to sensuality and greediness.

The ages-old fear of the infinite appetite for wealth, however, is still valid. For the desire for the universal means to the good things of life cannot and will not equate with the desire for a life of goodness. Our proneness to sensuality, display, and love of social superiority, as we saw in the last chapter, poses the ever-present danger that gain-seeking can be subverted into satisfying baser Values. Thus the striving for gain, for more income and wealth, which absorbs most of most people's lives, is both an essential energizer of an affluent economy and moral danger to the affluent. Mandeville reversed, public virtues seem to require private vices. Obliquely at least, the problem is that of defending affluence itself.

Resolving this dilemma must begin by reviewing the logic of affluence. The persisting experience of abundance begets the affluent attitude, the expectations of more income and more material goods. But the very fulfilling of such expectations generates more wanting, so that scarcity, if not intensified, is never alleviated, and economic output never matches economic wants. Consequently, a moderation which stifles the gain-incentive or represses wanting attacks economic abundance. A greater wisdom than expressed here may urge such draconian measures as the salvation of Western society. But those who so argue would do well to tally the social consequences not only in developed but in developing countries, and not primarily for the rich but for the poor.

The Dilemma of Affluence

Rather the approach here is more modest. It will not require fleeing abundance, forsaking industrial output, nor dismantling abundance but it will demand the more difficult moral art of balancing increasing wants within increasing satisfaction-possibilities. That is, the static notion of moderation of realizing one's Value priorities out of a given income is as outmoded as a surrey on a superhighway. For there is no amount of wealth, no level of income, no plane of living which a person can define as enough. At the same time, given the immediate possibilities, there is always at any particular time an intensity of striving which is too much.

Consequently, no cook-book or rule-book can determine the ingredients or define the limits of a moderated appetite for wealth. At best we can formulate some of the considerations necessary for a morally balanced attitude. Four elements in that attitude would seem important, three of which are suggested by the economic process itself: 1) To increase income demands curtailing wants; 2) More income will generate more wants; 3) The economy at any one time is limited; 4) Increased wanting is three-dimensional: given wants can be intensified; the horizon of wants can expand; and wants can be elevated to achieve higher Values. We will give some consideration to each of these four points.

<u>To increase income requires curtailing current expenditures.</u> While this idea goes against the grain of current Post-Keynesian thinking, it retains a fundamental validity. In macro-economic terms it means that the saving function is as essential for economic growth as the consumption func-

tion is for maintaining the level of national income and employment. The logic is clear and irrefutable. An economy cannot grow unless it acquires more capital goods, researches better production techniques and more efficient ways of satisfying wants, and invests large sums in improving labor skills. What is true of the whole economy holds for individuals and firms. That is, investment for growth demand prior saving. The expectation of increasing income, which is one of the essential ingredients of the affluent mentality, requires curtailing current want satisfaction.

This does not argue against going into debt. To the contrary, it implies more indebtedness because the people who save are not the people who invest, and consequently, the latter must borrow from the former. It does suggest that creating money and relying on Federal government credit, both of which could fuel inflation, are not appropriate forms of savings. The hope for larger future income imposes real saving on us all. We cannot have more cake tomorrow if we eat it all today.

This implies that most families must save and all must moderate their credit buying within reasonable expectations of future income. It implies changing some of the current mythology about corporate profits, seeing them as necessary to generate and encourage investment. Conversely, business decision-makers have the obligation to hold corporate profits in public trust as means to improve corporate performance, and to maintain sales, production and employment. It means also that we cannot make politicians' providing "goodies" for us, at whatever the cost to the common welfare, the principal condition for their political survival. At the same time, it imposes on political servants the obligation to administer public funds for public purposes and not to enhance their personal prestige or to appease popular appetites.

No economy can spend to the hilt today and expect more in the future, and no segment of the economy can exempt itself from this obligation. This is a particularly harsh statement under conditions of inflation when going into debt to buy now makes sense both because debts will be paid off in cheaper dollars and one pays a lesser price today for what one would pay a higher price tomorrow. Nevertheless, the rationale for saving is still valid, from the economy point of view, because such credit-buying itself further fuels the inflation, and from the personal view, because the inflation may be inducing one to buy for the sake of price and not in consideration of one's reasonable wants.

This conclusion is corroborated in two other considerations. The first is the very fact of scarcity in abundance, the realization that wanting increases faster than income. Hence, we can never have all we want right now: some very good and desirable goals must be postponed to future fulfillment. A policy to increase and spread income is self-defeating, in and by itself. What happened to New York -- the Big Apple -- is only the most dramatic so far of innumerable instances in households, businesses and governmental units of a self-defeating income's policy. For the bigger New York's income became, the bigger were the bites into it, some by graft certainly, but most by legitimate demanders. Increased income must always be tempered by greater, not a lesser, spending restraint.

The second corroborating consideration is the hard fact of the economy's production possibilities frontier. At any one moment, given the resources, the technology, and the will of the people to work, an economy can only produce so much. Consequently, every one's share in the national dividend, from the federal government's take to a teenager's allowance, is limited. The frontier can be pushed back, but to push the economy close to its present limits generates not more goods but higher prices.

This is the one inescapable explanation of the current world-wide inflation. The OPEC price cartel, Federal Reserve policy, senatorial spending habits, labor union demands are really only surface phenomena of the more widespread malaise that we all demanded more of the economy than it could produce. "The simultaneous rise of appetites throughout the world", writes Professor George Katona, "was a major fact in demand exceeding supply and a major explanation of worldwide inflation."[21] Economists have contributed by still emphasizing the Paradox of Thrift, that excess saving can cause a decline in saving and by not balancing that warning with the Paradox of Spending, that excess spending can result in paying more for less consumption.

Environmentalists and conservationists argue in the same direction. Too rapid depletion of the earth's resources or destruction of its habitibility are problems not to be taken lightly. Such groups' tendency, however, to dogmatize on incomplete knowledge of the earth's nonrenewable resources and on crude estimates of irreversible environmental damage is but one element in a climate of hysteria they generate. More dangerous is their disposition to insist on macro-controls, legal rates and quotas, on mining and drilling, on using non-renewable resources, on generating waste in production, and, most seriously, on birth rates. They almost disdain preaching self-restraint, reducing waste, or using known technology more efficiently, and all but scoff at price mechanisms which would encourage such moderation, all of which would substantially alleviate pressure on the economy while preserving individual economic freedom. The possibilities of environmental damage cannot be ignored, and, whatever one's disposition as to solution, provide another impelling reason for moderating one's own economic demands.

The Wanting Dimensions

The multi-dimensional wanting of affluence, our fourth consideration, is at the heart of the moral issue of a moderation for moderns. Despite our emphasis on the distincttion between the sense and wealth appetites, traditional ethics was correct in maintaining their relation: wealth is desired primarily to satisfy material wants. Moderating -- a self-control not a social suppression -- the wealth appetite in an economy which constantly generates more wealth, therefore, requires examining the implications of the affluent attitude on the three dimensions of wanting: want-intensification, want-expansion, and want-elevation.

Economic abundance provides more means to satisfy already established want-patterns, and thereby to intensify them. Ours is a sensate society and affluence enables us to cultivate a wide variety of sensuality and to carry them to extremes. A new industry, for example, aimed at the majority middle-income group, has grown up just to help people work off excessive culinary indulgence. The inefficiency of spending as much money and energy in taking off fat as was spent in putting it on is obvious and mildly ludicrous.

The cult of the comfortable and of the cosmetic spends billions annually in a ceaseless concern to avoid pain and inconvenience and to cover up body odors, blemishes or imperfections. Venereal disease, despite medical science, is in almost epidemic proportions. A too large percentage of the under thirty are crippled by drug addiction. More subtly corrosive is our national mania for violence in sports and entertainment. A rampant alcoholism openly or covertly affects as much as 10% of the total population. All peoples have faced similar problems in controlling the appetite for food, drink, sex and stimulants. Poverty and destitution in survival economies, however, effectively contain these problems. In affluent economies even the poorest can cultivate their favorite vices.

Just as affluence has greased the slides, it has increased the penalties. A drug-blighted life can cost millions of dollars in income lost, crime, and custodial and rehabilitation expenses. One night of drinking can cause an automobile accident costing hundreds of thousands of dollars. Sexual infidelity leading to divorce cruelly punishes the innocent and, when a family is abandoned, heavily burdens other tax-payers. Even simple and entirely legitimate pleasures -- a couple's weekly night out, dinner, movies and drinks -- can, if become a fixed pattern, absorb a substantial percentage of a good income. Affluence has, therefore, greatly magnified the problem of controlling the sense appetites. It has not, however, changed it qualitatively. The traditional ethics of moderation are still valid and relevant to contemporary living.

Want expansion, however, adds a new dimension to moderation. For the very essense of the affluent attitude is the ever-expanding horizon of wanting which increasing income and wealth encourages. Indeed, when abundance increases faster than population, want-expansion is inevitable. When it produces a fuller and more human life, it is wholesome and desirable. Its danger, however, lies in allowing a mindless proliferation of wants, novelties pursued for novelty sake, fads embraced to conform to the latest style, trivia purchased on impulse. These form the fabric of our throw-away consumer habits, which fill closets and attics to overflowing and make the garage-sale a suburban institution. They are symptoms of a rootlessness which cannot savor possessions once their novelty has worn thin. This undisciplined wanting of what allures and impresses may be called a carcinoma of consumption.

This craving for things is further fed by the desire to possess for prestige sake. The concern for image rather than achievement is the vice of the 'phony' and 'four-flusher' in every economic function at whatever level. In the neighborhood it produces the conformist who must have whatever others have. In business and government, it takes the form of pampering executive comfort and prestige. Business amenities are necessary for efficient performance. But pampering is evident when the plush of executive suites contrasts starkly with the miserable working condition of the staff and production people, who will, moreover, become the principal victims of bloated costs and poor profits.

Finally, the vices of wanting are tightened when want-proliferation is combined with want-intensification. For the will-of-the-wisp of novelty in sense-titillation counteracts the boredom of habit, and by spicing habits with the new and bizarre intensifies the addiction.[22] Thus affluence can contribute to the erosion of resolves and deflection from goals by proliferating wanting over a wider horizon of satisfactions and by rooting people deeper into vicious habits they already have.

These two vectors suggest the importance of the third dimension of wanting, want-elevation. The inevitable pull of increased income and wealth is downward unless counteracted. The affluent mentality tends to materialize Values and to coarsen character unless a person makes some effort to raise his Value-sights.

Thus our search into the effects of the affluent attitude has led us back to the original ethical insight, that the infinite appetite for wealth can be morally corrupting. We are daily scandalized by stories of the already wealthy and powerful, senators, tycoons, respected professionals, entertainers and athletes, who shipwreck their careers in grasping for one more bribe, one more money-making scheme, one more shady deal. But for most people the crisis of gain-seeking is seldom dramatic. For most people have no great ambition to amass a fortune or acquire power. They want more, surely, but because everyone wants more, and they gain simply as part of a growing economy. Whatever edge they acquire on others is hardly significant. The real issue with them is not their reasons for seeking increased income but how they spend it.

The important decision -- and it is seldom a dramatic break-through but a series of little decisions gradually producing an inclination -- is whether they dissipate increasing income on trivialities, on show, and in search of sensual pleasures, or whether they raise their Value-sights to more aesthetic, more spiritual, and more social Values. It means pushing for goals slightly beyond one's grasp, requiring sacrificing lesser wants and feeling the pinch of scarcity. Certainly any one who is sensitive to what happened to the American spirit can trace the malaise of the Seventies to the dissipation of the prosperity of the Sixties.

Thus moderation for moderns, for the affluent, has a third dimension. It not only must steer a course between indulging the sense appetites and puritannical repression of pleasure and insensitivity to the good things in life, but, because of income expectations, it must maintain elevation against the down-ward drag of materialism. It requires breaking the pattern of conformism, resisting pleas that everyone has it or does it. It demands a certain insouciance that family and personal goals differ from those of the majority. In business, it means hewing to reasonable expectations, resisting tempting quick-riches schemes beyond the business' areas of competence. In short, moderation is clear-eyed about objectives and goals -- whether personal, family, business or national -- which fit our particular needs and capabilities. Such differentiation in Values is one aspect of a dynamic moderation.

The other aspect is compulsion. Whether we would or not, our Value gradient is either rising or falling, lifting or slumping. It never remains the same. To change the metaphor, the affluent are on a moral treadmill: unless one runs faster, he falls behind. This may be the more disheartening aspect of moderation. It seems too contrived, too controlled and too rational, always seeking the better way to spend income. It seems to dampen gayety and spontaneity.

In fact, however, it does not. For there are at hand a vast set of higher Values which require no ingenuity to find. Sharing our surplus with others whose needs are greater than our own requires only a generous spirit, alert to others' distress. In a world where every nation's poverty is almost as well known as our own, the scope of liberality is unlimited.

The parable of Dives and Lazarus is instructive on this point. Dives was not condemned because he was wealthy or desired wealth. Dives was condemned because, being wealthy, he did not know what to do with his wealth. Specifically he could not see the good use for it, lying begging at his gate.

The terrible truth is that excessive wanting destroys gayety and spontaneity, because at the heart of affluence is scarcity and frustration. The more we have, the more we want. Yet we are wanting what is limited; we strain against a production possibility frontier. Moreover, the faster we make the economic machine whir today, the more certainly we slow it down tomorrow. These are hard, bleak facts, just as bleak as the drunkard's getting cirrhosis of the liver, or the promiscuous' contracting a venereal disease. There was a sad ballad which achieved some popularity several years ago in which a disillusioned demi-mondane bewailed the pleasures of life turned to ashes and longed for one more ride on the merry-go-round. This is the frustration inherent in an affluence lacking moderation.

More to be feared, the reaction to dissipation is not moderation but puritanism. The current hypocrisy which castigates profits and profit-seeking, while clutching at economic abundance, is just such a puritanism. The way of reason, of moderation, however, is not devoid of zest or lacking in spontaneity. The discovery of new and higher goals, of breaking from previous patterns can be even heroically spontaneous, like the simple decision of Mother Theresa to give up teaching to gather the dead and dying from the streets of Calcutta.

In the next two chapters, we hope to see more, how zest can be restored to affluence. Moderation as a brake on wealth-seeking, like a brake on an automobile, is meaningless considered in itself, unless we open our attitudes to dimensions' beyond ourselves and to meanings deeper than personal want-gratification. In the fifth chapter on justice, we consider the dimension of our social obligations and, in the following on spiritual poverty, the true meaning of wealth.

CHAPTER FIVE

JUSTICE AND AFFLUENCE

We all insist on fair treatment and at the slightest infringement of our rights rush to court seeking justice, heedless of Hamlet's warning that if we got our just desserts we would all be whipped. For implicit in the demand for justice is the obligation to treat others justly, the implications of which most people prefer not to explore. Yet no student should balk at the proposition that when everyone is seeking more income and more goods, making both scarcer, some principles of just sharing are necessary. The purpose of this chapter, therefore, is to review the implications of justice and then to re-apply this virtue to conditions of affluence.

Justice, says Aristotle, is being lawful and being fair,[1] meaning that it applies both to our general conduct in the community and to our particular actions affecting others. Justice, therefore, has several dimensions, intertwined of course because it is whole and not bits and pieces. But to capture the richness of the concept, these several aspects, like the themes and movements of a symphony, must be disentangled and viewed separately.

Students should realize that there is a vast literature on justice and an important requisite of the moral life is to be alert in our reading to sharpen our perception of justice. For a start Josef Pieper's short treatise, Justice, is recommended.[2] There Pieper draws out the radically provocative implications, especially for moderns, of a classical and medieval philosophy of justice. From its reading the student will appreciate that the treatment here of justice in economic matters is the smaller and less important part of justice's broad concern for our neighbor's rights as a person, as a sexual being, and as a citizen.

These cautions in mind, we will try to ferret out of the history of thought the three principal dimensions of justice: 1) as an internal harmony; 2) as a social virtue guiding actions which affect other individuals and the community; and 3) the dimension, emphasized in modern philosophies, justice as the power, hence obligation, of the state to preserve and to reconcile private rights.

This last aspect, though peculiarly modern, surfaced at the very beginning of philosophizing about justice. Thrasymachus in friendly debate with Socrates in Plato's *Republic* pin-points the universal feeling about the bitter-sweet nature of justice: however necessary it is for the community to enforce justice, nevertheless, the just person acts from disadvantage in dealing with the unjust, so that the best state of man would be to be unjust but to appear just in others' eyes, and the worst to be just but to appear unjust.[3] To Socrates this is *the* moral issue of justice and the *Republic* forms his answer. There he draws the analogy between society, in which each class harmonizes with the whole by each performing its functions well, rulers ruling wisely, guardians defending bravely, and general citizens contributing their services and moderating their demands, with the individual who achieves peace and harmony with himself and others by maintaining mastery over his anger, sensuality and greed.[4] In brief, justice is internal order and harmony, a good beyond all other goods. Socrates' definitive answer to Thrasymachus was his own equanimity and peace of soul in suffering an unjust condemnation and death.

Augustine casts this concept of internal rectitude in a Christian mold: "In the soul itself the reason must be subject to God if it is to govern as it ought the passions and other vices."[5] Thomas Aquinas goes further in identifying the Socratic original justice with the rectitude Adam enjoyed before his fall, a harmony which "consisted in his reason being subject to God, the lower powers to reason, and the body to the soul."[6]

Aristotle, while acknowledging this internal harmony as a kind of metaphorical justice, stresses that justice "is the actual exercise of complete virtue."[7] For him justice is the virtue by which we relate well to others in a general way by obeying the laws and customs of the community, and in a particular way by being fair, by not grasping more than one's due and rendering to each what is due to him. Thus justice in sharing the goods of community, material well-being, cultural benefits, civil rights and civic honors, calls for sharing proportionate to merit, while justice in exchange between private persons requires returning equal for equal received.[8]

Thomas Aquinas further fleshes out Aristotle's thought

with Christian and his own insights, setting the style among pre-moderns for a comprehensive treatment of the virtue which still has power to inspire. He founds his thought squarely on the fact of rights, but not on our own rights but those of our neighbor, since justice always regards the other person. Given others' rights, a debt or obligation arises whenever they are disturbed or infringed upon. Thus, Aquinas views justice as a continuous process of rectifying the external order which our actions have disturbed.[9] Justice, therefore, is a firm habit of the will to give everyone his rights, his due.[10] Such a disposition becomes a powerful force, informing all actions and attitudes in a general way with concern for the common good of all -- what Aquinas calls general or legal justice[11] -- and in a particular way rendering to each his due. Particular justice, as with Aristotle, safeguards the rights of others, giving equal for equal in exchange, commutative justice, and an appropriate share in the common good, distributive justice.

This magnificent edifice, which like Chartres must be pondered in whole and in detail to appreciate its organic dynamism, was one of the foundations of ethical theory over three centuries. With lesser minds, however, it hardened into dogma which could not accommodate the new facts of commercial gain and the new spirits of individualism, nationalism, and religious freedom. Intransigence begot skepticism and skepticism the search for certainty. This need was fulfilled by Descartes (1596-1650) who, setting out methodically to doubt everything, concluded with mathematical certitude that doubting was existing. The doubter, however, was only really sure of his own internal states of consciousness.

Radical Individualism and the Sovereign State

When Thomas Hobbes applies this radical individualism to the question of justice and rights, he finds that an individual is only certain of his own rights to existence, to bodily integrity, property and the like, and since they are universal and inalienable they conflict in a war of each against all with the rights of others. In the state of nature, says Hobbes, there can be no justice.[12] Justice is possible only when a powerful state, in the words of Spinoza (1632-1677), establishes "that climate of confidence" that everyone is "restrained by fear of a greater injury."[13] Thus unrestrained individualism is held in check by an all-powerful state which establishes justice by passing needful laws and by arbitrating the rights of individuals.

This combination of moral relativism and state totalitarianism becomes the issue for modern social philosophy. Yet it incorporates a social Value in Western Civilization, sharply different from the status principle of the Middle Ages, which philosophers strove to preserve, namely, the freedom of individuals to make their own way in life, in the economy, and in civil society. The varied attempts to derive moral principles empirically from an innate moral sense or from social utility were rejected by Immanual Kant (1724-1804) who otherwise accepted the Hobbesian world of atomistic individuals clashing with each other in pursuit of their rights.

Instead Kant postulates an autonomous will confirmed in goodness such that it acts not out of sense attraction, or purpose, or even the love of God but on such maxims which one could will as universal laws.[14] Such a will is an unconditional or categorical imperative. It is duty. Reason cannot comprehend its content but only its necessity as a law of action. As for justice Kantian duty would require entering "into a state in which everyone can have what is his own secured against the action of every other."[15] Critics point out the ambiguity: duty may be simply undeviating obedience to the laws and customs of the state or it may be an absolutely unique personal conviction, impervious to all other reason.

Resolving this antinomy became part of the ethical agenda of the 19th Century. Among many, two are representative of quite different approaches, reflecting perhaps differing national temperaments, the dialectical approach of G.W.F. Hegel (1770-1831) and the more practical and utilitarian approach of John Stuart Mill (1806-1873).

Hegel's dialectic is an heroic attempt to bridge the chasm between self and society. The interplay between the ego's subjective and objective phases is an organic growth in which "the mind in its freedom, the culmination of self-conscious reason. ... gives itself actuality and engenders itself as an existing world."[16] This reciprocating process of externalizing internal states of the mind, and internalizing external relations, described below, are not, however, phases in an historical sequence, like a string of sausages. Because they involve different levels of consciousness, these phases overlap and, though following a definite procession, may even occur simultaneously.

Man, he begins, is pure thought of himself, subjective, free of determinancy and hence universal, but in knowing itself the ego is determined as its own object. This moment of determined universality, of subjectivity-objectivity, is the concrete concept of freedom. Thus in relating to others, for example, in friendship or love, I know myself in my selfhood, different from them yet free and possessing formal and abstract rights to my body, to my actions, and to external objects. But my aims, purposes and good -- the sphere of morality -- are not bottled within me but must be realized externally, thus entering the realm of ethical action.

The first embodiment of subjective rights and moral action occurs naturally in the substantial unity of the family. As, however, the family dissolves, its members relate to others in civil society by using property to satisfy mutual needs, by embodying these rights in law and protecting them by public force and private association. This association for subjective needs in turn is objectivized in the nation state. In this higher ethical state the freedom of the individual is fully realized, for his rights are achieved in fulfilling his duties. The state, therefore, is constituted when its laws are rational, that is, protective of personal freedom and administered by a state which is for the well-being of all and open to the will of all, and when citizens are disposed to view its laws and constitution as immutable principles and their supreme obligation to subject their wills to them.[17]

In pioneering self-centered rights through the dialectic to social obligation, Hegel, however, presents no formal treatment of commutative and distributive justice as guide to the evolving relations between the two. Rather he looks to the end of the process where the individual will is confirmed in freedom and goodness precisely when it is structured in and by a totally rational and good social order. With Hegel Hobbes' Leviathan state does not just protect rights it fulfills them.

J.S. Mill, on the other hand, starts from the experience of justice, namely, that someone should be compelled to do or not do something. "Legal restraint", he says, "is the generating idea of the notion of justice."[18] From this is inferred that an individual can claim that something as a moral right. So the essential ingredients of justice is to punish a wrong done to another 1) because of feelings of self-defense or of sympathy for others and 2) because of the conviction that society should defend one's possession of rights. "Why society should protect individual rights?" he can give no other reason than general utility. For Mill Kantian duty becomes obedience to such rules of conduct which all rational being might adopt with benefit to their collective interest. The important Utilitarian conclusion that all rights are to be protected because they benefit the common good, may lead to the opposite, dangerous principle, that no rights are to be protected which appear to harm the common good.

This review could be carried up to the present, surveying the thought of Nietzsche and Dewey, Moore and Sedgwick, Rawls and Nozick, on and on endlessly. But the point of our concern is made sufficiently: justice permeates one's moral life. It is a Minister of Internal Affairs maintaining order among the various faculties and appetites under reason and especially a reason informed with love of God. But it is more specifically a Minister of Foreign Affairs guiding actions as they affect the common good and other persons, rectifying the social order which our actions have disturbed, in the first case, and restoring rights our actions have infringed, in the second. With the onset of individualism justice requires the power of the state to maintain individual rights and freedom. But that power itself obtains its moral sanction from the individual person's sense of duty. Indeed personal freedom and rights can only be fully realized in a totally rational social order and it becomes the collective interest of all members of society to defend the rights of each.

Of the key words which run through this survey, rights, duty, order, rectitude, sharing, and social, the last two are salient to a discussion of justice and the affluent attitude. They require stressing not only because affluence itself is a social phenomenon but more so because our contemporary self-centered sense of justice emphasizes what is right and fair for me, and not its social sense what is right and fair for someone else. Our first task, therefore, is to examine what social and society mean.

SOCIETY

We are social beings because we are related. We are conceived related to a man and woman in a trinity of intimate bonding. We are born related to their relations and grow up relating to brothers and sisters, neighborhood children, school mates, and work colleagues. We relate in a special way to friends, to inspiring leaders and masters, and uniquely to our spouse and those born of our union. Even in death we are identified by our relations. In short, we are social because we cannot exist unrelated. That is the basic fact of human sociality. Its good will take further probing.

This probe, therefore, begins with the fact of human relatedness. Society is, at minimum, this mesh of relations by which everyone is related in some way or ways to everyone else. Using this idea, we can dissipate some of the false and fuzzy notions about society in current usage. Hopefully in the same process we can delineate the notes of the true concept of society.

The fuzziest use of the term society is as some alien thing, standing in opposition to the individual, as in "Society is at fault because Johnny can't read." Now if we finger the causes why Johnny cannot read while other children can, we will certainly find Johnny at fault. In all likelihood too his parents, his teachers and school administrators share some blame. If the sentence means anything, it says that besides these obvious culprits, all people are at fault in not establishing a climate conducive to Johnny's learning to read. Whatever the truth of this may be, society is not alien to Johnny. Quite to the contrary, it is because he is related to parents, schoolmates, teachers and the like and through them to all others that he finds reading difficult and distasteful. Consequently, his problem is not his alone but that of all people, in various ways and to various degrees.

Society may also refer to a particular set of people as in, "Mary Smith made her debut into Society at the Charity Ball." Society here means a pecking order in which Mary must locate herself as she enters the marriage mart, and from which the mass of mankind is excluded. Society in our sense is indeed such a mesh of relationships but it is not exclusive but all-embracing. Willy-nilly, everyone is a member of society.

That is, society is not just a collection of individuals, Hobbes's conception of man in the state of nature. Society is not like a can of worms: individuals thrown together in no particular way, writhing over, under, and around each other, each seeking to disentangle himself from the mass, seeking moving room for himself. While any particular relation, say to one's spouse, is never fully comprehensible and most seem random and haphazard, nevertheless, one's most important relations are existential, arise from coming into being and giving life to others, and all relations, even the most casual, reflect a deep-seated desire for human fellowship. We are meant to communicate with, not to avoid other people.

Society also appears in titles of organizations, as in The Society to Prevent Cruelty to Animals. Here society means a group of people, voluntarily united for a common purpose. Although limited to members and in this sense exclusive, such associations spring spontaneously from a social impulse: people get together to achieve collectively what they cannot achieve individually. In principle, therefore, they are socially desirable, endangering society only if their purpose is contrary to the common good. But they differ from society in two important respects. No one joins or resigns from society voluntarily: we become members by birth and continue related even after death. Secondly, society has no purpose in a narrow sense of a defined objective. It has, or rather is, a common good. Since the social common good is the final focus of our effort, and because we have one more important confusion to disentangle, we postpone discussing it for the moment.

State and Society

The greatest bloc to a true understanding of society comes from confusing it with the state. Because they interpenetrate each other, they are identified. But society as the product of everyone's natural impulse to relate to others, leaps national boundaries, while, as a common cultural heritage, several societies may co-exist within a state. Thus not their extension but their internal constitution differentiates them. Society is more informal, more spontaneous, more inclusive of all men in all their human aspects. The state is formally constituted, more structured, founded on the narrower basis of maintaining peace, harmony, and order in society. The state, therefore, fosters and protects society but it does not constitute society.

This difference establishes a tension between society and state, which, however, need not be destructive of either but salvific for both. For in principle society, being all-inclusive, not only tolerates differences but flourishes on integrating them. The state, on the other hand, requires a certain civic homogeneity, at minimum general knowledge and observance of its laws. Society, therefore, without civic discipline becomes anarchical; the state without tolerance becomes tyranny.

In nothing do we reveal our inheritance of the Hobbesian chasm between absolute individualism and absolute national sovereignity than in our inability to square a respect for differences with the requirements of civic peace and order. In fact the 20th Century coined a word to describe monumental crimes of intolerance not by barbarians but by civilized peoples -- liquidation.[19] Nazi Germany and Stalinist Russia may be prime examples of the systematic elimination of those who differ religiously, culturally, racially, or ideologically, but few nations of either the developed or emerging world are totally guiltless. While such monstrous crimes are universally castigated, moral indignation, it seems, has become muted by the frequency of this crime perpetrated by states against society.

But closer to ordinary life, the melange of self-centered individualism and statism have confused the functions of state and society. People, for example, will badger police over every neighborhood nuisance but turn deaf and blind at crimes committed in their presence. Law officers have vented and do vent their prejudices under cover of the law. Officials are affronted at the efforts of community groups to help curtail crime and other abuses, while known criminals are turned loose endangering all. Radicals will use every legal trick available to defend actions contrary to law. People, who proclaim their devotion to the law, on the other hand, try to corral the powers of the state to institutionalize their intolerance. Individuals and groups make demands on government, which, whatever the good proposed, are uncompromising and regardless of harm to others. Above all, the majority have tolerated for centuries systemic injustice to minorities on account of religion, race, sex, or disabilities, and only with difficulty and reluctantly are constrained to right the wrong.

These are actions of people who are ordinarily decent to and considerate of others in their private lives, but who seem, upon entering the public sphere, to lose a sense of proportion between the demands of public order and the freedom of social intercourse. Much of this is a protective withdrawal from the mammoth impersonality of our civic institutions. But more is due to our failure to see that the social context of living is something between the purely private and individual and the machinery and structure of government. Europeans, for whatever reason -- a longer tradition of urban living, the experiences of war and conquest, or provincial pride -- seem to have more social consciousness, an indefinable respect and concern for the quality of social life. Our lack of awareness of this social reality threatens us with the paradoxical danger that in the name of individual rights we are using the powers of government to induce and to regiment greater and greater conformity. To protect our individualism we are becoming a nation of conformists.

Human Sociality

The viable alternative, as always, lies in the middle in seeing the social good as a true personal but an all-embracing public good, protected by, yet distinct from political law and order. It is not alien to the individual person but arises from personality in response to basic human needs. Society has no specific purpose, nor imposes a conformity, but it is a good in which all share and to which all contribute, each in a particular way. The health of society, therefore, is achieved not principally by social legislation imposed from above but from that which perfects the individual himself, the life of virtue. Hence, the obligation a man has to society reveals the true social character and dynamic dimension of justice, a dimension which echoes the dynamism of affluence. What society really is and what it obliges begins logically with the question what is man.

The duality of the human person, as we saw, is the crux of the human condition. Man is the walking paradox, both angel and beast. He can tie himself into a knot of self-centered sensibilities, or range toward the infinite. Rooted in the earth, he can aspire to the stars. In saying this we lay bare the heart of human torment. For despite this duality man is one: a toothache impairs one's ability to pray.

The human duality-unity, therefore, is not just a being with two distinct orientation, but the wedding of two different principles. Man cannot be truly material unless he is spiritual. Nor truly spiritual unless he is material. Possession of superfluous wealth often breeds sensuality and materialism. On the other hand, only some measure of abundance permits the flight of the spirit.

Because man is simultaneously material and spiritual, he is inevitably and radically social. Because man is limited, he needs other people to fulfill his needs, not only his biological and economic needs, but his transcendent yearnings. Because each person is unique, each is obliged to contribute to the common pool of humanness, each adding his mite toward the fullness of humanity.

Americans generally little appreciate this. They are still nostalgic for the rugged individualism and self-reliance of the frontier. "Out West" still has advertising-dollar potency and the rugged he-man astride his horse, silhouetted against the setting sun, evokes the heroic mood. Fittingly, the companions of such fictional heroes are bovine. In real life, the lonely guy probably wants nothing more than to get away from those "damn cows" and see some girls.

Another hero of American mythology is the unsophisticated person -- read "hick" more frequently than not -- who comes to the city or the army or high society. His unremitting goodness and home-spun wisdom lays bare their shallow sophistication and eventually converts all to the life of simple virtue. He himself passes through it all untouched, unsullied -- and unbelieved.

This 19th Century individualism has, in a sense, gone to seed with the "me-generation". When the only and ultimate realities are my feelings, my wants, and my "thing", all action becomes totally self-regarding. Such people seem almost in a state of social shock, fearful of any involvement with others, paranoid about any personal commitment unless backed by a contract which is enforceable in a court of law by the power of the state.

Reality is quite different from both attitudes. No man comes in contact with another without being changed. Nor can anybody be ignored if he does not want to be. Just stand at another's desk and say nothing. No matter how busy or how absorbed he or she might be, your mere persistent presence will force the query "What do you want?" Persons are truly the proper subject of our knowledge and love. As a material being his materiality attracts; as a spiritual being the mystery of his transcendence echoes to the mystery of our own. We come to know ourself in other people, and to love ourself in love of another. Each glimpse into another human heart reveals more of our own.

Beyond self-knowledge we pool our knowledge and experience through communication. As individuals we are limited to knowing directly what contacts our senses. We can expand our experience, however, almost infinitely by sharing in the common reservoir of human love and knowledge. Only through such sharing can we help slake our thirst for knowing and loving all things. People must share to be truly human. This is the true root of human sociality.

So varying, so all-embracing, and so connatural is this multi-dimensional net of human relations that we are not conscious of how they came to be. Some people we relate to formally and voluntarily like our spouse in marriage. Some are simply there, like brothers and sisters, neighbors or colleagues at work. Some are haphazard, like the victim of an accident seen in childhood who, though forgotten, still affects our conduct. What we are doing today has been conditioned by chance of birth and blood, by events of the past or distant present of which we know nothing. We are not masters of our fate in any absolute sense. For we are caught in a net of circumstances not of our will or choosing, a net which while it ensnares also supports us. But it is inescapably there.

Deprivation of one's customary social environment, either through change or through an egoistic turning into one's self, is disastrous for the human personality. Nostalgia for school or the old neighborhood is a mild but real psychosocial illness. Homesickness is often a heart-rending form of it. The Korean POWs who crawled into their bunks and simply ceased to care were acutely ill of this social malaise. Husbands and wives are literally killed by the psychological wrench of the other's death. For society in the concrete is the love binding parents and children, the mutual endearment of husband and wife, the common intellectual goals of a classroom, the rapport between artist and his audience, the sense of common purpose in a business or athletic team, or simply the spontaneous friendship of a neighborhood. It is the warp of which personal response and action is the woof.

o In brief, sharing in our common humanity is effected by means of an infinitely varied and changing network of human relations, uniting each to all. No one is so exalted that he or she can do without it; no one is so trivial as to be excluded. This is society -- not the mere massing together of peoples, nor the formal and legal relations of the state, but an ensemble of human ties by which every o person is related to everyone else materially, spiritually and culturally. It is natural, spontaneous, inevitable and good.

SOCIETY AS THE COMMON GOOD

Society, like the air we breathe, penetrates every phase of our life. For convenience we study society as a community of persons, a community of culture, and a community of things. In reality they are so interwoven as to be one. For the relations binding people are simultaneously personal, cultural and economic ties. But viewing each in turn and separately will reveal the important aspects of this many-faced reality.

Society as Community

As a community of persons society is the blending together of individual diversities. The root notion of community is not unity but differences, differences which can blend together in mutual support. It comes not from com-unitas but from com-munitas. Men form communities to complement and to supplement each other, and by so doing to achieve their individual goods in a good common to all. The fear that society suppresses individualism and enforces conformity is a fear not of society but of its ersatz, state totalitarianism whatever its manifestation. Human community is not achieved through an autocratic will, but by the free and responsible contribution to and personal sharing in common goals and purposes. The unity of such communion necessarily builds on diversity of talent and intention.

A hunter and his dog are a unity to the extent that the hunter imposes his will on the dog's skills and instincts. But they are not a community. A hunting party, in which some hunters beat ahead, some track, some are armed for the kill, and some perhaps only watch the camp, forms a community. Each hunter contributes his talents in his own way to a common effort and each expects his share in the prize.

So much is this an everyday phenomenon that we hardly avert to it. But the need for social communion is not fortuitous. It arises first of all from the diversity stamped in the body, emotions, and attitudes which distinguishes men from women. This most basic difference provides man with his profoundest religious analogies. Most of his artistic effort has been devoted to expounding its mystery. In a sense, much deeper than the biological, man must act on and find his inspiration in women and woman must act on and find her inspiration in men. Whatever a person's attraction to his own sex, a man is humanly incomplete unless he complements in some way his masculinity with femininity, or a woman her femininity with masculinity.

This complete complementarity is expressed and symbolized in the marriage act. Equality and partnership in marriage is stressed so much today that we often overlook the basic and inescapable fact of sexual diversity. But marriage is much more than the expression of biological utility. It is an interweaving of lives, a blending of personalities, a getting out of one's self and becoming involved with another -- an ecstasy in its deepest sense. True marriage fosters a society of friendship, in which each loves his spouse as himself. Such love will blend but cannot suppress differences; otherwise each would only love self. To the contrary, in an atmosphere of mutual love differences are encouraged to develop to their full beauty and perfection.

If this ideal seems impossible, so does the dynamics of running. The rarity of ideal marriages no more argues against the ideal than the rarity of four-minute miles denies that men can run. For even in the most tawdry marriages there is an inkling of this design. When they fail it is because husbands and wives fail to break out of their selfishness or vicious habits to reach that true communion for which they yearn.

Beyond the family, the infinite diversity of human characteristics is the foundation of the socio-economic community. We so differ among ourselves in talent, interest, training, experience, skill, physical strength and dexterity and we come to do what we do by such different paths of desire, ambition, necessity or chance that the socio-economic community seems only a haphazard collection of individuals each going his own way. Whatever unity here seems to be only a conformity imposed by the state. But in a way more basic than our political ties we are united each to everybody else by millions of invisible ties of complementarity and mutual assistance.

Diversity and Complementarity

We take this so much for granted that we identify ourselves not by what we are but by what we do. We do not introduce ourselves as the father of four children and a Methodist, but as a teacher, or accountant, or lathe operator, or housewife. In fact, the intense specialization of modern industrial life has so atrophied the skills needed for human survival that we fall into the opposite error of thinking that we participate in this community only to meet individual economic needs. But the initial impulse to economic, civic and social life arises spontaneously from the diversity and complementarity of men.

The more profound side of this is psychological. Families must mingle not only their blood but their views and values with other families. Psychological inbreeding is just as dangerous as biological, for it warps by accentuation family traits and characteristics. The isolated family, whether aristocratically turning in upon itself or clannishly driving away all intruders, is in danger of distorting its family mores into a dogma of madness.

More apparently, though we do not advert to it sufficiently, the impulse to community arises from the desire to improve the quality of life. The city has always attracted men despite its abrasive irritations and generally less healthy environment. People could survive isolated in the wilderness but human civilization is a tale largely of urban living. Such living together entails economic specialization which not only produces more but produces better. From it arises, first of all, economic exchange: a man acquires more shoes and food and housing not by making these himself but by making more automobiles. Specialization also provides the thrust behind economic progress. Whatever the contribution of the outsider, the specialist ultimately advances his craft. Emulation of others forces him to improve; knowledge of his materials and his clients' desires encourages change; ideas from other fields inspire adaptation; and above all experience gives an amazing proficiency.

However horrible a human jungle the modern city has become, diversity, complementarity and specialization are forces making for a better life, giving us more to read, more to see, more to hear, more to learn, more to experience and appreciate. That this profusion has not resulted in the universal improvement of life points up the obvious, that we have not learned to use it well. Nor will we, until we see that this socio-economic community is a true community of persons, mutually assisting each other to achieve a better life.

Even as urban problems flood us, we are challenged in another direction. Modern communication and travel has so shrunk the globe that no people can be a stranger and no nation, whatever its culture and history, ignored. History is a story of man's shameful treatment of his fellow human beings, through wars, conquests, slavery, through commercial and cultural imperialism. Nevertheless human development has advanced through the successive embracing of a greater diversity of people and through cross-fertilization of cultures. Isolation, intolerance, prejudice, cultural snobbishness, and unwillingness to embrace new ideas, on the other hand, dry up the vitality of a civilization. The challenge of peace, of poverty and destitution, of racial, religious, and cultural tolerance, however complex, are ultimately challenges to conceive all men of all nations as forming a true community of persons. They challenge our will to be social beings.

Communion and Communication

Society as a community of persons is founded on diversity, but its purpose is communion and its means communication. People are attracted to each other. They must share themselves with others and in turn share of them. They must express themselves. They must tell what they are and how they think and feel. But persons can only communicate with other persons. They can train and order animals, but only from other persons can they expect that look of comprehension and understanding which is the purpose and joy of communication. Such converse borders on love for it is essential to it. As the community of persons arises under the impulse of people's affections, so the *community of culture* responds to the needs of their intellects.

Culture in this broad sense is the whole net of words, signs, symbols and gestures by which we transmit our thoughts and feelings. In a more formal sense, culture is concretized in a people's language, its literature, art, sculpture, architecture; in its educational ideals, its religious symbolism and civic rites; in its civil, political and economic institutions; in the very style of dress and manners of its people. Above all the culture of a people is mirrored in its pattern of virtue: its laws to insure justice and preserve public morals; its support of and respect for religion; its encouragement of private virtue and morality. None of this can be achieved except in community, by means of public institutions, both those government supported and those privately sponsored. Churches, schools, public monuments and buildings, civic festivals, concerts and theaters, the city's commercial and industrial endowment, these are the social vehicles of culture.

Culture is sought as a personal good. Families develop their own rites and cultural pattern. But no one is immune from the pervasive culture of the city and nation. It is the public expression of ourselves to ourselves. Its vitality buoys and its aridity depresses personal aspirations. That Americans are increasingly critical of their tawdry cities, uninspired civic architecture and the institutionalized ugliness of commerce is due as much to the greater emphasis put on art and culture in schools as to the inspiration of civic beauty acquired from abroad. Society is a community of culture and no individual can be indifferent to it. Willy-nilly we are immersed in it, contributing to and sharing in it.

A Community of Wealth

Lastly, society is a community of goods, of wealth. Though only means, wealth is absolutely necessary to realize the community of persons and culture. We are related to each other and we communicate with others by means of things. For us this aspect of society is the focus of our concern. This concern takes added importance because our extreme touchiness about the rights of private property has blinded us to the social burden private wealth bears.

We can approach this important idea by clearing away one bit of sloppy usage. Private property has no rights. I have rights to possess things privately, but the things have no right. That is to say, property rights are personal rights and as such are preceded by many other personal rights, to life, to liberty, to knowledge, to follow conscience. Its importance, in fact, arises only from its being necessary to achieve these other rights.

Private property is not the only support of personal and civil rights. Their realization is and must be achieved also through our public patrimony of soil, climate, mineral resources, waterways and harbors; through our public ownership of highways, postal service, civic facilities, and schools; and finally through those vast social instruments of production, the corporate complex. This is nothing more than saying that our affluence, the staggering proliferation of economic goods, is the result of our combined efforts and contributions. Affluence is a social phenomenon.

But wealth is social in a more intimate sense. For wealth is nothing but the value of something in exchange for something else. Wealth is not measured by its worth to us. An older car may actually be more useful to us than a new one, but its wealth is determined by its Blue Book trade-in value. A Van Gogh which no one but its owner wanted fifty years ago was of little value. That same picture, giving no more personal enjoyment today, is worth millions simply because people are able and willing to part with many more things (read: money) to obtain it. Its owner is wealthy simply because other people want it. In a very real sense that wealth is owed to society. Hence, my wealth is not mine in the sense that I brought it into being, but only that I possess what is a social good.

We are a wealthy people today not because we work harder or better than other people or other generations but because our efforts exchange for more things, the necessities, conveniences and comforts of life. To say that I am more productive than my father or grandfather is an optical illusion unless by this I mean that the economy today is more productive and I share in this increased productivity. That is to say, our incomes and our wealth are a function of social productivity.

There is, besides, little wealth which can be enjoyed privately, in the strict sense that it gives no pleasure and bestows no benefit on others. This is true of even one's most intimate possessions. The clothing which enhances milady entrances the bystander, even the indigent "wino" shuffling by. It is especially true of capital goods which constitute the great bulk of private wealth. For to be true wealth they must be worked socially to produce goods socially to be sold socially. And society must share in the return. The modern miser can gloat secretly over his portfolio of securities in the double-locked womb of his safety deposit box. But all that paper is valueless without the farms, the factories, the railroads, and the immense marketing complexes of the economy, which earn the incomes which give that paper value.

What is true of the social character of private wealth is, of course, all the more so of public wealth. It is a characteristic of affluence that this should proliferate even faster than private wealth since there are greater demands on society for goods collectively consumed -- hospital services, education, travelways, recreational facilities and social welfare. All of these together are called the capital infra-structure of the economy which like an iceberg is nine-tenths submerged, and which belongs to the patrimony of the people as truly social wealth.

Thus the most private possessions as well as the most public lands are included, each in its distinct way and according to different functions, in a common pool of goods. Together they form a true community of wealth, the material means, by which men are united to men, share a common culture, and mutually service each other's material needs.

An affluent economy is also and pre-eminently a social good. Its structures, institutions, its network of goods and money are the means by which all of us service so lavishly the wants and desires of each other. This is the setting in which the productive efforts of hundreds of millions of people are coordinated and the benefits from this activity distributed. It is really society seen under its economic aspect.

The Individual in Society

Society then as a net of human, cultural, and wealth relationships penetrates every phase of life from the individual's most sublime aspirations to his most mundane preoccupations. For good or ill we cannot flee society. Its fibers begin to entwine about us at conception; its regulations determine the manner and place of our final disposition. In between our every act is conditioned, assisted, limited, disciplined, and in some way affected by the forms and Values of society.

If individuals cannot flee society, neither must they drift with its every new current. The type is familiar. One year they are "into" civil rights, the next into feminism, then environmentalism, then Zen Buddhism, then jogging. They are social flotsam. For them every headline is a nightmare; every change of fashion a trauma. They lack firm anchors in their own personalities. More tragically their social dither has no mooring in society itself. For in scurrying from one cause to another, they reject the mores of good breeding, rational political discourse and moral principles, which, however conventional they may become, nevertheless, are the very bonds which hold society together. They wear out their lives in frustrated attempts to change social structures and succeed only in weakening the foundations of society itself.

Virtue as always stands in the middle. Individuals fashion their lives both out of their inner convictions and the Values current in society. The thrust of their lives comes from within: their will to exist, their search for fulfillment in infinite reality, their sense of inner direction. But this thrust, like the flight of the arrow, must be conditioned to the social environment in which it occurs. Between it and personal strivings a constant dialectic is taking place.

Society, in summary, is an all-embracing milieu, an infinitely varied and varying network of human ties, ranging from intimate personal identification to casual knowledge and sympathy, which unites each to all without exception. Since it fulfills a radical need of human personality, society is the absolutely necessary medium in which and by means of which the individual person can find, can exercise, and can develop his human personality. Like the sea which engulfs the scuba diver it is, one and same, the environment against which a person must struggle and the support of his movement and action.

If the individual person cannot be indifferent to the good which is society, he or she cannot be indifferent to the obligation which it imposes. Just as people must make costly efforts to purify their physical environment, if they pollute it beyond the purifying powers of wind and sun and soil, or perish, so they are much more obliged to maintain the purity of their social environment. But here the analogy stops. For people pollute the world about them by living in it -- by breathing, by eating, by moving about, as well as by producing goods. They pollute their social environment in one way, by acting against their social inclinations. Only selfishness pollutes society. Who for friendship returns indifference, for love lust, for wisdom the maxims of self-seeking, the vicious person, who lives only for himself pollutes his social environment.

To the contrary, the man or woman of virtue purifies

and builds up society. For they return love for love, justice for justice, wisdom for wisdom, not in copy-cat fashion but transmuted and enriched by being their own. These Values, being filtered through their personalities, will reflect uniquely another facet of their beauty, goodness and humanness. Thus peoples' words, their art, their conduct and above all their regard for others will enrich the lives of those about them and through them all human relationships. Society poses no other obligation than the life of virtue.

The old canard about leaving the world a better place cannot be sneered away by an introverted cynicism. The simple people with an ancient wisdom born of obscurity, privation, and labor draw their principal comfort from it. Only affluent men and women, running on the treadmill of production or cowering before their technology, seem to have lost its meaning. Yet even their actions belie their words. For they can ultimately explain their straining after material success, their pathological worry about the state of the world only in terms of hope that their children will have a better time of it and a better world than they experienced. Their cynicism is subconsciously hope.

o In our striving for fulfillment, involvement and commitment, in our efforts to personalize and humanize social and economic structure, these conclusions should be burned
o into our consciousness. Society is people's common good par excellence. It arises as people seek themselves in others. It is a sharing of the love, knowledge, wisdom,
o as well as the material means of all people. It is all-embracing and all-pervasive, and imposes no other obligation than that people act truly virtuous.

SOCIAL JUSTICE

While a person's every virtuous act does indeed reinforce the ties which bind him to others, nevertheless, this disposition requires the additional consideration that such virtuous acting is really owing to others, if it is to become firmly fixed as habit. That is, we must try to live decently with others both as individuals and as members of society because the well-being of society requires it. This is meant by acting out of sense of social justice.

The term social justice is admitted to political discourse today where thirty years ago it was only on the lips of moral "cranks" and socialists. But as used it generally refers to an objective condition of society or implies the legislation and constraints necessary to obtain this. It connotes then the obligation of others and of government. Few make the transference to themselves: I must consider the good of society in everything I do and say.

The failure to make this transfer is often glaringly apparent in those who are most vocal about social rights and social justice. Generally the predominating feature in most civil litigation and social protests of this nature is a narrow individualistic sense of justice. Racial minorities, the poor and disposed, farmers and laborers, defenders of private education struggle largely to protect or obtain individual and group rights. Antagonists clutch possessively the rights they already enjoy; protagonists claw to get rights denied them. Both display what is the _leit-motiv_ of our age a defensive individualism appealing to the power of the state for protection or redress. Neither shows a true and genuine concern for how their demands affect the well-being of society as a whole, that is, for true social justice.

Social justice, in its meaning here, however, is largely identified with Aquinas' general justice, that virtue which perceives a social dimension in all acts, even those whose object is the most personal good.[20] This echoes Aristotle's thought that justice puts all virtues into practice, reflecting in turn Plato's conception of justice as in its root an internal order and rectitude. Hegel goes one step further, seeing this relation between man's internal state of justice and external acts as a dialectic, an organic interplay in which each fosters the other. While social justice is a constant will to see the social good or harm in all one's actions, it is not given but grows by evaluating actions in its light and rectifying one's attitude as criticism suggests.

Social justice is not constrictive, not narrow, but all-embracing, yet it is firm and unsentimental. It is, for example, not vindictive against the criminal but not wishy-washy about his crime. It is concerned about the criminal's rights and his victim's rights but preeminently about society's rights, about returning the criminal to society as a good and useful member that he may directly or indirectly repair the damage he has done. Social justice is not simply the jealous guardian of the letter of the contract or the _status quo_ but an intuition into the impact of every act on others. It is social consciousness, an awareness that every act is fraught with the good of society, a realization that what is owed to others is a healthy social environment which reflects and fosters the life of virtue, the life of culture, the life of political peace and harmony, and the life of economic abundance.

Justice seen in this light permeates every virtue by consciously rendering social benefit. It imposes no new activities upon a person but engenders a new spirit with which to perform his or her accustomed functions. Like a stereophonic over a monaural system, the spirit of social justice adds an enriching dimension of overtones to the most humdrum routine. Such consideration will not take away the summer stench of garbage containers but the garbage collector in realizing that he performs a necessary social service can perceive its hidden nobility.

The full-flowering of the obligation of social justice will do much to temper the violence which characterizes American life -- the blasting advertising; the sneaky slander circulated in political campaigns, the name-calling, bombing and rioting which passes for social action; the mad, thoughtless carnage on highways; the bullying exercise of authority; the staggering lawlessness; the disregard for the plight of others; in short, the manic insistence on rights regardless of consequence to others. Consideration for others will go far toward softening the abrasiveness of modern living.

It will do much also to purify our national purposes. For this insensitivity about how our conduct strikes others has indeed distorted our noblest Values and virtues. Because of it our idealism is often seen as bravado; our generosity has turned brackish to those we aid; the pluralism and toleration of differences upon which our democracy is founded has been corroded.

Social Justice and the Other Person

Social justice and social awareness must permeate and inspire every virtue and every act. But it cannot hang in mid-air. For one cannot be just to society. He can only be just to persons, as individuals and as social beings. The garbage collector owes it to _me_ to collect _my_ garbage, not only because I pay taxes -- perhaps I do not -- but because my uncollected garbage is a social menace. I must repay _you_ the five dollars I owe because they are yours but also because this debt uncollected threatens the relationship between us and perhaps endangers relationships you have with others.

Social justice is accomplished then when the individual is treated justly: when he is permitted to share proportionately in the common good of society and when he is given what is owing him in exchange. These most readers will recognize as the familiar distributive and exchange justice which specify and individualize the general obligation of social justice. Thus justice which is primarily concerned with preserving the social good is implemented by safeguarding the rights of individuals.

This view of justice also includes in its scope more than physical rights. It respects obviously others' rights to life, to their skill and talent, and to their possessions. It respects their more important claims -- in a sense -- to good reputation, to esteem in the eyes of others, to the love and friendship their virtues have earned. Greater injustice can be committed against these than against physical property. Undermining another's good name, racial and religious prejudice, contempt for others because of poverty or social position are very real injustices both to individuals and to society. The criminal abused by the police, the dullard ridiculed by his professor, the negro insulted because of his skin, these all suffer a justifiable sense of social outrage. For they are hurt precisely in their relationships to others.

<u>Such injustice when institutionalized tends ultimately to destroy society</u>. The law which bears heavier on the poor than the rich becomes an instrument of oppression of the poor by the rich. Welfare which is geared to discourage normal family relations or is demeaning to recipients makes poverty a social disgrace. Popular attitudes which prevent minority groups from sharing in national opulence breed a pattern of ignorance, poverty and social malevolence that widens further and further the gap of envy between the well-off many and the dispossessed few. Nepotism and favoritism in business, in unions, in politics and in all vocations impedes not only the aspiring outsider but lessens the productivity of the economy.

Nor can individuals throw the entire burden of responsibility on the makers and administrators of the laws. Indeed, contempt for law is so widespread precisely because people have acquiesced in institutionalized injustices in the distribution of the goods and burdens of society. The plea that the world was always so is harvesting the popular feeling that public and corporate property are proper prey for those who can steal with impunity and that anything from evading taxes to murder is all right, if no one is caught. When such popular sentiment coalesces with public and private institutions to exclude groups from economic abundance, it is only to be expected that such oppressed and segregated minorities will hoot derisively at pleas for law and order. Our generation is reaping the ugly tares of centuries of institutionalized social injustice.

Affluence and Social Justice

Affluence makes such institutionalized injustice doubly aggravating and the need for a more sensitive sense of social justice doubly urgent. Where the economy is constantly expanding and society ever-changing, the concern for justice must look beyond the letter of today's contract to its implication for future rights. The old narrow and individualistic sense of justice, the scrupulous paying and exacting of every cent owed, is simply one-dimensional in a multi-dimension dynamic. The pace of economic change also demands of officials charged with the common good constant surveillance that material well-being be broadly shared, that families caught in the economic back-waters be given the opportunity to contribute to and share in the ever-mounting economic abundance. Failure here could mean that today's maldistribution causes tomorrow's social cataclysm.

Affluence has made this concern an obligation for a broad segment of the population. Not only the wealthy but the very large middle-income group, the principal beneficiaries of affluence, owe to society that their surplus wealth be used beneficially for society by affording opportunity to the dispossessed, by assisting civic ventures and by aiding cultural life. Actually the notion of the stewardship of wealth, that the owners of wealth have an obligation to see that their wealth through investment or philanthropy renders social good, is a basic characteristic of American capitalism. Despite many and notable exceptions, this tradition has distinguished American from European capitalism and has significantly contributed to the broadly shared well-being which has been the benchmark of the American economy.

Affluence now broadens the scope of this obligation to

families quite modestly circumstanced. Too frequently the wide-spread cynicism, which likes to see the cloven-hoof of self-interest in every private philanthropy, is shown up as an hypocritical cover-up for consciences which fail to match proportionately the generosity of the well-to-do. By and large this new middle-class dissipates a larger part of larger incomes on trivialities, while excusing their own anemic charity under vociferous griping at welfare taxation.

Affluence has similarly made paying debts and observing contracts -- the acts of exchange justice -- more fraught with the common good. Business trust has always been recognized as essential to the smooth functioning of the economy. Nothing disrupts business so much as fraud, stealing, and refusing to honor one's word. Nothing slows business so much as the system of check and double-check. Nothing adds so much to costs as the endless litigations necessitated by men fundamentally lacking in trust. Where millions of dollars ride on split-second decisions, as in stock and commodity markets, welching on even verbal contracts would be totally disrupting. How much more does the tremendous volume of telephone business demand scrupulous adherence to contract?

Affluence has also made violations of exchange justice easier. The vulnerability of insurance companies, corporations and governments to liability is extremely tempting to the petty chiseler to squeeze a few more dollars at the expense of everybody else. The impersonality of marketing has spawned a new profession of super-market shoplifting. Fraudulent use of credit-cards and credit-ratings is practiced with seasoned nonchalance. Employees think nothing of appropriating company or government property. Amazingly, such people are often little conscious that they are taking from another, let alone forcing higher costs on everyone else.

Even businessmen who honor every contractual obligation frequently fail to see that injustice incorporated into a contract is socially disrupting. Contracts, which embody the power that the wealthy and unscrupulous have over the poor and undefended or the advantage one group can wring from another, produce a frustrated sense of outrage which, magnified by affluence, eventually corrodes society. Contracts which take advantage of another's weakness, ignorance, lack of aggression, or dire necessities foster a gnawing bitterness at both the injustice and the lack of redress through courts. Any one familiar with industrial disputes knows the difficulty of getting at the roots of worker bitterness. Labor's demands might be for wages but their disaffection comes from removing the toilet door. The riots in the inner core have their cause in a smouldering resentment, not in the inadvertent or even innocent act which sparked them.

So much of this bitterness, this rankling distrust and violent flare-ups could be prevented if people would universally act as imbued with a fully-developed sense of justice, a justice which treats persons in all their dimensions, not simply as hired hands which can be manipulated like machines, not like animals to be hounded by fear, but as persons living in society, each with his or her personal aspirations and his or her burden of social responsibilities.

JUSTICE, GAIN, AND DISTRIBUTION

Thus far we have seen that affluence adds an extra fillip of social obligation to exchange and distributive justice. The knottier issue remains whether the universal spirit of self-interested gain-seeking is compatible with a sense of social justice. At the personal level, it seems fair to say that, when wealth and incomes are increasing, an individual can strive for more without taking that which belongs to another, or depriving others of their fair share, or passing the burden of costs onto others. That is, self-interest in principle need not violate exchange justice. It is another matter, whether economic self-seeking is compatible with such sharing of the economy's output so as to preserve social harmony by allocating to everyone what is due as a person or citizen and not according to strict economic contribution. We would be shirking a duty not to attempt an answer, even though no definitive one may be possible.

Putting the matter into better perspective, we know that we practice such sharing all the time. Children, those who are disabled, the poor are regularly allocated more of the economy's output than what they contribute to it. No one takes St. Paul's advice literally, "If people won't work, let them not eat." We are appalled that anyone, even the most shiftless, would starve. Certainly, such sharing is done from the higher principle of love, but it is also a matter of justice. Parents who do not feed their children are hailed into court and required to do so. The issue of economic self-seeking is the tougher one of maintaining some balance in income distribution when incomes generally are increasing, a harmony and balance required by the common good. We can begin by taking a hard look at self-interested gain-seeking.

Justice, Gain and the Market

Self-interest, we obviously must acknowledge, can be greediness, lusting unjustly for gain at the expense of others and of society. But self-interest is not necessarily greed because it can as frequently motivate to get more from national income by contributing more to national output, as to get more by taking at whatever cost to others. Hence, self-interest can be operative in an economy which is geared to a just and widespread distribution of its product as well as in one in which only the strong and ruthless take as much as they can. In either case self-interest is the motivating force. This is simply to say that considered in itself, considered as the principle assumed at the beginning of economic analysis, self-interest is morally neutral. In itself it is neither just nor unjust.

The fact of affluence pushes us further to say that some self-interest is necessary. The ever-increasing flow of material goods is there like Everest to be had. It has to go to someone. It cannot exist in a vacuum, not to be enjoyed by and used by anyone. The alternative to self-interest and private gain is public interest and public gain. But even this is not a true alternative, for public interest itself can be realized only in individual use and enjoyment. The real alternative then is between a system of private distribution of the productivity of the economy or a public distribution by the government which is subject to private interest influences. Hence, neither private nor public interest precludes the other. Both public and private channels must share the function of distributing the social revenue of affluence.

The public role, of course, will predominate in a centralized economy, the private in a free-market economy. In both the question of relative weight given to private and public means must be answered. (The consideration of principles and social mores to make this determination is left to a later chapter on the relation between the economic and political orders.) But, granted that in a free-enterprise system most of national income is channeled through the private sector, self-interest will always be necessary.

For the market mechanism can operate only on the two bases of what is wanted and what is available. Income can be earned only by supplying what the public desires and will pay for. Product can be taken from the market only by paying the price to make it available. There is just no other way for the free-market to operate. It cannot recognize social worth or economic need. It can only recognize and reward economic contribution. This is to say that the market compensates self-interest. Those who best consult their own interests in supplying the goods and services most desired are the most liberally rewarded. Those who seek the better paying employment, get it. Those who shop for cheaper priced items, find them.

Harsh and unfeeling as this may seem, it flows from the same sense of justice which each of us ultimately appeals to in insisting on more remuneration for our productive services. Moreover, because it expresses a fundamental justice, the criterion of economic contribution produces economic order, efficiency and peace.

For the economy, viewed only as a system to alleviate scarcity, is an order by which individuals contribute to social wealth in return for private gain. Efficiency is served when those who produce or use their income most effectively enjoy the fruits of their efficiency. These together produce peace, as the harmony which arises from good order. For there can be no harmony without the general recognition and practice that economic return compensates contribution. To this extent, self-seeking is compatible with social justice.

In practice, this means that those who know how "to make a buck" will and should receive the highest income. It means that the market has no way of alleviating those most in need. It means that those who set their sights on higher Values, on goals more socially desirable though not so well remunerated, must be content with a lesser share of the national dividend.

This conclusion, though it exasperates those with a social conscience and seems to comfort those with none, stands firmly on the nature of the free market. To fault the market for not recognizing social worth or alleviating need is simply quixotic, a refusal to understand what it is designed to do. But far from shrugging off the problem, this conclusion points to the true answer: where worthy social efforts should be more liberally rewarded or distress alleviated, we should not attempt it by tampering with the market mechanism but openly and forthrightly through public means. In a much deeper sense, criticism of the supposed faults of the market lays bare a snobbish plutocratic spirit, that attitude most corruptive of a democracy that only wealth and income gained from the market are titles to social merit, that any monetary reward from government or society is somehow tainted with public charity.

Gain and Income Distribution

In this dynamic, therefore, the market mechanism cannot effect a broadly shared and socially just distribution of economic benefits unless economic gain is possible to a wide segment of the economy. Gain is an elusive phenomenon. It cannot be readily quantified, the one exception being profits. For profits can be expressed as the difference between two sets of prices, the prices a firm gets for the goods it sells less the prices it pays for the materials, energy, taxes, and human services necessary to produce, transport and sell its products. This amount is a very small part of the total gain from the economy. Corporate profits (profits from unincorporated businesses are impossible to determine with present statistical methods) after taxes were $10 billions in 1930 when GNP was $100b; they were $92b. in 1976 when GNP was $1,702b. No matter how these figures are refined -- and they need much -- the increase in corporate profits grew only half as fast as the economy.

The rest of total growth was distributed throughout the economy. Governments obviously gained since income taxes increase faster than incomes rise, property taxes increase as the value of property rises, and sales taxes as the dollar volume of sales. The general public in turn was recipient of more and higher-priced government services, especially in defense and education, but also roads, insurance and welfare generally. More people were employed by business at higher wages and salaries. The increase in the prices of securities and real estate yielded capital gains.

This widespread sharing in the growth of the economy demonstrates that gain-seeking, the desire to share in increasing national output is also widespread. The many faces of gain are matched by the many ways in which it is sought. The desire for business profits is gain-seeking, the expectation of more government revenue is gain-seeking, the hope for capital gains is gain-seeking, negotiating for a higher wage or salary is gain-seeking, and finally bargain-hunting by householders is gain-seeking. Business and government gain-seeking is obvious and measurable in sales, profits, and tax receipts. The other two, economic rent and consumer surplus needs some explication.

Economic rent is one of those confusing misnomers which arise from the fact that economic science started by explaining everyday experiences, and then proceeded to more and more precise and scientific meaning. Economic rent began as an explanation of land rent, the fee peasant farmers paid land owners for the use of the land. It still relates to this, as we shall see, but it has little to do with the ordinary monthly rent one pays for an apartment or business space. Economic rent is the difference between what a seller of a productive service or good receives and what he would be willing to take. It is dramatically illustrated in the sports and entertainment field, where fantastic salaries are earned way beyond what the athlete would be willing to perform for. It depends first of all on the demand for those services, the money people are willing to pay to watch Pele play soccer. It also depends on the uniqueness of the performer, that there are no close substitutes. From this it is easy to see how particularly good business locations can also command an economic rent.

But economic rent motivates all kinds and ranks of labor. For example, plumbers will advertise the importance of licensed plumbers while at the same time limiting membership in their union. Doctors and lawyers do no differently. In seeking a raise a person will argue his or her unique contributions to the firm. The argument has real force if the person has an offer from another firm. Union negotiators, seeing healthy corporate sales and profits, assume that the entire work force is more valuable as a consequence. This quiet persistent conviction that if the company is doing better, I must be worth more or if I am offered more elsewhere, I am worth at least that much here, is the force which has maintained the long-term split of the national output of 25% to owners of productive property and 75% to providers of human service, skill, and energy.

Finally, consumers also can share in economic growth. This is the phenomenon which Marshall first defined as consumer surplus.[21] It explains the difference in appraisal between a buy considered a bargain and a buy which is not. In a certain sense consumer surplus arises in every transaction because the buyer will not part with his or her money unless he or she values the purchase higher than his money. But consumer surplus becomes apparent usually only after reflection on a purchase made. It is the realization that one has actually received more service from a good than he or she paid for, or that what was paid was lower than prevailing prices. This produces a feeling of elation, a sense of achievement, a sense of having gained. Professional buyers will be able to express this in a sum of money. Most households cannot quantify their consumer surplus, but they are no less convinced of its reality and act on its basis, seeking bargains and avoiding mistakes. Indeed for some people bargain-hunting becomes a disease in which their bargains are only generic bargains but not bargains in those things that they need and will use. The motive of seeking to gain through consumer surplus is real -- recall the rush into Filene's basement -- , it touches all of us, and it effects a sharing in the national output.

An individual's sense of social justice would, therefore, come into play at this point by first recognizing the validity, the utility, and the necessity of gain-seeking as a motivator of economic actions. It would mean accepting as fact that corporations seek profits, governments more revenue, labor higher wages, and customers bargains. It means acknowledging that, since gain-seeking has no internal brake, peoples' desires for gain will go to excess and inevitably clash. Justice, therefore, will keep its cool in economic disputes and will consistently work toward reasonable compromises which will keep the business going, governments solvent, and households out of bankruptcy. Justice in recognizing others' right to gain will always hold open that possibility to contributors to the enterprise, to citizens who pay the taxes, and to customers who make one's market.

In a dynamic, multi-dimensional relationship which is the typical business enterprise, no one can determine precisely what is just compensation, what are just returns and just prices. But an attitude of social justice, a recognition of the right to seek gain, a spirit of compromise in the face of scarcity, a willingness to rectify past mistakes, and a dogged determination to keep things going for the sake of all concerned will come closer to a just set of solutions than any lesser effort. Difficult though it may be, an individual's self-seeking may be tempered with social justice. Call it "square shooting", "making reasonable demands" or "giving a fair shake", social justice can be operative in the economy.

Distributive Justice Policy

Such an attitude of fair play, though always vitally necessary, is limited to the sphere of personal influence. Beyond this lies the vast area where the power of the state must be invoked to effect distributive justice policies. This is the area, as we saw, in which modern philosophers were most interested. Here a personal attitude of social justice, while quantitatively insignificant, still plays an important role by learning the facts, formulating reasonable conclusions, and influencing public and legislative opinion.

The problem of income distribution policy is a hydra-headed. Three general levels can be distinguished: 1) The international distribution of income among the rich and poor nations; 2) The structure of institutions affecting the distribution of income within an economy; and 3) The ability of families and individuals to share in increasing national wealth within a given structure. These levels are distinguishable but not independent of each other. Simplistic, one-dimensional solutions will inevitably be wrong. Solutions which ignore the dynamics of value creation are going to do more harm than good.

This warning particularly applies to sincere people who are shocked at world starvation and poverty. Too frequently they think in crude mercantalistic terms, a mixture of nationalistic sensitivities and a primitive, materialistic concept of wealth. Then too a closer relationship must be established between the basic humanitarian impulse to feed and shelter the destitute and the steps which must be taken to generate and nourish the spark of economic growth in survival economies. This will largely consist in efforts to nourish the hope for economic gain.

The structural problem comes closer to our main concern, gain-seeking as it affects one's share in national output. The corporation and especially the corporate giants are institutions which gather economic gain into immense pools of funds. But labor unions and professional associations also channel gain toward their members. Finally, government through its taxing structure and also through its regulatory bureaucracy greatly affects the flow of gain throughout the economy. These institutions, both public and private, present a never-ending challenge to economists, to politicians, to labor leaders, to businessmen and to representatives of consumer interests to modify and to reform the ways in which institutions arrogate gain to themselves and their constituents. Again simplistic answers can be disastrous. Modifying the power of institutions to share in growth will affect those institutions contributions to growth. In the shifting scene of value creation no a priori blue-print is possible. Any plan must take into consideration the natural drive in all sectors of the economy to gain.

Thus, however, we approach the problem of income distribution, we must ultimately end with the personal problem of the gain motivation. For the man on the street the problem of income distribution is very intimate: Why can't I get ahead? or Why do others move ahead faster than I? No one seriously proposes to answer his second question by absolute egalitarianism, absolutely equal distribution of wealth and income. Even the most rigidly communistic societies do not propose this. The boldest proposals call for the same rate of sharing for everybody. This, of course, insures that the already wealthy will become absolutely wealthier. It may also impede or inhibit the growth of the economy itself, so that all may be sharing equally in zero gain.

The surer but entirely less intellectually satisfying way is to sharpen people's instincts to gain. Some broad structural changes would greatly encourage this, for example, a negative income tax, a school voucher system, and government sponsored credit insurance would do much to alleviate the initial disadvantages of people. But all can share in increasing affluence by more intelligent consumption, by achieving consumer surplus. This will yield real improvement in a family standard of living, but it cannot dramatically improve it unless family income itself can be increased.

The structural proposals above can help. But a large percentage of the population will still be cut off from any sharing because of a gamut of physical, social and economic disabilities: drug and alcohol addiction; poor schooling; mental retardation, blindness; social prejudice or a prison record; no job skills; or the burden of small children. These are the peoples left in the economic back-waters, little able to make a contribution to economic growth and consequently not sharing in it, and unable unaided to get into the main-stream. They lack the leverage to make their desire to gain effective. They are turned-off and discouraged, fearful of society and often bitter toward it.

They are in turn an enormous drag on the efficiency of the economy. No magic Washington wand is going to turn them into honest and efficient gain-seekers. Nothing can be done unless they will it. They on their part can do little without the support of a variety of social programs. These few remarks must suffice for now by way of putting the problem of income distribution into the context of growth and gain-seeking.

Gain and Growth

A final dimension of social justice might be called intergenerational justice. This is most conveniently analyzed under the two related problems of the desirable rate of economic growth and the rate of pollution production. These involve justice between generations, in the broadest sense of those already enjoying human existence and future generations still unborn. The nub is the right of the living to realize a higher level of well-being as against their obligation not only to continue the human specie but to provide conditions that the unborn can enjoy at least the same level of well-being as we do. Basically it comes to pitting our right to live well against theirs.

Too frequently analysis of these problems ignore the most fundamental issue implicit in them, that is, the questions whether human existence itself is good and whether that existence should be passed on to others. The basic issue is the right to life of the unborn and even the unconceived. That the question is being asked is one of the most trenchant commentaries on affluent people. We will proceed on the assumption that the answers are convincingly affirmative and leave the problem in the hands of theologians, philosophers, and psychologists.

The problem of the limits of growth relates to the income distribution problem because a badly maldistributed income is the surest way to kill the instinct to gain and to insure zero or even negative growth. This we have known since Adam Smith. Consequently, those who are despairing of income distribution are usually despairing of income growth. But the contemporary pessimism runs along the line that affluent economies will run out of raw materials, that people will procreate faster than the food supply, and that we will garbage and pollute ourselves to an economic standstill. They picture a planet some eons from now where the highest form of life has destroyed life itself. There is little value to these prophecies except as themes for late movies on TV. The warnings they imply, however, are worth heeding.

There is a sense in which the economy, even the most productive, is limited. This is what economists call its production possibilities, the aggregate amount of goods and services of all kinds which an economy can produce at any particular moment. This is determined by the technology which is currently used, the amount of raw materials and energy available, the skills and willingness to work of the people in the economy. Obviously all these can and do change, and consequently the production possibility frontier is always shifting.

Secondly, what an economy can produce is not a guarantee that it will produce at that level. Generally, there is some slack, some unused capacity, some unemployment or under-employment. Indeed, as students who recall their macro-economics will concede, economic growth itself upsets the economy. The shift of output from current consumption to goods used to produce other goods, investment in a broad sense, which economic growth entails, is always jerky and never perfectly coordinated. Thus the economy is always tending to under- or to over-produce its possibilities. There is a limit to growth which hinges upon the actual capabilities of the economy and upon the efficiency with which those capabilities are utilized. _But it is a shifting limit._ There is always enough on the immediate horizon, more raw materials, more energy and better technology, to shift the production possibility frontier outward.

Consequently, the real limit to economic growth is the limits imposed by human knowledge: understanding better the forces of nature, exploring the potentialities of the earth, and devising ways of producing goods and utilizing energy which is more conservative of energy and materials. We know little about the natural resources contained in the ocean. We have barely scratched the crust of the earth. The resources of the moon and the planets are virginal. Anyone can predict doomsday by keeping resources and technology constant while increasing population and wanting exponentially. That is a mathematical game which anyone can play. The key is whether persons will respond, will they rise to the challenge of resource and energy limitations by more exploration, more research, more implementation of knowledge for human use, and above all less wasteful use of available resources and more flexibility in institutions to effect these changes. If Earth is reduced to a burnt-out cinder, it will be due to a failure of the human spirit.

The above says simply that further growth is always

possible. It denies that growing economies must inevitably self-destruct. It does not deny, however, that the rate of growth, the rate of gain-seeking and want expectations can be excessive and with catastrophic results. The world-wide inflation is not solely or mainly atributable to a few oil moguls using their economic power to re-allocate the world's production of wealth a little more their way. Rather, it is a warning, like the chest pains of the week-end athlete, that we are pushing our economies faster than they can currently run.

The fault lies not in economic growth but in the rate of growth. Given the present limits of the production possibilities frontier, we collectively, congressmen who see no need to conserve the public purse, bankers who perceive every loan as profitable, corporate executives who see no end to their markets, labor leaders who demand ever-fatter pay checks, as well as the general public who sees no reason for curtailing their appetites for things, can and have been guilty of wanting more than the economy can produce.

The same argument is advanced for the problem of pollution. For a pollutant is only a good which cannot be put to use in its present form. When use for it is found, it is called a by-product not waste. Thus the problem of pollution is basically that of finding uses for what is now wasted. This is a basic principle of industrial production and has been implemented since man began. For every useful material was waste at one time. The process must be stepped up so as not to overburden the natural powers of climate, water and soil to return waste to useful resources. In many cases technology is available for utilizing waste but the technique is not economically feasible. This then becomes a problem of private or more generally public economic choice. Finally, new technologies must be devised and old ones improved. All in all, the problem of pollution reduces itself to the willingness of people to develop by-products, to re-cycle and re-use waste. One cannot be cavalier about these issues: they effect our well-being vitally; they are not amenable to easy solutions. But their solution, beyond the technical, call for personal awareness and response.

This problem and others in the chapter must be left as unfinished business. For the chapter was intended only to plant the seeds of an attitude which will grow and flourish in the struggle to reconcile our gain with what is right for others. Only the realization, that society is founded on the uniqueness of the individual, that social intercourse must take place between different and unequal persons, that common purposes are achieved only through specialization of contribution, will reconcile personal purposiveness with outward order and conformity. Only true and complete social justice, by according the person his due as an individual and as a member of society, bends every effort toward realizing the highest human good of a peaceful and humanizing social order. Finally, this sensitivity to the rights of others as individuals and as social beings flows from and confirms an internal harmony manifested particularly in directing the pleasure and gain appetites toward life's higher Values. Whatever his wider impact, the just person is at peace with himself and those about him.

Now affluence, which has accentuated the need, also provides the means. But we must face up to the need that our burgeoning wealth must be directed more to the good of others and less to our own. This may mean more governmental welfare but it certainly calls for more public, non-governmental philanthropy and private and individual giving. It means that increasing income be devoted less to shutting people off in their comfortable, gadget-filled homes and more to enriching and humanizing civic and social living. It means less sealing off the degeneracy and poverty of the central city and more dissolving the ghetto with the solvents of economic opportunity and personal acceptance. It means less building walls against the destitution and revolution in the world and more guaranteeing world peace through stimulating the growth of affluence in the developing nations.

Affluence inspired by social justice, and justice using the resources of affluence offer the best hope for a world torn by war, nations split by prejudice, and cities divided by unequal opportunities. This is not a solution, nor a program but an attitude from which programs and solutions can be devised. This attitude above all will become a source of strength when good programs seem to fail, when the intractibility of men and institutions test our patience, our tolerance, and our will to be genuinely just.

For the effort to act in the light of social justice will, at minimum, have a reflex effect in elevating our Value hierarchy and in confirming our mastery over tendencies toward sensuality and greed. Looking outward, social justice perceives a higher meaning for affluence beyond treating individuals fairly and sharing its benefits equitably here and now. We address this transcendent meaning of affluence in the next chapter.

CHAPTER SIX

AFFLUENCE AND THE SPIRIT OF POVERTY

The pause which refreshes also provides opportunity to survey how far we have come and whither we are going. Starting with the fact that our actions are a complex woven of many strands, what we called 'principles of action', we examined first the condition of affluence, an economic environment which provides many more goods and services than required for survival and indeed minimum comfort. We had no choice in the matter; being born affluent and experiencing nothing but economic abundance, we have an affluent attitude, an insistent expectation of more income, wealth, and economic goods. Further that drive itself creates more values and more wealth which not only perceptibly transforms our milieu and style of living but subjects us to sudden shocks of change.

With our environment promising no stability, we turned to our inner resources of personality. There we found that just as a tree grows by simultaneously raising its tower of branches toward the sunlight and spreading a deeper and more extensive net of roots, so too a person grows by raising his Value hierarchy and by deepening his insights into his own goodness and that of other things, and of other people. As applied to the affluent attitude, raising our Value sights was shown as the only effective control on the appetite for wealth and thereby checks our tendencies to sensual pleasures, to vain display, and to pride of power over others. More positively, the view of justice as social justice adds a dimension of concern for others, respecting their rights not only as individuals but as social beings, and opens up an entirely new set of obligation for the well-being of society, the human community itself. Thus affluence enlarges human possibilities, providing the means by which a person can ennoble his character by sharing his bounty with others.

This vista we have achieved with little aid other than the light of intelligence and good will. But such secular visions, whatever their grandeur, are not enough. For example, Marx's ideal of species man, the person who can identify his well-being with that of his brothers, is noble indeed in contrast to the self-centeredness which engulfs most lives. But such aspirations pose their own quandary especially for the affluent. On the one hand, they are painfully aware that an affluence feeding materialistic tendencies can debase them to a level which is less than human. On the other hand, however noble their aspiration to serve others, they are faced with the same spectres of physical deterioration, senility and death as those who seemingly have enjoyed the good things of life with little care how this affected themselves or others. Without meaning beyond this life, the struggle with affluence leads to despair.

Our analysis, though largely limited to the here and now, did point, however, to a transcendent dimension. In the very beginning Scheler's criteria of Value, the four notes of enduring, indivisible, most basic, and yielding the deepest contentment, when raised to the absolute level, converge in the goodness of a being which is not only immortal but eternal, which is pure spirit, the first cause of all, and an infinitely loving intelligence. The absolutely absolute Value may only be the absolutely human ideal, but if it exists, it can be identified with the Supreme Being, God, Allah, the Great Spirit, or the myriad names peoples have given it. If it exists, then its reflection in all creatures is revealed in the deepest penetration into and perception of their goodness. If it exists, then its law is the very substance of the internal peace and harmony which overflows onto others as social justice. If it exists, then a person's struggle to use his material well-being to elevate his character by helping others is not terminated by death but has meaning and fruition beyond this life.

Most people, who have a conviction of their survival somehow after death, have also made this leap of faith to the existence of a Supreme Being, of God. This chapter assumes, avoiding the psychological and theological issues attendant upon such a faith-commitment, that its student readers do so believe, and will draw out the implications of that belief for living the affluent life. Further it assumes that that faith-commitment as a principle affecting the acquisition and use of wealth is expressed in the religious attitude called the Spirit of Poverty.

Most people react to this proposition with incredulity. To them no two states of mind are so antithetical as the affluent attitude and spiritual poverty. Where one exists, the other cannot and no further discussion is possible. Yet students, who are alert to the paradoxes of affluence, should be daring enough to explore the possibility that the spiritual wealth flowing from the spirit of poverty may somehow redeem, fulfill, and give meaning to the ontological poverty found at the heart of affluence. If this should be so, the exploration would involve: 1) probing the ambivalence and ambiguities of our age for the emptiness at the heart of affluence; 2) extracting the riches of the concept of spiritual poverty by surveying its organic growth from its beginnings in Covenental history; and 3) reconciling, at least in principle, the spirit of poverty with the affluent attitude. This is a tall order for a short chapter. The student should expect little more resolution than some fertile suggestions for future thought and consideration.

AMBIVALENCE AND AMBIGUITIES

No living generation describes its place in human history with accurate objectivity, usually exaggerating its discontinuity with the immediate past. Nevertheless, there exists a universal feeling that our age is in transition, being most commonly described as post-Christian, post-industrial and post-whatever, essentially negative attributes. Karl Rahner, the Jesuit theologian, catalogues some of the more positive changes:

> "Our times have been described as the end of the modern age; as the atomic age; as the age of unification in one human history of all who dwell on the one planet; as the age of organized atheism; of world-wide industrialism; of the collective, of man in the mass, of the decline of individualism and interest in subjective personality; as the age of existential anguish, disillusion, and loss of belief in progress; the age of the denaturing of nature, the eclipse of the numinous in the world, the absence of God; of the substitution of the planned product for the natural growth, of addiction and anxiety, of the replacement of the given by the manufactured, of loss of the center; an age in which, for the first time, the release of the mind from its bondage to nature is really being accomplished."[1]

However, history will view this 20th Century, we do experience this sense of cataclysmic change and the need to hang onto youth, the present, at the risk of forgetting our past and not heeding the future. Rahner continues:

> "We really do live in a new situation, in comparison with which the whole history of humanity

> and of Christianity so far, despite all its vicissitudes and changes, really does shrink into a single period. The transition from one period to another lasts for a long time, longer than an individual man's life; we are inescapably creatures of yesterday and today and tomorrow. If anyone, impatiently revolutionary, seeks to cast off the historical necessity of living in this state of transition, he will merely fail in what has been appointed for him in history; <u>he will be serving, not the future, but destruction</u>; he will not be laying hold on the wealth to come but losing that heritage from his forefathers which he was meant to take with him into the future as something too precious to be lost."[2] (emphasis added)

Rahner locates the ambivalence, the amgituities, the moral confusion of people today in that which is the glory of the modern era, its freedom, not complete of course, from the bonds and limitations imposed by nature. Like young men and women who have cut the silver cord, modern man experienced the heady excitement of a larger scope of freedom but at the same time faced the terrifying facts of personal responsibility. Rahner is worth quoting in full:

> "Man used to be protected by what is imposed and inescapable, which is nature. He could not be everywhere, he had to be sedentary, whether he liked it or not; the abiding sameness of his environment forced him, without his observing it, to a traditional way of life. He had no weapons that would enable him to kill large numbers of people before being killed himself; he could not escape from the unity and closed structure of family and kindred without being swiftly punished by the loss of his biological existence; the number of his progeny was not something over which, in the concrete, he was in a position to exercise control; nationalism and internationalism were no problem in periods in which peoples were isolated from each other by empty areas; intellectual events had plenty of time to develop and ripen slowly, because, without printing, radio and similar things, it was not possible artificially to accelerate such developments and work them to death; man could not over-stimulate himself with addictions and sensations; he could not get away

from himself, he could not achieve the fearful discontinuity of modern life, because to a large extent he simply did not have the wherewithal, and because even small attempts to do so would be promptly disciplined on the spot by nature, with punishments going as far as death...

"Today it is different. Man is beginning to carry out the task, laid on him in paradise, of subduing the earth, on a hitherto unimagineable scale. There is nowhere where he cannot go. He can control his own breeding processes, he can make artificial materials that are better than those provided by nature; he can plan himself; he is even thinking of leaving behind this earth which God created as man's home; he bounces radar signals off the moon, which God set in the sky to be his light by night, and which men of an earlier age reverently contemplated as an unattainable heavenly image of a wholly other world, not subject to terrestrial change; he no longer knows of any starry heaven above him to fill him with the same awe as the moral law within his heart; he has no convictions which could not be confuted, not by arguments and in the light of higher truth, but by the right injection. He has been largely successful in protecting himself against nature, which he sees as cruel and heartless towards man; he has reared ramparts against her, against her climate and her bacteria, her animals and her power of death. <u>And behold, in protecting himself against nature he has lost the protection which she afforded him against himself</u>, and man is delivered defenseless into his own hands, to all the errant possibilities of his freedom, to his own hybris, to his everlasting temptation to be as God, i.e. to be someone bound by no reality outside himself, no law higher than himself."[3] (emphasis added)

The conclusion Rahner draws should be set to memory as describing the travail and, pray God, not the epitaph, of modern man: "Man, escaped from nature -- protective, nurturing, limiting, formative nature -- is handed over to himself, to his destructive intemperance and lack of intellectual bounds."[4]

Abundance in Balance

What Rahner writes of the modern era in general can be particularized in application to affluence. For the affluent with their wealth and technology have not only provided the most important means for economic progress, but their scientific and intellectual curiosity has been a world civilizing force. If at the heart of affluence we find an ontological emptiness, this must be balanced against its very real achievements.

The affluent have been the principal agents in the exchange of cultures. More of human history has been recovered in the last two hundred years than in all preceding ages. As a consequence, the affluent possess in the original or faithful reproduction the music, the art, the literature not only of their own heritage but of many other cultures. This legacy, moreover, is not the prerogative of the wealthy only but is available to the poorest. Libraries, schools, art and historical museums are at ready reach to most. Symphonies, ballet, good theater, and excellent civic architecture are found even in the provinces.

The affluent have mapped and measured the world, rediscovering civilizations which natives had forgotten. Their satellites, cables, and wire service have turned the world into a global village, making events in remote areas today's headlines. Their technology has allowed primitive peoples to leap hundreds of years of economic development. Their medicine has wiped out diseases which have plagued the world. The Christian message has been carried to more people than in any previous generation.

In affluent countries economic abundance has ameliorated the lot of the masses. By humanizing the condition of the majority, abundance has provided the means for greater personal fulfillment. It has opened many new ways for upward social movement -- sports, entertainment, politics, business, labor unions, education, and the arts -- which were simply not available two hundred years ago. The effects of this in venting the pressure of class envy and enmity is incalculable and often overlooked.

Economic abundance, therefore, still holds promise of alleviating the dire destitution of the billions of people in the developing world. That that destitution, the droughts, the plagues, the rate of infant mortality and starvation, is a world issue today and was not over thousands of years is due to the rising expectations of peoples who have seen and begun to experience some modicum of abundance. While Western intrusion into their economies, first through mercantile imperialism, then through colonization, and now with development aid, often perpetrated untold cruelty, injustice, and enslavement, nevertheless, it has been the main agent generating a world-wide economic revolution.

In the relation among nations, economic abundance played an important part in unifying Western Europe, thus defusing the cause of conflict of the worst international wars of the modern period. For the same reason, the super-powers have sidled away from direct confrontation, despite the myriad of opportunities over the last thirty years. By the same token the struggle of Third World peoples for freedom and the dramatization of their economic discontent are only possible with the support of affluent countries. No one can predict the irrationality of world leaders. But if the bombs are dropped it will be contrary to, not in accord with peoples' desire for economic abundance.

The Failure of Abundance

Yet economic abundance seems to have more failed than fulfilled the promises made in its behalf. Affluence has turned the United States into a neurotic trillionaire, jittery over every economic downturn and the more rapid growth and trading strength of friendly nations. We are becoming paranoid about our intractable inflation and the specter of a lower rate of growth. We are worried that Russia in successfully exporting its technology may export its ideology into developing countries.

Affluence seems rather to heighten than to mitigate domestic discord. The struggle for minority rights, of blacks, Spanish-speaking, Indians and women, however political and sociological, is at gut level a struggle for economic opportunity, for jobs and income. Affluence has spurred labor demands, especially of teachers and other public employees even at the expense of the public interest. It has vocalized welfare recipients, polarized renters and landlords, and sent consumers marching in protest. Yet our domestic discord, hot as it became at times, is mild in contrast to the 1967 uprising of students and laborers in France. Indeed, whatever the ethnic, religious or ideological roots of violence in Northern Ireland, in Beirut, in Cyprus, in Chile, in Lisbon, Angola, Mindinao and so on interminably, one can always find an economic factor looming large.

Economic abundance has not brought ease of mind, but to the contrary, the competitive rat-race, the pressure of neighborhood conformism, and the feeling that costs and debts mount faster than income. The young are disenchanted, the idealists dropping out of the system and the cynical conforming to take it for all they can get. Internationally we are embarrassed by our riches, feel guilty about our physical environment and abused by recipients of our generosity. But our social environment has fallen into greater chaos. More and more people crowd into megametropolitan areas seeking more money. There they enjoy fewer amenities and pay higher prices; suffer the dysfunctioning of schools and other civic institutions; exist at the mercy of any group which can disrupt civic life for its own purposes. They are bogged in traffic and fearful of life and property. Crime clogs the courts and jails, while suspected thieves, homocides, and rapists are returned to the streets to commit new crimes before they can be tried for the old. Cunning and rapacity are rewarded and honest effort scorned.

Accentuating this personal disenchantment is the feeling that modern technology has diminished the human person. We are caught up into vast productive, financial, and marketing processes which seem to run on abstract mechanical principles and allow for little personal influence. More frustrating are the vast bureaucracies which control these processes. Unless one happens upon a bureaucrat with human instincts, someone willing to take a personal interest in our problems, the process seems impervious to our needs. Greater frustrations await those drawn into the maws of governmental bureaucracies, which are supposedly set up to meet citizen needs and wants. The tax overcharge which can never be corrected, the relief check which never comes, the learning disability which can never be attended to can make one feel paranoically helpless. Like carrying a mattress without straps one does not know how to get at it. Granted that much of this is caricature, the reality is still pretty grim.

The Trauma of Change

To the frustration of hopes and the helplessness in the face of bureaucracy must be added the trauma of change. This more than the other may explain the affluents' feelings of life's transitoriness and impermanence. Change and risk are not unique to affluence. All business necessarily involves risk because costs must be incurred to produce goods and services for an uncertain and changing demand. Every change furthermore sets off a chain-reaction. Just as changing demand causes changes in the hiring of labor and other factors and, consequently, of their incomes, so too changing production patterns cause new buyer-seller relations, new employer-employee relations, new customer satisfactions and new income patterns. All of this is fraught with risk which must be borne by someone, by stockholders, managers, employees, consumer, or by the public at large, and in large enterprises by all together.

Affluence heightens change exponentially. Consumers with greater discretionary income can shift spending from one non-essential commodity to another as taste or inclination directs. The complexity of technique allows a bewildering flexibility in product lines, combining productive ingredients in an amazing variety of substantially the same things. Labor, especially at the higher levels displays this same mobility. Capital is the most fluid of all, flowing from corporation to corporation and within the corporation from one productive unit to another. The amazing diversification of 3-M Company is but one outstanding example of capital, labor, technology, and equipment constantly changing in response to new products and new demand.

The very susceptibility to change accelerates change itself. More planning effort is directed toward researching new products, building prototypes, analyzing changing patterns of demand, new technologies and potential sources of raw or fabricated material than in actually selling goods currently produced. Business must look to, not what is, but what will be produced. That is, the business to be successful must not only respond to change from outside but must initiate change, constantly updating its techniques, its product line and its marketing methods. Above all success requires keen vision to utilize the scientific findings pouring from corporate, university and government laboratories. It is a zestful struggle to stay abreast; a triumph to gain an inch.

But change and its attendant risk refuse to be confined to the initiating enterprise but spread throughout the economy. This is true in slower paced economies but it is accentuated in affluent economies for two reasons. First, the timing of change varies from firm to firm, from household to household, and from government to government and all of these from each other. Time is of the essence of the economic process. For every economic decision is a response to what has happened and anticipates what will happen. Thus the reaction time even to the same event will be different for households, governments, firms, and units within the firm. Secondly, all economic units are bound together in a web of economic relations so that change anywhere starts a series of reactions and reactions to the reactions throughout the economy. For these reasons the economy is characterized by a choppy, not fully predictable, seething.

This more than anything makes economists' predictions of the future so frustratingly uncertain. For the ordinary person it poses a real problem of insecurity. Not only does every economic unit vary in its reaction to change but everyone's response to change in turn produces its own waves of change throughout the economy. For sellers depend on buyers who in turn depend on producers of product and hirers of resources. This web of interdependence means that when one strand is plucked the whole system vibrates.

This may be seen more clearly in the large, in an event which affects the entire economy simultaneously like a tax cut. Take-home pay and disposable income of everybody is increased, in varying amounts. Spending on goods, more savings, and larger holdings of cash are all likely. Depending on the proportions, sales will increase and more funds made available for investment. Profits most likely will increase, as well as the profitability of investment, since interest rates may initially fall. Increased investment could mean more employment, more overtime, more income, more spending, more savings and so on. Higher profits and employment could spur labor unions to push for higher wage rates. Larger income means more tax revenue, cancelling some, maybe all, of the tax cut. As if by magic everything could be better, more income to spend, more jobs, business booming, government revenue rising.

That a tax cut scenario worked like this some years ago, however, does not guarantee that it will work that way again, as it did not in 1975. For every change, besides re-aligning economic relations, produces a permanent effect on the economy, in the industrial structure, in technology, in the composition of the labor force and capital goods, and in the potential of the economy. Just as lowering a swamp may increase cultivation, lowering it more may cause problems which nullify further gains. For the economy is a system in which all parts must be kept in dynamic balance with each other. Every change, therefore, produces a new balance. Set in the real world of war and international conflict, of social strife, of population movements, of scientific inventions, of discoveries of new sources of raw materials, the economy is in perpetual flux. Everything is fluid and everything affects everything else.

Consequently, no one and no firm is guaranteed a permanent position in the economic order. Though some are better insulated, no one is isolated from change. Even the industrial giants have no guaranteed place. Thirty percent of the 200 largest in 1954 were not on the list in 1968. Slightly more than half disappeared through acquisition; the rest because they grew at a slower pace. All but 22 lost or gained more than five places and only a handful kept their same position. If new markets, new products, new technologies, new management affect the largest corporations, how much more so smaller businesses of which millions are begun and die every year and whose average life is about five years?[5] For the individual, consequently, there is no ultimate security. Skills are eroded, jobs run out, divisions are sold to other firms. Opportunities or their lack force families to move on. Social status for most depends largely on the vagaries of economic fortune.

The businessman, with experience of and perspective on the inter-relationships of the economy, might be psychologically forearmed against the vagaries of change. But the vast majority of people drift uncomprehendingly on the sea of economic fluctuations: the housewife staring across the breakfast table at her worried but uncommunicative spouse; the shop or office force churned by rumors of lay-offs and cutbacks; the millions unskilled in reading the signs of economic change, even otherwise intelligent professional people, in a constant fret and dither over the morning's business news. Inexplicably their incomes rise or fall, their markets grow lush or fade, their jobs pay more or are eliminated without a change in their own skill, diligence, and effort. For everyone, change has become a condition of life: new jobs, new skills, new locations, new friends, new levels of living are all but forced on us. <u>This is the psychological uncertainty and insecurity which affluence has produced</u>.

The Poverty in Abundance

The greatest disenchantment with affluence arises from

the fact that it has not irradicated poverty, even after a "War on Poverty" and hundreds of billions of welfare spending. In fact, most feel affluence has exacerbated poverty. Exacerbated, not increased is the correct word, because every one is poorer than someone else, or at least, feels so. That is to say, poverty is always relative to others' well-being. Even formal poverty guide lines are relative to the prevailing plane of living. They, therefore, both overstate and understate the significance of poverty. They overstate when they imply destitution. For our poverty levels of $6500 for a family of four would buy at today's prices the goods and services which provided a comfortable living for an unskilled worker in New York in 1915.[6] This would be a terribly crabbed and pinched existence today but it would not be destitution.

On the other hand, the poverty guide-lines do not get to the real anguish of poverty, that of being so much worse off than others. In this sense, they understate the case. For example, the Catholic Committee on Human Development recently insisted that 50% of the median family income, or approximately $9000 today, is a more realistic figure at which to place the poverty level. Certainly, no one will consider that a family can live in plush on that income. But $9000 today is the equivalent of $2800 in 1950, which would have placed a family close to the fortieth percentile of the richest country in the world, in the history of the human race -- hardly poverty. But whereas in 1950, another $400 would bring such a family up to the median income bracket, it would take another $9000 to bring today's family to the median level.

Thus the poverty of affluent peoples means absolutely more economic goods and a higher plane of material well-being. At the same time it means being absolutely worse off than the majority. Both are very real aspects of the sociological poverty found amid affluent plenty. They emphasize correctly that the real poverty in affluence is psychological. People feel worse off, and these feelings are real not delusions.

Part of this is the universal human experience that all things material have at heart an ontological emptiness. They are always means to higher ends. To rest in them, to cling to them is purposeless and meaningless. But affluence adds a few overtones of its own. The first we have already mentioned: that affluence creates scarcity, that increased income by generating more wants always trails a widening wake of frustrated wants.

The second flows from the dynamic of affluence. For affluence not only generates more wants but arouses the expectation of more. This expectation radically differentiates the affluent psyche from the torpor of destitution. An affluent people from having more, wants more, and from wanting more, expects more. They expect that the future promises more than the present, because the present gave more than the past. Because of this expectation, the uncertainty of affluence produces both greater trauma and frustration, when unemployment, accidents, illness or any loss of income reduces one's customary plane of living or lowers it below what neighbors and associates enjoy. Affluence not only goads people to expect more, but by that fact sharpens the trauma of uncertainty and change.

A third aspect of the psychological poverty of affluence relates to our liberty. Affluence by widening the spectrum of choices and want-satisfactions has expanded our liberties, but the tendency of people to overdo things, to let wants get out of control -- again the infinite appetite for wealth and the *fomes peccati* -- invites social controls. The universal remedy for restricting the abuses of the few is to pass a law which restrains all. Thus affluence in enlarging our *liberties*, may actually occasion the erosion of our *liberty*.

Add these to the frustrations of an evanescent life, heightened by newly aroused wants and expectations, sharpened by complicated products promising more sophisticated and refined pleasures, and one begins to feel the tensions which shoot through the life of affluence. It explains why the affluent lash out defensively and protectively against anything which would seem to diminish their material well-being. It explains the Sisyphean frustration of so many, wearing themselves out in joyless dissipation of resources, energies, concerns and skills to overcome scarcity, while missing the joy and truly meaningful possibilities in the plenty they already have. Viewed from afar and against the backdrop of world destitution, the affluents' feelings of insecurity, of scarcity, and of poverty seem a ludicrous paranoia. But both the sociological and psychological poverty in affluence are real.

There is a certain madness about the situation. Affluence, that alluring good, which holds so much promise for mankind and the masses of destitute throughout the world, which is so desired by the peoples struggling in developing economies, seems to have turned to ashes in the mouth of those who have tasted it.

Yet even they will not surrender it. Indeed the affluent cannot shuck off their affluence. This the "flower" children quickly discovered. They were forced to live off its bounty, to scrounge from its refuse heaps, or to prey on its defenseless periphery. They could neither shed the habits of affluence nor live without its support. Those, who came to their senses before they were destroyed, realized this bitter truth and drifted away like a Frisco fog.

All of this forces us to the inescapable conclusion that economic abundance and affluence have no ultimate meaning in themselves. Consequently, neither self-control in enjoying the fruits of abundance, nor concern about the well-being of others in sharing our affluence will give it meaning, because at the heart of affluence is an ontological poverty. Affluence must propose a good beyond itself to have real meaning, a meaning which stands out above the ambivalence and ambiguities of modern life. This vision only theology, the science which takes as subject the ultimately transcendent, can give. Pushing paradox to the limit we will try to find a theology of wealth in that attitude which is fundamental to the religious spirit, wherever manifested, called spiritual poverty.

THE SPIRIT OF POVERTY

I was struck by this paradox some years ago when wandering through the ruins of Jumiege and St. Wandrille, those two great abbeys in the Seine Valley whose histories stretch back into the Dark Ages. These monasteries were richest and most flourishing when the spirit of dedicated poverty burned most fervently. They languished and became subject to spoilation and expropriation, when that spirit burnt low. When it died they were destroyed.[7]

This paradox, that poverty spurning wealth increases wealth, seemed to fit, like glove to hand, that other paradox, that affluence creates scarcity and very real poverty. The possibility of fit, however, runs into two seeming incompatibilities:

1) The spirit of poverty accepts, tolerates, and even encourages real and effective poverty, the possi-

bility of whose elimination is perhaps the only moral and social justification of economic abundance; and

2) the motive, fundamental to the affluent principle, to seek more wealth and income and to realize more want-satisfactions, seems to contradict that spirit which embraces doing without in preference to having the good things in life.

As a consequence, affluence seems to present an impossible condition to the contemporary Christian to realize Christian poverty as a truly operative principle in his life.

Yet the amazing vitality of the concept of spiritual poverty continued to intrigue. Versions of it are found in all major religions and quasi-religions. The very meaning of 'musilman' as the servant of Allah is fundamental to Islam. The goal of Buddhism to be absorbed into the Transcendent Reality implies leaving behind all material goods and sensate things. Even the Marxist Principle, from each according to ability and to each according to need, is really a secularized spiritual poverty.[8] Much of the dropping out of the economic mainstream, whether inspired by social service, social pessimism, or true religious feelings, embraces poverty as the better way.

In the Judaeo-Christian tradition, the spirit of poverty has passed through a sequence of deaths and revivals, woven into the history of economic growth and decay. Like the olive tree, the spirit of poverty has deep roots, which seemingly dead can renew itself with the grafting of each age. Even after its long dormancy in modern times, when it seemed to shrivel into a joyless jansenism or a cold welfarism, interest in spiritual and dedicated poverty is beginning to revive.[9]

The spirit of poverty is not a rational but a vital principle in an organic sense. Each re-flowering reveals another aspect of its vitality, yet it remains one with its embryonic manifestation in primitive Judaeism. It cannot, therefore, be defined. Rather it must be understood organically from seed through maturization and successive flowerings.

It is implicit in the formation of the Hebrew nation. These were several hundred thousands of agricultural slaves who toiled in the Delta of the Nile. They were largely Semitic but apparently not all descendants of Abraham, Isaac and Jacob. Centuries before they had drifted to Egypt or been herded there as prisoners. All alike gravitated into the condition of persecuted social outcasts which their name seems to imply. Jahwe, through an educated but outlawed Hebrew named Moses, decided to call this people out of Egypt, to form them into a nation, promising them land of their own on condition that they were faithful to his Law and the promise of a Savior. Of all the ancient peoples no more motley crew could have been chosen, but that is God's way and His privilege.

Unlike modern sociological treatises, poverty is never defined in the Bible. Rather it is the interweaving of three lines of thought. The most fundamental is that poverty is a scandalous state, testifying to the wealthy's neglect of their duty to the poor. The second theme, more muted, is that poverty is divine retribution for Israel's unfaithfulness. Finally, in the Wisdom literature it means a middle state between wealth and penury, the state most conducive to virtuous living. But in the dynamics of Biblical thought this complex of ideas acquired a religious aura: the man of poverty was the client of God, who not only depends on God but furthers His aims.[10]

As one of the seminal concepts of the Old Testament, spiritual poverty is organically linked with the Alliance and Justice. The three flow from the same spirit, 'nuances' in Gelin's[11] word, of the faith of Israel. For faithful Sion is the covenantal people, set apart as witnesses to Jahwe. They are those who, upright and irreproachable in their own lives, seek the justice of God. Consequently, they are the poor of Jahwe, his clients, trusting his promises, welcoming him, open and available to him, and humble before him.

Drawing from this rich matrix, the prayer, the songs, the hopes and the life Israel celebrate spiritual poverty as a main theme, a leitmotiv of covenental history. Each phase of the history of Israel drew a greater richness out of the seminal idea. Grelot[12] perceives three stages in its maturization: its germination in the covenental period from Exodus to the Prophets; its interiorization in the post-exilic and prophetic age; and Christ's reformulation and practice.

At the heart of the Alliance is God's literal promise

to bless Sion with material well-being if she remained faithful. Since the promise is made to a people and not to individuals, communal sharing of her material wealth is integral to Israel's faithfulness. Real poverty in her midst was considered a scandal. Sometime such poverty was viewed as divine retribution. So Job's friends chided him in his adversities. The more frequent theme was that the poverty of orphans, widows, and underprivileged bore witness to the failure of the rich to practice social justice and charity. Judges and prophets were scathing in their castigations, denouncing even kings to their faces. This obligation to share was thus a warning against the seductiveness of wealth. At the same time it implied that a moderate well-being, the mean between extravagance and destitution was the desirable standard for all. From the beginning, therefore, spiritual poverty was a theology, not of poverty, but of wealth.

The interiorization of poverty flowered during the era of Israel's subjugation, her exile and schism. In experiencing persecution the faithful, the Remnant of Israel, came to realize that the divine promises would not always and immediately be fulfilled. Thus forced to accept real poverty, the faithful interiorized poverty, abandoning themselves to God's will, silent under injustices and persecution, hoping in and humble before God. At the same time, their confidence that God's justice would eventually rectify their plight drew the people of God together in a union of hearts, helping each other in their needs thus encouraging one another with God's faithfulness to Sion. In this period Isaiah produced that most beautiful pre-figurement of Christ, the Suffering Servant, who by bearing the sins and suffering of others frees his people.

Christ, the incarnation of the Suffering Servant, added a new dimension to the interiorization of poverty, that of seeking and preferring poverty. While he simply accepted the socio-economic conditions of Jewish society, Christ's life was paean of praise to poverty. He was born in a stable in a strange town, grew up in obscurity, living the life of a village artisan, and on his mission he took whatever was offered him, water from a prostitute, a fine meal from a rich man, an ass from a stranger to make his triumphal entry into Jerusalem.

Yet he has nothing against the wealthy as such, counting many friends among the well-off. One consistent accusation against him is his consorting with publicans or tax-collectors, the group most hated by the Jews for their avariciousness. Indeed he blesses the household of Zachaeus and uses the figure of a publican as exemplar of true humility. But his teaching warns decisively and uncompromisingly against the seductiveness of wealth. Nowhere more so than in the four maledictions of St. Luke 6, 24-26: "Woe to you rich... Woe to you who have your fill now... Woe to you who laugh now... Woe to you of whom the world thinks well..." These echo repeatedly in the parables and comments about the rich and their undoing.

To the contrary he preaches the preferability of poverty. Do not worry about your shortcomings or even your material needs. For God will provide. Rather prefer seeking spiritual wealth to accumulating material goods. Sell all and give to the poor and come follow me. Take up your cross and follow me for I am meek and humble of heart.

The apostles and early Christians, according to Humbert[13], took Christ's words as applying to all and not to just the spiritual elite. All considered poverty, appropriate to their circumstances, as essential to salvation. Yet they did not surrender their property upon becoming Christians. The Jerusalem situation was unique, so far as we know. Yet even there the surrender of private possessions was voluntary not mandatory. Indeed the Jerusalem Church always seemed to have a peculiar burden of poverty, requiring the creation of the original ten deacons to dispense charity to the poor, and inducing St. Paul to beg constantly from the newly founded churches among the gentiles to help the brethren in Jerusalem.

While the apostolic Christians confirmed by their lives the goodness of material things, the appropriateness of private property, and the necessity of work as the way to economic sufficiency, they were wary of the passion for possessions heeding St. Paul's warning against unrestrained wanting. The ideal they held to was that of complete detachment, of using wealth as the caretaker of God's bounty. Wealth was for the good of all, a way to unite not to divide the community of men, a means by which each person could reach his full development as man and as Christian.

As a principle, the Spirit of Poverty, is integral to the Christian life and vision. At times it seems to languish only to revive freshly vigorous and contemporary. Each new flowering displayed another aspect of its attractiveness. The spirit of detachment from worldly goods and honor gave strength and nobility to the Christian martyrs. The desert hermits originally fled the urban turmoil, seeking freedom from worldly cares. Yet remarks Christopher Dawson, "It is a remarkable paradox that such a movement originating as a protest against culture and an escape from culture should become one of the characteristic institutions of Byzantine culture and later of Western Catholicism."[14]

Benedictine stability was founded on the vow of poverty. Yet from that vow and stability grew the great agricultural, cultural and charitable centers which dotted Europe. The Abbey of St. Germain de Pres in its glory days had the care and organization of 40,000 dependents.[15] Each renewal of the Benedictine Spirit, as with Cluny, Citeaux and Solesmes, was implemented by a flight to more primitive economic conditions and with the same results, economic growth and influence.

The son of an affluent merchant of Assissi revealed a new aspect of My Lady Poverty. Francis, wishing to imitate Christ in all things, literally stripped himself of his father's wealth, and embraced the joyful bohemianism of the begging brother, preaching the love of God and unconcern for worldly goods. This was an entirely new kind of dedicated poverty, a monk whose stability rested on having nothing at all of his own. Yet Franciscans were soon teaching on University faculties, founding hospitals, and setting up small-loan shops for the urban poor.

Ignatian poverty, though as severe as Franciscan, was more practical. Doing without was not seen as an end in itself, but in all things Jesuits were to live in an ordinary and contemporary manner. This practical poverty expressed concern for the economic well-being of primitive peoples, inspiring such experiments as the Paraguay Reductions. At the same time in Europe it was effecting an academic revolution.

Luther, Calvin, and Wesley went further in laicizing the spirit of poverty, holding it up as a practical idea for lay men. Much of the fervor for religious renewal and reform derived from this appeal to the urban poor. The Calvinist Layman's vocation, to work, to be sober, and to watch for the coming of the Lord, proved ingredients for a moderate kind of economic success and seemed to sanction it. However much this Protestant Ethic is maligned today, it did give a moral meaning to wealth accumulation when modern man was dizzied by the vision of increasing abundance.

This laicization of the spirit of poverty was not just pious cant but sparked real concern for the poor. Whatever exploitation is associated with the rise of capitalism and the industrial revolution, the modern era witnessed a vast extension in educational opportunities, a revolution in hospital care and the conquest of disease, the elimination of human slavery, and a tempering of the brutality with which prisoners and destitute were treated. Figures like Don Bosco in education, Vincent de Paul and Florence Nightingale in care of the sick, John Howard and Elizabeth Frye in prison reform, and Thomas Clarkson and William Wilberforce in abolishing slavery shine bright during the last two centuries. At the same time, however, the spirit of poverty was progressively secularized by the forces of individualism and nationalism. Reviewing briefly the steps in this declension is worthwhile just to highlight by contrast the gracefulness of true Christian poverty.

First Puritanism and its Catholic counterpart, Jansenism, cast a pall of bleakness over the life of virtue, including the spirit of poverty. Phrases like 'honest poverty' and 'laboring poor' became almost cant in excusing real sociological poverty. This played into the secularizing spirit of Utilitarianism which became the most effective social ethic, based on the principle that pain was bad and pleasure good. Thus welfare became a public obligation and charity a civic virture. Marx carried this secularization to the ultimate stage in that capitalist society itself necessarily created poverty and generated the increasing immizeration of the working class. His ideal Communism may be viewed as the coming into being of a completely secularized and universally lived spirit of poverty in which each contributes according to ability and shares according to need in a bountifully productive society.

By contrast, the pale pragmatism, which prevails in most non-Communist societies, has little power to inspire. Foreign aid to poor nations must be motivated by the hard criterion of national self-interest, exorcising all humanistic or humanitarian impulses. Community charity drives, truly marvelous social but non-governmental efforts, must be sold not on the basis that we are helping those most in need, but that we are helping ourselves. For the most part, however, charity today is a government function. Indeed few private charitable efforts can continue without government assistance. Above all we are urged to war against sociological poverty, not out of concern for others but because poverty breeds crime, disease, civil disaffection, and now, too many children. Poverty must be eradicated because its eradication now will cost less in the long run than remediating its effects. Where in this immense effort the true spirit of concern for others shines through, it is considered quixotic.

Granted that the last paragraph was drawn in bold strokes, the modern secularist is little prepared to see in the spirit of poverty those features which make it so attractive and necessary for an affluent people. They see it as an attitude condoning sociological poverty and not as a theology of wealth. For the secular mind is prone to despair not to hope. It cannot sing of wealthy America as Isaiah did of a Jerusalem, brought to its knees by schism, exile, and the loss of political freedom:

> Since the riches of the sea will flow to you,
> the wealth of the nations come to you;
>
> Camels in throngs will cover you,
> and dromedaries of Median and Ephah;
> everyone in Sheba will come,
> bringing gold and incense
> and singing the praise of Yahweh. (Isaiah 60, 5-6)

The history of the spirit of poverty in the heroic living of it by men and women in every age has successively revealed new aspects of its moral richness. The spirit of poverty is enobling of character, it insulates from worldly care, it provides an inner core of stability amid turmoil. It is joyful yet practical in doing good. It is for all men and women, each in his own way. It has eradicated some of the worst brutality which people have perpetrated on people.

Far from being harsh, joyless, and despairing, Christian poverty celebrates dependence upon a <u>bountiful</u> God, a God, above all, overflowing with spiritual riches but also with material wealth which both symbolizes and serves as means to these spiritual goods. In imitating the Divine bounty Christian poverty is open to the needs of others, for God is bountiful not only to his people but to all men, raining his mercies on the just and unjust alike. Consequently, the desire for material well-being is moderated, a mean between penury and extravagance, characterized primarily by a willingness to share by those who have in excess with those who lack. It goes beyond this in urging us to bear the burden of others' needs at the expense of our own.

Christian poverty requires detachment, a willingness to part with material goods when they stand in the way of a higher fulfillment or when helping others is more urgent than satisfying our own needs. But such detachment from wealth implies no denegation. For there is no virtue in detaching one's self from what is worthless or evil. At the same time it warns against the seductiveness of wealth, and of seeking more income and wealth. For this reason, it urges the preferability of poverty to wealth, of doing without to doing with, of not having to having. The spirit of poverty cannot exist where there is no real wanting. For those who have all they want can experience no sense of dependence upon a bountiful God; they have proven themselves impervious to the needs and deficiencies of others, and they are snugly content in possession of their wealth.

Yonick's conception of effective poverty summarizes with a cross-sectional cut the three features of spiritual poverty in its manifold manifestations. First, it views the paupers of this world, by this is meant anyone needing our material or spiritual help, as having a sacramental function, for in them we encounter Christ himself. Second, it implies a commitment to the divine will, whatever one's state of riches or deprivation, but cautious that care for the things of this world make such total commitment difficult. Lastly, effective poverty is not confined to "acts of charity" but is as all-embracing and creative as life itself. These features, sounded in their profundity, constitute spiritual poverty.[16]

This description of spiritual poverty, summarizing as it does Christ's own preaching and practice, starkly contrasts its spirit with the spirit of affluence. Their reconciliation, therefore, becomes the agenda for the rest of this chapter.

RECONCILIATION

In sweeping once again across the landscape of affluence, we should now be able to conclude that what the affluent most desperately need is a sense of stability and an orientation, a realization that just as people in the past found meaning to life despite their destitution, so affluent people can find meaning in their affluence. Consistently, the development of the preceding chapters urged toward the conclusions that only the spirit of poverty, as a deeply felt confidence in God, can calm the restlessness affluence produces, that only the spirit of poverty, as a mandate of concern for others, can both inspire and inform sharing our worldly goods with the poor and disadvantaged and thus fill the emptiness at the heart of affluence. Such considerations lend hope, like recollections in January of green fields and soft breezes, that affluent people can allay their anguish and find meaning in their abundance and from that meaning find peace of soul.

The answers, however neat, are neither simple nor simplistic. To the contrary, rather than solving anything they initiate a radical dialectic within one's most intimate affections. Confidently, patiently and intelligently followed wherever it may lead, this dialogue will not conclude to shunning industrial abundance as an unmitigated evil, nor to selfishly plucking its fruits whatever the consequences. It will conclude to neither of these simplistic answers but to the more tortuous and difficult one that abundance and affluence offers a new dimension for achieving a more human living. As such the answer is open-ended and the question never finally answerable. It begins a pilgrimage of which we only have the most general directions. Those directions can be analyzed according to the five critical features of affluence: as a principle generated by economic abundance, as an attitude implying social productivity, as a principle of gain-seeking, as a dynamic, and as causing scarcity.

Economic Abundance

Affluence, as a principle generated by economic abundance, means that the fear of destitution has been wiped out for much of mankind and extends a realistic hope to the rest of the world. The evils of affluence are largely due to its success and not to its failures.

Spiritual poverty has no qualms in celebrating this great human achievement. Unlike much secular wisdom which really suspects that material well-being demoralizes the generality of mankind, the spirit of poverty has always proclaimed the goodness of wealth as symbol and expression of the providence of a bountiful God.

Accepting affluence for the good that it is will banish that feeling of guilt about our abundance which seems to paralyze our willingness to share it with others. This does not imply a complacency about the exploitation, ugliness, and pollution industrial abundance has produced. Much less does it mean taking the material benefits of abundance for ourselves, oblivious that modern technology provides the means by which we can at last lift from people the dehumanizing burden of destitution.

Industrial growth, whatever its ill effects, marks an entirely new chapter in the story of mankind. For, however much destitution in the past was spiritualized by a stoic acceptance of God's providence or lovingly embraced by heroes of poverty for the sake of others, it is no longer acceptable as the lot of people. In barrios, in slums, and in primitive villages, people have seen economic abundance, and having seen it, are restless until they have it. The poor of the world have, so to speak, lost their primeval ignorance and innocence. As a consequence, where the means are perceived as possible, mass impoverishment has produced more human brutality and less love of others, more materialism and less liberality, more war and less peace. The possibilities of technology and economic abundance must belong to the substance of hope for a better world. In no way does this contravene the concept of God as a loving Father.

Social Productivity

Affluence is a function of social productivity to which all contribute and in which all must share. No one's economic success can be claimed as due exclusively to his own abilities, effort and skill. Honest and hardheaded appraisal of one's success reveals that much, if not most or all, was due simply to the fortuitousness of being in the right place at the right time, that one's success is importantly attributable as much to one's circumstances as to one's ability. That, in fact, we simply shared better than average in the general social productivity of the economy.

The spirit of poverty underlines this by reminding that the promise of material well-being was made to all of the Poor of Jahwe. Thus those who are well-off fulfill this promise by sharing with those less fortunate. As a consequence both extremes of extravagant wealth and destitution frustrate divine providence. In this, the spirit of poverty is in hearty accord with the secular wisdom that a nation, or for that matter a world, which is half rich and half poor is heading for disaster. To the contrary, a true love for the poor animates and warms the rationality of secular wisdom with a lively spirit of human and spiritual fellowship. It takes this obligation out of the realm of civic dutifulness and makes it a matter of personal charity.

For indeed the obligation of generosity is thrust upon affluent people. Will they or will they not, affluent people will be the instrument by which the surge of rising expectations, domestically and internationally, will be implemented. A sense of justice will corroborate this, for intuitively the just person will conclude that justice has not been realized where a part of the world is sated with goods and the greater part exists in dire need. A willingness to share fellowship with the little one's of God will urge a person to pledge that at least none shall starve, that national and international economic assistance will be supported and, if possible, one's own time and talent will be given.

Not so paradoxically these insights coincide with conclusions reached by hard-headed businessmen in search of profits. The inner thrust and drive of industrial development demands the opening of new markets, the involvement of a larger labor force, the elevating of human skills, and the thawing of the material hopelessness of the peoples of the world. Economic abundance cannot be self-centered and isolationist, it must be expansive and sharing. The lowest of reasons why affluence cannot survive in a sea of destitution is fear of the envy of the impoverished majority in the world. A more positive reason is that the dynamism of affluence demands expansion. The most exalted is concern for social justice and the mandates of Christian poverty.

A System Requiring Gain

Affluence, as motivating action, requires that men and women desire to gain. While this implies a certain service to acquisitiveness, affluence gives no clues whether such service is as to a master or to a servant. The whole thrust of this book has been to demonstrate that the ambiguity of secular wisdom today arises from a kind of enslavement to an affluence which more and more shows itself hollow and purposeless.

Seen in this light, the seeming contradiction between the acquisitiveness, premised in economic analysis, and the spirit of poverty is found to be a spurious problem. For economic self-interest lies entirely in the order of means, while theological poverty is primarily concerned with end or purpose. Consequently, there is no incompatibility between the two in practice. At the level of means, to participate in an abundant economy is to intend to gain. At the other level, the end and object of the religious impulse is not a niggardly but a lavish God. He, who provides for birds and animals so bountifully in their natural habitat, and is so carefree with the beauty of rocks and trees, of water, clouds, and light, does not begrudge man the hard-won rewards of his halting mastery over matter and energy, provided always people respect their own habitat with grateful care and are willing to share their abundance with others. To suppose otherwise, it would seem, strikes at the very essence of the spirit of poverty and especially at Christian poverty.

This insight will relax us on the treadmill of affluence. It can slow the pace of acquisition and purge us of the frenzy of getting. For though affluence requires gain-seeking and growth, as we have seen, it does not require a frenetic pace. It need not prevent our taking the time to derive more pleasure in each new thing as acquired, to savor a greater joy in helping others, to take more time in what benefits our family, neighborhood, business, church and the civic and cultural life of the city. We can come to the calming realization of how much we can do without, and yet, without skimping, lead a fuller life.

Affluence as a Dynamic

Affluence as a *dynamic* principle implies change and risk-taking. This dynamic guarantees place to no one, and the faster its pace the more traumatic becomes loss of place. The spontaneous response to this is insurance, and no age has witnessed a comparable growth and proliferation. Yet there are still great risks which cannot be covered by insurance and which are beyond personal control. When such disasters strike there is only the raw hope that another job, another career, other markets can be found. Conversely, much of our success is also fortuitous, being owed more to our stars than to ourselves. Pete Rose, whose annual income probably exceeds Ty Cobb's career earnings, would be silly to consider himself by that fact the better ball-player. In some final record book he may be listed ahead of the Georgia Peach, but his earning capacity is a function largely of his time in history.

The spirit of poverty, however, locates its trust not just in the economy but in God. It sees Providence, in Teilhard's beautiful words, "as brooding over the world in ceaseless effort to spare that world its bitter wounds and to bind up its hurts".[17] This is the final test of detachment. While respecting work, property, and gain as part of God's plan for human well-being, the spirit of poverty, in concern for transcendent well-being, takes what God gives humbly, confidently, and calmly.

This ontological humility before a God, now seen not as the Just Avenger but as Bountiful Father, will manifest itself in a calm confidence amid the vicissitudes of affluence. In this context the admonition to be "like the lilies of the field" loses its ironic overtones. For those words can no longer be used as text for an apathetic complacency at one's lot in life, and even less for the miserable lot of others. It can no longer serve as an opiate for the masses. For reliance on Divine Providence now affirms the trust that one can find the social and personal resources to surmount barriers, to recover from set-backs and to push quietly ahead, and implies the obligation to help others do the same.

Finally, the dynamics of affluence offer daily opportunities to bear the role, which seems so distasteful to those concerned about their rights, of the suffering servant. Change reverberates through a highly interdependent economy unequally and impersonally. Individual lives are drastically affected in ways beyond personal control or responsibility. There is little the individual can do about such inequity. One can bear it with equanimity or disgruntedly, but either way one becomes a suffering servant.

This can happen in a harrowingly personal way which forces one to put his Values on the line. For example, school administrators, public officials and realtors had little to do with the great migration which brought the negroes from the rural South to northern cities. Caught between the pressures of the blacks for equal rights and the fears of the prejudiced, they were forced into decisions in which they were damned if they did and damned if they did not. That these people refused the role of suffering servant, and each of us in our way, is attested by the meager achievements in opening housing, by the chaos in inner city schools, and by ghettos becoming almost human jungles.

But ordinary living provides no end of hard decisions which individuals are forced to make which drastically change the welfare of others. The family which must retrench to meet an astronomical medical expense or to develop a child's unusual talent is offered the opportunity to practice the spirit of poverty -- a calm confidence to find the means, a humble acceptance of the obligation and a real sacrifice of personal wants for the sake of others. All the more so, executive decisions involving the lives of thousands of people requires a motivation informed by something more than the calculation of immediate profit and loss, or the mere animal zest for struggle or self-glorification as tycoon. A university president faced with a declining budget, or a corporate executive, contemplating the need to shift resources from one division to another, can proceed in either of two ways. They can brush away with a callous unconcern the effect of the decision on the lives of their subordinates, or they can make sacrifices to mitigate the blows, hoping that doing the decent thing will eventually recoup its costs. In no way would a lively sense of spiritual poverty introduce the unreal, the maudlin, or the pollyannish into these hard decisions.

Such examples demonstrate that the spirit of poverty is effective in handling the ups and downs of daily life produced by affluence. Destitution, the bleak awareness that economic disaster lurks around every curve ahead, is obviously conducive to trusting in Divine Providence. But affluence is just as salutary. Peer into the frustrations of the affluent, their sense of insecurity and their feelings of transitoriness, and one finds conditions requisite for such humble trust. Examine the real nature of Christian poverty as a dependence on God and willingness to accept the role of suffering servant, and one finds the salt to savor economic abundance.

Affluence as Scarcity

The final note of affluence is scarcity: affluence heightens, it does not reduce scarcity. This is the most important linchpin between affluence and the spirit of poverty. A worldly prudence -- as the recent recession has forced many to do -- could come to an understanding that doing without is inherent in the affluent condition. If so, it would counsel patience in getting, that nothing worth having is without sacrifice, that there is no such thing as a free lunch. It will also concede the inevitability of poverty, because the dynamics of affluence measure out greater wealth and income to some and less to others. It will recognize that even if all incomes increased proportionately, at the same rate, smaller incomes would increase by an absolutely smaller amount than larger incomes.

Secular wisdom may concede all this, the scarcity and inevitable inequality. But it has no spiritual resources to stomach it. For some it will hold out the chimerical hope that more will be better, that more affluence will cure its ills. More frequently secular wisdom is accepting the radical critique, turning to an emasculated kind of Marxism, that it is preferable that all have less than that, even though all gain, some gain more than others. We recognize this for what it is: envy is at the root of the contemporary malaise with the very success of economic abundance.

Here spiritual poverty draws from the deepest well of Christ's mandate of the preferability of poverty to wealth. It counsels, flying seemingly in the face of affluence, that having less is actually having more. For the spirit of poverty knows the poverty that lies at the heart of plenty, which no amount of material goods can satisfy. In accepting that proliferation of material goods only increases dissatisfaction, the spirit of poverty seeks rather to relish what is had than dissipate yearnings on what is not.

But Christian poverty urges one step beyond. It says rejoice in the good fortune of others. It counsels all not only to accept the role of the suffering servant but to seek it and embrace it. It commands that we commit our abilities and our goods to the service of others and through them to God. It mandates this on all who would call themselves followers of Christ, maybe not in the heroic fashion with which it has flowered in Christianity from the martyrs to Mother Theresa, but nevertheless really and effectively in our everyday life.

Far from being the bleak spectre envisioned by secular wisdom or the opiate for human misery of Marxism, the spirit of poverty is really a theology of a bountiful God and of a loving Providence. As such it caps the effort in this first part of the book to develop a philosophy of the use and meaning of increasing material abundance. The affluent psyche, therefore, does not in itself deny the spirit of poverty. To the contrary it enables man to imitate that most conclusive manifestation of God's love for mankind -- his lavish generosity. Christian poverty, on the other hand, can not only tolerate increasing wealth but it alone can give it teleology and ultimate meaning. In the day to day discipline of living, it alone can prevent wealth from sucking man into a sybaritic search for pleasure, and post warnings against acquiring wealth for the power it gives over others, for the sheer animal joy of material success, or -- most senseless of all -- for the mere sake of accumulation itself. The spirit of poverty alone can fill the ontological poverty at the heart of affluence. It alone can give meaning in the radical frustration affluence generates. It alone can answer the inevitable disillusion: "Now that I have so much, what good is it to me -- or to anyone else?"

With this we conclude Part I which introduced the affluent attitude as a principle of human behavior, set in motion by the experience of economic abundance and playing a decisive role in continuously modifying the multi-dimensional web of economic relations. Using the insight into the Value-utility as both a determinant of economic values and a mean to other Values, we examined the impact of the affluent attitude on Value and character formation. More importantly, we saw that raising our Value sights became an essential third dimension in moderating our sensual and wealth appetites, and that social justice in considering what we owe to others as social beings and to the human community opened a vast area where both self-interest and concern for others could find scope. Finally, we concluded that the transcendent dimension given by the principle of spiritual poverty could alone give this effort an ultimate meaning.

You may find the schema concluding this chapter helpful in sorting out and summarizing these relationships. But this first Part will fail in its purpose if you only perceive it as an intellectual exercise. For its purpose was to help you form an attitude and to develop a sensitivity, that affluence posed particular moral dangers and thus needed a moral response specific to them.

On the other hand, do not feel you have failed if you cannot buy all that was presented. Your moral life is unique: you come from a unique background, your approach is unique, your problems are unique, and your growth and development are unique. You cannot possibly agree with everything I say. Should only one idea strike you as significant, that is enough to begin moral growth. Nurture it, explore its implications, make it a principle of your actions, it has power to transform your entire attitude. For all that was discussed forms an organic unity -- and if it had been well done, this would be apparent -- so that you can achieve the whole, given good will and time, by coming at it from any one aspect.

Your moral life is like your biological life: key events _reveal_ that you have grown (or grown old) but real growth occurs quietly, microscopically. Life is but a concatenation of minutiae which only all together have tremendous significance.

SCHEMA OF PART ONE

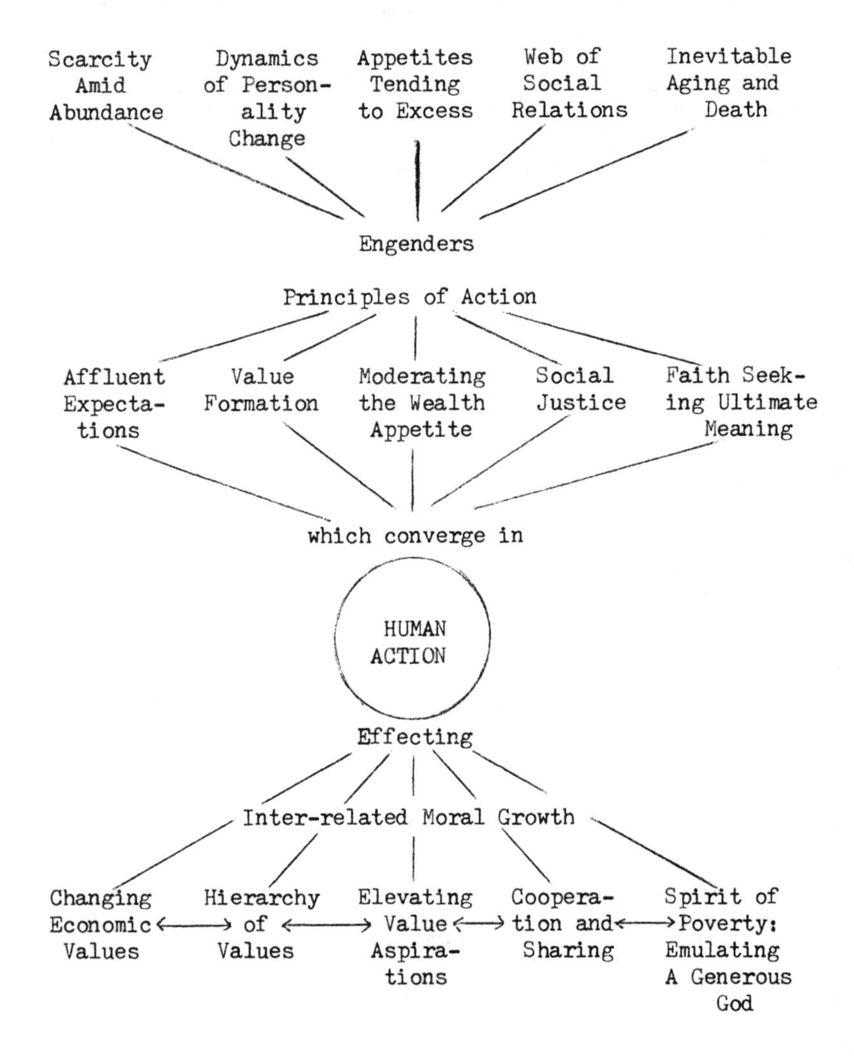

CHAPTER SEVEN

THE CORPORATE AGGREGATE AS SOCIAL INSTITUTION

Harmonizing the principles which are the ingredients of a right attitude to affluence is an essential preliminary. But they must be put to the test of reality, for conscience is formed by personal convictions encountering the world as it is. A right conscience regarding affluence then must be shaped in struggling with precisely those elements of our industrial society which differentiate it as an economy of abundance. This is the task of the second part of An Ethics for the Affluent.

No claim is made here that the features discussed are all-inclusive, nor apologies offered that they are not. The hope is that those chosen are sufficiently broad to provide a sweeping vision across the landscape of affluence. Nor is it claimed that the statements of the problems and the solutions proferred are definitive. Where the pace of change is so rapid, any insight makes but one comment in a continuous effort to bring principles face to face with reality.

The most prominent feature of an abundant economy is the corporate aggregate, those huge industrial, commercial and financial complexes which are the founts of material abundance. Chapter Seven examines them as systems of social power, of social productivity and of social property. Such institutions, social yet private, require a form of wealth which is a contractual claim to future income. Hence, credit-debt pervades the economy, becoming both its most serviceable kind of wealth and its means of exchange, its money. This phenomenon with its moral implications is explored in Chapter Eight. In logical sequence, the principles and techniques for sharing social productivity are the subject of Chapter Nine.

Just as the corporate giants concentrate enormous economic power, so too power coalesces in labor unions, government agencies and non-profit institutions. In view of such institutional power preserving personal freedom and responsibility becomes of paramount importance. This is probed in Chapter Ten. From this there is but a step to considering in Chapter Eleven the role of the individual as citizen and economic participant in the interplay between Big Business and Big Government in the Mixed Economy. The concluding chapter by exploring the interface between economics and ethics in action will tie all together and will set the students on the life-long adventure of integrating their economic ambitions with their moral aspirations.

We begin then by examining the large corporate aggregate, this chapter's purpose being to achieve a balanced view of this institution which is distinctive of an abundant economy. Because these huge productive aggregates touch everyone's life constantly and at many levels, as consumers, as employees, as suppliers, as managers, and as civil servants and public officials, one's attitude toward them becomes the emotional touchstone of one's attitude toward the economic system itself. Those who are most disaffected with the market, the free-enterprise, system are at root fearful and distrustful of the large corporation. Moreover, since they benefit from the material bounty of corporate aggregates which they are reluctant to surrender, their ambivalence extends to an ambivalence about affluence itself. The student can engage in no more useful exercise to clarify his own attitude to the world he will enter than to appraise calmly and objectively both the dangers and the benefits the corporate aggregate poses for society.

THE CORPORATE AGGREGATE

While our gaze will center on the large commercial, financial, and industrial corporations listed in the *Fortune 500* which together form the skyline of American business, some other landmarks should be kept in mind for perspective. These giants are already being crowded by hospitals, universities, research institutions, state and federal agencies, and professional organizations. In fact, they are dwarfed by several federal bureaucracies both in budget and employees. Nor has their size destroyed the vitality of small businesses. According to Neil Jacoby, "Small companies hold an important position in the U.S. economy. It is a serious error to assert that giant corporations 'characterize' or serve as 'prototypes' for American business and that medium and small companies are transient institutions that will ultimately vanish."[1] Nevertheless, these corporate giants are awesome. Their annual sales are greater than the national product of most nations. Literally millions of families depend on them for income as employees, as suppliers, as retailers of their product, or as stockholders or creditors. While no one of them accounts for as much as 1% of the U.S. gross national product, altogether they are the principal fountainhead of economic abundance.

Allis-Chalmers Corporation

Among these giants of the corporate world, Allis-Chalmers Corporation is only a mini-giant. In fact, it is practically unknown to most Americans. For this company, which has been described as one of the world's largest machine shops, has no product, other than its Simplicity line, which directly services consumer wants. Yet so wide is its range of products in materials processing, in agriculture, in electrical products, materials handling, and power generation and transmission that it is impossible to imagine a household in the United States which has not indirectly benefited from Allis-Chalmers' equipment.[2]

Despite this, its assets of $1.5 billions and annual sales of $1.7 billions ranks it only 164th in the Fortune 500 list of industrials. Still its 33,000 employees and 30,000 stockholders would fill a good-sized football stadium. It operates over 35 manufacturing plants in the U.S. and another 25 throughout the world. Its network of over 3,000 dealers and 10,000 suppliers ramifies its economic effect throughout the United States, Canada, Australia and indeed the world. It runs joint ventures with both Fiat of Italy and Siemens of Germany.

Yet this widely-flung but integrated system has no dominant owner or ownership group. For the largest individual shareholder owns about 1% of its 13,600,000 outstanding shares. The top corporate officials together own about .5% and all other employees another 1%. Of its $76 millions of net income in 1978, $18.7 was distributed as dividends and $57.3 retained in the company. Total taxes paid exceeded $60 millions and its annual payroll approaches $.5 billions, including a wide variety of fringe benefits.

Although Allis-Chalmers Corporation would be dwarfed next to Exxon or General Motors, nevertheless, its economic impact is woven into the fabric of the U.S. economy. More symbolically important, its philanthropic functions demonstrate that its corporate officers conceive the company as having a deeper social role. Besides encouraging employees' participation in civic activities and assisting them to further their education, the company has a wholly owned subsidiary, Allis-Chalmers Foundation, Inc., which dispenses between 3/4-1% of company earnings before taxes -- an amount close to the national average -- in a wide range of community welfare programs, the United Fund, Boys Club, Scouts,

Junior Achievement and the like. It helps independent college associations and awards matching-grant scholarships to children of employees. It provides health and hospital support in cities of Allis-Chalmer plants. In all this it follows a national pattern. It was unusual in pioneering a program to combat and cure industrial alcoholism.

While the history of Allis-Chalmers over 130 years is a fascinating story of far-sighted applications of engineering principles and of growth both internal and through acquisitions to implement these insights, its story would probably only provide a footnote in the history of U.S. industrial development. That illustrates the fact that each of the corporate giants has its own history, its own development, and consequently a unique organizational format and purpose. Each has its particular impact on the U.S. economy. There is, consequently, no stereotype which fits them all.

History of Capital Aggregation

Yet there is one common note to all such corporate aggregates, which is the ability to accumulate and organize large amounts of capital. The genesis of this feature can be traced to the Medieval trading partnership. Merchants organized such consortiums to trade at the great fairs or to equip ships for foreign trade. Initially temporary, they gradually acquired permanence as the trading corporation of the town. They often served as both town council and chamber of commerce. They were in fact a kind of exclusive partnership, limiting members to those who were acceptable to other members, who were willing to abide by corporation regulations, and were able to buy into it. Completely natural to the Medieval commercial spirit, they were amazingly varied. Some like the Hanseatic League became international in scope with trading stations throughout the North Sea.[3]

With the growth of nationalism and the re-opening of trade with the Far East and with the New World, merchants formed Merchant Adventurers companies which obtained patents of monopoly, royal charters granting exclusive trading privileges in a particular area. They became immensely wealthy, owning fleets, depots, warehouses. Some like the English joint-stock companies became in fact the English government in the lands under their sway. The English East India Company waged war, signed treaties, maintained an army, set up a training school for its employees and established a civil service. Company policy became English foreign policy as it related to India. Robert Clive could not distinguish between his concern for the Company's interests and his conception of Britain's imperial policy.[4]

Although Company stock was sold on the exchange, the East India Company and other chartered companies retained many of the aspects of a partnership. Indeed the Company probably demonstrates the limits of viability of the partnership form. Like the dinosaur, the partnership outgrew its environment and survives now mainly in less unweildy and imposing form. Nevertheless, the trading company demonstrates one characteristic of large capital accumulations: even though private property, they are fraught with public responsibility. The trading company was a public institution in its effect on the lives and income of so many people, in its impact on the country, and in its influence on government policy.

Transmutation, as often happens in the evolutionary process, did not occur in such companies. Free trade killed their exclusive trading rights; imperialism their governmental functions. In fact, the principle of incorporation, that the corporation enjoyed a legal existence apart from the real existence of its owners, was first applied in this country in the famous Dartmouth College case of 1819 to a non-profit organization. But as a business principle it took roots more rapidly in manufacturing than in trade. For there the technological revolution in requiring the integration of manufacturing processes called for larger and larger outlays of capital. Incorporation became an ideal way of raising capital without diluting control. Corporate entrepeneurs were abetted in this by states' vying to pass easier and simpler laws of incorporation. With the outlawing of the trust and cartel and the courts' ambivalence about bigness, corporate acquisitions and mergers became the only viable method for quantum leaps in growth. In 1901 the first corporate super-giant was formed with the merger of Carnegie Steel Company and several smaller companies around Pittsburgh with a capitalization of $100 millions. While only modestly large by today's standards, United States Steel began the era of the corporate aggregate.

The Role of the Corporate Aggregate

Keeping in mind the continued vitality of small and medium businesses and the huge governmental agencies, nevertheless, we can agree with the general perception that the large corporate aggregate plays an overwhelmingly important role in the economic well-being of the country. The 200 largest corporations own more than 25% of the income-producing national wealth and the 500 largest industrial corporations have more than 50% of manufacturing and mining sales.

Yet their bigness does not guarantee a permanent place at the top. What happened to Studebaker, A and P, Montgomery Ward and the New York Central can happen to other corporate giants. The largest firms, concludes Scherer, retain their position by "a willingness to adopt new product lines" or "by becoming more diversified, hedging against shifts in demand."[5] That is, a large company can survive only by being able and its corporate management being willing to service a mass market, both of which demand enormous capital resources to change production and to risk in new products. Big business is big because it can marshall large amounts of capital. It will yield to government enterprise when even a consortium of the wealthiest companies cannot risk the capital a venture demands, for example, mining the oceans or colonizing space.

For our generation at least the corporate aggregate will continue to produce the product, provide the jobs, amass the capital which an abundant economy requires. They can best utilize the mass production technology needed to service such an economy. As such then we must learn to live with them, not allowing them to tyrannize us but at the same time respecting the benefits they bestow. And if they must be modified, changed, or tamed even, these changes must accord with what they are. That is, they are systems of economic power, they are systems of social production, and they are complexes of social property. These aspects we shall now analyze, starting with the last which is the most fundamental.

A THEORY OF PROPERTY

The term 'private property' is used so confusedly in conversation that, like a tangled fuse-box, it generates more heat than light. A basic cause of this confusion is forgetting that no two kinds of property have the same degree of privateness. A simple comparison can help guide our discussion. An automobile is not private property in the same sense as a pair of socks. For not only must an automobile use public roads and parking but it is subject to much more public regulation, even to being comandeered for public use. Socks are such an intimate apparel that they have practically no public function. To talk as if each is mine in exactly the same sense is false and confusing.

To disentangle the confusion and more particularly to define the corporation as property, we must begin with some basic realities as expressed in the terms, dominion, possession and property.

Dominion, Possession and Property

Dominion is the exercise of power over something or someone. One who dominates another effects or affects what another is or should be. Dominion then is dynamic. While it may leave a permanent mark or impress on that which is dominated, dominion strictly speaking ceases when the act affecting the being or purpose of another ceases. Only God, the Infinite Being, exercises absolute dominion because he not only continuously sustains the existence and orients the purpose of his creatures but he in turn is in no way affected by this exercise. Human dominion, to the contrary, is not only intermittent but mutual. In the dominion of one person over another, even in that most complete dominion of parent over child, the dominator has no absolute but only a delegated and limited authority. Moreover, the dominated can assert his own good and thus react upon and change the exercise of authority. That is why most children have two parents, to even the odds between dominators and dominated.

Man's dominion over material things is somewhat different. Like divine dominion it is absolute in the sense that man gives ultimate direction and purpose to material things. It is spasmodic like personal dominion in that it ceases when a man stops exercising purpose, and mutual in that even material things react upon its user. Man's dominion over material things is not without a struggle. For all things, even those which have no free will, resist changing from what they are, animals more so than plants and plants more so than minerals.

Domestication, man's dominion over lower creatures, is not only for his own good, but in freeing their latent potentialities for their good. A dog in its wild state has no other purpose than to survive, to produce other dogs and to be food for stronger animals. It acquires a higher, an almost human, purpose when it is domesticated. It is taught to herd sheep, to guard children, to hunt, to guide the blind. Under man's tutelage it becomes faster, stronger, healthier, more cunning, intelligent and brave than its wild brother. Far from being unnatural, domestication gives meaning and purpose to non-human things. Destroying or mutilating things for no or trivial reasons, therefore, is wrong not so much because they are abused but because in some way they are rendered useless to other men. Our reaction, for example, to the silly sentimentality of clothing dogs in cashmere (while little children are without jackets) is basically of the same kind: it abuses the dog by changing its natural relationship to man.

Further, man is absolutely dependent upon this domestication, this refining of natural things to serve his purposes. As an embodied intelligence he must use things by giving them purpose. Domestication then bestows dominion. One who fashions a hatchet from wood and stone dominates the wood and stone by giving them purpose and use. The wild horse broken to the saddle or carriage belongs to his conqueror and master.

Such dominion is called possession. Natural things belong to him who has appropriated them for his own use, or acquired them from another. Such dominion is never permanent. Since man is not the cause of the stone and wood but only of its shape and function, his dominion lapses when his agency and purpose lapses. A piece of stone became a statue when Rodin shaped it to his design. Should this be effaced it reverts to a piece of stone. It is no longer Rodin's since he has ceased to exercise purpose over it. Should he sell it or give it away, his original purpose, while remaining, becomes subordinate to that of the new owner.

The power of possession then is not the power to abuse things, nor in the strictest sense not to use them. It is the power to have for use. Such use might mean destroying them, as a man by eating destroys his cow, or it might entail laying it aside for eventual or future use. To possess things we need not use them continuously, otherwise we are possessed by them. We need not keep them always at hand but only accessible to our claims upon them.

Such possession is absolutely essential to man's purposes but more importantly it gives him a place of reference in the material universe. Man is at home where his possessions are. This is the root sense of property, the material things appropriated by and proper to a man. In a real sense man cannot be deprived of all possessions for his ashes at least claim some resting place. But short of this, to deprive him of material things is to destroy him. This is the paradox of the human condition: man who comes with nothing and leaves with nothing and can absolutely speaking call nothing his own, must be surrounded at all times by a vast array of material possessions in order to live like a man. God, on the other hand, who has absolute dominion over all things, needs nothing. Half the world's woes and strife is distilled in this paradox.

Its obvious resolution is that God, the master of all, destined material things for man's use, not to this man or that, not to men of this age only, but to all men of all ages. No man, no group of men can deprive other men of possessions necessary for survival and human existence; no generation can disinherit succeeding generations. Men are not simply caretakers of the material world. They can and must use material things and in so doing must destroy some of them. They are rather tenants of an estate which they enter with nothing and leave with nothing, but in between enjoy its reasonable use. However they have improved or destroyed the estate, it will eventually pass on to others.

The Paradox of Property

From these trite and elementary observations two conclusions, both of profound importance yet almost contradictory of each other, are forced upon us. God as the absolute owner of the material universe has destined it for the benefit of all men. Individuals by the right of dominion can at best possess things temporarily. On the other hand, to benefit from the material universe men must enjoy material things individually, and things to be used must be used individually. The resolution is all but forced upon us: inherent in material possessions, is both a principle of communality and a principle of individuality. Benefit must be common, use individual.

This paradox is deepened when it is looked at from the side of the material thing. For a thing can be used by many and yet only by one. It can be used by many, for nothing is inevitably and ineluctably destined for one particular man. There is no inevitability that I or the socks I wear should exist. Granted that I and socks do exist, there is nothing about these socks which destined them for me. Thousands of men of my size of foot could wear them with equal comfort and convenience. But still the socks can only be worn by one man at a time. Nothing can be reduced to human use unless it is used by an individual. A particular vista in a public park in the morning sun can only be enjoyed by me, for only I can stand on this spot on this morning. No one has nor will behold exactly the same thing. All the more is this true of things privately owned. This can of beer can be drunk by only one man at a time. This automobile driven by only one driver -- a fact some wives forget!

Since nothing in nature, neither of things nor of men, inevitably destines this thing for this man, to use material things paradoxically demands their being separated and divided into yours and mine. Since nature offers no guide toward resolving this paradox, men must agree to share by dividing up material things. This is the conclusion of profound importance: the problem of distribution cannot be solved automatically; men must work out agreements and conventions to achieve common benefit through individual possession.

Such agreements and conventions are expressed through the laws, customs and practices of a people. However sanctified by tradition and ingrained in the fibers of society, such customs are always conventions, particular human determinations to solve a problem. They are never absolute but always relative to human need. Hence, they can always be criticized and modified to better meet changing needs. Such criticism and modifications must satisfy three standards: <u>community of benefit</u>, <u>individualized use</u>, and what flows from the two, some <u>stability in the right to use</u>, having things available even when not in use. These criteria at the same time are the characteristics for categorizing what kind of property a particular material possession is. Each criterion deserves a little expansion.

The material universe must support the needs of all men, minimally, that no man is deprived of subsistence and, ideally, that every man have that amount of possessions so that he and his family can live decently according to prevailing social standards and the current level of affluence. To do this, individual goods must be made available to individual men. Men must truly have the use of things and the right to use them. Not only must community possessions be made available to all and not reserved for the few, but private possessions must not be accumulated senselessly in kinds and amounts which the possessor could never use. (Clothes which are never worn and household furnishing never used while others wear rags and live in hovels bear witness to an infantile love of possessions for their own sake. Such people are like little children who cannot go to bed without their "bunkie".) Finally, a man should enjoy a certain stability in his possessions. That possessions are intended for use does not imply constant or even daily use, but only reasonable expectation of future use. For stable personal and family living a great array of things must be accessible and available to be really useful. They must be at hand when needed or the need is never met.

Public or Private Property

The broad classification of possessions into community ownership and private ownership, however useful, should never obscure the fact that all property is simultaneously common and individual. The distinction in a particular case can only mean that one or the other feature is prominent. The most cursory glance over the range of normal possessions reveals this blend of the two, displaying a continuous spectrum from the most intimate private possession to the most public national monument. A suit and an automobile are both private, but it is not likely thata suit would be commandeered for military or civic use. A home and a shop are both private property but the latter is subject to more regulation because it is more accessible to the public. A highway and an official limousine are both public property, but the extent of their public use is drastically different. Loose categorizing of everything into public and private distorts honest and correct thinking. Everything must be assessed on the basis of what it is and how used.

Everything, too, must implement the three objectives of property. Private property seems better adapted to fulfilling the objective of individualized use and stability but not community benefit. But this is only seeming. For just as a man's most private acts are social, so his intimate possessions, the food he eats, the clothes he wears, the TV he watches, must be socially useful. Individual enjoyment cannot be divorced from the social good of becoming a better spouse and father, a more effective business associate, and a more perceptive citizen. Indeed social reasons may be more compelling than personal, as is the case of the dress and appearance of prominent people who are expected to be elegant.

Public property, on the other hand, must be adapted to individual and relatively stable use. National forests, while preserved as forests, must be made available to all to whom they belong. Restriction on their use cannot be subject to the caprice of officiousness. The limousine, which guards and presents the President, must be adapted to his personal requirements. The congressman, out of favor with the administration, cannot be deprived of office space in the congressional mausoleum. Driving on national highways cannot be denied owners of foreign imports. All property, public and private, must realize all three objectives to be truly and validly property.

This will undoubtedly upset cozy patterns of thinking but it alone reflects reality. So much is written on the sacred right of private property and the dangers of creeping socialism that the necessity of looking at each form of property to determine its precise blend of public and private cannot be stressed adequately or often enough. To cry "Socialism" every time a new regulation is passed affecting property which bears some burden of the public good has become almost a conditioned reflex in certain business circles. Too frequently those who bewail most the erosion of private property are mute when laws are passed which invade the privacy of the home and the intimacy of the family.

There are arguments and very strong ones for preserving as much property in private hands and subject to private decisions. Private property promotes peace and order, since the lines separating my things from yours are clearly drawn and enforceable by law. Private property promotes industry and efficiency since a man will normally work his own goods more diligently and keep them more carefully than what belongs to others or to all. For his diligence is immediately rewarded in his property and his carelessness immediately punished.[6] But none of these arguments adds up to an unconditional right to private property, to its use, non-use and abuse to the harm and deprivation of others. All are on the level of practical wisdom, convenient and efficient ways of achieving general benefit through individual use.

None of these arguments eliminates the need to judge in a practical way whether public or private administration of a particular kind of property is most socially beneficial. Appeals to extreme ideological positions, total abolishment of private property or the absolute right of private property, render such judgment impossible. Nevertheless, a tension between the two poles of public and private inheres in every material good. Debate between those who are concerned more about social benefit and those who care more for private use is good and implies a healthy scrutiny of particular types of property. Too frequently the fear of stirring an ideological hornets' nest has prevented objective appraisal of whether a public program could more efficiently revert back to private administration, or whether a private business could benefit from more public assistance and control.

Finally, arguing from such ideological position obscured the real scandal of property, both public and private. This is refusal to share an unused surplus. In the presence of economic scarcity such surpluses necessarily deprive others of economic benefit. While more frequently appearing as private wealth they exist in communal property as well. Here, however, they are camouflaged as the peculation of private suppliers and the corruption of public officials. For both the bribe-taker and the fraudulent contractor divert public funds to private use. Even when the amounts are smaller, the crime is greater since they steal from the common patrimony.

The dialectic between the principles of dominion and the modes of possession produce the amazing variety of property rights. Dominion may be either public or private, and property in the private domain may range from the intimately personal to the social. What is actually possessed may be an animate or inanimate thing, or may be a right to its use or to the income from it. Benefit from property rights may be almost exclusively individual or may in varying degrees be shared in by others. The purpose of property may be for consumption or for production, and its intended use may be immediate, like a bowl of strawberries and cream, or for a life-time, like a lawyer's library, or for future generations, like a family estate or a country's mineral wealth. Ideological mind-sets, casting all property into the rigid molds of public or private, radically impairs the ability to see a given property right as it really is with all its nuances of dominion and possession.

With these preliminaries we are better prepared for a hard look at the most important type of property in an economy of abundance, the large corporate aggregate. From this we determine to what extent the general public sanctions and accepts it as a complex of social property, as a system of social production and as a system of social power.

CORPORATE SANCTIONS

The basic sanction enjoyed by corporations is incorporation itself which has been legitimized by law and accepted in practice. Because by incorporation a business acquires legal personality and enjoys perpetuity, and its stockholders are protected by limited liability, the corporation becomes in a unique way a public thing. For this reason the large corporate complex is best described as social property.

Legal Personality, Perpetuity and Limited Liability

Of the three legal personality is fundamental. The corporation is recognized as having certain rights of citizenship: it can sue and be sued; it can be convicted of crimes and forced to pay taxes; it can enter into contracts; it can own and dispose of property. Allis-Chalmers Corporation does not really exist, except in the eyes of the law. What does exist is a complex of buildings, machinery and inventory, and, more pertinent to this point, a group of people who make decisions and 'act' in the name of the corporation. Their decisions, literally affecting the entire economy, are reached by a process to which outsiders are not privy. These men and women, who enjoy economic power that would make Caesar envious, remain all but anonymous. Their actions, whether wise or woeful, are attributed to the corporation. Even their misdeeds, unless their personal responsibility can be proven in court, are by and large covered by the corporation.

On the other hand, such legal anonymity frees corporate officers from legal harassment which would make corporate decisions impossible. In a vast and complicated enterprise demanding millions of decisions daily, involving the income and material well-being of millions of people, that corporation executives should be held personally responsible would be incredible. No man's will or fortune would be adequate to the challenge. This would be like holding the President of the United States accountable every time a top-sergeant maltreated a mule.

Legal personality then, while a boon for business

enterprise, makes the corporation peculiarly a creature of the law. And what law has created, law can destroy. Such dependence upon public legislation removes the corporation as a piece of property from all other kinds of private property and invests it with a public character. The law's recognition of my automobile as a licensed vehicle did not cause it to be, but the law's recognition of General Motors did bring it into being.

Perpetuity is a natural consequence of legal personality. Just as a corporation's legal life is distinct from that of its owners and managers, so its existence in law is not dependent upon any one's or any group's continuing as owner or manager. That is, the corporation maintains its legal identity through ownership and management changes. This further implies that while stockholders own the corporation, the corporation itself owns the assets. Thus a manager, whose stock holdings may be quite modest, will have more to say about the disposition of corporate property than a stockholder whose invested millions do not constitute a controlling interest.

On the other hand, stockholders are not saddled with the corporation. If they sell their holdings they can do so without putting the entire business up for sale. Historically what has resulted is the transformation of the stockholder in the very large corporations from ultimate sources of authority over directors and managers, to an uninformed and unweildy rubber-stamp, and finally to, in many instances, a positive embarrassment and nuisance to the executive team.

The final effect of incorporation, limited liability, is best known because of its dramatic influence on capital accumulation. Since stockholders or corporations bear financial responsibility only to the extent of their original investment, preserving the rest of their estate from attachment in the event of company bankruptcy, great numbers of people can be induced to buy stock and immense sums of capital invested.

But at the same time limited liability attenuates ownership for it shifts part of the risk of enterprise from the legally recognized owners to an heterogeneous group of corporation creditors, including not only bond-holders and creditor banks, but employees who may be owed back wages and pension rights, suppliers of material on credit, retailers who have committed investment in order to sell the corporation's product, and even governments to whom taxes are due. In a very real way corporate bankruptcy shifts risk onto the entire economy. As a consequence, corporate executives are responsible not only to stockholders but to this wider circle of interested parties.

Thus limited liability has gradually eroded not only the stockholders' effective ownership but their sense of ownership. The overwhelming majority of stockholders in the largest corporations cannot acquire the knowledge nor have the inclination to exercise ownership-decision. Their psychology is little different from bondholders concerned principally about return and market value of their securities.

Whatever the legal definition of corporation ownership, the reality is that stockholders are only one of many groups which has an interest in the large corporate aggregate. This conclusion strikes at the root of the myth that these institutions are private property in any accepted sense. They are indeed so involved with the good of the entire economy that an entirely new category of property is called for. The term, social property, neither governmental nor strictly private, best describes reality.

Social Property

The term cannot be applied to all forms of incorporation. For in our legalistic society incorporation has become the most convenient form of organizing many diverse types of properties. It would apply to some of these like churches, schools, religious committees, fraternal societies and philanthropic foundations because of their strong social character. To others like the incorporation of an individual or the incorporation of a small or medium-sized business in which a discernible stockholder group exercises ownership, the term would not be applicable.

Wherever the line might be drawn, the idea clearly fits the corporate super-giants who in terms of annual payroll, annual production, annual investment, taxes paid, and dividends distributed set the tone of the economy and whose collective health or malaise determines the prosperity or depression of general business. They are sanctioned by law and popular acceptance as social property.

Social Productivity

The sanction of corporations as social property anticipates their popular legitimation as immensely productive social property. Enough has been said here and there throughout the book simply to mention that large corporations, by socializing production, have tremendously increased output. By organizing vast complexes of men and machines and capital, they service the wants of mass market profligately. Without disparaging the productiveness of American agriculture, the importance of smaller business, or the role of government agencies, we can affirm that the industrial, financial, and marketing giants are essential to our affluent well-being. _And we accept them because they are._ Because some may hanker for the simpler life before the Generals, General Motors, General Electric, General Dynamics and the like, an analogy may help make the point.

One of the most perceptive students of the modern corporation, Adolph Berle, has developed in his _The Twentieth Century Capitalist Revolution_,[7] a useful comparison between the super-corporation today and the great feudal baronies of the early Middle Ages. Like the dukes, earls and margraves of that age the modern corporation is a popular institution. Both were founded on principles fundamental to the social organization of their times -- the contemporary industrial giant on the principle of legal incorporation, the Medieval barony on the principle of investiture. (Incorporation we have already seen. Investiture was the recognition by the suzerain of his vassal's hereditary rights of sovereignty over a fief in exchange for a vow of personal fealty and loyalty.)

Both were responses to the needs of their age: the modern corporation to harness the productive potential of the scientific revolution; the feudal system to organize defense in a beleagured Europe and to maintain some balance of power against internal rapaciousness. Both delivered on their promises. The 20th Century corporation is the great engine of affluence. The proof surrounds us, our tables burdened with food, our sumptuous automobiles, our inexpensive mass entertainment. Less understood is the civilizing influence of feudalism. Enough is said in stating that it saved Europe from barbarism; it settled agriculture, pushed back the wilderness, organized colonization; and despite internal feuding withstood external aggression and maintained sufficient law and order that trade could grow, towns develop and the civilizing mission of the Church have scope.

Both were natural in that they display, despite a basic uniformity, the diversity in structure and style of natural things. Each baronial house developed a tradition of its own, reflecting and conditioning provincial differences which persist today. This is illustrated vividly in the women of such families who, even those from rival houses, displayed the most ferocious loyalty in defense of the feudal rights and prerogatives of the family into which they married.[8] The same differentiation is occuring amongst modern corporations, reflecting the firm's technology and markets, the philosophy of founders and the competitive conditions in the industry. Executives, even those wooed from rivals, are expected to display total identity of fortune and interest with their corporation. Such identification leaves its mark on the style and address of corporate officers. There is a subtle but real difference about an IBM man or a General Electric man.

Ethic

The result for feudalism was the evolution of an ethic of *noblisse oblige*. Though tenuous and frequently violated, the obligations of knighthood were taken seriously. Men swore by it and took pride, even in those rude times, in living up to its obligations. So too corporate executives are conscious of social responsibility, however individuals might publicly dispute this to preserve the fiction of private property. They are aware how the outpouring of corporate production affects every part of the economy and how corporation style sets national style and establishes the material conditions of life. Willingness to take Washington assignments at great personal loss, a sense of statesmanship about investment, a touchiness about public relations and corporate image, acceptance, even if reluctant, of unions and collective bargaining, and most recently admission of government intervention as necessary for economic stability and growth, all attest to a growing sense of corporate ethics.

Whatever hypocrisy might lurk behind it, the shock expressed at the revelation of executive malfeasance points to an unconscious fostering of the business image as one of fàir-dealing, efficiency and probity. Everyone is aware that businessmen are human and faced with great temptations. The very fostering of such an image, therefore, indicates a move toward an ethic expressing awareness of the possession of great economic power and a responsibility to use it well.

Corporate Professionalism

However cynicism or skepticism might dispute the development of a corporation's ethics, it is universally agreed that the modern executive has become a professional business manager. They are recruited from universities and colleges, trained in all phases of the corporate processes, and encouraged to take advanced degrees. They mature in anonymity, removed from the eye of the public and stockholders both. Their handling of responsibility and authority earns promotion when noted by higher executives in their own or other companies. They are loyal, though not committed, to their company. Their hallmarks are discretion, efficiency, hard work, interest in their jobs and a quiet enthusiasm for command. They are generally pleased with the economic rewards. Advancement depends much upon their getting and making the most of breaks and a willingness to sacrifice personal interests for the sake of their job. Wheeler-dealers may vault into top spots in corporations but for the most part executive suites are filled by a somewhat mysterious process of internal promotion. All this says is that the executive-type is the professional-type.

This professionalism contains a discernible element of community concern. Through years of association they have developed a sense of the role of the company in a community. Whatever their personal feeling about civic and public service, loyalty to the company motivates them to foster the company's image as a good neighbor and citizen. Company philanthropy, even when reluctant, is demanded by this image. Personal conviction, as well as concern for company interests, motivates them to make the community a good place to live in. This feeling, progressively diluted perhaps, is expressed also in company policy at the state, regional and national levels.

The essence of their professionalism, however, lies in their function within the corporation. Besides their production decisions, indeed at the heart of them, are their distribution decisions. For corporate executives, to the degree of their over-all authority, are arbiters of the distribution of benefits from an aggregate of property against which many claim a variety of incomes. Claims for taxes, for employee wages and fringe benefits (including their own), claims for bonded indebtedness, claims for customary dividends and for capital gains of stock, claims for dealer assistance and customer good will, claims for nongovernmental, public charity press against the corporation from a variety of sources, law, contracts, unwritten custom, or the desire to present a company image.

Living at the center of this vortex, executives see that none of these demands can go unsatisfied without harming corporate productivity. At the same time they see that none can be fully satisfied unless the property they administer is made more efficient and productive, unless new markets are established and old improved, unless the company researches new products and better techniques, unless in short they live up to their responsibility to the corporation as a social entity and instrument of affluence.

They sit then at a focus of a dynamic tension, pulled this way and that in ways that affect the entire economy, a tension which they must translate to their entire organization. In this era of affluence the company which goes slack goes broke. Thus no matter the degree to which top officers might be motivated by self-aggrandizement or social responsibility, the demands of the public upon the corporation have become compelling and impelling forces for increased corporate productivity.

Social Power

The sanctions corporations enjoy of social proprietorship and social productivity in effect sanction their social power. This is the bone which sticks in the throat of those most disaffected with the free-enterprise or -- as they would call it -- the capitalistic system. That private individuals and groups can arbitrarily, it seems, affect by their decisions the life and well-being of so many offends their deepest convictions about personal freedom. The most idealistic, recognizing that corporate power is part and parcel of economic abundance, reject the modern industrial state. These are rare birds who survive mainly in monastic-like communities. At the opposite end and almost as rare are doctrinaire libertarians, who deny that corporations bear any more social responsibility than private individuals, and this minimally. In between, the vocal minority -- and some quietly determined in government -- would entangle corporations in a thousand regulatory strings, forgetting that impairing corporate profitability impairs their productivity. Neither they nor the large and largely silent majority will forfeit their affluence. The latter, while acknowledging the bounty corporations bestow, are overwhelmed by their bigness, fearful of their impersonality, and alienated by actual or seeming experience of power arbitrarily exercised.

Within this last group legimation of corporate power will be determined, and the good will advertising aimed at them by corporate giants recognizes this fact. Too frequently, public relations departments forget that good will is really the public's perception of the corporation using power responsibly. The recent flap over substituting Chevrolet for Oldsmobile motors tarnished General Motors' image of probity immeasurably. Most people were rather gleeful that rectifying its "cheap trick" cost the automotive giant much more than levelling with their customers in the first place would have.

The problem of corporate power is not amenable to easy solutions. It will come up again in each of the next four chapters, for corporate credit resources is an important prop of its power; in industrial bargaining corporate power has necessitated the counter-vailing power of labor unions; corporate power is a dominant feature in the landscape of affluence; and is the critical element in the power-relation between government and business. The issue, therefore, is protean and can not be solved by a prior dogmatism. The essence of corporate power is control over highly productive social property, and such control is always subject to abuse and misuse.

The alternative to constant vigilance by court or consumer action is to eliminate the possibilities of abuse. There are three options: 1) breaking corporate giants into smaller units at the risk of losing the cost advantages of size; 2) trammelling corporate actions with regulations which like barnacles will slow production and which in curing some abuses will encourage others; or 3) transferring corporate economic power to government which will burrow power irresponsibility under one more layer of bureaucracy. In effect, the alternative to large concentrations of economic power is a 19th Century standard of living, and that Century was not noted by the absence of abuse of the powerless by the powerful.

Concluding, we see that the modern large corporate aggregate presents a set of serious problems on what kind of property they are, how they enhance the material well-being of people, and, especially, to what extent they should enjoy power in this regard. These are practical, not moral questions. Moral principles neither legitimize nor condemn these features of corporate aggregates. They o are sanctioned insofar as they contribute to material well-being, to the social common good, and to political and personal freedom. But these issues are not divorced from o morality. Our conduct toward corporate aggregates as consumers of their products, as contributors to and sharers in their productivity, and as managers of their productive o power are modified by the sanctions they enjoy. Our conscience, therefore, regarding them is fashioned from a dialectic between the moral and economic principles we have o been studying and this view that corporate aggregates are power-laden and highly productive forms of social property.

THE CORPORATION AND CONSCIENCE

The correct attitude toward corporations begins with a true conception of the economy, not as just a set of financial arrangements nor even as a set of interrelated property relations -- certainly, it is both -- but as fundamentally and essentially as a network of human relations, a complex process of exchange by which we, each contributing his skills, know-how, talents as well as property, mutually service each other's wants. Where people possess these skills to a high degree, they can satisfy a higher level of wants. Where they lack them, their level of living is lower.

Post-war experience demonstrates this. The German and Japanese 'economic miracles' were not miracles at all. Industrial capacity was destroyed, commerce was in shambles, and farm output unavailable to people. But the know-how, the industrial discipline, the organizational skills were not destroyed. Once given funds to rebuild, to retool, to return to production, their economies quickly moved into high gear, two of the most advanced in the world. On the other hand, the far greater oil-earnings of Persian Gulf countries and foreign assistance to India have not been able as yet to transform them into self-sustaining economies because their people, though of ancient and high culture, do not as a whole possess modern economic skills.

We are so used to measuring, as we must, the economy as producing so many bushels, pounds, and units of material goods, or their money value, that we forget that economic relations are human relations, people acting on and with people, and, therefore, moral relations also. If moral relations, then moderation, justice, spiritual poverty and the like apply.

The Corporation Viewed Morally

What applies to the economy, applies to the corporate aggregate. For it does nothing more than organize the highly productive skills of men and women to effect a tremendous outpouring of goods. Cybernetics, computers and automation which have hurtled us into the electronics age do no less. The skills required have shifted away from physical energy and even manual dexterity to those of taste, intelligence, judgment and decision. But automation still organizes human talents to satisfy human wants. The fear that machines will take over is really the fear that the few who command the machines will dictate to the many.

Fears that the greater capital aggregation which automation demands will depersonalize and standardize life are equally unfounded. Production will demand more not less human judgment just as the driver of an intercontinental tractor-and-rig must exercise more judgment and display more skill than a whole train crew a hundred years ago, or the operator of a caterpillar than a gang of ditchdiggers. Electronically geared manufacturing will not only permit a truly customized mass-production, that is repetitive production of tailor made items, but the increased wealth and leisure men will gain will demand much greater concern about the quality of life. The real fear is not depersonalization by machines, but the inability of the masses of men and women to rise to the responsibility of fashioning their Value priorities, moderating their wants in conformity with their Values, and thereby determining the material conditions of their lives.

This is not wishful thinking. As late as three decades ago it was a cliche that economic efficiency and ugliness were inevitably paired. The factory produced ugly products fashioned in ugliness, dirt, and noise. Today no such alternative is seen as inevitable. Not only has affluence given us the resources to afford beauty but the esthetically pleasing is found to be more efficient and economical.

The corporate aggregate, as the principal instrument of economic abundance, will not dehumanize life unless we let it. Our insistence can force change, just as the insistence on automobile safety and greater economy has forced change. Though the corporation in producing affluence fosters change, manufacturers', nevertheless, resist it. They fear risking capital on unpredictable products, hoping rather to persuade the public to buy what they are geared to produce. Buyer resistance and buyer articulateness are indispensable weapons for forcing corporations to engage in the tremendous efforts to explore the changing wants and desires of people, to improve their product line, and to experiment with new offerings. In short it means that we should know what we want and insist that we get it. Conversely, like our political leaders, we get what we want.

At the same time, economic moderation always warns of the fact of scarcity and the production possibilities frontier. Neither the economy, nor any one corporation, no matter how huge, is an unlimited cornucopia. If we demand more than what can be produced, we pay for it with higher prices and at a sacrifice of the future.

Since corporations are social property which is burdened with social responsibility they themselves are an important part of the common good. The cynical contradiction of condemning them for preying on society, while enjoying all the benefits their productivity provides, flows from viewing them as private property. More disturbing is the widespread practical conclusion that since they prey on the public they themselves can be preyed upon.

A look beneath the private property facade of corporations to their true social nature lays bare the social injustice of managers or in-groups who exploit the corporation for their own gain, of customers who chisel on liability claims or steal from supermarkets, and of workers who stock their home work-shops out of company stores. Each raises the cost of living for all of us, individually microscopically, collectively very substantially. In fact, by nibbling at large corporations which are the principal material support of society, they prey on society itself.

Viewing the corporate aggregate as a common good from within, management decision-makers are presented with knottier issues of social justice. The reference here, however, is not to the typical justice issues which arise in business, prejudice, favoritism, demands for sexual favors, payoffs, conniving with competitors, product fraudulency and the like. However hard the choice because jobs and careers may be on the line, the question what is just is relatively clear-cut.

The almost insoluble issues of justice relate to the corporation as the center of a vortex of demands from stockholders, unions, customers, suppliers, and government, all presenting legitimate claims which cannot be met *in toto* because there is not enough economic gain to go around. In this situation distributive justice may shade into pure pragmatism, buying off whatever group is most threatening just to keep the operation going. Yet there are two principles, derived from the nature of the corporation as a common good, which may help. 1) Because the corporation is an economic common good, all involved with it expect and have the right to expect economic gain and 2) the viability of the corporation requires that all who share in must contribute to its profitability. While too broad for precise determinations, they provide guide-lines within which an overall attitude of justice can operate. Such an attitude in turn opens one to more ultimate considerations of the role one's corporate life plays in total life. This we explore now as implications of spiritual poverty.

The Spirit of Poverty

Most people will find this hard to take. Indeed nothing seems more removed from spiritual poverty than the thrusting towers of commerce and finance and the voracious jaws of mills and factories, gobbling up men and machines and materials to spew out product. The overweening physical presence of such structures seem to speak more of man's perennial aspiration to be like God than a humble stance before Infinity. The awe they in turn stir in us is often an overwhelming dread like from a Frankenstein's monster.

But removing once again the physical facade reveals a more marvelous reality within, the exceedingly complex interaction amongst men of the most diversified talents and abilities, organized for the one simple purpose of servicing our wants. Even the greatest corporate giants stand on the narrow basis that we accept their products. No doubt such aggregations can marshall immense political power, can deluge us with advertising, and can set the conditions, often demeaning us, for the purchase of their products. But all the shouting about consumerism -- how we are being noodled with goods we cannot use well, which clutter our lives, and distort our Values -- forgets the very simple and basic fact that we can say, "No, thank you." The hand-wringers about consumerism refuse to assert the basic difficulty that we are not disciminating buyers.

On the other hand, the insight which the spirit of poverty gives will also recognize that if we enjoy the benefits of mass production mass marketing, we must accept the premises of mass production. It is difficult to attune such organizations to individualized promotion and service. Human error and carelessness can sour any sale. Inertia and resistance to change is as much a reality of corporate as of personal life. This is not to say that we must accept such things meekly. But in our insisting that the corporation fulfill its primary purpose of service, we should keep our cool. Even when our protests seem to get lost in bureaucratic channels, we can retain a healthy humor that no one specifically intended our inconvenience or discomfiture.

From the corporate side consumer sovereignty provides sobering considerations. No corporate aggregate is guaranteed a place at the top. Corporations, who have wheeled and dealed throughout the globe, have shriveled to a fraction of their former size when their products and services lost favor with the public. Other giants have run tail between legs for government help or seen foreign subsidiaries nationalized with scarcely a ripple of protest from home. On the other hand, corporate power is sanctioned because corporate aggregates can amass and venture vast amounts of capital. Projects like the Alaskan Pipe Line, however, are demanding investment which only a consortium of giants can risk. More are on the horizon which only governments can finance. The corporate aggregate will continue to play a large role well into this generation's future, but no corporation can ignore the well-being of its constituencies and survive. Even so, history may make them obsolete.

The modern corporation executive might read with some humility the lessons of feudal decay. When ducal families became more concerned about aggrandizing their holdings than in preserving peace, and when the nobility as a whole became more touchy about their rights and powers than in administering justice and fostering economic growth, they lost the support of the people to the centralizing power of the monarchy. When business executives lose their sense of responsibility to their customers, workers, client firms, and to the general public, they invite government intervention not only in the form of more peripheral regulations but in curtailment of effective management and decision making. If a sense of humility -- read, spiritual poverty -- does not motivate a more lively social responsiveness, businessmen had better act responsibly from a sense of survival.

In the stratosphere of executive power where mergers and acquisitions are effected or fended like trading Monopoly cards -- in the two years, 1967 through 1969, Allis Chalmers fought off no less than four serious take-over bids, and since then acquired a few companies and subsidiaries themselves -- wheelers and dealers can easily forget that the zestful game of corporate power has serious consequences for people's lives and income. The Cash McCalls make headlines and become subjects of novels and movies but their careers like those of the "young wonders" of the sixties present a completely distorted picture of corporate command.

Spiritual Poverty and Corporate Command

There are other elements in the complex of executive command which can find their completion, their crown and profoundest meaning in poverty of spirit -- not a Milquetoast meekness but an inner strength, a reserve of moral purpose during periods of trial and of decision during adversity. Purely secular success certainly can be gained without the spirit of poverty. But it is also invalid to assume that spiritual poverty dulls business acumen and blunts the will to risk. It is further proposed that the true attitude on spiritual poverty will give meaning to a pattern of actions, more humanizing and more satisfying than merely the thrill of playing the game successfully. Finally, while much of this presentation seems directed at top management, nothing prevents its application at all levels. In fact on levels, where pride of accomplishment and recognition come but rarely, the sustaining power of poverty of spirit might be more needed.

The three elements in command which can be sublimated by poverty of spirit are: the motive of <u>service</u>, the fact of a <u>community of effort</u>, and the <u>loneliness of command</u>. Service may be for "suckers" in the vocabulary of the "con artist" who works a territory and moves on, but for a business hoping to pitch its tent in a community and to stay awhile it is the foundation upon which its business reputation rests. Amongst all enterprise none is so vulnerable to the charge of lack of service as the large corporation. Beardsley Ruml, who could philosophize authoritatively about the ingredients of business success, says bluntly, "The greater the service, the greater the profit."[9] Corporations survive on the basis that their products are good, are up-to-date and reasonably priced. While advertising can shore up a faulty product, the word of mouth of pleased customers eventually makes the difference.

To be of service to others is always humbling, and sometimes humiliating. It means making the positive effort to see the other man's needs and wants. It means suppressing one's own tastes and preferences and prejudices. It means being disposed to others' will and subject to their complaints. A corporation whose personnel cannot or will not do this loses customers. The obvious relief from this galling duty -- and all who deal with the public admit this -- is to think of service as precisely what it means, doing good to others, doing their will and suiting their fancy. Without demeaning one's self, the obligation of service, even for profit, can be an act of charity. This involves no hypocricy or schizophrenia, for love is that psychic movement which has two terms, self and another. The moral personality is not split by being conscious that service simultaneously renders a good to others and is profitable.

Poverty of spirit can make vital the sense of corporate community. A corporation is nothing if not a cooperative venture. It displays on a smaller scale all the diversity of human talents, inclinations and aspirations of society itself. For its success it can use every kind of background and experience. It has a hierarchy of command and of earnings. The plant superintendent bears more authority than the maintenance crew foreman. A research chemist earns more than a janitor. But the lack of janitorial services or poor maintenance would bring production to a halt. No activity is so trivial that poorly done it does not lower the efficiency of the whole. On the other hand, no function can be more easily dispensed in the day to day operation as that of the president or chairman of the board.

No man's task is so menial that he cannot be praised for his contribution and no one so indispensable that his sloppy performance cannot be criticized. Many a boss would be a more human leader if he remembered that the shop or office would run much better if he performed as well in his position as some of his subordinates in theirs. The executive who looks with complacency at his own success could well pause, now and again, to consider how much that success depends upon the faithful performance by innumerable people under him, that he himself functions only with the confidence that their tasks will be performed without his constant surveillance and direction.

A chain of command is as strong as its weakest link. The trust that each link is as strongly motivated as he who first gives the order can only have two possible bases, the force of the command itself and the punishment or rewards meted out, or some force transcending this like a sense of duty, justice or personal convictions which logically find their basis in God. Hence, it is not impossible to see in the community of action of a corporate an analogy with the community of spirit, the fraternity under the fatherhood of God, which is basic to the poverty of spirit.

However far-fetched and foolish it might seem to introduce the divine into mundane matters of business, there is one aspect of corporate command when the believing man instinctively turns to God for assistance and when the non-believer tastes the loneliness of complete self-reliance. This is the time when a real decision has to be made, not merely the reiteration in different circumstances of previous policy but something entirely new. For no matter how computerized the business, no matter how brilliant the research staff, or wise his counselors a man must eventually come to a clear 'yes' or 'no'. This is the real loneliness of command. Unlike executives on lower levels where responsibility can be shifted upward, the top executive can appeal no further. He is answerable only to some amorphous thing like public sentiment; to a court of law, perhaps, or government agency on legal points not precisely defined; to the reaction of his workers or of the stock market.

The man, who feels the loneliness of command and with it the weight of responsibility for affecting the incomes and hence the lives of many people, will himself be more tolerant of mistakes of subordinates. He will appreciate that authority demands experience in command and risking mistakes. Such a man will take the sting from mistakes by assuming some of the responsibility himself, if not publicly at least privately. He will defend his subordinate against detractors. Such a man, no matter how shrewd and hard-nosed, is well in the frame of mind to take inspiration from that master tactician of men, Jesus Christ, who encouraged all "Learn of me for I am meek and humble of heart."

The psychological complex which is poverty of spirit, does meet a need in businessmen. It seems further to resolve the dilemma which William Whyte posed in his perceptive book on executive psychology, The Organization Man.[10]

There Whyte draws the contrast between the Protestant

and the Social Ethic. Management trainees and junior executives are trained in corporate life in the Social Ethic: the conference table, the path of committee agreement and group decision. From this cadre, nevertheless, must be drawn the top executives who are nourished on the harsher diet of Protestant Ethic: self-reliance, individualism, personal responsibility and decision making. From the one how can be gotten the other? From amiable conferees how can be born the self-directed, hard-driving chief which the corporation demands?

A true sense of community, a commitment not only to one's own ambition but to the needs of others and in particular the needs of subordinates would seem to fill the psychological demands of both Ethics without splitting the human personality in two. For a person who bears authority in a responsible way not only for his own purposes but for the good of others can be self-reliant without despising the advice and counsel of others. His sense of community will urge him to seek consensus but he is not enervated by its lack when a decision must be made. His inner moral resources give him strength to bear the burden of mistakes and errors of judgment. Thus he can become a true captain of a team, personally self-reliant, a leader whose vision spurs him on to efforts greater than that of his men, but also encouraging, sympathetic to weakness, but not slack in authority.

Idealistic, of course, but nothing truly worthwhile and truly human is other than idealistic. It can be achieved only by those who see corporate property in its true perspective, freighted with tremendous social responsibility, the means by which many men achieve their diverse ambition, the source, par excellence of society's material well-being. Management of such property is not the task for petty men, men confined to the covers of a ledger, or wrapped up in their own financial ambitions. It is a task which demands men who can see the effects of their action on all of society. Only the rarest of mortals could perform well in this way without an attitude of reliance and dependence on God.

Conclusion

If the student still harbors ambivalent feelings about the large corporate organization, this would not be abnormal. The corporate giant is a unique kind of property, neither dominantly private nor dominantly public, and each corporation is unique in its development, organization and ethos. Consequently, there can be no stereotype response to all, neither all love or all hate. The ultimate sanction of their power, a power, moreover, which is vulnerable to changing public preferences, is their ability to produce abundantly. As such they are an element in the common good. To use them unjustly or to abuse them by excessive demands on them, therefore, is to violate them as a common good. All the more is this an obligation of managers who bear the responsibility of maintaining and directing them as a community of service to the public. So there is nothing sacrosanct about the large corporate aggregate. As human organizations they play both an economic and a moral role. They survive because they perform the first reasonably well while allowing scope for people involved with them to act morally, if they so choose.

CHAPTER EIGHT

MORAL DIMENSIONS IN MODERN CREDIT

The second feature distinguishing affluent from destitute economies is the all-pervasive and all but invisible phenomenon of credit. The simple act of borrowing-lending is a basic expression of human community and as old as the human race. When I borrow from you and you lend me $10, a special debt-credit relation comes into being between us: you trust me to the extent of $10 and I am beholden to you for the same amount. It is an act of exchange not a gift, but an exchange in which the lender defers his _quid pro quo_ over the time of the loan, and thus includes a stronger element of benevolence than simple exchange.

Yet it happens everyday. It is the rare student, in these days of astronomical educational expenses, who has never borrowed. The financial statement of the typical family consists largely of such credit-debt claims. While its assets include such physical property like a house, a car, furnishings, clothing and the like, its most valuable assets are its credit claims, rights to social security receipts, to insurance proceeds, to pension payments, its checking and savings accounts, and holdings of securities, and its liabilities are debt obligations, its mortgage, installment debt and personal debts. Government and especially business financial statements present the same picture, only more so.

Tell us something new, prof! That is the point: the chapter will present nothing new. We will simply look at an old phenomenon in a new way. We will look beneath the concrete facts of borrowing-lending and of credit-debt to a somewhat mysterious reality called credit-worthiness or, the term we will use, credit-ability. If I borrow $10 from you, then I enjoy your trust. Indeed I had _credit-ability_ before I borrowed, otherwise you would not have lent to me. The facts of credit and the economic and moral implications of credit-ability are the subjects of this chapter.

CREDIT AND CREDIT-ABILITY

More than a fact of affluence, credit-ability is a key to it. The man who commands credit is a new hero of legends. Like the knight with his magic sword, Excalibur, or the Texan stalking a frontier town, hand quick to his six-shooter, the man who is adroit, swift, and sure in the use of credit stands larger than life, a favorite of the gods. At his call the temples of finance open. When he prowls, boardrooms tremble.

However he achieves it -- being born to wealth, scrambling up the corporate ladder, pioneering a dynamic market, wielding political power, or clawing through the back alleys of crime -- the man who commands credit is set apart from lesser mortals: men and, in particular, financial institutions are willing to lend large sums of money to him. Better than the actual possession of wealth, the command of credit lends a certain aura, a smell of success, a materialistic charisma.

A Credit Cavalier

Illustrative is the career of a modern, though really a minor, cavalier of credit.[1] He begins, in Alger-fashion, as a fourteen-year-old boy, leaving a South Carolina town asleep in the shadows of the Blue Ridge mountains, to become a Senate page. In Washington he catches the eye of several prestigious senators and in twelve years has become secretary of the Senate. By 1956 he has a $20,000 a year job, some real political power, but no assets. He cannot raise even $250 to buy into a general insurance agency.

But that same year, he gets his grub stake, swinging a deal for $30,000 of stock in a mortgage insurance company by peddling small amounts to friends. Two years later he acquires $10,000 more of the stock by borrowing from a friend. In 1961 a vice president of a Texas construction firm borrows $64,000 from a Dallas bank, on their joint behalf, for more of the same, and another $111,000 to buy stock in one of the largest mutual funds. All -- particularly the insurance company stock because of a favorable tax interpretation -- pay off handsomely, netting him profits estimated at over a quarter million.

He branches out. He borrows, without collateral, another quarter million from a Baltimore savings and loan association to buy a third interest in a plush motel on the Maryland shore. When difficulties arise he arranges a $53,000 loan from the Small Business Administration. The opening of the motel in the summer of 1961 is a "smasheroo" -- champagne, girls, and crawling with government dignitaries.

Not content, he forms a partnership with a man, well connected in the booming aircraft industry, to organize a vending machine company over which they have controlling interest. (Among others involved is an operator of a gambling casino in Las Vegas.) The company, thanks to contracts with two aero-space giants, has, within months, realized profits sufficient to purchase the plush motel for a reportedly million dollars.

In all these maneuvers our hero's sure hand at credit has parlayed his political job into a fortune variously estimated between one-half and $2 million. In less than a decade he has acquired stock in 22 corporations and been able to borrow from 18 banks and 5 other lending institutions in more than a dozen different cities. As one banker reasoned, a man with so many and so high connections was a good credit risk for a mortgage, unsupported by collateral, to build a $127,000 home.

This tale, however, hangs heavy with the spoor of call girls and abortions, political pay-off and favoritism, larceny, fraud, and income tax evasion. It trails through the Senate and dangerously close to the White House. It ends predictably, though not inevitably, with his forced resignation as secretary of the Senate, indictment and eventual conviction for income tax evasion, larceny, and fraud. He is, of course, Robert G. (Bobby) Baker. Like another Prometheus, reaching for the sun, he is cast down and after years of appeal, imprisoned.

The Two Edges of Credit

Credit is a two-edged weapon. Just as a magic sword subjects its wielder to the warning that he who takes the sword will die by the sword, and the fastest draw in the West survives only until a faster comes along, so he who grows wealthy by credit can just as easily be bankrupted by credit. For the great temptation of the command of credit is an overweening euphoria that all doors are open, that more can always be borrowed as long as the facade of wealth is maintained -- more spending, more wheeling and dealing, more financial juggling, no retrenching, no pulling back, grasping every means to get funds, plunging further into debt. Once again, whom the gods destroy, they first make mad.

Eventually creditors become restless. First the little ones, the paperboy, the milkman, the tailor. Then friends strapped for cash, department stores, and utility companies start to press. Interest payments are missed, notes fall due, credit companies start dunning. Finally, banks and loan companies hear of his financial discomfiture and cut off his lifeline of credit. Now the pack is in pursuit, yapping, snarling, biting at his heels until he falls. Those who cannot handle credit, succumb to it.

But he never falls alone. He embroils his family, his associates, his friends, creditors, governments and sometimes, in widening circles, financial houses, their stockholders, and their creditors. In other words it is not a game like Monopoly. Real people are really hurt in their real wealth.

Tragedies, like Baker's, repeated less dramatically every day, prompt the conclusion that credit and its use is a devil's device. Moral outrage tends to conclude from such careers that the easy availability of credit, so contrary to the virtues of hard work, keeping free of debt or repaying it promptly (which were the moral sources of past prosperity), corrupts a sense of justice, hurts the innocent, and lures men to their ruin.

Heightening these almost medieval superstitions is an uneasiness bred from incomprehension of the facts of high finance. People, reviewing the quarter century since 1950 and seeing public and private debts increase 7 times from $555b. to $3800 b. while gross national product increased 6 times from $286b. to $1700b., do worry about an orgy of national indebtedness.

In 1976 the Federal debt of $597b. loomed large, more than doubling, but all other sectors in the economy increased their indebtedness ten or eleven times over the period: state and local governments from $25b. to $236b; corporations from $167b. to $2521b; and households from $104b. to $1107b., a sizable portion of which was farm and small business borrowing, but over $900b. was in mortgages and consumer loans.[2] Considerations like these tend to dissolve the rosy tableau of affluence into a grisly picture of national bankruptcy.

All these elements -- moral outrage, incomprehension and fear -- are coalescing into demands for legislative and institutional reform.[3] Reforms, by all means, are called for, but not such which proceed from an irrational fear of modern credit and without realizing what our stake and our role in the credit industry is. The chapter begins by examining what credit is and what it does: 1) that it is a real economic good; 2) that it is the most desired form of wealth and productive of wealth; and 3) that some of it is money. From this basic understanding it will derive a few general moral attitudes which modern credit requires.

CREDIT: AN ECONOMIC GOOD

Credit in essence is the confidence a borrower inspires in a lender to entrust him with his property. Such accommodation is a spontaneous and natural response to human community, for it frees property of its exclusiveness while preserving rights of ownership. Lending-borrowing, even when motivated by self-interest, does for material possessions what love does for spiritual goods. The first insight into credit, therefore, is that it has two faces: borrowing requires lending, just as buying requires selling. (If we owe $3800b. of debt, we own $3800b. of credit claims. The "we" is not the identical collective in both cases, but there is considerable overlap.) The reality is hyphenated: credit-debt. A person commands credit when others are willing to lend to him. He is a man who can go into debt.

Modern Credit

Where modern credit differs decisively from the past is that most borrowing is not from individuals but from businesses. Modern credit is institutionalized. Corporations make it their business to accept deposits of money from anyone and to lend to whoever gives promise of repaying. From this two conclusions can be deduced: credit is a generic good and these institutions are founded on a trust, broader than that between individuals, a public trust.

Unlike a diamond necklace, a collection of records or a favorite chair, modern credit has no specific use or desirability. Specific goods may be loaned but their specificity limits their loan-ability. There is no such restriction on credit for it is money or can be easily turned into it.

Furthermore, because credit-debt is generic, it is an objective good: a good for the borrower who gets purchasing power and a good for the lender who gets a claim to a future return. A loan is an exchange of real economic goods: the borrower sells his credit-ability for money and the lender buys it. What is unique to this exchange is that each activates the other's good in the exchange. The borrower's credit-ability and the lender's credit-claim become valuable simultaneously.

This point is crucial to understanding the role financial institutions play. Since credit-debt depends on personal trust, it cannot exist between strangers. Banks and savings companies by interposing their own credit-worthiness between ultimate borrowers and lenders not only relate strangers but improve credit-relation between them. For just as these businesses pool small savings into larger, more useful amounts to lend, so they buttress the credit-ability of individual borrowers with their own public trust. In a real sense they manufacture billions of dollars of credit-ability annually.

Such institutions have existed almost as far back as recorded history. The most prominent were associated with religion or government, the temples of Delos and Adelphi in classical Greece, the Aerarium of imperial Rome, the *montes pietatis* of the Middle Ages. But as early as Nebuchadnezzar, individuals and private groups have enjoyed this public trust. From the time of the Renaissance private businesses more and more predominated -- the great Lombard banks, the Fuggers in the era of Hapsburg domination, the Bank of England at the beginning of England's greatness, and later the Rothchilds and the Morgans. Though run for private gain they were always more involved with and responsive to a public trust than were other kinds of businesses. Raymond de Roover describes the many facets of public trust upon which the Medici Bank of Florence based its manifold operations.[4]

The Credit Industry

Today a vast industry, employing over 4 million people, services the exchange of money for credit-ability, translating annual savings by persons, businesses and governments, into amounts and forms which may be borrowed to buy capital or consumer goods, or credit instruments. Since these last may be bought and sold many times in the course of a year, the best guess would put the annual dollar transaction in the trillions.

The credit industry is an enormous market reaching every corner of the economy. In it every borrower and lender preference as to amount, interest, maturity, marketability and risk can be satisfied. It is dramatized in the milling and shouting around the horseshoes beneath the Big Board, in the frantic calls to brokers, in the cool trading of hundreds of millions by crisp phone calls from executive sanctuaries.

But these are only crests on the waves. The deeper reality is the annual flow and accumulated pools of the economy's savings and investment. The biggest stream is the $66b. of household savings, pouring annually into vast pools of financial claims -- the $610b. of life insurance and pension fund assets, the $506b. of time deposits, the $111b. of U.S. savings and other bonds, the $436b. of savings-and-loan and credit-union assets, the $272b. of government and private pension funds, the $51b. of mutual funds, and the $36b. of social security and unemployment compensation reserves. Other funds seeking investment come from the $179b. of undistributed profits and capital consumption allowances of business and $20b. from governments and the rest of the world.

For buyers, the merchandise is varied and alluring. The U.S. Treasury offers some $164b. of treasury bills, $257b. of notes and bonds and another $72b. of savings bonds in all amounts and maturities. State and local governments hawk another $35b. new bonds every year to finance highway construction, schools, utilities and other capital improvements. Corporations also sell $42b. of a varied inventory of new bonds. In 1976 the total of all bonds increased by $120b.

Stocks proliferate, blue-chip and growth, common and preferred, voting and non-voting, stock rights and options, mutual funds of every description. Registered exchanges sell over $175b. annually and what dollar business over-the-counter markets do is anybody's guess. For other tastes there are $87b. more of mortgages, $15b. more of automobile loans, $12b. more of notes issued against installment purchases each year. In addition, banks lend $552b. to individuals and businesses in short-term loans.[5] Name it and this great "bazaar" has it, or will shortly get it.

It is not a market for just financial houses, businesses, and the wealthy. Over 25m. people own some stock and 4½ million own $5000 or more. Almost 90% of all families own life insurance; slightly more than this are covered by social security, and about 60% by private pension plans. Credit unions have almost 25 million members claiming some $45b. of assets. All these forms of institutionalized saving are buyers in the credit bazaar.

While these figures tend to swamp the imagination, they

do sketch in that vast network of debt and credit by which each of us, directly or indirectly, simultaneously owes and has claims against everyone else. In essence as simple as borrowing a cup of sugar, the financial market is a spontaneous elaboration, following no blue-print, of new ways of translating savings into borrowings according to the economy's needs. Through this sytem flows the largest part of accumulated national wealth.

Personal Credit-Ability

How much of this generic wealth an individual can command is determined by the three C's of credit -- cash, collateral, and character. Under Cash is included not only funds at hand but expected income. The larger and the more certain the flow of cash, the higher the credit rating. Collateral are those assets which can be turned into cash. The more marketable they are, the greater their value for borrowing.

The third, Character, is the most important. Though character refers to business, not moral qualities, it includes ingredients not inconsistent with a good character as ordinarily understood: the ability to withstand the temptations of credit, moderation in seeking the good things in life, and most especially a keen sense of justice. Business differs most from moral character in that it is motivated by a worldly self-interest.

The two principal ingredients of business character are a willingness to risk and a reputation for meeting one's obligations. Of the two the willingness to risk is initially the more important. Unless one has a sure hand in the use of credit, can smell profitable situations, and is clever enough to convince others, he can never command large amounts of credit. Over the long run, however, trustworthiness is the more significant because this alone dissolves creditors' reluctance to lend. The reputation for honoring debts is acquired with difficulty and only through persistent good behavior. It is easily lost, as once happened to young ladies, by the slightest hint of scandal.

Because these factors constantly change, one's creditworthiness constantly changes and it changes not homogeneously but varyingly in quality. One's best credit is sold first. Therefore, the less the indebtedness, the more that can be borrowed and at lower rates. Just the opposite is the case for people deeply in debt, as they discover to their dismay when consolidating debts at Friendly Finance! Like businesses and governments, households can benefit from periodic financial check-ups to estimate how much credit they command and what its quality. Overestimation can produce financial disaster. Underestimating one's credit-worthiness is to neglect an important and very real part of personal and business wealth.

CREDIT: PRODUCER OF WEALTH

Credit is not only wealth but productive of wealth. Take the everyday example of a man with a $50,000 home, free and clear, which he pledges against a $100,000 loan from a bank to build an apartment. When completed he sells it for $125,000, the buyer financing it with $25,000 of cash and a $100,000 mortgage from a savings and loan association. The seller now pays back his loan with interest, redeems his home and pockets the difference.

Of the original wealth items, the builder has his home: the bank returns to its original asset position; and the cash has changed hands. What is new are an apartment, obviously new wealth worth $125,000 and the $100,000 mortgage. This must also be counted as wealth because it earns income for the savings and loan company and can be bought and sold. To get net additional wealth, however, this $225,000 must be reduced by $100,000, the owner's indebtedness, by the $25,000 of cash which simply exchanged hands, and by the $30,000 of materials used in building the apartment. The $70,000 remainder is new wealth.

Part of this, of course, is represented by wages paid construction workers, contractor fees, permits and other labor costs totaling $50,000. But labor and management skills were actualized, began earning income, only when put to work. Subtracting these incomes still leaves a net addition to wealth of $20,000. Thus credit was the instrument by which potential wealth was actualized and new wealth created. In the same way, from this wealth more can be made.

This is the legerdemain of credit -- wealth drawn from wealth, drawn from wealth endlessly -- which confounds the uninitiated and tempts the bold to their ruin. Credit-ability's very unsubstantiality -- the trust a man enjoys from others -- makes it hard to conceive credit itself as wealth. But it is real, it is costly, and it can be bought and sold. It is not unlimited and free but commands a price, an annual return of five, ten, twenty, even fifty percent.

The Usury Debate

The realization that credit is wealth did not come easily. Philosophers and economists, for two thousand years beginning from Aristotle wrestled with the questions, "Why and How interest can be charged?" The usury debate during the Middle Ages, far from being obscurantist, represented a tremendous intellectual effort, considering the question from all sides, theological, philosophical, legal, sociological and economic.[6]

The common man did not resent the usury prohibition as imposing unnecessarily an unwieldly burden of conscience on businessmen. To the contrary, these strictures answered a deeply-felt fear of usury whose deadening clutch had blighted the development of village and town economies in other civilizations.[7] Usury laws did much toward saving Europe from theocracy by preventing bishoprics and monasteries, which were the most important reservoirs of wealth, from becoming lending institutions. Last, they nudged business away from consumption loans to gain-seeking through productive investment.

This intellectual struggle is pertinent to the present discussion, precisely because the Scholastics saw usury as a charge for nothing. Money, they argued in following Aristotle, did not change in value over time. Moreover the use of money could not be separated from its possession. Therefore, a dollar loaned today is equal to and justly recompensed by a dollar repaid next week or next year. Any added use-fee (usury) is unjust. This reasoning not only accorded neatly with the Biblical counsel to lend expecting no gain, but articulated popular sentiment.

Such conclusions, however, increasingly ran into two difficulties: 1) people, especially the poor, needed regular sources for loans;[8] and 2) businessmen did borrow productively, that is, they used money as a tool for profits.[9] Late Medieval analysis, consequently, moved toward finding an interest of the lender in the monies loaned. This interest would be valuable and compensation could be justly demanded. Each such title to interest was controverted: the cost incurred in making loans, especially the ordinary return as a business; the risks involved in the business of lending; and the loss of gain which the lender might reasonably expect to realize if he had not loaned.

Over this last -- lucrum cessans -- the greatest battle raged, ending in exhausted stalemate in the 17th Century. In this seeming retreat of moralists from previous dogma, contemporaries failed to see how society benefited from their intellectual efforts and how close they came to finding the analytic key to the thorny problem of interest. Interest becomes a real and valid claim to wealth when the universal possibility of gain becomes a reality and thereby transforms credit from a nebulous good-will into an income-earning wealth.[10]

Businessmen of the time were already acting on this basis and taking interest on all loans even those to the poor. What conscience they had about this was salved by assuming that the poor somehow shared in the general gain. (This assumption has in a general way been justified since industrialization has not produced the wholesale mortgaging of the masses, to the wealthy few.)

Credit and Economic Growth

Universal gain, therefore, not only is an element in the explanation why credit earns income but provides the clue as to how. For credit fuels economic growth. Lenders rely on a rising economy to assure that their loans will be repaid with interest, and borrowers to justify the risks and costs of borrowing. The gain-motivation of each is rooted in the hope and expectation of sharing in economic growth.

Besides stimulating, credit-debt helps maintain the tone of the economy. The dynamism of an economy flows from an organic tension and balance between what stimulates and what depresses it. An economy is sick when it is afflicted by either the "slows" of unemployment, or by the hyper-tension of inflation -- and sometimes by both. All spending, especially spending beyond income such as installment buying, government deficit spending, and most importantly business net capital investment, accelerates the economy. Saving, on the other hand, non-spending of income by business, government and households, depresses or slows the economy.

Between these forces there is a continuous organic interaction. Saving, with one important exception, provides the only source of funds for those who would spend beyond their income. Spending, in turn, and especially capital investment, which is spending to expand the economy's productive capacity, increases income and makes more saving possible and probable. Intimate to this process of balanced growth, the credit system, like the circulation of blood in the animal organism, translates savings into loans and back into more income and more savings. Its health, therefore, is a precondition for a healthy economy.

This analysis of credit as wealth resolves the paradox of increasing affluence and increasing indebtedness. In a healthy economy saving, investment, and indebtedness must increase simultaneously. The rate of going into debt is determined basically by the rate of economic growth, and vice versa.

CREDIT AS MONEY

The last and most remarkable feature of credit is that some of it is money. Not all credit is money, but all money is credit. The nonchalance which accepts this statement is usually matched by resisting it as a fact. This resistance is eroded only by a patient review of every-day financial facts.

On Becoming Money

Money has a sensuous sound which perks up even the jaded. It wrings deference from the most reluctant. For its sake half the world's crime is committed. Yet for all this mystique, the student knows that almost anything can become money, and almost everything has -- cattle, salt, fishhooks, beads, tobacco and tulip bulbs; cigarettes, nylons and K-rations, iron, copper, gold and silver; huge stones and pieces of paper.

A thing becomes money when it does what money does. It first must be desired for itself, but beyond this it must be wanted generally, even by those having no immediate use for it, because others will take it in exchange. The fundamental function of money is to serve as surrogate, a medium in exchange. Once generally acceptable in exchange, it becomes the unit by which wealth is counted. Its decisive transmutation, however, occurs when a thing, in Marx's felicitous phrase, "crystallizes value", when it becomes valuable in and for itself, irrespective of any useful or desirable characteristics of its own. The process is completed when as a store of value, the thing can be borrowed and lent, when it keeps its value over time. Fulfilling all these functions -- a medium of exchange, a unit of accounting wealth, a store of value, and a means of payment over time -- only then does a thing truly become money.

No government can decree this. The people alone by their daily usage transform a thing into money. What becomes money is what the people want to be money. One of the first attempts by a modern government to induce the acceptance of a new kind of money was undertaken by Louis XV of France under the influence of the Scottish financier and adventurer, John Law. The wild speculation resulting is known as the Mississippi Bubble.[11]

What things become money is determined by such characteristics as their bulk, transferability, ease of safe-keeping, convenient divisibility and, above all, their limited utility. A thing which satisfies many different wants makes a poor money because these uses compete with its use as money. Smoking a cigarette in Berlin after the War was literally burning money. For these reasons as commercial economies become more complex, accelerated, and extensive, money is progressively "de-materialized" from bulky "natural" goods like boats or cattle to metals, to paper-surrogates of coins, and finally to credit.[12] A completely automated money of credit cards and a national computer-controlled accounting system is already on the horizon.[13]

Credit-Money Today

By all criteria credit is a happy choice. It is flexible; it can be transported as rapidly as electricity; it is made out of nothing more material than trust; it has no other use than to be exchanged. Safe-keeping alone poses problems. Consequently, only the credit of institutions, whose lending is carefully controlled and limited, becomes money. What these are is easily seen by what we pay bills with and receive in payment. Coins are the credit of the U.S. Treasury for that, the larger part of their face value which exceeds the market value of their metals; paper currency is wholly the credit of Federal Reserve Banks; and checks of commercial banks. Checking accounts, for reasons obvious to all, exceed the other two in popularity by a 3 to 1 ratio.

This listing excludes the $11 billion of gold at Ft. Knox because gold cannot legally circulate as money. Moreover as an international money passing between governments and central banks, it is a pledge for the several hundred billions of dollars held by foreign banks and businesses and international agencies. Consequently, it provides no practicable backing, for the $320 billion of coins, currency and checking accounts which constitute the domestic money supply.

How checking accounts became money is, like the acorn becoming an oak, beyond adequate explanation. The process starts from the basic contractual agreement of commercial banks to pay legal tender (coins and paper) on demand. All banks in turn have checking accounts, called reserves, with other banks. Small banks have reserves at larger banks and these at the twelve Federal Reserve Banks, so that all banks are integrated into a system of reserves which serves the individual bank just as a checking account does its customer. As a consequence no bank needs to keep any but a small fraction, about 1%, of its demand liabilities as currency in its vault.

Because people are confident of getting currency whenever they want it, paradoxically almost, they prefer checking accounts. This popular preference for checks has in a real sense germinated the reserve system, so that trillions of dollars of checks are "cashed" each year with only $80 billions of currency. In effect and in fact checking accounts are money in the bank.

The reserve system, while making bank-money possible also controls individual banks when tempted to increase and to proliferate their accounts. Millions of checks are cleared daily, some in favor, some against an individual bank. If this tally runs persistently against a bank it must replenish its reserve by transmitting currency or, more likely, by selling some assets. Either way its business is curtailed. Experience, therefore, and now law, dictates that reserves be a certain percentage of checking accounts. This reserve ratio varies by State and size of bank but averages 16% nationwide. The Federal Reserve sets the ratio for its member banks and, beyond this broad control, actually modifies the size of their reserves. Since member banks own 85% of bank assets, the Federal Reserve can effectively control the banking system and, consequently, the money supply.

How banks can change the amount of money in the economy is so utterly simple that people cannot accept it as fact. Even business students need re-telling to translate their theoretical knowledge into operational understanding. But take the ordinary example of a man borrowing $4500 from a bank to buy an automobile. In effect he has exchanged his credit for bank credit. Notwithstanding, the automobile dealer takes the check, banks it and writes checks against his deposit. From bank to bank the $4500 circulates as new money, alternately being deposited and checked out. Just the reverse happens when the loan falls due. The borrower writes a check against his account, redeems his credit and, just as surely as burning forty-five hundred dollar bills in his fireplace, destroys $4500. Banks make and destroy money by monetizing and demonetizing the credit of individuals, business, and governments.

Confirmation of this is afforded by a glance through any issue of the Federal Reserve Bulletin.[14] In the Consolidated Banking Statement for December 31, 1977, for example, one finds that banks owe governments, businesses and individuals $377b. in the form of checking accounts and $545b. of saving accounts. In turn they have extended $257b. credit by buying corporate and government bonds and another $657b. by lending to governments, businesses and individuals. Banks make money by extending credit.

In other words, banks have a money tree, granted not by law but by popular preference. They enjoy this privilege because, better than coins or Federal Reserve currency, checking accounts respond faster to the economy's needs for more or less money. More money, like gasoline in an engine, is wanted when the economy accelerates. Less when it slows down. Banks meet this need, because borrowing from banks tends to increase when spending increases and loan-repayment when spending decreases.

These minute-by-minute fluctuations produce that overall tone of seething in the money and financial market. The many facets of this can only be mentioned. First, borrowing from banks entails no previous saving -- the one exception to the limitation on borrowing to previously accumulated saving. Though quantitatively seldom exceeding 5% of total annual saving, borrowing from banks like a highly volatized fuel is high-powered: it is spent immediately. This is further charged because banks make profits by lending. They tend, as a result, to expand loans excessively during boom periods and to be overly cautious in contracting credit during recessions.

Other facets relate to the astronomically mounting use of checking accounts over good years and bad; to the drive to devise constantly new techniques and new ways of channeling funds; and to the pervasive influence of banking. Changes in banking policy affect all parts of our economy; can have drastic effects in the securities and mortgage markets; change an important source of European liquidity; and have repercussions on total world trade. A life-time is inadequate to understand the ramifications of the banking system.

Trying to ride and steer this vehicle, the seven governors of the Federal Reserve System -- the mandarins of high finance -- have the worrisome responsibility ultimately of regulating the money supply. They have not performed perfectly. Historically, the Fed's financial philosophy has lagged well behind academic consensus and even that of the banking community. The money market's state of constant flux as well as the political influences from Congress and the White House make difficult developing that experienced foresight necessary for effective policy decision. That the Governors maintain their continuous and conscientious analysis of the economy and of the overall viability of the monetary system, has, if at times worsening situations, prevented crises from degenerating into chaos.

Thus credit-debt as money annually moves close to 2 trillion dollars of goods and services from firm to firm and on to ultimate users. This must be its most important accolade. Born of mutual trust, hence of its very essence social, institutionalized into a new, all-pervasive wealth, traded in a fantastically complex market affecting every organ of the economy, debt-credit is often the only and always the necessary means to further wealth. It is dynamic, indeed mercurial and evanescent, subject to rapid increase and just as sudden declines. It has grown enormously, but it is still scarce, the demand for it far exceeding its availability.

If even this is unconvincing, wander through the financial district of any major city. The fanes of finance are built impressively, marble-lined and with expensive decor. Reverential ritual and elaborate safeguards are maintained largely to protect names and numbers in a book or computer printout. But this is no facade of fantasy but the setting for deadly serious dealings in enormous sums of wealth.

CREDIT AND CONSCIENCE

All this is preliminary to a few reflections on the moral dimensions of credit. Suggestive rather than definitive, they invite further moral discussion. Implicit in them is the hope that moralists and ethicians would come to the market-place, as did the late Scholastics like Lessius and Biehl,[15] to experience first hand the complexities of trading vast amounts of this mercurial good. Contrariwise, they should not be so ready to lump easy credit with sexual libertarianism, revolt against authority, lawlessness, and crime as just another sign of moral cancer. Moralists can take encouragement in this enterprise by the renewed interest in business ethics, the debate over the social responsibility of business, and the renewal and extension of regulatory law, much of which finds its roots in the moral principles incorporated into Medieval common and commercial law.[16] In short, they should realize that, while easy credit means abundant wealth, the moral issues lie not in credit's abundance but in its use or abuse by men.

While this invitation suggests correctly to students that the moral dimensions of credit are still a somewhat unexplored land, nevertheless, the student is not without some moral guide-posts. He must not let his conscience be determined by the pragmatics of conventional wisdom or, worse, formed by the struggle between the unscrupulousness of the mighty and the equally a-moral vigilantism of those supposedly speaking for the masses. Specifically, the chapter suggests that man's attitude, his conscience regarding modern credit, is no different from that applying to other forms of wealth. Such a conscience is a complex woven of three considerations: a sense of balance in using credit; concern for the rights of others in its exchange; and the root ontological response to credit as good for, but not the substance of, well-being. Translated into familiar terms these are moderation, justice, and spiritual poverty. What would be new are the modifications and emphases suggested by those characteristics, stressed in this paper: credit's reality, its sociality, and its scarcity.

Moderation and Justice

Credit, like any wealth, must be used in moderation. Unlike other goods, however, credit cannot warn of misuse or abuse by physical satiation. More likely it warns by a kind of light-headedness about the possibilities of amassing wealth. This signal is clearer in its collective manifestations like a wave of mass euphoria, as in a speculative fever gripping either the business community or an entire populace. It can be the relatively wild ebullience of a long rising market, the ferment of land or gold speculation, or the mass hysteria of the Mississippi Bubble[17] or of the great Bull Market of the '20's.

However its manifestations, such mania violates credit itself. For it forgets that as a wealth, possessing economic value and commanding a price, credit must be scarce. Though credit is creative of more credit and of more wealth, it is still limited by income, investment opportunity, habits of saving and, above all and most importantly, by public confidence. Put bluntly, lack of moderation in using credit hurts its users and destroys credit.

Considerably more stress must be placed on the justice aspects of credit transactions. Exchange justice obliges honest representation in applying for loans, repayment in full and on time with a compensating interest, usually at the going market rate. Such obligations of borrowers are clear enough; not nearly so clear are their rights.

Their primary right is to protect their credit-ability as personal property. Credit-ratings, which are business's measurement of credit-ability, should be open to scrutiny and subject to challenge. Falsehoods and misrepresentations in these do hurt a person in his financial wealth. Irrelevant criteria like religion, sex, race, or place of residence violate justice when they force individuals to pay higher interest under more onerous terms than their true credit-ability warrants. Such reforms could go far toward eliminating such ridiculous instances as this told by a black businessman. He was refused a $1500 loan to purchase inventory but could and did get the same amount from the same bank to take a vacation.

Public credit-ratings do involve questions of invasion of privacy which has become a very sensitive issue. If, however, banks and lending institutions charged rates of interests on personal and installment loans scaled to a person's credit-rating just as they do businesses according to their Dun and Bradstreet rating, the service could become viable entirely on a voluntary basis. People would be encouraged to check their credit-rating as they do their health. They would of their own accord supply the facts which demonstrate better credit-ability.

Such public credit-ratings, based on objective standards and challengeable in court if necessary, would be one of the most far-reaching institutional reforms, acknowledging credit-ability as a real form of wealth and encouraging a healthy competition in its purchase and sale. Truth-in-lending, a clear statement of the total cost of borrowing, is only half the truth. It must be complemented by an accurate, objective and public statement of credit-worthiness. The Fair Credit Reporting Act of 1971 is a step in this direction, but until it is implemented by ordinance on the local level where credit is formed, its principle has limited applicability. Moreover until credit reporting becomes so standardized that lenders compete for loans with terms commensurate with the quality of credit-worthiness, simple exchange justice will not be achieved.

Such reforms would also help correct a related and almost institutionalized abuse, that of loan favoritism. Credit, extended to insiders in a grossly favorable way or to friends for business and political favors, violates the public trust which credit institutions enjoy. A more subtle favoritism is giving more credit to large borrowers in order to shore up their weakening credit position. This usually does no more than throw good credit after bad. It is favoritism in that the declining quality of the borrower's credit-worthiness is not matched by higher rates and more rigorous terms.

On the other side of the coin is the advantage taken of the weak credit position of the poor. Until quite recently, little moral outrage was expressed at the usury practiced, in defiance of laws, against the poor. But loan-sharking, sleight-of-hand credit salesmanship, and credit misrepresentation are no less heinous than other forms of strong-armed robbery. What is worse, they prey upon the meager wealth of the defenseless. Respectable institutions which abet the credit positions of usurers or even connive at their practices are no less guilty than those who leech the income of the poor.

More blatant forms of credit theft are using another's credit, kiting checking accounts and passing bad checks. That better control in issuing credit cards, better surveillance of accounts and the introduction of the bank overdraft would eliminate much of this is no defense against the plain fact of dishonesty. To say that no one is injured is simply not true since all must bear higher overhead, surveillance and insurance costs. In this category of thievery must also be included the gain realized by insiders and those privy to advanced information who use their advantage to buy or sell the securities of a firm. That it too is hard to police is no defense against its dishonesty.

All such injustices against individuals' or institutions' credit have another dimension in that they attack the credit system itself by weakening the public confidence upon which it rests. Howevermuch credit-ability is a form of personal wealth, it is in essence the trust inspired in others; it is also a common good.

Credit as Common Good

This thought opens another vista of rights and responsibilities. The credit system is a public good, fostered like education by the institutions of society. Everyone, therefore, who contributes to the economy has a right to share in the generic goods of credit, that is, the credit-ability of credit institutions. Where individuals are prevented from making such contribution by unemployment, layoffs, work disability, or what is worse, social prejudice, unequal opportunities, low employability and economic despair, they have the right to call on government to shore up their low credit-ability with the stronger credit of the government. The demands of social justice in guaranteeing loans or even assuming part of interest charges have long been recognized in farm programs, in subsidizing industries or home ownership, but they always stopped short of being applied to help the very poor and most disadvantaged.

Inflation reveals a deeper implication of the social nature of credit. One of the unfortunate residues of the New Economics was the emphasis on spending to buoy up national income at the expense of saving as a pre-condition for productivity growth. The intractable inflation of the '70's may hopefully teach the lesson that the two must be kept in balance. Just as recession eventually touches all segments of the economy, so does inflation, at least the private sector. For it not only erodes fixed and annual incomes, but discourages savings, makes capital investment more hazardous and sets the income-dog chasing after the prices-tail. Worst of all it encourages legislators and bureaucrats that their essential role, because governments' property and income taxes increase faster than expenses, is to provide more spending programs and more generous salaries. This psychology along with that of households' and business' to spend now because today's dollar will buy less tomorrow generates an inflationary mentality which is just as pathological as a recession or unemployment psychosis.

The burden of responsibility to contain inflation falls on the Federal Reserve. In this they will inevitably fail if they are mandated to hold the line on interest rates, which themselves rise with the rate of inflation, rather than on the money supply and banks' ability to create money. Even this, however, is impossible against the counter-sweep of the entire economy. If the Federal budget runs huge deficits in years of prosperity, forcing the Federal Reserve, in order to maintain interest rates, to increase member bank reserves by buying their holdings of government securities, then government becomes not only the greatest beneficiary but the principal cause of inflation. But households by spending to the hilt and beyond, businesses by increased borrowing from banks, labor unions and professional groups by pressing for higher wages, salaries and fees, all contribute to inflation. The fault lies not with just the technical failures of the Federal Reserve; the entire economy is indicted.

All are guilty of ignoring the basic economic rationality, that rising prices warn demanders to slow down their buying. All should have been concerned about over-heating the economic machine, that too much money was chasing too few goods, and that increasing the economy's productive capacity could not take place overnight. This is really mass social irresponsibility since everyone and every group is driving to get all they can regardless of over-all economic consequences. It reflects a narrow and constricted view of credit as a matter between borrower and bank with no social consequences.

In addition bad loans and too easy credit strain the credit system itself because good credit runs out. The one fact most ignored during inflation is that credit is scarce and subject to decreasing quality. Though the system is a money tree, it must be carefully cultivated to produce more and better credit. The amount of serviceable <u>credit is limited</u> by the productivity of and savings performed by the economy, and it, consequently, is never enough to meet all demands for it. This is the real reason for its price and for the rationing of credit by price. As a result no one can get all that he would want.

This, moreover, is the basis for the judgment that

demanders of credit have an obligation in social justice to be concerned about the productivity and savings of the economy. In the contemporary context the need to save goes beyond the need to accumulate a little nest egg against an uncertain future to the more positive attitude of investing in future growth by contributing to it. There then is a real obligation, however difficult to specify in individual cases, on all in the economy to save some of their current income, if they expect future increases in output and income.

These implications of moderation and justice conspire to add a dash of sober seasoning to the credit euphoria. A cold, rational analysis would conclude similarly that credit is not a new magic nor an ever bountiful font of wealth. Simple business prudence cautions against the illusions of speculative fevers. Responsible use of credit -- that is, with moderation and justice -- is the strongest corroboration of what a worldly prudence advises.

Spirit of Poverty

A far greater difficulty is relating the use of credit to the spirit of poverty. The difficulty arises not only from the gossamer quality of credit itself but more so from the complex nature of this profoundly religious attitude, variations of which are found in every philosophy and religion.

What I mean here by the spirit of poverty is essentially an attitude of existential humility of the finite being before the infinite. It is a loving not a debasing humility which, contemplating the common finiteness of all men, leads to true community of help to and assistance of others. In short, it is simply recognizing one's own dimensions vis-a-vis God and other people.

Such an attitude regarding credit may be awed by the vast elaborations of the credit system but at the same time recognize its profound humaneness. It will acknowledge modern credit's fragility and viability, its great good and its dangers.

Such an attitude will perceive that credit is a decisive mutation in the evolution of money and an irreversible stage in the development of economies. For there is no other good available to service the ever increasing and more complicated transactions within and among modern industrial nations. Economies, dependent upon gold and silver like the late Roman empire, suffered money anemia when their mines gave out, but new sources of species could rejuvenate them. If credit is destroyed, however, nothing could take its place and, literally, modern economies would grind to a halt.

Such an attitude, while acknowledging the great good of credit, will know that it is not a new providence, but like everything finite and material, subject to the same law that there is but one infinite reality. More biting is the realization that when credit becomes a people's idol, no jealous Jehovah need destroy it and its cult with fire. For, as every speculative fever in history has demonstrated, credit bears its own self-destructing mechanism which only needs human abuse to be activated.

Balancing these somber considerations is admiration for credit's remarkable resiliency. After every debacle and crisis, credit has shown new life and new strength as wealth and as money. Despite men's blundering misuse of it, credit continues to draw vitality from its deep ontological roots in human community and fellowship and, in fact, has proliferated into every phase of economic relations. Credit can be destroyed and may be irretrievable, but this can only happen if something radical will have happened to the human species, that brother cannot trust his goods to his brother.

The corporate empire builder, surrounded by executive plush and basking in the glow of his latest financial coup, may well scoff at thoughts like these. But the hard fact of the matter is that in using credit he used a powerful instrument which was not mainly of his making but a good which was generated and sustained by the economy itself. If this does not sober his euphoria, reviewing the careers of the Bakers, the Insulls, the Wolfsons, Lings and Vescos and the rest, all who vaulted with credit and fell when it collapsed, might have this sobering effect.

At a more mundane level, the suburbanite, sleek with the success his work and investments have given him, can well be more modest in assessing his personal achievement. Undoubtedly hard work at his profession or in business earned him a comfortable living. Undoubtedly too he had to take risks, maybe of a modest, but perhaps his only, stake. But where his pay-off was more than the 3-4% average annual rate of growth, the credit tree paid off more handsomely to him than to others. This pay-off would have been impossible without the supporting institutions of the economy. His more than average return, moreover, meant that others could not reap the same golden harvest, and maybe nothing at all. This is what credit's scarcity really means.

This humbling consideration that he was at the right spot at the right time with available funds should temper his congratulations on his own acuity and efforts. This consideration should make him more willing to acknowledge the working of a transcendental Providence, that like flotsam he rode the waves to shore while others became waterlogged at sea. A cold rationality or fatalistic conviction in a lucky star would yield the same conclusion. This conviction becomes more heart-felt in the light of a lively sense of spiritual poverty and more strongly motivating of a moderation and justice in the use of credit.

In conclusion, every one of these suggestions needs elaboration, debate and clarification. Even so there are vast vistas of implication left unexplored. Credit, as a wealth, as a producer of wealth and as a money, does not yield easily to accurate verbalization and concretization. It is a reality in which personal and social elements are so intricately blended and whose abundance is so illusionary that its moral dimensions are hard to pin down. The student, however, in view of credit's vast implications for modern life, will find that continued reflection on credit and credit-ability will yield dividends of insight into the workings of the economy, greater rationality in the use of credit and greater peace in facing the queer turns of fortune.

CHAPTER NINE

PROFITS AND PRODUCTIVITY-SHARING

One's labor and how it is rewarded are two abiding concerns of life, no less for the affluent than for the non-affluent. That affluence has not blunted but rather sharpened emotions about work and income was dramatized in a vignette captured on television a number of years ago.

Shortly before his death Mr. Walter Reuther, who had spent his life battling for union rights and had put his career on line in fighting off a Communist take-over of the Ford local, had just negotiated what most agreed was a very successful wage increase for his auto workers. But it was no hero's welcome which greeted him at union hall. Instead he had to elbow his way through a cordon of angry workers, abusing him and shouting, "Whadda you care about us and our families? You get your big salary!" In an instant fists were swinging and the police called.

Who were these workers? What their complaint? They were not workers from other industries who would now pay higher prices for automobiles. They were not poor, struggling along the poverty line. They were not veterans of the labor strife of the 30's, but young men predominantly, skilled craftsmen from his own union, inheritors of one of the highest wage rates in the world. Their "beef" was simply that Mr. Reuther had not effected wage increase relatively as good for them as for the semi- and unskilled workers. Whatever the justice of their complaint -- and this is not the issue here -- the incident illustrated that affluence heightens emotions over labor income questions.

Why the issue should be more volatile deserves analysis into the nature of labor and especially into its economic aspects, some inquiry into the sources of industrial dispute in an abundant economy, and some suggestions how justice and economic efficiency may be better realized in a dynamically productive economy.

LABOR, WORK AND WAGES

Both terms, labor and work, bear many meanings. Labor can mean physical or mental toil, the particular function in the economic process of providing human skill, energy and effort, and the class of economic participants who provide such services. Work and worker can convey these same meanings but can also refer to any kind of effective effort even that which is not performed for economic return. In addition and uniquely work can mean the effect, the product, the thing resulting from labor. We will generally use labor to mean the human activity which enters the economic process and work to mean the effect of that effort in some product. That we will frequently deviate from this general usage simply highlights what the many connotations of the terms imply, that the reality is a complex of many aspects. Our brief look at these will be organized under the two categories of the economic and non-economic dimensions of work and labor.

The Non-Economic Aspects

Labor as one kind of human activity has all the dimensions of action given in the Introduction: it is physical, biological, psychological, social, political, spiritual, moral, and economic. We will look at some of these aspects by considering labor and work as necessary, as social, and as befitting the dignity of man.

The necessity of labor has never been questioned -- except perhaps by teenagers asked to help around the house. St. Paul was terse and to the point in dealing with the early Christians who were neglecting daily affairs in expectations of the imminent end of the world: "If they will not work, neither let them eat." The difference between an abundant and a non-abundant economy lies largely in the amount and quality of labor expended by people. But man must work not only to sustain himself and to obtain goods beyond subsistence but also to realize his potentialities as a human being. "Man," says Viglino, "is the mean between the physical and spiritual world. He does not wander a strange shadow in that realm of becoming: we are not alien in the world but at home, for it is of our own substance.... It is precisely through work that man carries out his mission in the cosmic order of the material-spiritual and the material world is united with the spirit."[1]

Labor has always been a social activity. Economic work, a commodity or service, is intended for the use of others. On the side of labor, workingmen have at least as far back as the City-States of classical Greece combined in fellowships, often begun as religious sodalities, to further their craft interests and to pass their skills on to succeeding generations. This social impulse has evoked an almost continuous traditions of societies, mysteries, guilds, craft corporations, workingmen's associations up to contemporary labor unions and professional associations. The modern office or shop by its very nature becomes a work community which is an important ingredient in an individual's content or discontent with his job.

The dignity of labor and work comes easily to the lips but, in fact, its realization in an operative attitude encounters prejudices which have deep roots in Western civilization. The Jews apparently were unique among ancient people in accepting labor and work as the normal lot of all mankind. While labor's drudgery resulted from man's disobedience, human work was considered "the counterpart to God's work."[2] Among the Greeks and Romans husbandry was accorded a certain respect. Nevertheless, the work of supplying daily necessities was mainly relegated to those classes which were under necessity, that is slaves and to some extent women. Thus Cicero judged that only agriculture and large commercial enterprise were labor truly worthy of free men.[3] With feudalism serfs acquired a status slaves lacked, but they were still a breed clearly inferior to warriors and clerics. While the monk could sanctify necessitous work as prayer, peasants and craftsmen performing the same work outside monasteries could not, because they lacked the higher aim of charity and purifying the inner life.[4] Even with monks contemplation enjoyed pre-eminence over intellectual and manual labor.

The monastic ideal was not, however, lost on the laity. Throughout the Middle Ages heretical sects arose especially among the working poor, the Cathari, the Waldensians, the Fraticelli and others, who emphasized the ascetic value of work in counteracting the sins of the flesh. Martin Luther and John Calvin in making their appeal to the urban poor and to the rising middle class, in a sense, laicized the monastic "laborare est orare!" Every person served God in the vocation to which he was called, God using man's labor as a sort of mask to bless man with what was really God's. Thus work and success in one's work symbolized God's favor. When the symbolism evaporated the Puritan Ethic became the Work Ethic, the purely secular dignity of work for its own sake. Karl Marx saw a new society evolving out of the purely materialistic dialectic between exploiting capital and exploited labor. The proletariate was the agent creating a world of unlimited production and universal brotherhood.

The Church was tardy in countering this Marxian vision.

Even Leo XIII's On the Condition of Labor emphasized more correcting the abuses against the dignity of labor than analyzing in what that dignity consisted. Over seventy years later Vatican II addressed this deficiency with the Church's official statement on work as the obligation to construct a more human world.

> For when, by the work of his hands or with the aid of technology man develops the earth so that it can bear fruit and become a dwelling worthy of the whole human family, and when he consciously takes part in the life of social groups, he carries out the design of God. Manifested at the beginning of time, the divine plan is that man should subdue the earth, bring creation to perfection, and develop himself. When a man so acts he simultaneously obeys the great Christian commandment that he place himself at the service of his brother men.[5]

In summary, the dignity of labor and work consists 1) in completing the plan of creation, 2) in fulfilling one's self as a person and 3) in serving others. Besides specifying labor and work as human Values, the statement re-iterates the other non-economic aspects of labor we have considered, its necessity for human survival and fulfillment, and its social nature. These are chords which will weave into and around the main economic theme of the chapter.

The economic aspects of the work-wage relationship we shall consider are four: 1) identifiable authority over the product; 2) the diversity of interests and responsibilities in producing and selling a commodity; 3) wage and salary as the basic income for the workingman's and his family's survival; and 4) labor productivity as the ultimate criterion for hiring and paying labor. Upon each of these factors a theory of income distribution has been built, each wanting in some respects, yet each reflecting some aspect which must be preserved in any final theoretical formulation.

Ownership and Profits

Production is a complex process into which long-range engineering, personnel, financing, and marketing projections must be fed. Production is a cooperative venture and one subject to an infinity of vicissitudes both from within the firm and from without. Clear-cut authority, therefore, must be vested in managers to make decisions to produce, to scrap, to market and to sell the product. This is best achieved when the product is owned as private property, that is, when the incorporated business, whether for profit or not, owns the product by buying off all claims against the product in process. Nationalized and employee-operated businesses can, but with greater difficulty, set up comparable lines of authority, and must to function as a business. If suppliers, workers, and creditors can press ownership claims against the product in process, managerial decision is impossible.

Secondly, because this complex process takes place over time, it necessarily involves risk and produces a residual income, which in its broadest definition as net income we call profit. Since costs must be occurred in buying off, prior to final sale, claimants who have contributed to production, there is always the chance that the final sale will not reimburse these prior costs, or, just the opposite, may reimburse them more than was anticipated. In either case a net income is realized, negative in the case of a loss and positive in the case of profit. Since suppliers, creditors, and especially workers are justifiably reluctant to wait upon this chancey outcome, the business itself must bear risk and suffer the loss or rejoice in the profit. (Nevermind that we are dealing with concurrent flows, so that suppliers of capital, resources, and labor for tomorrow's output are really being paid out of today's sale of yesterday's production, the causal sequence, the risk and the residual income remain.)

The oldest and most simplistic theory of income distribution -- usually assumed rather than formalized -- simply states that, once claimants are bought off at their respective going rates, the residual belongs to the owners of the enterprise which is the owner of the product. This tidy theory, while clearly preserving managerial authority, makes two assumptions which may be questioned: 1) that the firm and its owners alone bear the risks of enterprise and 2) that owning and having authority over the product in process should entitle the owners, by criteria either of efficiency or of justice, to have sole claim to the value of the product, and thus to the profits.

The second assumption touches on the key analytic concept of the chapter and will be postponed for discussing in its proper place. We can briefly address the first. We have already seen that the large corporation -- and to lesser degrees all businesses -- spread risk throughout the economy. Supplying capital and product to companies always entail some risk, which may or may not have been adequately compensated. But clearly workingmen assume risks of endangering their health, life or limbs in taking employment. Moreover and more generally they risk their earning capacity because skills may be eroded by technological change, because jobs may be lost due to changes in demand for the product, because businesses may turn belly-up due to poor management. If risk establishes claim to profits, then workers have a claim.

Diversity and Industrial Bargaining

From the same fact of the complexity of production flows the second consideration, that the enterprise incorporates a diversity of interests and responsibilities in production and, consequently, a diverse sharing in its fruits. The point has been made several times that a business is a cooperative venture and that it has a common good which for business for profit is profit itself. Despite this, those who work on product and those who manage and own the business approach production from differing points of view, the latter having a view and responsibility encompassing the whole business, the former limited largely to their particular contribution and its reward. Thus a tension necessarily exists between labor and management which can only be resolved through negotiation, and, that failing, through a test of might. Were a company run democratically, so that those who work on product have some managerial say-so, the tension may be defused somewhat in the process of reaching management decisions, but not entirely and with the possibility of open conflict.

As an historical fact, however, industrial negotiation of wages and working conditions arose as a countervailing right of labor to ownership's sole claim to profits. The fact of conflict thus gave birth to the principle of industrial bargaining and the negotiated wage, two rights backed by economic might, the strike and boycott by labor, the lock-out and blacklisting by management. This industrial strife, titanic at times, inevitably invites intervention of government as umpire.

The last generation has seen an entirely new branch of law sprout from Federal and state laws, local statutes, court decisions and practices, and National Labor Relations

Board decisions. This law, while regularizing the pragmatic test of might, has at the same time recognized and legalized the industrial struggle.[6] Implicitly it also affirms, what we are all aware from personal experience, the public nature of this method of dividing the fruits of enterprise, that all of society is concerned not only in what division is effected but how.

What the principle of negotiation has brought clearly to light is that there is a diversity of interest in the business and differing views on sharing its output which often can be settled only through negotiation. Furthermore, individual workers cannot stand alone against the corporation but must negotiate in concert. Finally, negotiation must be an open process because it bears a great burden of social interest, and consequently public and social pressure are legitimate presences at the bargaining table.

This principle, in practice, also demonstrates that industrial warfare like all warfare is enormously wasteful. Strikes and lock-outs and boycotts hurt not only the individuals involved but can seriously affect the national interest. We have not hesitated to approve the use of massive Federal force to prevent such disasters.

What is not generally seen is that the tides of this war are constantly shifting with the acceleration and deceleration of the economy, that boom strengthens the demands of labor and recession of management. In addition the presence of government in the struggle shifts the balance of might from one side to the other, depending upon the political complexion of the Administration and Congress, or membership on NRLB. This does not necessarily prevent an equitable solution. But every negotiated settlement is a compromise, and, no matter what the equity, where the compromise is arrived at under external pressure, feelings on one side that they are being had will arise. Necessity might suppress them but they continue to rankle and will break out with greater force once advantage shifts.

Thus, while the conduct of industrial warfare today is more genteel, the strife has not really been ameliorated. It frays tempers more easily and makes industrial peace a pipedream. It weakens the economy by artificially stimulating or depressing inventory accumulation, by affecting industries far removed from the conflict, by straining welfare resources of communities. Above all it perpetuates the tradition completely inimical to free-enterprise that the economy is founded upon a struggle between social classes, between those who work with their hands and those who let their property. Such a view is archaic today when the vast majority of people enjoy some direct and a large indirect ownership interest in the economy beyond their labor-income.

However this may be, wage bargaining predominates as the accepted means of distributing the national product. Recent years have seen its spread into areas previously considered legally off limits to it. Its conquests in the municipal services and teaching fields shows the continued vitality of industrial bargaining and promises that it will remain on the industrial scene.

Family Living Wage

The principle of collective bargaining, however, has been subtly modified by two other principles. The first is that of the family living wage. The idea that a living wage was owed in strict justice was a hot issue twenty or twenty-five years ago, especially amongst Catholic economists and sociologists. Occasionally still, a moralist will get some publicity mileage by urging the demands of justice for the family wage, but he gets the newsprint only at the expense of setting a ridiculously high figure for the minimum need for survival.

The minimum family wage, however, is inherent in the wage contract. While one can argue the moral value of work -- that most of us need the discipline of working for another -- a man's productive powers are an economic good. He has just so much time in which and so much energy with which to work. In selling this to others, he should in the course of his lifetime be paid sufficiently to support himself and to fulfill his social obligations, the most burdensome of these the support of his family. Whatever else a person wants from work, he or she wants a decent wage.

This minimally acceptable wage is also implicit in the vision of all economists who aspired to say something socially significant -- in Smith, Marshall, Keynes, in Ricardo and in Marx. Nor did they conceive this as a fixed bare minimum, but growing as the wealth of the economy grew. The pressure of wants upon even increasing income is so intense that we forget the very real achievement in raising the socially acceptable minimum in the lifetime of this generation. The most obvious gain has been in leisure, more vacation, more holidays and early retirement. But even during the slower growth of the past decade, the moderate family budget increased over $700 in real purchasing power.[7]

While employers were and still are reluctant to admit the strict justice of the family wage, few argue with the proposition that every worker -- at least here in the United States -- is worth a decent wage. The fact that only half of $18,000 average family income is needed for survival means that a family living wage is simply built into most labor contracts.

But the doctrine is not a dead letter. The family wage idea has put pressure under legislation to raise the minimum level and to extend its scope. In addition, it has been transmuted into the widely held conviction that all families should participate in affluence in a minimally decent way. Schemes, like the guaranteed annual income or the reverse income tax, are premised on this right.

Productivity-Wage Guidelines

The second, more recent modification of bargaining theory is the argument that wage increases should parallel general economic growth. This proposition underlies the wage guide-lines of recent and uncertain reputation. That wage guide-lines have not worked too well in practice, however, is no argument against their theoretical importance. For they have advanced bargaining theory by amalgamizing the practical wisdom of unions' ability-to-pay argument -- that if a corporation enjoys good profits, it can and by implication should pay a higher wage -- with the more defensible theoretical arguments.

The micro-argument for productivity-wage guide-lines is used more frequently to temper union demands. Labor can demand to be paid what it is worth, but no more. If wage rates are driven too high relative to sales and productivity, corporate managers are faced with the alternative of crippling losses or of substituting machines and automated equipment for man-power. Conrail, for example, had to face up to the painful decisions that, along with investing $2.5b. to update rolling stock, rails, and yards, it had to trim its work-force so that the high wages paid workers were justified by the revenue produced. Conceding this logic, the brotherhoods lent their cooperation.

The shifting of spending from labor to capital goods is going on all the time. There is, however, an obvious limit because no machine nor electronic device can substitute completely for labor. Someone must start and stop the machines, oversee their operation, and maintain them. Moreover, improved efficiency may by lowering costs improve sales and thus increase employment. In the decade 1967-76, while industrial blue-collar workers, upon whose jobs automation would have its most serious impact, declined from 26% to 25% of the total work-force, nevertheless, their absolute number increased by 2 million.

The more positive justification of productivity-wage guide-lines is that as the economy grows, the income of all sectors of the economy and especially the largest portion, that of labor, must increase with it. If not, the product produced will not be taken off the market. This logic is inescapable to managers of firms who produce for a mass market. Howevermuch the corporate giant would like to reduce its own wage bill, it readily recognizes that all firms could not do the same without serious decline in its own sales. In no way did American capitalism distinguish itself from European than in the early vision of Henry Ford that mass production necessitated the "five-dollar day".

Where wage guide-lines fail is in their use as a statistical average. First, any average growth rate figure will vary with the period chosen and none will coincide with the recent past or today. Even less so will an economy average match an industry's or a firm's recent average growth. To be absolutely just in application, wage guide-lines would have to admit so many exceptions that they would cease to guide. Consequently, to be really effective and just they would invite so much government intervention to the bargaining table as to, in effect, destroy the bargaining process. Nevertheless, they provide criteria for moderation. In time of crisis, also, the general good of the economy may justify the many inequities a blanket rule may perpetrate. Thus productivity-wage guide-lines like the other principles of distribution display glaring weaknesses as effective instruments for income distribution.

- Yet the guide-lines like the other theories of income distribution make positive contributions to final formulation. Such must preserve clear-cut managerial authority.
- At the same time, industrial bargaining, given the complexity of production and the diversity of interests, will always have a role in negotiating wages and working

o conditions. Such a formulation must be frank about the nature of the wage contract: people work for money, and want enough to support their families decently. Finally,
o the level of wages and salaries depends on labor productivity in turning out goods which sell. To pay less lowers aggregate demand; to pay more threatens a com-
o pany's survival. A viable formulation of income sharing must incorporate all these realities of industrial relations.

THE NEUROLOGY OF CONFLICT

A final formulation -- if this is ever possible -- must also be capable of neutralizing the fears and prejudices which can seethe beneath the surface of a work-community. This simmering pot of neural responses, thought clichés, and accumulated animosities, a brew of both economic and non-economic ingredients, can make intelligent confrontation of labor relations almost impossible. We will try to scoop up some of the causes of worker disaffection and have a look at them.

Problem of Craftsmanship

First, the question of craftsmanship. No one denies that modern technology has changed the sense of craftsmanship. It is difficult to see how a worker whose task is to inspect bottles of beer streaming past on a conveyor for defectives can achieve a sense of fulfillment. Or how a man hopping from chassis to chassis to put in a headplate can have a sense of craftsmanship. Automation performs no more humanizing role than to eliminate such boring, moronizing routine.

But in deploring the decline of hand craftsmanship, critics often forget the tremendously increased demands which the complex production of today puts upon human judgment and responsibility. From the man at the controls of a wrecking crane, to the girl punching cards in the office assembly line, to the inspector on a production line, craftsmanship has shifted from hand manipulation to judgment and care. When a leaky valve can destroy an Apollo rocket, the lives of astronauts and millions of man-hours of expensive effort, the individual bears an enormous burden of responsibility, however little he might derive a sense of satisfaction from his efforts.

Then too in lauding the marvelous craftsmanship of the past, what people frequently forget is the brute labor these crafts demanded. The bulk of the human labor to build a cathedral was expended in quarrying and dressing stone and putting it in place rather than in carving capitols and engineering construction. Machines have largely alleviated this effort and freed human work to go off in other directions.

Work skills have acquired many new dimensions. For many it consists in controlling vastly more sophisticated capital equipment like steering a tractor-and-rig through traffic, operating a modern combine, drop forge, grader, or word-processor. For other workers it means analyzing complex physical, psychological, or industrial conditions and making life-or-death decisions what to do. Millions are involved in the demanding tasks of managing people, persuading them to buy, capturing their imagination and interest, motivating them to perform. The skill-demands of modern industrial living are such that they seem rather to over-tax human abilities than otherwise. Clue to these increased demands is that the skills of the past, from chipping flint tools to hand-weaving, are acquired as leisure hobbies. The real problem seems to be to find jobs which the physically handicapped and the mentally retarded can perform productively and with dignity.

This conclusion is borne out by the continuing shift in the composition of the employed labor force from routine manual labor to labor demanding personal skill, judgment, responsibility, and/or contact with the public. Over the period 1954 to 1976, the three categories of unskilled industrial labor, machine operators except in transportation, and private household workers declined from 27% of total employment to 18.6%. Contrariwise professional and technical employment increased from 8.9% to 14.7% and employment in services industries from 8.2% to 12.7%. While the increase in clerical jobs from 13.1% to 17.7% may represent an increase in routine work and the decline of farm employment from 10.1% to 3.1% of the total meant the loss of 3.6m. jobs demanding a variety of skills, the other categories of managers and administrators, sales, skilled craftsmen, transportation operators all increased or kept pace with the creation of 25.6m. new jobs during that period.[8] In effect, therefore, practically all the new jobs were of the kind demanding a higher level of skill and responsibility.

Despite these changes in the nature of craftsmanship,

pride in work well done is so spontaneous that where this is missing generally in a plant, office, laboratory or school, there almost always exist causes more fundamental than the carelessness of individual workers. This pride can be corroded by the acid of indifference stemming from the engineering of the product downward through a whole series of decisions about materials, production, assembly which are satisfied by slapping a coat of covering-up paint rather than by pulling an item from the line. More frequently a management, which discourages, penalizes rather than rewards, the conscientious worker, nor solicits the contribution of his know-how, is at fault. The easiest excuse is to blame the worker for indifference, and often he is at fault. But too frequently the system itself is at fault. There is, in short, no linking of reward with a general spirit of conscientious effort.

Diligence Rewarded

Man works for reward. Only the exceptional person continues to work regardless of honor, esteem or pay. Honor and esteem are valued rewards whatever the field of endeavor. But while a mother who slaves for her family is satisfied with the esteem of her children, and men of strong social consciousness for the honors of political or civic life, man in his economic life wants a material gain. Honor without the money is hollow, not because the honor is worthless, but because business is entered for the sake of material return. This is not cynical but clear recognition that the purpose of enterprise is profit and gain. Peer respect is accorded just as much to the weekly pay-check as to the corporate profit and loss statement. Words of praise and esteem are really worth something only if they presage a higher income, a better position, or some other tangible reward.

Bob Newhart caught this neatly in his wry sketch of the office clerk who, losing his inhibitions in the wine at his retirement dinner, contrasted his "cr-crummy watch" to the hundred thousand of company funds "sweet Miss Simpson" absconded with to Mexico.

Rewarding effort, however, must be rational. Its purpose should be not only to compensate past work but to elicit further effort. It should be forward looking. A system, offering no hope to increase one's income, squelches a sense of craftsmanship, dampens enthusiasm to advance, and turns the ambitious away to other than the normal paths of advancement, perhaps through the labor union, to another firm, or into an altogether different kind of work.

Less but, nevertheless, also corrosive of personal drive is rewarding solely on the basis of longevity. While senority increases are a practicable means for rewarding experience and hence of worth, it is based on the assumption that duration on a job is true experience. But routine repetition is not experience, unless there is a conscious process of appraisal leading to improvement. It demands personal effort. Wage and salary increases which reward routine performance equally with true experience soon discourage the latter. Supervisors should be especially quick in recognizing and rewarding the development of unique competences. That this should occur should cause no surprise, paralleling as it does the business's own drive to develop uniqueness in its product. We all are keenly conscious of our own individuality, that even in a standardized performance there is something different about our touch.

Thus the second nerve of worker disaffection is laid bare. Workers can identify with their company if its reward system spurs them to contribute not only greater but personal effort.

Worker-Company Identification

Probing this ganglion touches another sensitive labor nerve. A system of rewarding individual conscientiousness is easily subject to the charge of favoritism. Special treatment always leaves the individual prey to the ill-will of his peers: refusing to talk to him, letting him eat alone, ostracizing him from the group, under-cutting him in every way ingenuity can devise. The overall disappointment of expectations from incentive pay, piecework and special bonuses schemes to increase productivity should have been anticipated by anyone who realized that the shop or gang is a social grouping. Recognizing this by group rewarding and bonuses, instead of by individual preferments, takes the pressure of group envy off the stand-out performer. Instead of under-cutting him from envy, others will applaud and emulate him since all profit from his performance.

Besides the morale factor, group rewarding will tap the deeper roots of craftsmanship. Where the individual in his individual performance cannot develop a pride in work well done because his own job is but a microscopic part of a whole, he can develop pride in the performance of the crew as a whole. Both group morale and craftsmanship are further bolstered when reward follows conscientious effort to increase output, to care for equipment, and to reduce waste. The company need not compete with union loyalty. While workers will still look to their union to negotiate basic wages, general fringe benefits, over-all working conditions and grievance procedures, they can also identify their own success with the success of their gang, their shop, and eventually their company.[9]

The Dynamics of Profit

Nevertheless, the very dynamics of profit-seeking pose barriers to such identification. We can look at two of them. First, the profit-seeking, which by spurring American economic growth since World War II maintained the over-all stability of the work-force, generated greater uncertainty for the individual worker. This is not so paradoxical as it seems. The economy's record is really remarkable: in the 22 years from 1954 to 1976 it created 25.6m. new jobs, increased average compensation, wages and fringe benefits, at a real annual rate of 2.5-3.0%, while doubling the number of paid holidays and days of vacation. Despite the 40% "baby-boom" increase of the non-institutionalized population over age 16 from 116.3m. to 156.0m., the number of new jobs more than kept pace. Thus employment statistics point to conclusions diametrically opposed to Marxist dogmatism of the increasing immizeration of the working class and the generation of a reserve army of the unemployed. For the very growth in the number of the unemployed from 3.5m. to 7.3m. demonstrates the success of the economy in persuading a larger percentage of the total population, especially married women and teenagers, to go job seeking.[10]

Yet as we saw above, this overall growth was achieved only by changing the composition of the work-force. Thus the factors generating growth, changing demand, production innovation, new technologies, automation, cybernetics and the rest, pose threats to the stability and continuance of workers' income. Work stoppages, strikes, shortage shutdowns, market slow-downs, and recession lay-offs hit the individual wage-earner all the harder because of the high wages he earns, which neither a strike fund nor unemployment compensation can adequately replace. Beyond this continuous threat looms the possibility that changing technology may render his skills and his job obsolete. However diligent his personal effort, the worker may be rendered temporarily or permanently superfluous by causes beyond his control. Nor do efforts to retrain or relocate alleviate all the trauma.

Related but deserving special highlighting is the problem of occupational injuries. Despite the wide-spread and generally successful campaign of the '40s and '50s to reduce industrial accidents, work-related fatalities and crippling disabilities are on the rise, particularly in production involving the use of new chemical compounds. The annual figures are grim: 9000 work-related deaths, 400,000 people who contract an occupational disease and about 6m. reported work-accidents.[11] This, coupled with the fact that workman's compensation awards are pitiful in comparison to wages lost, has raised worker's consciousness on matters of safety. In the ten years from 1965 to 1975 the number of work-stoppages due to physical and hazardous working conditions has increased from 1.5% to 6.6%[12] of the total. Thus poor safety and health conditions becomes another issue accentuating the workingman's feeling that he is a pawn in corporate profit-seeking.

Finally, labor's mistrust of profit-seeking is compounded by misunderstanding the dynamics of profit. For profits are always expressed in the past tense, as the difference between costs incurred and sales made in the year or quarter past. Profit-seeking, however, looks rather to the future than to the past. The dynamics of profit-making, therefore, involves a process of constantly pressing into the future to improve present methods, to turn out more product, to strive for higher sales. This is the heart of the industrial matter, the inmost drive which gives a business form and structure. This is enterprise in its bare essence.

This semantic issue lies, too, at the heart of the distribution problem. For today's labor which is paid out of today's sales is producing tomorrow's product. But today's sales is of product worked on yesterday. To restrict today's labor income to what yesterday's efficiency has earned is to clamp the dead hand of the past upon today's hope. While the business as a whole is looking into the future, labor must be content with what has been earned. No wonder labor always feels that it is constantly catching up on its due returns. No wonder too it is content to stick with the methods of the past and to resist change. Change offers no hope to them. Here we cut closer to the crux of industrial conflict: management looks ahead, investment, innovation, new markets, increased sales; labor looks at the past, last year's annual report.

All this can become hardened into two opposing views. Management finds it galling that workers claim an increased share in increasing revenue when productivity increases are due to forward-looking investment, research and development, innovation and risk-taking, all management functions, while labor is a reluctant cooperator, slowing the pace of change, feather-bedding, even sabotaging improvements. Labor, on its side, sees its gains as a reluctant minimum wrung from management. What is, therefore, given with reluctance deserves only reluctant work. The company, in effect, is made for fleecing, deserving only the sloppiest work tolerated, the minimum effort spelled out in the contract.

Both views deny the essential, cooperative nature of business and argue from a myopic sense of justice and near-sighted individualism. Both miss the point of scarcity in an affluent economy that wasting resources and misusing human labor is more unpardonable because the very profusion of affluence creates more wants than it satisfies.

Alienation

All these elements of dissafection are cited as evidence of a general malaise, called alienation. For Marx, however, alienation has a precise scientific meaning of a condition inherent in the capitalistic system. Since all the labor neuroses above may arise in whatever kind of enterprise, profit or non-profit, authoritarian or democratic, socialist or free-enterprise, it is better to restrict the term alienation to Marx's meaning.

Briefly then, Marx confines alienation to capitalism[13] because only in that mode of production the worker not only works under another's control but on that other's property. Thus the worker is robbed of that which is specifically human in work, his own creativity. Under capitalism, therefore, the worker is estranged from the product which is not his own creation, from the production which is controlled by another, from the customer because he works not to satisfy the buyer but to appease the capitalist, from his fellow workers since each works independently of others under the boss, and, worst of all, from himself for work has become a bondage and hated toil and not an activity in which he can develop as a person.

But more than begetting alienation, capitalism perpetuates and intensifies it. For Marx recognizes that possessing labor skills can be a lever of insubordination and the very massing of workers together can increase their resistance to domination. But the capitalist by means of exploiting labor's surplus value is able increasingly to mechanize his operation, thus obviating his reliance on skilled labor, substituting women and children instead, and by replacing workers with machines creates a surplus army of the unemployed who serve as a threat to keep employed workers in line.

Marx's bleak picture, however lacking in historical verification, nevertheless, places the warning signs how a work-place or a business system can disintegrate, once workers lose a sense of common purpose. A healthy personnel policy will heed their warnings. Marxian alienation also brings into relief the neuroses we have discussed: the problem of craftsmanship, the rewarding of personal and group diligence, the difficulty a worker experiences in identifying with his company, and the need to overcome labor's mistrust of the dynamics of profits. Against these rather somber considerations we advance some suggestions how a more just as well as more efficient production can be achieved.

PRODUCT AND PRICES

The nub of the issue is the distinction between product and its price. Simple enough! But simple distinctions have a way of becoming complicated upon close examination. Indeed this distinction lies at the heart of the unfolding of economics as a science: is the worth of a product due to the labor and other factor inputs or is it due to its ability to be sold? This, students will recognize, is the critical difference between a Labor Theory of value and a Marginal Utility Theory of value.

The Product and Its Value

Yet this distinction, which runs through all of business, is accepted as an everyday occurrence. Ask the president of a company what they made last week and he is likely to respond, "One million dollars". Ask the plant manager and he may say, "Twenty castings". Ask an accountant what a certain purchase order is for and he will reply, "For $310". Ask the shop supervisor and he will say, "For 10 tons of steel scrap". Though each answers differently, each is correct -- depending on the context. Both refer to the same reality but differently, one to the product itself, the other to its price or value.

The language of business is full of words with both a value use and a product use: productivity, labor, capital, sales, output and so forth. Their meaning is determined from the context only. Other words like price, cost, salary, profits, and revenue are clearly value words. Terms like craftsmanship, work, machinery, engineering and commodity are product words. Even product itself is bi-valent, a value word as in Gross National Product and a product word in, for example, "This farm's largest product is corn."

The confusion arising from this usage is not such that we cannot live with it. If we talk to machinists, personnel officers, engineers, and transportation officials we use the language of real production. When we talk to accountants, budget people, and financial officers we talk value production. With purchasing agents, sales managers and presidents of firms we are likely to interweave the two.

The real problem, since value production and product production are obviously related, comes in determining what is the relationship between the two, which has primacy in the firm, how is the tension between product-oriented people and value-oriented people resolved, and finally (what this chapter is most concerned with) what is the respective ownership claims against the value of the product and against the product itself.

To begin, therefore, a product is the commodity which is being fabricated and eventually sold -- an automobile or a home or a song. It is the result of combining many inputs of planning, engineering, labor skills and effort, raw material, machinery, promotion and selling. (This definition includes services. For example, a lawyer's product is the legal opinion he renders, the application of his knowledge and experience -- his labor skills -- to research into the facts and legal precedents -- his raw materials.) This effort fixes certain qualities of usefulness in the product; hence people desire it.

Value, on the other hand, is simply what a commodity brings when sold. There is always an element of the fortuitous here: sometimes the price is higher than anticipated, sometimes lower, depending on the product's market. For this reason we are ordinarily sure of the value of the good only when it is actually sold.

But goods-in-process also acquire and have value. The difficulty is that since such goods are seldom saleable as such it is hard to get an accurate fix on their true market value. Accountants consequently use the convention of evaluating them at the cost of labor, materials, energy and overhead which had gone into them up to that stage of production. This convention, however inaccurate, is based on the presumption that the formation of value parallels the fabrication of product and is impossible without it. What the convention does tend to obscure is that the quality of production, the efficiency and craftsmanship of the productive process, is at every stage increasing or decreasing the final value, even though this will not be determined until the final sale. It is clear, therefore, that through all stages of production the contact between value- and product formation is constant and close.

Profits, Values and Products

Which has primacy in the firm, is a knottier problem. The firm seeks profits and without them dies. Since profit is solely and clearly a value reality, value-formation is the firm's primary purpose. That and that alone explains why materials are bought, labor hired, and the wheels set in motion. The whole process is senseless without the profit-motive, all sentimental and romantic nonsense to the contrary notwithstanding.

This is not the whole story, however. No profit is possible without a product. Even the profit from stealing needs the product-services of the thief. Productivity further conditions profitability in that the better the product, all market condition being the same, the more the profit (or the less the loss). More than this, for society consumption is the end and purpose of production. A firm must produce what people will buy. We seem then driven to the opposite conclusion that product-formation, not value-formation, is the primary end of business.

But this is not an impasse. There is an alternative:

not a slick philosophical out but a true insight into a complex reality. <u>Product-formation and value-formation are processes simultaneously means and end to each other</u>. Product is a necessary means to achieve value, the hope of value being the end or purpose of production. But looked at from the side of consumption, which is the end of production, the product is the end and the value the necessary means. Like male and female they mutually fulfill each other.

From this mutual interdependence flows most of the tension within firms -- the scraps between engineers and salesmen, between accountants and production people. It is not a fight between idealists and realists but between two sets of half-realists who see only an aspect of the whole. For sales people cannot sell (if today, not eventually) a poorly engineered product. But they are equally handicapped by a product so engineered that it is priced out of the market. This tension then is built into the firm; it is the very force which makes the company go. Emphasis on value-formation to the exclusion of product-formation means that the company will sell a poor product simply to make money; emphasis on product with no concern for value means no profits. Both spell eventual bankruptcy.

This tension exists in all human institutions. Take that which should be least concerned about profits, a church. The pastor whose sermons are so ethereal and his attitudes so angelic that he turns off his people decimates the collection plate. The pastor, the predominant theme of whose preaching is money, drives the spiritually hungry away. Even here people pay -- according to their means -- for value received.

Ownership and Value

Establishing the distinction between the product and its value legitimizes the question, "Granted that the business owns the product, can others lay claim to part of its value?" To answer the question, the student will excuse our reviewing briefly some ideas discussed in Chapter Two and elsewhere.

A commodity has two values, a value-in-use, the usefulness perceived by potential customers, and a value-in-exchange, what people are willing to give up to get it. Obviously, value-in-exchange implies scarcity: no one surrenders anything for a good so plentiful he can have for the taking. Conversely, the rarest good which no one wants is valueless in exchange.

Utility, this perception of usefulness, is central to exchange, the market value being but the conjunction of the subjective evaluations of many sellers and many buyers. Utility, therefore, is the primary cause of value but those who fashion the product with these useful qualities also contribute to its value. (This priority marks the decisive difference with Marx.) If labor, therefore, has some claim to the value of the product, it comes in here.

But to ferret this out, we must begin with consumer demand, to satisfy which is the purpose of production. Given that consumers have the ability, they are persuaded to buy upon perceiving the product's useful qualities in contrast to those of substitute or competing commodities. The greater this competition, the more the price of the good must be lowered to sell more of it, and the greater the fall in sales if the price is increased. Just the opposite, the more distinctive a good is perceived, the greater the freedom to lower or raise prices. This change in the dollar volume of sales, marginal revenue, with a change in price is a critical consideration for business in deciding its level of production and hiring of labor. What firms can sell, therefore, depends on customer expectations of satisfaction relative to price in contrast to competing goods, and that _expectation is largely conditioned by their past experience of the product_.

The scene now shifts to production, where labor, raw materials, energy, machines, supervision are blended to make the desired product, the cause of the product being, therefore, this blend and not any individual factor of production. Labor especially is a _sine qua non_ and, given a system of capital goods, more labor will be hired if the added output can bring in enough additional revenue at least to cover their wages. That is, businesses can increase their profits by hiring more labor right up to the point where this marginal revenue product equals the wage rate. Thus the three determinants, consumer demand for the product, labor's productivity, and the wage rate simultaneously set the amount of labor hired. A change in any one affects employment, demand and productivity directly, the wage rate inversely.

While this neat mathematical model, which the student can review in any standard principles text, simplifies out a great range of social circumstances and a bewildering variety of jobs, many of which are not susceptible to quantitative productivity measurements, nevertheless, it concentrates our attention on the factors determining labor productivity. For quantifiable output piece-rates and gang-rates are standard incentives and sales work typically has a bonus feature. But for supervisory, staff, and office work the quality of performance must be evaluated. While production and sales can share in productivity increases, nevertheless, even here quantity output can be pushed to the detriment of quality productivity. Thus the quality of work performance poses the big problems.

We will consider two factors, minimizing scrap and servicing the customer. Minimizing scrap increases output by lowering costs, but wasteful scrap takes on many forms. There is the obvious, a botched casting, and then the not so obvious, wasted effort, reports which have to be done over, the thoughtless "chewing out" which turns an employee sour, the incorrect billing generating additional paper work, the misdirected shipment, all are forms of scrap which more conscientious work could have turned to profitable output. The second more difficult part of quality performance is the attitude of keeping the ultimate customer in mind. It is more difficult because most employees never meet the ultimate customer. Whatever else the consumer movement has achieved, it should make manufacturers more conscious that defective products have a diminished value. When a car window, shimmed into place to pass inspection, falls out in a customer's hands, the sloppy work besides earning customer ill-will slashes the value and the profits by the cost of the repairs. Again surly salespeople, indifferent nurses or nurses aides, improper credit procedures, late deliveries and the rest produce their toll in customer reluctance to come back again. Mistakes will be made and carelessness occurs but a consistent pattern tells of a management policy which tolerates such habits or cannot motivate its personnel to catch the mistakes as they would slip by. It tells of a general attitude of indifference for the final product and the customer.

Applied to our original distinction between the product and its value, all these factors, managerial policy, diligence of the work force, the attitude of care for customer service, make a difference in the value of the product in that more can be sold at higher prices or at lower costs. Thus no matter who owns the product, the entire firm as a working unit can lay claim to part of the profits. For, o while wages and salaries buy off the workers' claim to the product, the value of their effort is not finally assessed until the commodity is sold. At that time there

o exists a legitimate claim to share in profits which their productivity made possible. Upon this idea the philosophy of profit-, or better productivity-sharing is based.

JUSTICE, EFFICIENCY AND PRODUCTIVITY-SHARING

One of the quiet successes of American industrial relations has been the phenomenal growth of profit-sharing plans. From the 37 corporate plans in 1939 over 185,000 plans were in existence in 1976. In addition more than 200,000 corporations have established pension plans for their employees. With profit-sharing slowly gaining popularity among the corporate giants -- over 40% of the 500 largest industrial corporations now have some kind of a plan -- perhaps 20% of all U.S. workers share in corporation profits.

The Productivity-Sharing Idea

Productivity sharing is not a single technique but a philosophy of compensation ranging over plans with modest stock option rights to full-fledged sharing annual profits, some with employee thrift and contributory features and some without, some blending pension programs and others profit-sharing only. Corporate advocacy varies from the fervent apostolate of Mr. James Lincoln of Lincoln Electric Co. in Cleveland to tepid hopes to turn an inefficient firm around (usually failing). While most plans were established after the War, Procter & Gamble's and that of Sears, Roebuck and Co., two of the most successful, were set up in 1887 and 1916 respectively. The Sears' plan has been phenomenally successful: its 310,000 employees currently own Trust assets of almost $3b.

A 1976 study by the Profit Sharing Research Foundation of the 38 corporations with the largest profit-sharing trusts suggests that taken as a group they out-performed their non-profit-sharing competitors in return on sales and return on equity capital.[14]

Productivity-sharing is no new idea. Its theory was worked out mathematically and in practice by the Prussian economist and land-owner, Johann Heinrich von Thünen (1783-1850). Years before Marx he demonstrated that the wage rate was and should be the harmonic mean between the cost-of-living and workers' share in the increasing output of the economy.[15] John Bates Clark (1847-1938), the great American economist, showed almost clairvoyant foresight when he wrote in 1892 of the troubled labor conflicts of his day and his conclusions apply with no less cogency today:

> "Upon arbitration, profit-sharing, and full cooperation must be our dependence for the solution of the labor problem. These measures are named in the direct order of their availability, and in the reverse order of their intrinsic excellence. Arbitration is the easiest, and will doubtless have, in the decades immediately coming, the greatest extension. It is, however, only the more radical measures, those which merge classes now hostile, that can insure a reign of permanent peace in the industrial world. Profit-sharing makes the workman, in a sense, an employer; and full cooperation makes him both an employer and a capitalist. In neither relation is he a disturbing element, for in neither can he well fail to receive obvious justice."[16]

In our approach, linking justice and efficiency to productivity-sharing, we will use as key the distinction between value- and product-formation. Besides showing how profit-sharing implements the logic of economic theory, we will show how it fulfills the thrust of earlier distribution theories, alleviates the fears of progress, and ameliorates industrial conflict.

The Productivity-Sharing Solution

This is a tall order for a short section but we need only gather together the bits and pieces which have been carefully prepared in the preceding sections, starting with those residues of solid truth derived from earlier distribution theories. Put briefly these concluded:

1) That clear ownership to the product is essential for management;
2) That a fluctuating residual return (profit or loss) is an inevitable form of business income;
3) That approaching an essentially cooperative process from differing points of view, the union and management must negotiate on wages and other industrial issues;

4) That the family living wage alone satisfies minimum justice; and
5) That the overall good of the economy demands matching labor's return with productivity gains.

The distinction between value- and product-formation can be seen in these conclusions. Conclusions one and four look on the industrial process as product realities. Two and five express value concepts and three, the differing approaches of workers and managers to the whole process. Thus the conflict implicit here can be ameliorated, or at least put on a more rational basis, if the other inconsistencies are resolved.

Profit-sharing preserves the ownership rights of the company to the product. In fact and in law it recognizes that the worker's claim to the product is bought off when the firm pays the agreed wage or salary. Implicitly it affirms the impossibility of management and of profit-making unless this is so. The right claimed in profit-sharing is to the profits from production not to the product itself. Clearly then profit-sharing is founded on the distinction between product-formation and value-formation.

Profit-sharing preserves the family living wage idea as compensation owed in strict justice. The moral claim of workers to the product is not bought off until they are compensated sufficiently to afford an adequate diet, shelter and clothing according to the minimal acceptable standards. The most important and largest part of the real costs of production is precisely this necessary compensation to the workers. Regardless of what the product sells for this minimum family wage is still owed to the worker. At the same time this is not necessarily a fixed minimum. For profit-sharing recognizes that this level can be moved upward as contemporary standards change. The clear affirmation of the family wage is possible only in maintaining the distinction between value and product.

Profit-sharing, in going beyond the family wage to value realities, moreover overcomes the limited applicability of the family wage principle. The family living wage, defined, for example, as the legal minimum wage, can itself be a barrier to employment for the completely unskilled. So defined also, it is hardly relevant for most wages in the United States today. Consequently the principle is largely at a dead end as a solution to the distribution problem and, more importantly, misses the broader social justice implications of wage-productivity guide-lines.

These are implicit in profit-sharing for wage-productivity is of the very essence of profit-sharing. Profit-sharing, however, avoids the straight-jacket of national or even industry guide-lines. Instead it focuses on the profitability of this firm, of this division, or even of this department, relating the profits from this particular line to the efficiency of this particular fabricating process or staff function in the firm.

Obviously profit-sharing, in affirming the necessity and reality of profits, as a form of fluctuating residual, orients the entire distribution policy of a firm towards realizing profits. At the same time it recognizes that profits are partly fortuitous and dependent on social and objective condition in the economy, in the industry, and in consumer demand over which the firm has no control. Hence, profit-sharing must recognize society's claim to profits in the right to tax it and its claim to commodities which service wants and are reasonably priced. But most of all it stresses the appropriateness of sharing this social gain with the workers who made it possible.

For profit-sharing bases the right of workers on the fact that profits are importantly increased when a firm can elicit from its labor force more effective and careful cooperation in cutting waste and scrap, in responding positively to new technology, in initiating improved techniques, and in general upon the individual worker's sense of motivation, a high shop morale, a communal sense of craftsmanship and a general desire to service consumer wants. For all of these lower the costs of operation regardless of changes in the marketplace. Here above all, profit-sharing affirms the justice of the worker's right to some of the profits and points out the rationality of effecting a more efficient operation by implementing this kind of elementary justice. The rights to profits are clearly founded on the distinction between, yet interweaving of the real and value elements in production.

Profit-Sharing and Productivity

Profit-sharing does not introduce an alien element into the logic of production. All it attacks is a gratuitous assumption, an assumption based on the confusion between product and its price, that the owner of the product, be it a company or a private individual, has the same absolute ownership rights to the profits of production as it does to the product itself.

Profit-sharing in itself will substitute an element of stability for the uncertainty produced by improving technology and increasing abundance. For even though their work skills may be eroded, the workers are being compensated by increased sharing in the gain produced by improved technology. More importantly, however, they can more easily recognize that if technological innovation reaps a return, it should bear the costs of progress, in this case, the relocation or retraining of workers whose jobs and skills are eliminated by the innovation. Both worker morale and efficiency is improved by so locating the costs of technological unemployment precisely in the profits created by technological change. Retraining and relocating programs rather than the brutal surgery of the pink slip, will do much to alleviate the workers' fears that progress is nothing for them but the shifting sands of job elimination and skill erosion.

But the principal benefit of profit-sharing is that it spells out more rational lines for industrial bargaining and negotiation by directing the eyes of both labor and management toward future returns. It is not a panacea for industrial peace, no more than Christian charity dispels all family disagreements. Union and management do look at the industrial process differently, but they have the same goals, economic gain. This is the firmly imbedded tradition of American unionism -- and thank God for it -- a healthy gain motivation, relatively unmixed with the political and social ideologies of European unions.

But they have been seeking gains differently. Like two horses they have been pulling together but each leaning to its side of the traces. Managers see profits as of the future. Today's costs affect tomorrow's profitability. Labor sees profits as yesterday's gains. If the company had a profitable year, they can afford to raise wages this year. The two are simply out of step: management complains that labor is a drag on progress, labor that it can never catch up with the past. What profit-sharing does is to direct the hopes and the concern of labor in the same direction as that of management. In thus establishing a closer identification of the workers' interests with that of his company, productivity-sharing pulls the intellectual roots of alienation.

Historians of American industry will recognize this as in line with the best tradition of American Capitalism. Economists will see in it a practical implementation of the marginal revenue productivity principle, that profits are maximized when the worker is paid his worth in value-productivity. In fixing workers' interest in the well-being of corporations, not only will industrial disputes be mitigated, the need for government intervention lessened, but workers' concern will become an important bulwark in preserving the corporation as social property. The man on the street will recognize in profit-sharing the convergence of economic efficiency with social justice in distribution. All of the above will help in restoring the aura to some very battered and tarnished American Values, like profits and profit-seeking, gain-motivation, industrial craftsmanship, and productive cooperation.

CHAPTER TEN

POWER, FREEDOM AND COMMUNITY

The demand for power smouldered beneath most of the hot issues of the last decades. Depending on what or who was burning, the flames blazed in varied hues: black power, green power, grey power, student power, woman power and always power to the people. These demands by groups lacking power, or so perceiving themselves, contrast to the obvious presence in industrialized societies of centers of immense power. Such centers, however manifesting power as military might, political clout, control of technology, or manipulation of public opinion, always possess some amount of economic power. Indeed one of the differentiating features of abundant economies is the presence and exploitation of economic power.

While all people want power and the majority of us relish those few moments when we have exercised it, we rather fear than cherish the power the few in our midst possess. Instinctively we cheer the individual who challenges a corporation or government bureaucracy. Above all we fear the power of powerful institutions, perceiving them as threats to our freedom.

This chapter, therefore, essays to walk out the dimensions of economic power in the U.S. economy, not with any hope of resolving the conflict between power and freedom, far less to advocate emasculating economic power, but only to advance some suggestions on how to live with power while preserving at least one's inner freedom.

POWER AND FREEDOM

Though lacking more precise formulation, the issue calls for closer examination of the two phenomena, power and freedom, and how they relate to each other.

The Features of Power

Power has many faces. It is protean and elusive. Because power is derived from many sources, moral, intellectual, physical, political and economic, it is difficult to determine who bears power and the relative strength of that power. That is, power is generally partial. Seldom does one person control another totally as in slavery.

Power here simply means the ability to effect one's own purpose. As such it is <u>good and necessary</u>. The individual could not survive without some power. Here we must sharply differentiate between possessing power and enjoying the trappings of power. It is much like the difference between sexual virility and machismo, between initiating an act of physical love and, perhaps, a new life, and dominating another person for personal pleasure. In affecting one's own purpose, a person does affect and influence others. But this can be done in a way which respects others' freedom or by way of dominating and lording it over others. (The other trappings of power, the big display, the big stir, the big name are vanities which may be based on real possession of power or may be illusionary.) So possessing power is not in itself evil, no more than sexual potency is evil. Power becomes evil, as does any means, when it is put to evil uses. The specific evil of power, even when used for a good purpose, comes from violating the freedom of others.

While we all need and have some power, it is not egalitarian. Power must be <u>unequal</u> at least with respect to a particular purpose, or stalemate results. Thus the Constitution of the United States establishes a balance of power among the three branches of government, but they are not equally powerful in effecting, implementing, and judging the laws of the land. To the contrary, the balance of power is achieved precisely because Congress, the Executive and the Courts each enjoys greater power than the other two in one of the three functions of government. The analogy holds for interpersonal relations, ability in one respect is balanced by ineffectiveness in another, one's power to command is complemented by another's power to implement.

Power is <u>personal</u>. Berle is precise: "Power is an attribute of man. It does not exist without a holder."[1] Nevertheless, power is elusive. While all want power it is difficult to determine in circumstances who actually possesses it. Some proclaim their power and sacrifice much under the delusion that they possess it. Some disdain power though possessing it. Others do not know the power they do have. Some exercise power by positive action; others by veto. In group or corporate decisions, while it may be impossible to pin down legal responsibility, and decisions seem to arise, consciously or unconsciously, from group consensus, some one or some few ultimately formulate the issue and make the decision. With modern weapons individuals or small groups can briefly possess a terrifying power, even holding a city or a nation at bay for weeks. In most cases they are acting out their own despair; in others they are acting from a fanatic dedication to an idea or cause. However manifested, power is ultimately traceable to a person or persons.

Power, finally, is never absolute, and none can be rendered so powerless as those possessing enormous power. The last days of Howard Hughes comes to mind. But in societies characterized by centers of tremendous power, economic and otherwise, the obvious fact is that power, though enormous, is _fragmented_. This is much more apparent in an open society, but it is no less true in a closed and totalitarian society. For in any complex society power depends upon the ability to command revenues and to implement ideas and intentions. To the extent that others can do the same, any particular center of power is limited. In sum, therefore, power is good, it is unequally held; it is ultimately personal; and it is fragmented.

Freedom: Its Content and Essence

Freedom, like human life and action, exists at many levels simultaneously. Freedom is the scope of action, the less confined the more freedom. Thus space, the _lebensraum_ for acting, is the context of freedom. One's experience of space, however, is governed by one's Value-perceptions. The person, for example, who perceives all things in the light of the absolute Value, Scheler's Holy or Sacral, is at home everywhere. All things, all persons, and all actions, even those personally distressful, speak of the Infinite Good. Such a one experiences no confinement and at this level of being is simply free. To the contrary, the person whose highest Value is sensual pleasure, is bound to the object of sense gratification. The drunkard, we say, is a slave to drink and to that extent is not free. The higher the Value-espousal, therefore, the greater the scope of action. Utility gives more freedom than pleasure, the vital more than utility, and so on up Scheler's Value hierarchy, the beautiful, the true, the good, the holy.

Since we live at all levels of human reality simultaneously, we experience the various degrees of freedom simultaneously. Freedom is and is not all of a piece. The dimensions of freedom are not compartmentalized; they interweave. The loss of freedom at the lower sensual and utilitarian levels impairs the higher intellectual and moral freedoms. Political tyrannies inevitably become totalitarian, controlling the arts, censoring ideas, persecuting religion in addition to and often by means of dominating the economy. Yet the inmost core of personal freedom is impervious to tyranny. The saint may experience ecstatic contemplation while imprisoned, and the alcoholic may achieve a fuller life by means of his humiliating addiction. The student should keep this dynamic in mind in our discussion of freedom in its ordinary societal sense, social, political and economic freedom.[2]

Freedom in this sense means doing what one wants to do. Like all things human, however, freedom has a <u>material content</u> and an <u>essential element</u>. The <u>content</u> of freedom is defined by and limited to the range of possible choices, what can be chosen or be done. This range of possibilities expands as we know more about human capabilities and the forces of nature. Today we can decide to go to the moon. Fifty years ago this choice was impossible. That is, technology, broadly conceived, expands and by that fact also limits the range of possible choices. More fundamentally, the limits of choice are defined by the human condition, that we are biological, psychological, political, social and economic beings. A couple has some choice to have a baby or not, but they cannot draw straws as to who will bear it. For while doctors can change sex, they cannot as yet transfer male and female fertility. The point is clear: at any moment there is a limit to the possible but this limit is not fixed once and for all. Thus the most obvious relation of freedom to power is simply that we are free to do only what we are able to do, what we have the power to do.

The <u>essential</u> element in freedom is purpose. I act freely when I act to achieve my own purpose, goal, good or Value. The act may be deliberate, either in the instance or implied from a previous determination, or it may be unintended but a consequence of a previous determination. The person, whose 'one for the road' is 'one too many' is responsible for the accident caused by his impaired driving. A free act, therefore, is one for which I am responsible. Though responsibility is never 100%, we are responsible if the event would never have happened without our having freely chosen to act. Freedom, therefore, is not an unmixed blessing. It means acknowledging an act as one's own. It means bearing responsibility.

Alienation

At this essential level the opposite of freedom is not powerlessness but alienation. This certainly is at the root of Marx's conception. The alienated act lacks purpose and all the more so, when another's purpose is imposed upon us.

Not all acts done for another or to accomplish another's purpose, however, are alienated. One may act for love of another, identifying the other's good or purpose as one's own, e.g. a wife acting against her wishes to please her husband. Second, one could voluntarily act as agent to achieve another's purpose with the intention of also achieving one's own good or purpose. This typically happens in the contract for hire: the worker does what the employer wants for a wage, for the goods he wants to buy. Alienation, it is obvious, can creep into both relations. If a wife is simply used by her husband who takes what she does for his own selfish good and not for their mutual good, he reduces her to a means and instrument to his wishes. Similarly, an employer may use an employee with no consideration for the worker's own good, but simply to accomplish his own. Both the loving service of the wife and the faithful service of the employee is alienated. An act, therefore, is alienated when one person is used solely as a means to accomplish another's good at the expense of his own.

Purpose and Possibility

The relation between purpose and possibility is not fixed once and for all. While attempting the impossible is quixotic and fool-hardy, the seemingly impossible is seldom an absolute barrier. For the impossible often means that no one has done it, that no one has stretched current techniques and technology to that limit. Pursuing the 'impossible dream', though often failing, does stretch technical limits, suggests new techniques, and expands the frontiers of human possibilities. Purposiveness is limited by possibility but also expands it. In this sense and to the heroic, the impossible is never an ultimate and final barrier to freedom.

In concrete circumstances, however, freedom to act means controlling the means to act. It has always been the case that those who control technology, production, income, and wealth have greater power to impose their purposes and Values on others lacking these means. Thus they have increased their own freedom and diminished others. Since abundant economies have both expanded the range of human possibilities and by that very fact generated centers of immense economic power, we can now formulate our question in a better exploratory fashion: Has economic abundance by creating huge concentrations of economic power widened the horizon of the humanly possible by actually diminishing the freedom of the general populace?

Affluence and the Context of Power

Before addressing this question, we can profitably recap the features of abundance and affluence which have changed the context of power. First, because affluence arises from abundance, even as abundance increases the range of possible satisfactions and human fulfillment, it has raised the stakes much more. The challenge to power is more costly, because the risks are greater and because centers of power have more resources at their command.

Second, affluence as a habit of expecting more income and more goods, generates scarcity. Every choice demands a greater sacrifice, a larger trade-off. While the cost, that is, the value, of any good is the opportunity cost of the next best alternative, what next best good one must forego, each good in the chain of possibilities is valued at the opportunity cost of the next so on down to the last which has no alternative, no opportunity cost and, hence, no value. But if the chain expands, then each alternative is increased by the opportunity costs of the added alternatives. Just as the more children are included in a crack-the-whip line, the faster those last in line will sail, so the longer the chain of economic choices the greater the value of each in the chain. This is true in the ordinary economic sense of scarcity, that in spending a given amount of money one foregoes many more alternatives. But it is more obvious in a more ontological sense, that the decision on how to use one's time, expend one's energy, or exercise one's skill and knowledge becomes more complex the greater the range of alternatives. The trauma of the very bright in choosing their vocational direction is very real and can be heart-rending.

Third, and this comes to the precise point of the chapter, economic abundance is a function of socialized production. The immense production of industrialized economies require mammoth economic and governmental institutions to produce the goods, to finance their distribution, and to control their flow. In industrialized economies those who control these institutions possess the greatest power. At the same time, while power is more socialized, it is more inter-dependent. While locked in a struggle to expand, corporations and government agencies counter and limit each other's power aggrandizement, nevertheless, each power-center is dependent on the others. Government power is helpless without the vast incomes generated by private businesses, and these in turn need the stabilizing influence of government. This view of a kind of stratosphere of power, where vast institutions strive with, yet support, each other, has generated the greatest fear that the overwhelming majority of people in industrialized societies are really powerless pawns in a struggle among titans.

The Fragmented Individual

This fear is enhanced by the feeling that the life of the affluent is fragmented. For in fact, an individual makes contact and derives much of his well-being from many of these huge institutions, the corporation he works for, the union he belongs to, super-markets and shopping centers, and a host of government, police and social agencies. But he makes contact and derives his well-being only at one aspect of his total being. This may even be true of traditional institutions, such as family, church and school. He belongs only according to one facet of his life and is not integrated into them as a complete person. Thus the individual can be dominated by many institutions simultaneously. Like Br'er Rabbit, a person feels he or she can survive only by beating the system, that is, by playing one power center off against the other.

However successful in this, the individual is still fragmented. By contrast, in simpler society, the individual was incorporated wholly into a number of supportive institutions, the family, the parish, the school, the neighborhood, the work community. They were so interlaced with each other, that where one failed or was inadequate for an individual the others could act as surrogate. The most obvious examples are the school acting 'in loco parentis' or neighbors giving moral guidance to children neglected by their own parents. Today, parishes and school have retreated from much of this concern for the whole person. Even families have become little more than groups which bed and board together.

"Behind the growing sense of isolation in society," writes Robert Nisbet, "lies the growing realization that the traditional primary relationships of men -- family, neighborhood and church -- have become functionally irrelevant to our State and economy and meaningless to the moral aspirations of individuals."[3] Thus the individual seems suspended in a multi-dimensional web of social, economic and political relations, none of which relate him to others as a whole to wholes. Being thus fragmented, the individual has lost power to act freely.

While fragmentation of the individual has occurred concomitantly to the growth of power vested in mammoth institutions, this chapter will advance no plans to dismantle the power structure and to emasculate the power elite. Rather it will move in the direction of reconstituting a new sense of community better adapted to an abundant economy. Before doing so we must take a closer look at the phenomenon of economic power itself.

ECONOMIC POWER

Having examined power and freedom and their relation in an affluent context, we can turn to the more specific notion of economic power.

Economic and Market Power

Economic power is the ability to achieve one's own economic good and in the process affecting the economic well-being of others. This then is a more encompassing concept than the narrower notion of market power discussed in Chapter two. Market power is the ability to affect the prices of goods and services to one's own advantage: a corporation which can maintain high prices because it dominates production of particular goods or controls the supply of particular resources; or a labor union which can restrict the supply of particular labor services; or governments which can change market prices by taxing. All forms of market power exemplify economic power but the two are not proportional. A monopoly general store in an Eskimo village may have, for the market, almost absolute market power but it does not possess much economic power. On the other hand, a large corporation like American Motors Corporation may have great economic power but little market power, because it is too small relative to others in the industry to affect product prices, wage negotiations with the unions, and the price of raw materials. Thus the actions of businesses to relocate, to hire and to fire, to change product lines in order to become more competitive with more powerful rivals may not have much impact on the market or market prices but will have economic impact on many people and even on whole cities. Our concern is with the more encompassing phenomenon of economic power.

In so doing, we do not restrict our vision to large manufacturing and financial corporations. There are many centers of economic power -- a few powerful families and individuals, labor unions, some non-profit institutions, and above all government agencies -- besides corporations. In all cases, however, the primary source of economic power rests on the ability to command large reservoirs of funds, not necessarily one's own, but clear-cut legal control.

A usual second ingredient, though not essential, in an open society is the power to persuade, that is, the ability to disseminate ideas convincingly. Groups wishing to bring a public issue to a head, the youth movement and the Vietnam War for example, the power of money was not nearly as important as the power of the press. But without the money to maintain the pressure for change, the hippies and yippies did little to change the economy and consequently society. Their leadership was absorbed into the establishment (where they may actually have more power today) or fragmented into groups of revolutionary cranks. On the other hand, organized crime shuns the press -- cannot exist in the light -- yet controls billions of wealth and income and thousands of lives. Complete cynicism might conclude that who controls money controls the press. But without yielding that much, everyone can see that having money gets more media coverage than not having it.

Centers of Economic Power

This present rather sketchy sweep across the landscape of economic power is not really necessary for subsequent analysis but it will paint in the back-drop for further discussion. Nor is it necessary that the reader agree with the estimates expressed here as to who or what groups possess economic power and how much. For all such estimates are very subjective, including this one. The purpose of the following survey is to demonstrate that a hierarchy of power exists and that relatively powerless individuals must live and maintain their freedom within its context.

Some individuals possess large amounts of economic power. Names like H.L. Hunt, Paul Getty and Howard Hughes come immediately to mind. But their power comes not from their fortunes but their control over institutions. "The rich man has little power because he is rich", writes Berle. "If he wishes a power position, he must find it outside his bank account."[4]

There are family groups which collectively possess much power, the DuPonts, Rockefellers and Mellons. While families of the very rich today enjoy a style of living which isolates them from the commonality of mankind, the families themselves are memorialized and remembered through their endowments of schools, museums, and symphonies. If they possess power, they do so because of the corporations and banks they control. The DuPonts may seem to hold Delaware in fief but their power and influence resides largely in control of DuPont Corporation. The Mellons without their influence over Mellon National Bank and Alcoa, or the Rockefellers without Chase Manhattan, the Rockefeller Foundation, and Exxon would only be a group of very rich people whose power extended to the range of their several personal influences.

Modern family power contrasts sharply with that of the great Medieval families. Then control of land controlled people. Then vibrant families, like the Savoys or Hapsburg, forged through marriage, investiture, or conquest mighty blocs of land-holdings which endowed them with both political and economic power. Generation after generation preserved the family's power by subordinating personal to family ambition.

But as commercial, manufacturing and, finally, financial power grew and was invested in the new bourgeois class, the economic power of land waned. Land itself became a commodity which money could purchase. Thus power passed to organizations which could command large funds of money and credit. The last family to dominate Europe was the Bonapartes, who carried the principle of family aggrandizement to the point of caricature, trying to wed republican sentiments to family sovereignty.

Berle is worth quoting in full:

"Most power in the later twentieth-century

world has been and is given through operation of institutional structures. Such operations confer power on individuals at the top and determine hierarchical delegation all the way down to the lowest ranks, through secondary chiefs, administrators, bureaucratic heads, and their deputies, agents, and subagents. They enable power holders in each echelon to exercise power with the range assigned them. Instituions perform a double function: they confer power and they are the instruments by which it is used. Achievement of power normally is accomplished by winning the designation of the institutions accepted as having the power-conferring function."[5]

However it is viewed, the modern corporate aggregate is a center of great power. The very largest have annual incomes which dwarf the Gross National Product of most national economies. Through advertising, their internal house organs, political and lobbying pressure they possess immense power to persuade. Yet they are not monolithic. They differ among and within themselves. Seldom does any individual possess top power long enough to make it a personal preserve. Rather individuals move up corporate ladders, acquiring more and more of a power fragmented through departments and divisions, each striving to grow in a varied context of fellowship and animosity, cooperation and competition, community and diversity.[6] Seldom can an individual or a cohesive group grasp it whole and entire. The power of huge corporations, in turn, is importantly conditioned by internal tension or laxity and by response to external stimuli, and like an elephant herd in the veld variously placid or rampant.

All of this applies preeminently to multi-national corporations. But their situation in developed or developing countries importantly differentiates their power. In developed countries the multi-national is usually but one among many huge conglomerates, and at least initially it may be struggling simply to get a foothold in an alien environment. Generally, it adds a healthy stimulus to domestic competition, as foreign auto sales has pushed Detroit into the compact market. Quite otherwise is the case in developing countries. There the mother company's financial resources gives the subsidiary, even in its fledgling stage, a great edge over domestic competition. For this reason multi-nationals have thrown their weight around, even to dictating political policy, and thus invited nationalization.

Labor unions, that is, organized labor which numbers less than 20% of the labor force, in little more than a generation have acquired enormous economic power over both wages and working conditions and frequently financial control over retirement funds. All have house organs to propagandize the union point of view. Most can marshall political clout at the various levels of government. The power of labor unions tends to be more monolithic both because leadership, despite or because of the democratic method, tends to be more permanent and because, given the shorter chain of command, successors can be hand-picked according to ideological purity. A change in union top command becomes a national event. Yet union power is not static. Locals increasingly chafe at national policy, insisting on the resolution of local issues at the local level. Furthermore, union membership is constantly being eroded by the replacement of labor by machines, forcing internationals to move into new territory.

Comparable in power to the great labor unions, professional associations like the American Bar Association and the American Medical Association and to a much lesser extent the American Association of University Professors and a host of even smaller professional groups, maintain the income levels of their membership, pronounce upon and influence public policy, and maintain a variety of pension and insurance benefits. Some have become labor unions. The National Educational Association has in effect narrowed its professional role to increasing teachers' salaries and lobbying for larger fiscal hand-outs for public schools. The greatest union advance in the last decade has been in the previously off-limits area of local and state government employees. Membership there has increased four or five times and earnings twice the rate as in the private sector. Indeed with both greater security and higher income government employees are rapidly becoming the labor elite.

Placed against the economic power of government, this may be the most frightening development of power in the power hierarchy. This growth of government power at the state and local level is dramatically captured in the increase of state and local tax collections, from under $15b. a quarter century ago to over $110b. today. Most of this goes into the expanded employment for services provided by government mainly education, health, and welfare, the areas most sensitive to personal freedom. At the federal level employment has only kept pace with the private sector, but as has been described here and elsewhere many times, enormous centers of power exist; in the hand-in-glove arrangement between the Defense Department and major suppliers of military hardware, which Eisenhower warned against almost twenty years ago; in the incomprehensibly complex regulations of the Commerce Department over transportation rates; in the power of HEW to direct funds according to that bureaucracy's policy preferences into welfare, education, and housing. The Federal Reserve Board exercises decisive authority in regulating the flow of credit. The Justice Department, by its zeal or lack in pushing anti-trust actions, is an important barometer for corporate aggrandizement. Across the entire spectrum of decision-making businesses and households fall under the influence of government regulatory agencies. In sum, Berle writes, "Major American administrative officials may well come to have more direct control over more human beings than did any Renaissance despot at his zenith."[7]

Of the institutions which seem to have lost economic power, Chambers of Commerce have tended to become the voice predominantly of smaller businesses, though it continues to serve the public with its Better Business Bureaus. Social clubs, like the Masons or Knights of Columbus, have probably lost the economic significance they had a generation or more ago. Churches, despite some sizable investments and the use of modern techniques of fund raising, seem to have little discernible economic power. The same may be said of Foundations, even those with hundreds of millions to spend annually. Charities are largely dependent on organized community giving or government subsidy. Their incomes, therefore, are a function of felt needs, hospitals doing far better than orphanages and half-way houses. Altogether foundations and charities dispersed some $25b. in 1975, less than 2% of disposable income. Gambling by contrast ran over $50b.

(The economic significance of Churches and Charities may not be measured by their cumulative budgets. For they touch people at their deepest levels of motivation. A foundation, for example, with but a few millions to spend may purchase the interest and effort of the most important intellectuals to propagate the Values and ideas it espouses. In the long run this may have more economic import than the billions the Defense Department spends. But by and large these institutions have not overtly sought power and hence exercise little.)

The Open Dangers of Power

Power can be dangerous. While power need not corrupt, its possessors are exposed to greater temptations. This, in one sense, is greater in an open than in a closed society, because there power tends to be reclusive. By shunning the light even the legitimate use of power shades into abuse.

Some exercises of economic power become clandestine because they have been declared illegal. First, the monopolizing tendency has been legally constrained. As we have seen, this tendency is an entirely normal reaction to intense competition. Many forms of price discrimination are accepted as entirely just; much product differentiation is welcomed as beneficial. Even price leadership is considered preferable in oligopolistic industries than the kind of competition which drives weaker firms to the wall. Nevertheless, monopolizing of certain kinds and degrees is viewed contrary to the public good and declared illegal. Yielding to the temptation necessarily becomes conspiratorial.

Second, some kinds of gross political influence is illegal. Supporting financially the party and candidate of one's choice is generally held praiseworthy in a democracy. For without such support only the very wealthy could stand for office. Yet the danger of large contributors' so dominating candidates and office-holders, to the contributors' economic advantage, has brought more and more complex law to hedge in political contributions, with the intent to preserve the independence of elected officials. The result is an unending dialectic between loopholes and legal plugs.

A more serious subversion of power lies in the personal enhancement of those who exercise legal power. No one, except those who view organization exclusively as flowcharts and tables of organization, is surprised at this. A police chief takes personal umbrage at every accusation leveled against one of <u>his</u> officers. A social worker in dealing with <u>her</u> clients acts like Lady Bountiful. Executive privilege become a personal right, and worse, power and authority are subverted for private economic enhancement. A senator abuses his immunity to cover personal derelictions. Political contributions shade into pay-offs for immunity or favors received. Regulatory agencies are stacked with industry representatives so that the agency regulates for the sake of the regulated. It is a universal failing of government that foxes are hired to guard the henhouse.

A final obvious danger of power becoming abusive is the ability of groups to hold the public to ransom. The basic techniques in industrial disputes, the lock-out, boycott, and strike, achieve leverage by inconveniencing, even harming, third parties to the dispute. Such techniques may be justified. Indeed customers and the general public may be beneficiaries of unjust wages or unsafe working conditions and this fact, that they benefit at the expense of others, should be brought home to them. Obviously, however, the technique is subject to abuse unless tempered with justice. This includes acknowledging that withholding a service or product harms some people more than others and requires providing some means to handle emergencies.

The most notorious perversion of power in open societies is that of organized crime. Far from glamorous, it is a sneaky, clandestine business which cannot exist without the venality of some officials and the indifference or fear of ordinary citizens. It is a government with its own law and law enforcement, even when it operates within the structures of authorized government and legitimate business. It is a perverted government which always takes much more than it gives, big criminals preying upon little criminals who prey upon the most defenseless in society. The pimp fleeces his whores and pays off up the line. The fence pays dearly for protection and waxes rich on the risks of the petty thief. Organized crime -- as opposed to the free lance criminal -- reaches into all of society only because ordinary people yield to the streak of vice or illegality in all of us and thus fall into the power of professionals.

The Hidden Dangers of Power

The insidious effects of power may actually be more dangerous. Power has an insulating effect, allowing the powerful to disregard others. In organizations for profit this can take the form of managerial sluggishness, laxness in implementing orders, avoidance, even suppression, of change. Profits become a function, not of service, but of market power and the lack of competition. In a dynamic, open society the danger is less because above-normal profits always lures competition. In nationalized industries that threat is often effectively removed and change must be forced through the political process. Too frequently such industries are so hamstrung with regulation that the rules themselves prevent change. The British railway workers hopelessly snarled commuter traffic simply by following the book to the letter.

Related but deserving special mention is bureaucratic impermeability. Where correct performance rather than results is the criterion, customers or clients petitioning for redress can be shuffled endlessly from one office to another, because no one is able or willing to take the responsibility to make a decision. It is like punching a water-bed; everything moves but nothing changes. What is true of corporate is all the more so of government bureaucracy. Indeed, even in organizations devoted not to profits but to charitable service, this kind of run-around has been raised to the fine art of elevating abstract principles over human well-being. Ask any student who has tried to get answers to simple questions at a large university!

Since power tends to be used to the advantage of the powerful, it generates greater social imbalance. In a purely economic sense, power widens the gap between the rich and poor. This is especially true where economic power is a function of political or moral power. For wealth accumulation is not only morally sanctioned but almost sanctified. Nothing saved Medieval Europe from a completely theocratic rule than the early and decisive prohibiting clerical usury because profiting from lending violated the spirit of charity which their role professed.[8] But any power which is insulated from erosion generates a surplus wealth from which more can be gained, piling Pelion on Ossa, even at the expense of the dire poverty of the masses.

More to the point in modern economies, where even great corporations, must compete for sales dollars and income in mass markets, economic power can have a decisive effect on social Values. This is obviously and frequently the case with large firms catering to mass markets. Their advertising, but more effectively obsolescence built into products by frequent style changes and costly repairability, has a great, if not decisive, influence on popular taste and social Values. By producing for the fads, they effectively limit choice, even though present computerized technology could cater to a much wider range of individual preferences.

More so than private businesses, government agencies influence social Values. Anyone is naive who thinks government is even-handed in the disposition of funds. The operative ideas, the issues touted in the press and funded for research, are those which fit the fancy of the policy makers in government agencies with large funds at their disposition.

While many such ideas have an initial grass-roots propulsion, they achieve respectability with media coverage and money, much of it governmental. Thus the in-ideas are foisted off as societal Values even against popular aversion. It is an occupational hazard of a priestly class, whether sacral or secular, to assume consecration bestows wisdom.

The economic power of both government and corporations is expressed in a general carelessness about the effects of growth. While corporations may be the greater offenders, governments may be no less indicted, not only for neglecting the impact on the environment of people but also the more intimate elements of well-being. Economic growth itself tends to generate social tensions because it entails the erosion of job skills, elimination of jobs, and expansion of production and commercial facilities. In all these respects the poor are more adversely affected than middle-income classes and, the wealthy least of all. For the poor live in neighborhoods adjacent to factories, trucking firms, railroad yards and expressways. Their skills are more likely to be automated away and they for one reason or another find it more difficult to retrain. Since most are not homeowners, their housing is more tenuous, their neighborhoods short-changed of civic services and they lack the political clout to prevent re-zoning and even total eradication. The history of urban renewal and expressway construction is one of governments' running rough-shod over poorer neighborhoods with an almost cynical disregard for the human suffering they have caused.

Nisbet was almost prophetic in assessing the effects of slum clearance:

> "To be moved from a slum, which, after all, if it is old enough, has a culture and more or less natural gathering places, to an architecturally grim, administratively monolithic, housing project may indeed 'clean up' the streets for a time and give surrounding areas higher economic value to absentee owners. But the ultimate consequence, a depressing amount of experience shows all too often, may be a new type of slum, one with little of culture or community, one in which gangs and violence as well as alienation will be the logical and predictable consequence."[9]

Corporations may even be somewhat more humane than government agencies in this respect. Nevertheless, their moves into and especially out of communities causes considerable uprooting of families and up-ending of communities. There are many factors causing the destruction of central cities but an important one is the movement of business to the suburbs and to other regions to take advantage of tax breaks or cheaper labor costs. Given the freedom of enterprise, little can be done to restrain the free movement of corporations, nor on the other hand of development authorities from competing for the relocation of businesses. Certainly, the negro migration into northern cities and the countering movement of business people into the Sun Belt has from an overall point of view been socially desirable in lessening the differences between the South and the North. We are economically more homogeneous than we were. But the change has trailed a wake of human suffering. More careful weighing of alternatives, more concern for the effect of change, more consideration of the problems both of corporations and of the community could have lessened the problems.

Nothing speaks clearer of the carelessness of economic power than what might be called the rape of the environment. Particular instances can be reeled off in reams so that an overall impression may actually be more accurate. The impression one gets when traveling about the country, in contrast to Europe for instance, is of a scarred landscape. Cities which have existed for over a century seem to have mushroomed any which way and any moment could be abandoned like mining town reverting to desert. Few cities have real charm. Fewer have that look that anybody cares. Most seem designed to make income not a living. The last decade has clearly demonstrated that if large cities are to survive as places where people can live and not simply as prisons for the poor, they must become attractive for living. Heroic efforts have been made with many pleasant results. Too frequently, however, the renewal has a cold, institutional look with few of those personal touches which tell of private development and personal response.

Regarding natural resources generally, the struggle between environmental and economic growth advocates misses the point that arguments on both sides are valid only to the extent they defend human rights. People have a right to enjoy the wilderness and the right to have an automobile. That is, profits and better living are not mutually exclusive. To the contrary, they enhance each other: environmentalism will become more effective as it becomes more profitable; greater wealth makes the wilderness more accessible to more people. The ultimate sanction, and criterion for judgment, is the good of people.

Before concluding this section, two further perspectives would help foster a balanced view. The exercise of power in the past was both more romantic and more brutal than today. When Prussia and Austria in 1763 joined in invading Silesia, for example, the rape was played out against the pageantry of war, movement of armies, colorful uniforms, the heroics of battle, fighting for king and country, manifest national destiny, repelling the enemy and the other sounding shibboleths of nationalism. However colorful and zestful, the action was no less brutal: men died horribly, peasant farms were destroyed, and whole peoples swept into a hated allegiance.

The take-over of Strauss and Co. by the XYZ group is, by contrast, drab and unheroic, its counters money and voting rights, its purpose profits. Fortunes are made and lost, managements change hands. But sales continue and employees remain at their jobs, not knowing whether the take-over will eventually benefit or harm them. From the view underneath, there is no less a feeling of helplessness, that ordinary folks and ordinary employees are only pawns in a power struggle. But today people experience a greater personal danger from their neighbor's drunken driving, the arsonist's can of gasoline, or the madcap's Saturday night special than from the power of top management to affect their economic well-being.

In de-glamorizing as well as de-brutalizing the struggle for power, however, the affluent spirit may actually have increased this sense of helplessness. By shunning headlines, the beneficial use of power is not easily distinguished from abusive exercise. Since people fear what they do not know and since possession is always a temptation to abuse power, there is a strong popular disposition to circumscribe the transfer and abuse of economic power. Businesses could do much to de-fuse this fear if they were more willing to explain their actions and to operate in the open.

o In concluding this review of the phenomenon of economic power, we saw that an abundant economy like the United States contains many centers of power. While individuals always exercise power, they derive that power not from personal or family wealth but from control over large private and public organizations. These power-brokers undoubtedly form a power elite, but their turnover and o the competition among power centers argues forcefully against a theory of a monolithic possession of power. However power centers may be tempted to collude, power

o in fact both grows and dissipates. More frequently, power centers countervail each other.

This evaluation is critical for further analysis. For where power is both abusive and monolithic, the only solution is revolution by oppressed classes against their oppressors. But where power, no matter how immense, is diffused, and power centers, though supportive, nevertheless, compete with and countervail each other, the recourse is quite different. Individuals then can play one center against the other, or they can attack abuses one at a time, or they can set up countervailing centers of power. Individual action, therefore, is both possible and necessary, but obviously some collective response is almost always necessary in fighting the abuse of institutionalized power. Fundamental to such collective action is a sense of community.

INDIVIDUAL ACTION AND COMMUNITY

Before getting into this, it may help to recall earlier comments about freedom and power. Freedom is limited to what is humanly and technically possible. Such limitations are not absolute but relative, because the dreamer and the heroic in challenging push back the limits of the possible. But that is not the issue here. Rather we addressed the social problem that institutionalized power, implemented by command over wealth, influence, and technology, becomes the context for individual action and thus limits its scope. The real question then is whether the individual can preserve his or her personal freedom within this context. We examine first what resources the individual can muster in countering institutional power.

The Strength and Shortcomings of Individual Action

Basic to this assessment is the frank acknowledgement that the affluent mentality, unrestrained by the principles discussed in Part One, is probably a major contributor to the growth of governmental and private institutional power. We tend to feed the very Frankenstein's monster we fear. Politicians are elected on the basis of the length and richness of the list of promises made to their constituents.

Labor leaders survive by outbidding challengers in getting higher wages and more fringe benefits. Corporate management keeps control by generating greater profits, more dividends, and capital gains. Any hope for controlling the power of private and public bureaucracies requires cooling down the pressure-cooker of affluence. This does not argue for no-growth but a slowing of the present frenetic pace, a willingness to modify demands particularly by those leaders in government, corporations, and unions whose examples receive national attention.

No one expects individual restraint to accomplish this. Whatever the good will, the complaint, 'Why should I take less while everyone is grabbing more', is valid. What is sadly lacking is a competent and persuasive moral leadership from churches, universities, and the press to convince people that pressuring the economy beyond its capacity not only will endanger it but feeds the very monsters of power we fear. Too frequently the fear of private power evoked a call for more governmental power, raising the more frightening spectre of a huge governmental monster to restrain the battling among smaller private monsters. It is the same Hobbesian solution of Leviathan. It is a solution particularly favored by social planners who naively assume that once a problem can be fixed in words and the words in a law, the problem is resolved. This mind set seems impervious to the history of past failures. Perhaps the Volstead Act did not increase alcoholism but it did not solve it. Instead by making what was legal illegal, the law exposed habits, ingrained in human history, to the clutches of those quite willing to violate the law for profit.

To this general warning that individuals collectively have contributed to the problem of power and that once created there are no quick and easy solutions to it, we can join another warning that individual action will always be bothersome and often borders on the heroic.

We now turn to what the individual can do to preserve his individual freedom. First and foremost a person must maintain an inner space of freedom, an inner sanctum of peace, against which he must resist encroachment.

> "The individual can stay free in this society of super-powers," Peter Drucker insists, "only if he creates his own area of personal freedom, the area outside of organized power. He must have a personal and inalienable membership in the

human race and in its heritage outside and distinct from the affiliation through his organization. This of course means first the religious and spiritual life of the person. But it also means the intellectual and esthetic life. A man who plays chamber music in a string quartet twice a week, albeit as an amateur, has a sphere of freedom which no corporation, no trade union, no bureaucracy can take away from him."[10]

In the area of social actions, however, the struggle is never that conclusive. In analyzing it, we will examine his power in terms of money and the media, applying these criteria to action against both government and private organizations.

Against government agencies, the individual's money power is almost non-existant because their funds are budgeted from tax revenues and no performance criterion are applied in the matter at hand. Certainly, agencies can be reviewed and tax-payers theoretically can vote for or against particular tax uses. But this is almost exclusively indirectly by voting for or against legislators. Withholding a portion of one's taxes is at best a symbolic gesture and usually fraught with penalties. Some few states allow putting tax monies in escrow until the disputed forms of spending are litigated in court. Again the gesture is mainly symbolic although it can be temporarily embarrassing to a state.

The easiest form of tax protest is to support private social and educational institutions which compete with governmental agencies by contributions for which income tax deductions are allowed. The allowance is, however, always considerably less than the support. (Another instance where one pays for Value espousal.) Consequently, only a long-run and collective resistance to taxes can impair government's money power against the private citizen.

In such disputes the media is usually ambivalent. It is, like popular instincts, against sin and taxes. It responds too to the struggle of David against the governmental Goliath. But on the other hand, the media, especially what is called the Liberal Press, tend to favor public agencies affecting a larger and more public good over private agencies which service a private or sectarian good. The most glaring example is the general support of high-cost public schools over lower-cost private schools because the former in theory is for all and particularly for the poor, while the latter services only sectarian interests and the rich. That public schools have perpetrated great injustice against the poor, the ghetto child, and minorities is ignored in supporting the anomaly that high-cost education is for the poor because they cannot afford anything better and low-cost education is for the rich because they can afford the freedom to choose the kind of education they prefer. Debate, whether better education at lower costs and greater freedom could be achieved by some other form of public financing than the present, is stifled by a huge public-school vested interest which swamps reason in emotional appeals to religious bigotry, our American heritage, separation of Church and State and the like. In all this the Liberal Press connives.

In dealing with large private organizations the individual has a better chance of resisting injustice. For the ultimate vulnerability of for-profit as well as non-profit organizations is the final sale. "Their essential charter of continued existence," Berle concludes, "lies not in their power, but in their capacity to supply -- perhaps stimulate -- the growing and manifold wants of a population affluent by all previous standards of comparison."[11]

Thus just as affluence has fostered institutional economic power, it provides a powerful weapon for controlling that power. For no one is really forced to buy from them or to contribute to them. Even though this veto power is less effective for goods in daily and essential use, one could still shop around. For non-essentials the veto power of not buying is absolute. Such resistance involves inconvenience, however, doing without, waiting for sales, complaining about shoddy goods or poor performance, not just to innocent sales persons but to top executives. Like all bureaucracies the private firm is resistant to the individual complaint but total victories have been won.

Successful complaints usually require some collective action which is highly-publicized. A word about both. To bring a corporation to heel one need not engineer a complete boycott. Profits are realized on the last 10% of sales. A boycott need only affect that small percentage of sales above the break-even point to make a large corporation hurt. Then too, publicity of concerted action is more easily obtained because in the public's and the press's eyes the corporation is always a "bad guy". This is even true when the newspaper's own business office squirms for fear of losing advertising revenue. TV 'gripe' programs seem to be particularly effective. One person could write to the president of a corporation about its defective goods without much results while a complaint on TV of even lesser difficulties can effect a complete replacement of the item.

For those within a corporation their ability to resist undesirable company policy is fraught with greater ambiguity. The fine line between compromising personal integrity and contributing to corporate profits is hard to draw. For both are good. For profit-decisions benefit not only stockholders, managers, employees but ultimately customers. Not to make profits violates the very rationale of business. The ethical question is not about profits but how they are made, quick profits or long-run profits, and by what means, by service, or by violating employees' integrity and customer ignorance. The answers are seldom clear-cut, nor is the individual employee's response free of ambiguity. When the matter is peripheral, one could protest it, if that would help, but continue with the business. Where the matter is substantial to the business, personal integrity may call for resignation.

When Meredith Corporation in 1975 took on the contract to publish Viva and Penthouse, two publications which differed drastically from their usual line, in order to shore up sagging profits, they began to cater to a substantially different readership than their usual. Now Meredith did nothing to create the pornographic market and without new business, it would undoubtedly have to cut back on employment. Nevertheless, it refused to accommodate the pressmen, whose conscience forbade their working on the Viva and Penthouse materials, with assignments on other jobs. Such a classic confrontation between conscience and profits can only be resolved in the larger arena of sales. If Meredith readers are sufficiently incensed at Meredith's cavalier decision not only to change its product but to force this change upon its employees, they can cancel their subscriptions to Meredith's respectable publications, thus forcing the company to make the profit decision which market, the pornographic or non-pornographic, it chooses to service.[12]

The role of the corporate informer is fraught with even more ambiguity. The one who blows the whistle on illegal or immoral practices is always suspected of betraying confidences, of disloyality, or of turning informer to save one's skin. Sometimes such a person's reputation for integrity contributes to his being kept in the dark about doubtful practices. Very frequently, a person may decide to lay bare the evil after considerable, knowing or unknowing, complicity. In any case, the informer is never free of suspicion, and his future is clouded with doubt.

Judgment in such cases should not be confused by a moral prissiness. Moral integrity, like good health, is not preserved in a sterilized environment but in overcoming temptations and amending failures. Then, too, one can temper judgment of business' sins with acknowledging one's own derelict conduct toward those one loves. Finally, in balance the evils attending business, greed, fraud, chiselling, even sexual randiness, pale before the moral occupational hazards, like intellectual pride or moral hypocrisy, of other more respectable callings. The real danger of such moral prissiness, which the young employee should especially be warned against, is rationalizing a cynicism about and indifference to moral issues. In business, as in all walks, a person pays for integrity. While he may be banking daily small amounts of respect, these may or may not prove of economic value, or gain business good will, advancement, or a more responsibile position. Its only perceivable Value is peace of soul.

Such integrity takes real courage. It may cost a job or subject one to being misunderstood, to being suspected, and even to expensive law suits. Hardest to bear is the terrible aloneness of integrity precisely because one's own integrity is absolutely unique and may be ineffable. The person of integrity is often shunned and kept in the dark when doubtful schemes arise. At the same time, because of his sensitivity, he needs more wiliness and adroitness to survive without compromising principles and, for fear of compromising others, must go it alone.

The examplar, par excellence, of the man of integrity is Thomas More. As portrayed in the play A Man For All Seasons, More tried to avoid forcing the issue of the King's marriage, but his very reputation for integrity made Henry put him to the ultimate test. In refusing to budge on principles, Thomas forced the hand of his accusers to condemn him. In this terrible ordeal More was alone. Neither wife, nor family, nor friends understood his obstinancy. Few could survive this heroic aloneness without the comfort and consolation of being understood by others, without a sense of community.

Indeed, Thomas More had such a sense, for he appealed

for support to a larger community than the kings, nobles, churchmen and intellectuals of his day. He appealed to all the saints and scholars and common people who had affirmed the meaning of Christendom. It is this sense of being at one with others, of sharing common Values, of working for a common goal which is meant by community. It is this sense of being supported by others in the individual's resistance to the abuse of power which strengthens personal integrity. We turn to this phenomenon now.

The Power of Community

Delineating a true sense of community is extremely important at the outset because there is a terrible hunger for community today, because there are many bogus forms of community about in the world today, and because the struggle for institutional reform can easily degenerate into narrow sectarianism and special-group interests. Though they are not distinct, a word about each.

The hunger for community, "its values, properties, and means of access," according to Nisbet, "is the major intellectual fact of the present age."[13] This hunger is best illustrated by the Youth Movement of the last decade. Since it was largely negative, however, when Vietnam disappeared, the youth sense of community dissipated, leaving residues in communes, in the flare-up of the Jesus Movement, in the Moon phenomenon, in a handful of leaders living underground. But though young people conform more to accepted patterns, they still form a world apart from the mainstream. Ostensibly living with their families, attending school, entering the work force and marrying, they still protect themselves within the cocoon of their own sub-culture, which is still largely incomprehensible to older generations.

A recent high school experiment illustrates this chasm of incomprehension as well as the deep hunger for community. A social studies class, with administration approval, was organized into a Nazi-like movement which the students were told was sweeping the country. Complete with uniforms, salutes and all the props, the group soon organized the whole school and the few dissenters were shunted to the library. Apparently the faculty and administration had no intellectual or moral resources to show up the bogus nature of the movement and to satisfy the students' hunger to belong.[14] Equally frightening is the proliferation of hotlines for individuals' experiencing troubles beyond their ability to cope. Is there no one a troubled person can turn to except an anonymous voice at the other end of a telephone?

Because of this deep hunger people are entrapped in many kinds of bogus community, most of which require surrendering personal freedom and responsibility. One can exaggerate the significance of the many commune experiments, the Manson family, motorcycle gangs, Jesus communes, the Moon movement, or the increased visibility of Nazi-like parties, but whatever their significance they exploit the need to belong, to seek others' support. They are exploitative to the extent they require surrendering personal freedom.

Of greater concern is that the need for institutional reform, particularly in their economic aspects, may generate a narrow sectarian and class-interest bias and forget the larger social picture. The union man looking only to his own wages and fringe benefits forgets that these can only be funded if the company, industry, and economy are doing well. The neighborhood council in emphasizing their needs may ignore the problems of the whole city. Private school people in fighting for their rights cannot walk away from the mess in education generally. Such perspectives require an attitude considerably broader than a mere collectivity of self-interests. It demands an attitude flowing from understanding man's inherent social nature.

This attitude must also be differentiated from the sense of community which prevailed under pre-affluent conditions, the kind of community which older people look upon with nostalgia. Such community was pre-conscious, spontaneous and informal. It arose out of one's natural state: one was simply born into a family, grew up in a neighborhood, followed the religious and cultural practices of family and friends. No one was voted into such groups. One belonged because one was there. Such community also was holistic: the total person belonged and was accepted as belonging, no matter how ill-fitting he or she might be. Group Values tended to take precedence over individual Values. Wants and desires were controlled within the economic possibilities of the group. There was a stronger sense of obligation to the family, to the church, to the school and to the neighborhood. Everyone, for example, baby-sat everyone else's children. Families rallied around at difficulties and each shared what little it had. Nostalgia can gloss over the bitter hatreds, the cruelty to non-conformists, the stereotyping of people, but people were not indifferent to each other. Everyone belonged, no matter how comfortably or inconveniently.

These early relationships, based on kinship, neighborhood, or religious communion, lost their ability to communicate moral standards and to provide for psychological security because they ceased to be significant in the larger societal arena of economics and politics. "Family, local community, church, and the whole net-work of informal interpersonal relationships have ceased to play a determining role in our institutional systems of mutual aid, welfare, education, recreation, and economic production and distribution."[15]

Today, as a consequence, a person must become a member of a community in a more conscious way: one elects to belong. If one finds oneself uncomfortable in family, church, school, neighborhood and the like, a person can seek a new social habitat. The old spontaneous sense of community is not destroyed, but effective community is likely to be the conscious grouping of people sharing common Values, seeking a common goal, and requiring contributions to and sharing in common action. These features of community we turn to now.

An important half-way step to such community is suggested by one of the most fascinating phenomena of recent decades -- the tremendous proliferation of causes. Now a cause is not a community, though community, at least initially, demands a stimulating cause. For a cause is only a common purpose, a common goal, and comes in every shape and size and for every conceivable purpose. Some causes are as short-lived as a group formed to elect an alderman; other are as national and comprehensive as the feminist movement.

A cause develops community when it manifests the other two characteristics: when it draws upon deeply-espoused Values and when it elicits a general contribution to and sharing in the common goals. Such seemed to be true of Saul Alinsky's famous Back-of-the-Yards program in Chicago during the thirties and the present-day Roxbury Action Program in Boston. The Values they drew from are the obvious, that it is good that people live together, peacefully and protected. They succeed because their support is broadly based on diverse loyalties of people to their churches, labor unions, social clubs, nationality groups,[16] and because all the neighborhood can perceive the change for the better. By contrast most urban renewal projects were brick-and-mortar conceptions, imposed on high, dispersing people not drawing them together.

The jury is out on many other causes national in scope. Many have a narrow sectarian (not in the religious sense) scope. Others, like the feminist movement could generate real community with even most males enthusiastically supporting it. But the movement, while espousing solid Values like equal humanity, equal citizenship, and equal right to employment, has tended to fly in the face of other cherished Values, the physiological differences between men and women, motherhood, and the greater emotional sensitivity of women. Too often advocates took an anti-male and even anti-family tone, or, hoping for easy results, rushed into legislation and courts, generating opposition rather than gathering cooperation. Much the same criticism can be leveled against the 'gay' movement. Rare is the homosexual that blesses his or her parents' heterosexuality. Granted the deeply-ingrained biases these movements encounter, they have tended to be divisive and not uniting.

Quite to the contrary Alinsky and others, who have fostered a true sense of community, drew support from broad communitarian themes, family feeling, religious convictions, school spirit, and neighborhood attachment. Rather than destroy they strengthened them by establishing a tier of association between them and government. Thus they were able to countervail against institutionalized government and corporate power by fostering, at the same, the natural habitat of community.

Because the spirit of community "springs from some of the powerful needs of human nature--needs for a clear sense of cultural purpose, membership, status and continuity"[17] it is the true countervailing power protecting free and responsible action. This is the real meaning of grass-roots power, the attitude that I am not alone in my struggles and problems, and I can draw support and human comfort from others, that there is a mechanism by which I can tap the resources of the community to solve my difficulties and that, as a consequence, I have an obligation to foster and contribute to that sense of community. Such an attitude is nothing more than the realization that one is a social being in the very roots of one's being and one's social nature is only fulfilled in the full flowering of those virtues and principles discussed in Part One.

A sense of community posits a higher Value than the satisfaction of one's affluent wants and desires -- what Berle calls a "central idea system".[18] It says that it is better to belong to others and be supported by others than to satisfy all one's material wants and that, in fact, without a sense of community, more income and more want-fulfillment miss the deeper satisfaction of sharing. Further, moderation, as the best protection of personal integrity, warns that unrestrained wanting of sense goods and income lays us open to being preyed upon by the more powerful. Also a sense of community nourishes and is nourished by justice. For the just person is sensitive to what is due to and right for others. Knowing his own need for human support, he is willing to render the same to others. Above all he realizes the need for institutional support, that kind of social ambience which makes it easier to be virtuous, to be compassionate, and to be generous than to be vicious, indifferent and stingy.

Finally, a sense of community requires and disposes one to assume the role of the suffering servant, that is, an active manifestation of poverty of spirit. For community is not achieved without effort. One must be sensitive to the needs of the group, catalyzing the vague and unconscious wants into common Values. This implies an organization, as simple as a family discussion or as far-reaching as a national movement. In either case, someone or some few must take the initiative, must put themselves out, must be willing to make the sacrifice of time, energy and money, must be willing to bear the suspicion that they are grabbing for power, or the vilification for causing social unrest. Without such a cadre of self-sacrificing entrepreneurs, who risk much for the sake of others, the spirit of community dies in wishful thinking. For, howevermuch the sense of the community is something of the mind and will and heart, its natural impetus is to affect the ways people live. Its Values are social Values.

Thus though personalism initially eschews social activism and institutional reform, it comes to that in the sense of community. A true community is always reform-minded. But, because the reform flows from a sense of community, the reform takes place in a context of what is possible and thus binds people together and does not tear them apart. It proceeds rather by persuasion than by coercion. Thus it is ever mindful of self-interest and consequently of the coercive help of law. But it uses law as a means of channeling self-interest into socially desirable courses of action. In other words, law must respect and perfect freedom, not repress it. But this opens a whole new perspective, the relation between the political and economic order which is the subject of the next chapter.

Conclusion

We have seen that power and freedom are inevitably twined: we are only free to do what can be done. At the same time, freedom to try, even to fail, expands the range of the possible. But the problem of power we explored is not at this ontological level but at the level of social action where institutionalized power is seen to inhibit the freedom of individuals. Such power in an abundant economy resides primarily in the ability to command income and to persuade others. While the power we fear most is that of private and government institutions, this power, however anonymously, is exercised ultimately by individuals. Finally, we rejected the thesis of a conspiracy of power, acknowledging that centers of power cooperate but mainly compete with each other. Indeed, they compete because wielders of power realize their self-interest by variously exercising their power.

At last we explored how a sense of community was the principal bulwark of individual freedom. There is a hunger for community, much of it bogus and inhibitive of freedom, which has resulted in a great proliferation of group-help and group-interest organizations. But these often fall into divisive sectarianism unless they draw their strength from communitarian Values and bind people into contributing to and sharing in a common good. Such a sense of community brings to fruition the principles and virtues discussed in Part One and is, consequently, the ultimate bulwark of personal freedom amid the mammoth structures of power in an abundant economy.

CHAPTER ELEVEN

MORALITY IN A MIXED ECONOMY

The title of this chapter may seem to promise, like the posted regulations in a coed dormitory, a list of do's and don'ts for moral behavior in a mixed economy. Such it will not be. Rather the chapter's purpose is to help students clarify their thinking and form their attitudes for living and acting morally in a social matrix of bigness, the emphasis here being on the relation between Big Business and Big Government. Since, as we saw, the latter grew in response to the former, government inevitably over the last two centuries acquired an increasingly economic purpose and its functions became inextricably intertwined with those of business generally and of large corporate aggregates in particular.

This chapter will neither denounce the mixed economy nor counsel fleeing it. Rather it accepts as fact that our mammoth political and economic institutions grew as the result of millions of past acts of preference. Neither Exxon nor HEW sprang full-blown like Athena from the mind of Zeus. However we may now regret what the past has wrought, these institutions waxed large as the result of millions of free choices which people placed in the hope of achieving some good. Conversely it assumes that no single decision will do such institutions out of existence. Rather their power, if people perceive it socially undesirable, will recede--as it grew--by millions of expressions of preference for alternative products and other political services.

Nor does the chapter propose to critically evaluate particular economic and political institutions. Such evaluation is a never-ending task, an especially worthy subject for business and political historians and a more general duty for all citizens. The chapter hopes more modestly to lay out in an orderly fashion some of the principles which everyone should consider in contributing his or her mite to this ongoing evaluation.

The chapter, consequently, makes these assumptions: 1) that the present mixed economy is the result of a largely preconscious and inevitable human process and serves human well-being as well and as evilly as politico-economic systems of other eras, the Greek City-State, the Roman Empire, the Feudal System and the Renaissance Nation-State; 2) that, however intertwined, the economic order, the economy, and the political order, the state, arise from distinct sets of principles and propose distinct human goals; and 3) that the ends and Values of individuals and of society, conceived here as all individuals in their manifold relations to each other, are both dependent upon the functioning of each order and yet transcends them. Put another way, our individual and social well-being is very much conditioned by how well the economy thrives and how peacefully political change is effected, but that these are only means to and do not constitute our ultimate well-being. Nevertheless, since the economy and the state contribute to and are necessary for our final end, we have a moral obligation to see to their functioning well and to their functioning harmoniously together.

SOCIAL VALUES OF MODERN DEMOCRACIES

The mixed economies of modern democracies are variously conceived as government interfering in business, or business using government for its own ends. However this may be found to be, our personalist orientation will focus on the tripartite relation of the individual person (in all his social relationships) to the state, to the economy, and to both in their relations to each other. This set of relations might be conceived as a triangle in which we as social persons draw income from and provide income to business, supply the means and grant authority to government to provide us with social goods and to bind us with legal obligations, and, finally and trickiest, we empower government to legislate and protect business and obligate business to support government. Unlike a triangle where, given the sides, the angles are fixed, these relationships are in dynamic tension, constantly adjusting and re-adjusting to each other. We will examine each of these relations in turn. But the chapter title suggests that the relation between state and economy is critical, implying that both a too close working arrangement as well as hostility between them is inimical to personal and social well-being.

Challenging understanding as these relations do, nevertheless, our purpose is the further one of seeing their moral implications. We will, consequently, first examine them in terms of the three social Values, liberty, equality and fraternity, which are explicit or implicit purposes in the constitutions of most of the nation-states which since 1776 have transformed the face of the globe. Of the three only equality and liberty are explicit in our own Declaration of Independence, which was the first such formal statement of political freedom. "We hold these truths to be self-evident," the well known words continue, "that all men are created equal; that they are endowed with certain inalienable rights; that among these are life, liberty, and the pursuit of happiness." Fraternity, however, is implied in the very fact of thirteen contentious colonies uniting against a government perceived as tyrannical and in the unanimity of the signers, who on all other points wrangled among themselves, in mutually pledging their lives, their fortunes and their sacred honor. This Value triad became explicit in the rallying cry of the French revolutionists, who drawing their inspiration from our own Declaration of Independence, formulated the Declaration of the Rights of Man and Citizens.

While nourished by the secular rationalism of the Enlightenment, these Values have roots in Christianity: Christ's redemption freed us from the slavery of sin and the tyranny of Satan; he redeems all men because all are equally loved by his Father; and being freed we become sons of God and brothers and sisters of Christ and of all other people. Thus liberty, equality and fraternity may be espoused in the more secular sense or with a Christian inspiration. In either sense they form the moral context and ideal for acting as citizen and as economic agent in today's mixed economy.

Liberty

Besides their possibility of being informed with a Christian meaning, this triad of Values fits well into a Schelerian hierarchy which thus provides a schema to review their interdependence. Obviously, the chapter can only outline these interrelations, hopefully sufficiently to help students formulate their own Value system.

Liberty fits into the second mode of vital Values in the Schelerian hierarchy. Freedom, we saw, was the scope of our acting, what we can do and, therefore, are responsible for doing. We possess freedom, however, at many levels from the wide-ranging freedom of the sons of God to the narrow freedom of choosing between two pleasure-giving goods. Thus freedom is always instrumental: freedom to pursue some good, the good defining the freedom.

At the economic level, freedom implies the right to possess property, to sell and buy it, the right to work for pay and the correlative right to hire and fire, the right to produce for gain, and to spend one's income or not. As citizens we claim rights to affect the political process, to vote and to stand for office; we rightfully expect protection of our persons, property, and good name; as free citizens we enjoy the right to move about and to settle where we will, saving the respective rights of others. In a personal sense, freedom implies right to worship, to thought and expression, to associate with others, especially in marriage, and, in sum, the right to be ourselves, to be different from others. Throughout freedom implies security in possessing these rights and thus imposes the obligation to defend them, and, more importantly, to defend the rights of others. Consequently, the scope of free action is always limited by the freedom others possess and by the good proposed. Spiritual goods bestow a wider range of freedom both because they are spiritual and because they impinge less on others' rights. To repeat, liberty is an instrumental Value to a higher Value.

Equality

Equality is a moral Value. It relates to justice and equity. Originally political revolutionaries sought political and social equality, the right of every one to be counted as equal before the law and as citizen, denying distinctions between categories of citizenship. Economically, equality forbids discriminating between customers except in ability to buy, workers except in ability to produce, between products except in the price and ability to satisfy wants. At the personal level, all are seen equal in freedom and self-responsibility. Our basic equality arises from sharing a common humanity. From the Christian view we are all equally redeemed by Christ and bathed in an infinite love. Thus equality is the protectress of liberty in its higher reaches, equality as citizens, as human beings, as sons of God.

Equality, however, cannot be taken with mathematical literalness through all levels of human existence. Different persons cannot be equal for the very fact that they differ. Citizens with the same access to the ballot box differ in their political influence. Incumbents seeking re-election usually enjoy an edge over candidates out of office. People come to the marketplace with different incomes and wealth, different skills, experience, natural talent, and connections. Firms and economies enjoy comparative advantage over competitors. Personally, we start life differing in physical powers, mental abilities and emotional sensitivity; we differ likewise in family background, education, personality and opportunities. The very uniqueness of the individual, an historic event which will never be repeated, defies absolute identification of any one person with another. Applied to the lower levels of human existence, equality destroys differences and, hence, freedom.

Thus the Value-equality presents the problem area. Individuality denies absolute egalitarianism, which when imposed becomes tyrannical. Both liberty and fraternity imply equality in a common humanity but not a mathematical identification. For my freedom is respected only if my differences from others, my differing scope of liberty, is acknowledged. Likewise, fraternity flourishes best among equals but not between identities. For I can love another only if that other is distinguishable from myself. The very notion of justice, which is the root Value of equality, requires treating people in accord with what is right for them both as persons and as individuals. That is, justice demands equity not equality in treatment. The potentiality for tyranny which every system carries in embryo lies in their disposition to assume away and to minimize differences. A system which cannot accommodate equitable as opposed to equal treatment becomes inhuman.

Fraternity

The egalitarian thrust, dramatized in the political, social and economic efforts of minorities for equal treatment, largely tells the tale of the innermost tensions tearing at modern democracies. This struggle is highlighted -- crudely, of course -- by contrasting the Liberal and Libertarian mind. Both, appropriate for their names, espouse first and foremost the Value-liberty. They contend over the Value-equality. For the Liberal denies the possibility of liberty when groups are not treated alike; the Libertarian when individual differences are not respected. Carried to extremes, both mind-sets would destroy freedom. This conflict cannot be ameliorated without the third in our triad of Values, fraternity. Clarence Walton gets to the essence of the matter:

> "...to dwell on notions of justice, liberty, and fraternity is to recognize how much and how long Western man has talked of the first, more recently of the second, and almost never of the third. Even James Fitzjames Stephen, who published the classic study in 1876 on Liberty, Equality and Fraternity,

confessed that he could understand men wanting liberty and justice. But brotherly love? Scarcely, because fraternity is not conveniently translated into law and politics. Indeed it is quite possible that contemporary liberal political thought which supports egalitarianism is essentially individualistic and unfraternal, and that fraternity is discussed by moderns in the sense of Cain and Abel."[1]

Fraternity, as a kind of love, manifests itself in as many ways as the relations which unite us to others. Since fraternity like love is motivated by whatever is lovable -- the good, the pleasant, and the useful -- the Value-fraternity can be located in any of the Schelerian modes, from the sensual, to the useful, to the sacral or be some combination of these. As a civic and social bond, fraternity would not imply that intimate union of love between spouses or between parent and child, for it would admit some mixture of mutual usefulness. Nor would it bind as closely as comradeship in war which combines a mutual help with a respect born of common sharing in hardship and danger. Social and civic fraternity, therefore, while admitting a stronger element of utility, nevertheless, is a love uniting citizens because they share common citizenship and common humanity. Thus while not a pure love of friendship, fraternity is respect for others as good in themselves.

Fraternity is not absent from American life. Wars and national crises, even local and personal disasters evoke fraternal response. What is lacking is the widely-shared conviction that this Value is essential to mediate the demands of liberty and of equality. For fraternity -- human community, civility, friendship, love -- is a spirit which binds citizens into an organic unity. For though each differs in his contribution to and sharing in the public good, all are one in sharing common citizenship. Less apparently but no less essentially, the economy is a cooperative enterprise. Suppliers need demanders and demanders suppliers; workers need firms and firms workers; borrowers need lenders and lenders borrowers. Whatever the competition for scarce goods, resources and income, resolving scarcity as a social condition requires mutuality in both contributing and sharing.

At the highest level of personal action, friendship not only requires differences but guarantees freedom to differ. The family, the most intimate of friendships, so intimate that it can violently explode, is a unity founded on differences, male differing from female, parents from children. The very power of the spirit of fraternity is to preserve the freedom to differ, while blending these inequalities into mutual contribution to and sharing in a common good. That true community is lacking in most families, neighborhoods, work places, and the like simply confirms what Walton says, the need for and the implications of fraternity have not been explored and consciously espoused as a social Value.

Nor is fraternity exclusive, for its very dynamic of creating unity from differences opens a healthy friendship and a healthy sense of community to the larger world and avoids the evils of turning in upon itself. If a family is so introverted that no friend of its members is admitted into its circle, it is destroying the very individual difference upon which it was founded. A clique of friends becomes a menace to its members if it closes off contact with the larger peer group. A neighborhood council which ignores the larger civic issues destroys its own rationale. A patriotism, jealous of other peoples' and other nations' achievements, loses the vivifying ability to recognize its own.

Summarizing we see that the very interplay among this triad of Values itself constitutes the person's moral attitude in his role as citizen and economic agent. None of the three can be omitted or neglected. Without freedom, fraternity becomes 'smotherlove' in all its manifestations, and equality a tyrannical conformism. Without equality -- equity and justice -- liberty becomes license, trampling on the rights of others, and fraternity becomes exclusive, favoritism and discrimination. Without fraternity, the power of welding diversity into unity, equality becomes a cock-pit of competing demands and liberty narrows itself to self-satisfaction.

Obviously, the foregoing could not plumb the depths of the vivifying inter-action among these Values. Yet even this superficial treatment should spark students' further contemplation and, for the immediate agenda, its application to analysis of the three relations of individual person to the state, to the economy and to both in their relating to each other. We explore each of these in turn.

PERSON AND STATE

The impulse to unite with others in a political union is so natural that the decision to change political allegiance is always traumatic. One thinks of Solzhenitsyn, neither welcome in Russia nor comfortable in America. But for most there is no such thing as a formal contract of union; one simply grows into citizenship, accepting benefits and responsibilities, as one grows into adulthood. Even a formal constitutional change rather confirms continuity with the past than establishes a new political order. For whatever its new form, a government must govern what is, the social relationships already existing among individuals, between families, within neighborhoods, municipalities, work-shops, churches and other institutions and social groupings.

Social Foundations of State

So the vast paraphenalia of a modern state rests upon and draws its strength and viability from a deeper reality, the multi-dimensional complex of personal, cultural and economic relationships which we earlier described as society. People spin this complex web by being born, by their own choices, or by happenstance but in no way by leave of the state. They are natural, not political relations.

Such spontaneous proliferation is subject to disorder, to some taking advantage of others, to people acting either maliciously or inadvertently at cross-purposes with each other. As in a Roman Plaza during the evening rush, someone with authority is needed to sort out the flow of traffic. Even in the simplest societies, an individual or group will make decisions affecting the good of the community as a whole, not particularly because people are at each other's throats but simply to coordinate diverse interests and abilities. Thus the basic need for political government to maintain peace and harmony in peoples' dealings with each other arises from the very fact of man's social nature and condition. An important part of this is providing the means to work out disputes and to enforce justice. Just as important is providing defense against external or internal enemies. For these reasons government inevitably becomes the only legitimate user of violence, granting citizens this right only when lawful authority cannot provide protection.

The peace and order necessary for people to go about their business and to live their lives is obviously good for them, but, just as obviously, it is a good which no one person can achieve on his own. It is a general good, a common good. But this political common good must be distinguished from the social common good which we discussed in

Chapter Five. There the social common good was seen flowing from people's inherent relations to each other, from their deep need to communicate with others, and from their sharing in producing things necessary for survival and useful and convenient for living. The political common good is more superficial, the condition of peace and harmony necessary for realizing this more fundamental social well-being. Hence, it is instrumental, a means to a higher common good. But being essential, the peace and harmony of social intercourse rightly demands our concern, our effort and our resources. The state takes its dignity from society but being necessary for society has a dignity in its own right.

From this duty to maintain healthy and flourishing social relations, the modern state has acquired many more functions than preserving order, justice and defense. Where the requirement for health, safety, and education, in short the welfare of citizens, exceeds their reasonable effort and ability to provide for themselves, and, more importantly, to some real impairment of society itself, the state becomes the resource of last resort to provide the means to attain these goods. (Note: providing the means, not the goods. More on this later.) Similarly, where people's economic well-being is impaired by conditions beyond their control, recession and inflation, lay-offs, industrial injuries and illnesses, physical disability, lack of marketable skills or more important responsibilities like caring for children, the state has the obligation to help, so as to prevent the creation of a class of economically dispossessed. From these simple considerations flows the vast proliferation of government programs by which we all by more ways than one have become welfare beneficiaries of government.

The Welfare State

The modern state's aggressiveness, however, in assuming these functions constitutes probably the single most serious threat to society itself. Forgetting its essentially instrumental role, the state more and more absorbs duties which private organizations, perhaps with some state assistance, can perform more efficiently and more humanely. More dangerously, the state is intruding into areas where the individual and, in the case of children, the family has primary responsibility. Alexis de Tocqueville over a century ago described the situation today with almost contemporary insight. His prophecy is worth quoting extensively.

> "Above this race of men [citizens of a benevolent democracy] stands an immense and tutelary power which takes upon itself alone to secure their gratifications and to watch over their fate. That power is absolute, minute, regular, provident, and mild. It would be like the authority of a parent, if, like that authority, its object was to prepare men for manhood; but it seeks, on the contrary, to keep them in perpetual childhood; it is well content that the people should rejoice, provided they think of nothing but rejoicing. For their happiness such a government willingly labors, but it chooses to be the sole agent and the only arbiter of that happiness; it provides for their security, foresees and supplies their necessities, facilitates their pleasures, manages their principal concerns, directs their industry, regulates the descent of property, and subdivides their inheritances; what remains but to spare them all the care of thinking and all the trouble of living?
>
> Thus, it every day renders the exercise of the free agency of man less useful and less frequent; it circumscribes the will within a narrower range and gradually robs a man of all the uses of himself."[2]

What de Tocqueville describes is a massive erosion of personal freedom. Moreover, he puts his finger on the cause: "The principle of equality has prepared men for these things; it has predisposed men to endure them, and oftentimes to look on them as benefits."[3]

The massive growth of welfare programs since WW II has been lauded as an increased sensitivity for the plight of the poor and concern that they share in increasing economic abundance. Certainly, this fraternal impulse motivated many citizens and legislators in approving such programs. Analysis, however, of the growth of welfare expenditures faces the bitter conclusion that these programs did not represent a massive shift of income from the wealthy to the poor. In 1950 total (Federal and State) welfare expenditures were $23.5b. or 13.4% of gross national product. In 1976 they had increased 1400% to $331.4b. or 27.5% of gross national product. Given some 10 million families below or struggling along the poverty line, dividing the welfare pot among them would have given each family a $33,100 annual income.[4]

Clearly that was not the case. Conceding that administering such vast sums requires a huge bureaucracy, we find that indeed total government employment increased from $6\frac{1}{2}$m. in 1950 to over 15m. in 1976. Granted then that 60% of welfare taxes paid the generous salaries, fringe benefits and office expenses of the bureaucracy, there would still be enough to give every poor family $13,000 a year. Clearly this also was not the case. The inescapable conclusion is that welfare payments were largely re-distributed among the large group of middle-income families against whose income the bulk of welfare taxes was levied in the first place.

o While these programs did help the poor substantially, so that at least they maintained their relative share of increasing national income and allowed others to escape
o the poverty syndrome, nevertheless, the predominant effect of government welfare programs has been to entrench a bureaucracy with larger numbers and higher salaries, to
o make all citizens more dependent upon governmental handouts, and to raise the suspicion that the modern welfare state from being hand-maid and instrumental to society has
o come to dominate it and to determine its Values.

State and Social Values

Whatever one's judgement that the welfare functions of the modern state are inadequate for social justice or that they manifest totalitarian tendencies, how to preserve one's Values of liberty, equality and fraternity is still a personal problem. People do develop a welfare mentality and, by no means, is this confined to the poor. Grantsmanship can become a way of life for academics, businessmen, municipal officials as well as for those disinclined to gainful employment. Many such, for good reasons or shoddy, try to milk the welfare system for all it is worth. Generally they forget that recipients of government bounty dance to the tune government plays and that subservience is no less subservience that the collar and chain one wears is velvet.

This is not to say that all such dipping into the public pail destroys personal integrity and responsibility. All welfare programs have a social benefit rationale. Ideally they are intended to aid individuals over difficult periods so that later they may pay back through higher taxes on increased earnings. Take that with which most college students are familiar, state and federal tuition assistance. Certainly few students could pay for college entirely out of their own resources, with no family or government help. Whatever the source, students can preserve their personal responsibility and freedom by choosing a school and program challenging their abilities and by attacking their studies seriously. This largely repays in gratitude for the help extended. In addition, however, beneficiaries of government tuition assistance bear another burden of gratitude, to fulfill the loan contract by repaying as soon as they can. This involves no more loss of freedom than does a company which meets its obligation to investors by successfully managing the capital they entrusted to it.

Similarly the integrity of equality and fraternity are preserved. Equality, in the sense of social justice, motivates the graduate to maintain the viability of the student loan program by his repaying his loan, so that legislators are disposed to continue funding loans to future students, giving them the same opportunity which the graduate enjoyed. One's sense of fraternity is sharpened by recognizing the general obligation that as one was helped so one should help others, that the 50% larger lifetime earnings a college degree will realize is not entirely due to a person's own efforts and can only be repaid by paying higher taxes, by savings for one's children's education, and by contributing to private efforts to assist future students.

That many will scoff at the above as pollyannish, insisting that such programs only work by constantly checking for fraud, by coercing students and schools to live up to their obligation, and by hounding graduates who are welching on their loans, only attests to the fact that people are not universally inspired by the Values of freedom, social justice and brotherly love. That sad fact, however, does not relieve me of my obligation, whatever the example of my peers and however the sacrifice required of my personal wants. The conclusion the student should draw from government benefactions he has received applies, as differing circumstances dictate, to all welfare recipients.

A more effective way of preserving personal Value integrity against the tendency of the modern state to dictate our concern for others is by our generosity to private groups and societies who compete with government in providing the same social services. In that competition private education and private welfare services are a shrinking part of the total welfare picture. While expenditures here have increased from $4.8b. in 1960 to $18b. in 1976, their percentage of total expenditures fell from 6% to 4%.[5] This fact testifies that the vast majority of Americans make but miniscule contributions to private programs in contrast to the taxes they pay to support public programs. The diminishing role of private charity is lowering the most effective barrier to the totalitarian tendencies of the welfare state. Fears of this possibility force us to acknowledge that affluence and economic abundance give us the means to blunt this thrust, and that our sacrifices for private agencies is the surest way to preserve the social Values of liberty, equality and fraternity.

PERSON AND ECONOMY

One of the anomalies of American politics is that among all its burning issues, right-to-life, integration, education, defense and international relations, the touchstone of political sentiment, differentiating Conservative from Liberal, is whether one more fears Big Government or Big Business. This attitude is almost an anachronism because in a mixed economy the two have more in common than in dispute -- a subject we will discuss shortly. Nevertheless, one's place in the social order does present a radically different view of the two. Looking up from below the poverty line, Big Government is certainly Big Brother, assisting with food and income, costly health care, and education of a sort, while Big Business is Big Ogre, charging high prices for the sake of profits, the reluctant employer of one's skills, the creditor demanding usurous rates. Looking down from some height above the poverty line, Big Government is Big Tax-taker, Big Waster, Big Regulator, while Big Business pours out goods in profusion and provides income, pension and bonuses.

Economy as a Social Order

Putting aside these prejudices as best we can, let us gaze fixedly for a moment on our relations to the economy, the economic order. For it is an order, an organization of many parts toward a purpose. That purpose is obviously to satisfy wants by providing material goods and services. Just as obviously it implies cooperative effort, for few individuals throughout history have satisfied their wants entirely by their own efforts. Even Robinson Crusoe, the paradigm of the complete individualist, used the ideas and techniques which he learned from an earlier life in society. But satisfying potentially unlimited wants in a world of limited resources, reluctant effort, and inadequate technology implies scarcity, that our wants as a whole exceed our ability to satisfy them. As we began, we stress scarcity once again and its implications: every scarce good has a cost, that cost is what one must sacrifice to get a good, and what one gets must be bid away from others who are competing for the good. Though bored with the repetition, the student can never forget that these basic conditions, scarcity, costs and competition, are unavoidable, as people go about their ordinary business of satisfying wants.

This struggle with scarcity likewise tends to obscure the reality of an overall purpose of the economy. Certainly, that purpose is not planned in the sense that a football team prepares a game plan in order to beat the other team. Quite to the contrary, the economy in a free-enterprise system, at least, appears chaotic. What is produced, who is hired, what firms survive in producing goods seem almost haphazard. From another view, money-making seems so to dominate that satisfying wants appears almost incidental. Yet wants are satisfied, people live and live well, production is organized to respond to people's unpredictable and uncoordinated desires for goods and services. Somehow the millions of individual aspirations are translated into sales of goods which firms have already produced by previously hired labor, previously purchased materials, and previously invested capital. The only intellectually satisfying explanation for this marvelous process of committing resources in anticipation of sales is that the overall purpose of satisfying wants motivates every stage of the way.

This discussion of purpose incidentally brought out the other overriding aspect of the modern economy: its amazing complexity, versatility, changeability. Millions and millions of people of the most diverse abilities are organized to fashion things and produce services for sale, which income in turn enables them to buy what the economy has produced. So highly differentiated are these skills, that most would hardly survive if torn from the technological processes by which they earn income. Yet these skills are blended together to provide a level of living which the most farsighted seer a century ago could not predict.

Set this complexity into a setting where people's wants, industrial techniques, labor skills and supplies, availability of materials and energy are constantly changing and the marvel is heightened that anything is done right. The economy, however, has devised an ingeniously simply communication system, again by no one's planning or foresight, but a spontaneous elaboration of signals based on the simple principle that all economic goods have a cost. Economists call this system the pricing mechanism. It is appropriate to call on the Nobel Laureate, F.A. Hayek, to elaborate:

> "We have come to understand that the market and the price mechanism provide in this sense a sort of discovery procedure which both makes the utilization of more facts possible than any other known system, and which provides the incentive for constant discovery of new facts which improve adaptation to the ever-changing circumstances of the world in which we live. Of course this adaptation is never as perfect as the mathematical models of market equilibrium suggest; but it is certainly much better than any which we know how to bring about by any other means."[6]

Such is the economy, a bewilderingly complex but completely natural and spontaneous cooperative process for organizing abilities and resources to satisfy mutual wants. We have already viewed it as an aspect of society, as our relationships with each other by means of scarce material goods, but it might be worth while to draw out these implications further.

Being natural and spontaneous, the economy is not a creature of the state. It takes its origin from man's relatedness, from his social nature. But since it arises from human relations through the mediation of material things, it arises from man's physical wants and needs. Consequently, it is strictly a means to people's higher vital, aesthetic, spiritual, moral and religious Values. Economic goods may limit the realization of these higher aspirations but they cannot dictate to them. However successful companies may be through advertising in shaping consumption to production, people's preferences, and ultimately their Values, determine what is produced. Correlatively, production which destroys lives, which disrupts families and communities, which dehumanizes labor can expect a backlash from the individuals and groups affected. This failing, it can anticipate that the power of government will be invoked. Though independent of the state, the economy is subordinated to the good of society and thus is subordinate to the state as custodian of the social common good. At the same time the state is dependent on the economy for the same physical means,as is the individual, to perform its own functions.

Economy and Social Values

This intermeshing of our social, political, and economic good means that we can and should expect to realize the Values of liberty, equality and fraternity no less in our economic relations than in our social and political relations. In a free-enterprise economy the Value-liberty is paramount. However successful corporations are in corraling consumer buying power to their own ends, consumer sovereignity is paid not just lip-service but is decisive. Even the largest and wealthiest company must bow to it. General Motors has surpassed Ford and Chrysler, and Volkswagen can compete against the Big Three better than Kaiser, Studebaker, and American Motors for the simple reason that they enjoy consumer preference for their product, and upon this their economic power ultimately rests. For the same reason freedom to compete in production is still operational, though this Value's constantly threatened existence is maintained only by constant vigilance to preserve competition. Freedom to work is probably most threatened for the reason that vocational opportunities are so unequal.

Again the Value-equality poses the problem. For if there is freedom to choose one's vocational goals, there is equally the freedom of firms to hire or not hire. Since people enter the job market with unequal talents, unequal experience and unequal training, they do not enjoy equal employability. And for this reason those who do hire must minimize, and hopefully eliminate, criteria for employment like race, religion, sex and sexual preference, and age to the extent that they are irrelevant to the job. That judgments about these criteria's relevance and candidates' potentialities as opposed to their experience may differ, only accentuates the difficulties. Gross discrimination, that is, discrimination in hiring and pay based on factors clearly irrelevant to job capacity, violates both equality of opportunity and freedom of access to the good of the economy and of society. Nevertheless, a valid discrimination is of the essence of economic preference, consumer sovereignity, freedom to hire, freedom to offer services, and freedom to produce.

Thus fraternity becomes essential. This Value, we have seen repeatedly, is not alien to the free-enterprise system. For that system is founded equally on cooperation as on competition. A lively sense of fraternity, of concern for the good and rights of other people, will inspire employers to establish working conditions, health and safety safeguards, and times for work which enhance not impede labor productivity. A sense of fraternity will care for retraining or placing loyal workers in new positions when technology or other economic conditions displace them. Fraternity, furthermore, will develop a concern for satisfying the ultimate consumer, that in paying the price the consumer, however only imagined, deserves a product which he or she rightfully expects. Finally, a keen appreciation of fraternity, as a Value which should inform all social relationships, will inspire a sensitivity toward those who are left in the backwaters of economic growth because of prejudice, physical or mental impairments, or even because of their own personal disaffection and unwillingness to make personal effort. Fraternity cannot overcome all the differences in sharing in the good of an abundant economy, but it can support such public programs which offer an opportunity to so share, equal to the capabilities and willingness of individuals.

STATE AND ECONOMY

We turn now to the knottiest issue the chapter addresses, the relation of the individual to the state and the economy in their relation to each other. The preceding may seem to have skirted this issue, but in reality discussing the person's relation to the state and to the economy separately is preparatory to discussing his relation to them together.

Because our biases against Big Business or against Big Government or perhaps against both, the subject provides a number of pitfalls. One may be inclined to cheer government on in whipping business into socially responsible behavior until business becomes simply an appendage of public political policy. One could hail every business gain as a victory for freedom, reducing government to a committee of the bourgeoisie as Marx held and as Calvin Coolidge believed: "The business of America is business." Or like Mercutio one could wish a "plague on both your houses" hoping that each would destroy the other or, at least, leave the individual to go about his business. A hope which will prove fatal as it did for Mercutio.

The Social Triangle

The student should be aware now that there is no ultimate resolution to this struggle. Society, the economy and the state are locked in a dynamic tension, each guarding its own good and purpose, yet each dependent upon the other two. The political good as well as the general economic welfare derive their ultimate meaning from and, consequently, are ordained to sustain the social good, those personal and cultural ties by and in which people realize their full humanity in family life, neighborhood and work community, education, art, and communal worship. Yet, these in turn, are dependent upon public order and a prospering economy. Finally, while the economy draws its rationale from society and not from the state, it operates within the public order and thus its good is subordinated to the political good.

The triangle, as we have already used, easily comes to mind in pre-figuring these relationships. In all the four figures below, state and economy are drawn as supporting society. The angles may be thought of as the social Values of liberty, equality and fraternity holding the three sides together.

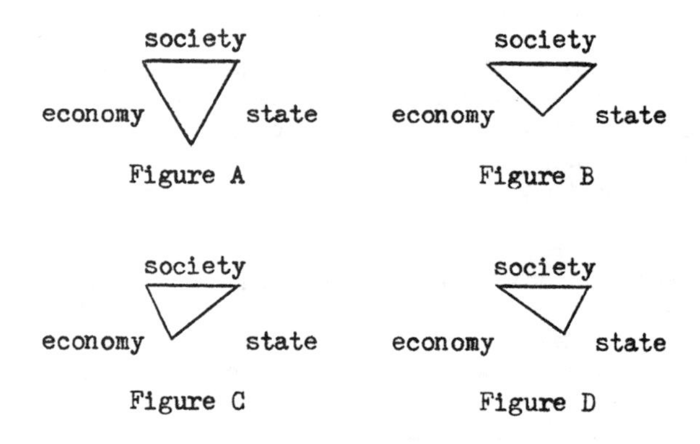

Figure A

Figure B

Figure C

Figure D

In figure A, the ideal is depicted. The state and the economy mutually and equally support society. In figure B the burden of society is shown overwhelming both an anemic state and a faltering economy. The more likely situations are presented in figures C and D. In the former the state in absorbing the functions of the economy tends to make the political good the predominant social good. Such happens in the totalitarian state, whether of the left or of the right. In the last figure, social Values are reduced to economic values when the functions of government are attenuated to supporting business, minimal government preserving property rights, enforcing contracts and defending capital against the demands of labor. This figure depicts laissez faire capitalism, at least as assumed in theory.

o Keep in mind, however, the dynamic tension, the shifting aggression and resistance of each against the others, so that these relationships are never fixed once and for all.
o Kept in mind, this dynamic highlights the role social Values play. Emphasis on liberty, to the neglect of social justice and fraternity, produces the society where busi-
o ness predominates. Equality, to the neglect of personal freedom, generates the welfare state with its totalitarian tendencies. Only the three Values, with especially a vivi-
o fying sense of fraternity, holds the three goods of society, economy and state in healthy balance.

This dynamic further suggest that two people, equally objective and knowledgeable, may differ in judging whether figure C or D is more representative of reality. With the interdependencies outlined above, however, social critics at least have a common format for discussing the facts, no matter how they differ in interpreting them. In addition, they have another set of clues from analyzing how efficacious the social Values of liberty, equality and fraternity are in energizing this dynamic. For the individual, these Values are touchstones in determining his own moral attitude toward society, state and economy, and in making his own contribution, whether as legislator, civil servant, businessman, or householder, toward maintaining this dynamic. To this we now turn.

Bigness and the Social Values

Frank discussion of this necessitates some analysis of the biases we have against Big Business, Big Government or both. Such analysis will inevitably find these biases rooted in the fear of bigness. We distrust the megacorporation because it seeks profit regardless of workers' welfare, quality of its product, and effects of its actions on the community. That is, it is impersonal in decision-making, its policies are not fully comprehended and above all it is big. We tend to be more sympathetic with the lower wages and fringe benefits of a small machine shop, whose owner may actually earn a handsome return on capital invested, than with the larger wages and fringe benefits which may be forcing U.S. Steel out of lines of production because it cannot compete with foreign imports.

We fear the workings of government agencies. They go

'by the book', regardless of individual needs. They lack flexibility, they are inefficient, and above all they are big. Paradoxically we are more worried about the general policy of an agency far removed from us than with the local agency which directly affects our welfare. We tolerate the ineffectiveness of the local principal whose leadership directly affects our child's education, while swamping HEW with letters over a change in national policy.

The anomaly was mentioned before that large corporations are tapped for executive personnel to head up community drives and alumni appeals, and to serve on the board of charitable and cultural organizations, yet 7 out of 10 Americans harbor a low opinion in general of big business.[7] Equally anomalous a stint in Washington or the state house has become entree to a handsome position in private business. Both anomalies point in the same direction: we distrust not the people who direct Big Business and Big Government but the bigness itself.

The problem with bigness, of course, is that it is big. Big things crowd out little things. Big corporations and big government agencies sprawl, intruding into our private lives. We meet their products and services at every turn; we depend on them for income, a goodly portion of our labor going to help them expand. How they are doing largely determines our own material well-being. They set the tone of our cities and make possible our style of living. We turn to them for education, for health insurance, for tiding us over crises, and for retirement income. They are the principal factors in determining whether our accumulated savings are worth much or little.

In face of such bigness we feel caught between two juggernauts. We are fearful of our personal freedom, convinced that neither government nor business will or can deal equitably with their clients, and expect, least of all, to be treated with human consideration or friendliness in our dealings with them. To be perfectly frank there is probably little that private citizens can do to make these huge institutions assume a more humane manner without a drawn out, widely publicized, and costly public effort. This is true even though there exists considerable sympathy for the effort within the institutions.

Nevertheless, there still remains an area of privateness in our lives which can be preserved and enlarged. Affluence does provide the resources for even the poor to follow activities for which we are not beholden to either government or business. Developing a hobby, cultivating an artist taste, following a sports program, obtaining further education can be pursued by paring one's non-essential spending and with no by-your-leave of government. Many have a consuming interest in their home or garden. Private charities have already been mentioned. Volunteer work and association with others in causes to effect institutional changes expand the range of one's life. To those whose jobs and the pleasures permitted by public order absorb their lives, all of these are simply palliatives to a trammelled existence. But to those who perceive life as transcending political and economic relations, such activities open large areas of private freedom and responsibility through which they can extend their interests, cultivate new friends, and give a new character to their lives.

This freedom to be private is guaranteed only if all can claim an equal right to it. For otherwise, the state can discriminate in granting the right to some and withholding it from others. But the Value-equality degenerates into egalitarianism when it is suffused with envy. For the envious would reduce all to their own level, defaming another man's virtue, expropriating another's wealth. Envy, unlike ambition or emulation, prefers to have less than that another have more. Egalitarianism, far from protecting freedom, jeopardizes it. The danger of affluent expectations for more is that it can, by stimulating envy, bloat the egalitarian spirit into a monster which will destroy freedom.

Much of contemporary egalitarianism, it seems, is motivated by this baser kind of envy. It insists on its cut into every welfare program. Envious of business success, it wants it kept in its place, preferring shackling it even if the economy suffers. Envy turns justice from equity, a fair sharing according to desserts, into equality, equal distribution regardless of contribution. Envy blinds to the good one already has by longing for the larger share another possesses. Ironically envy is equally blind to the burdens which accompanies the larger income and wealth another enjoys. Many an underling would welcome return to his lower status were he forced to bear for even a short period his boss's responsibilities.

Once again a sense of fraternity is the conjunctive Value between the tendency of liberty to go off on its own and of equality to look askance and enviously at anothers' good fortune. For fraternity can see another's good as one's own. A worker can rejoice at his employer's success because that spells more work for the shop; in turn, the employer is appreciative of the loyal industry of his workers who makes his success possible. Fraternity has the power to transform liberty into working for a common goal and envy into emulation. Universally, fraternity acts to bind groups into a community of effort whether in families, work-places, schools, congregations or social societies. By doing so it extends the individual's range of freedom into areas not dominated by large business nor policed by the state. It is suggested here that preserving and enlarging these enclaves of privateness within the larger arena of public struggle is essential to making life livable.

Indeed if we look honestly at our situation, contrasting it with that of most of the world today and of our fathers and grandfathers before us, we would concede that the scope of free society is larger than ever. It is limited, but as much by our own failings, our vice and crimes, and plain human 'cussedness' as by big business and big government. Gabriel Hauge, drawing on wide experience in teaching, government and business, may paint a triumphalist picture, which will not set well with the millions disheartened in ghettoes, reservations, and rural slums nor with the millions of youth turned off on school and turned onto drugs, but he does affirm in a reasonably realistic way that, by and large, the state and the economy have served the overwhelming majority well:

> "A free society is a kind of miracle whereby each of us can pursue his separate ends with due regard for the rights of others to follow theirs. Government is an essential creation to mediate and compromise the inevitable conflicts between the rights of one and the rights of another and widen opportunity for all. Business supplies the fuel of freedom: the income, the wealth, the infinite variety of goods and services, the wide range of remunerated occupations without which most of our ends would prove quixotic. Its role, its goals, are not in conflict with other legitimate aspirations. Our society is big enough for many dreams and many destinies; business places them within reach. It has made great strides in solving the problem of producing wealth. The use of this wealth is up to us, in our private decisions, and in our collective choices through government."[8]

The Government-Business Struggle

We address, at last, the relation of government to business because it forms the context, though not the essence, of a good life. In so doing we must keep perspective. They do struggle, but their struggle is not chaotic. There exists a larger area of agreement than disagreement. Consequently, in trying to set right what is wrong between them, we should proceed cautiously lest greater harm to society result.

While the government must have a considerably longer time-perspective than any particular business, the political and economic goals of people are co-terminous, neither set can be achieved without the other. There exists, therefore, considerable consonance between the needs of government and the needs of business. Both need overall economic stability and steady growth. Both need technological development and improving human skills. Both benefit from the discovery of new sources of energy, from improving ways of exploiting the earth's original deposits of minerals and metals; both benefit from conserving their use. Both require an orderly money and credit market. Both need to peer down the road to plan for future expectations. As spin-offs from the preceding, both have an interest in furthering education, in improving the health of citizens, in stimulating scientific inquiry, and in sustaining economic incentive.

This consonance of needs indeed poses the real danger that such an alliance between them may cause the private and social goods of people to be subsumed into the overall goals of an industrial society. Statism, whether of the right in which the private interests of the business community become the public interests of government, or of the left, where the public interest becomes the private interest of business, is equally totalitarian and presents the danger that the two bureaucracies act in concord to preserve their interests and to impose their Values as social Values. When one's political acceptability is dependent upon economic status or one's economic status on political acceptability, the range of private freedom and the scope of social relations is reduced to what the state deems permissible. A hand-in-glove coziness, whichever is hand or glove, between business and government is as disastrous for society as the temptation to effect it is insistent.

Some tension between government and business is, therefore, desirable. It should arise from their respective goals, the economy's to satisfy material wants, the state's to maintain peace and order in social relationships. It should arise from the differing discipline to which each is subjected: governments must operate within a pre-ordained budget; business acts on the basis of expected revenues and costs. Politicians and political appointees face the judgment of elections; managers the judgment of profits. Tension, most of all, arises from their differing modes of procedure.

The political common good is always a compromise, the infinite wisdom of legislators extending only to the ad hoc, what will keep things moving in an orderly fashion in the present situation. Consequently, the legal procedure is a synthesizing process. Government is the art of compromise, a reasonable resolution among conflicting rights and wrongs, worked out in response to a de facto situation. Compromise is achieved by definition, by formulating a law or by court interpretation. The resulting law, therefore, is universal, applying equally to all in a particular category; it is fixed, remaining on the books until amended, superceded, or simply forgotten; it is objective and known, becoming a fact which must now be taken into account. To be effective it must have a sanction, an appropriate penalty for its violation.

The economic process, on the other hand, is no less a compromise, arising from the clash of self-interests (competition) in exchange. It differs principally from the political process in being a continuous adjustment to changing anticipations and expectations. What was affects the exchange rate only in so far as past experience shapes future expectations. By compromising subjective expectations, the exchange rate becomes an objective fact, the current market price, the going wage, today's interest rate, but becoming objective people respond to it and responding change it. One final point: the exchange rate is complex, not just a price but a cost. The difference is that price is only the money cost of goods while cost includes sacrificing many other goods than money, time, effort, convenience, honor, moral virtue, eternal salvation etc.

Thus we have laid out the scenario of frustration which awaits legislators, being for the most part lawyers and not economists, when setting legal prices. First, people will respond to the legal price, some buying more, some less than before, some selling less, some more, but all changing as the result of the price-setting itself. More frustrating, since the law can only fix the price and not the costs, the costs will significantly change. A moratorium on rent increases, for example, will cause landlords to let maintenance slide and to be choosier in selecting tenants; it increases renters' cost, therefore, by decreasing their mobility, tenants preferring to put up with bad situations rather than to risk not finding another apartment. While good arguments can be made for setting a legal price in particular situations, legislators should expect that the law will never fully achieve their hopes because costs can be shifted in ways no legislator could conceive.

It is apparent, consequently, that business and government clash over their respective dynamics. Government grows in response to constituent demands for more social goods, more roads, schools, hospitals, welfare generally. Special economic interests also beat to Washington and to state capitols, often under guise of the general welfare, but really to obtain government favors, betraying the general freedom of the economy for the sake of their particular interests. Both kinds of supplication are abetted by and abet the general drive of government to impose political rationality on economic activity. For the political mind can only perceive order as coming from authority on high and not arising from a seeming chaotic conflict from below.

The economic dynamic is gain-seeking, realizing a greater value after exchange than one had before. Given scarcity, gain-seeking is competitive, a pressured search for advantage in a context of constant change. Obviously, consumers, workers, companies seek surcease from this pressure, room to manipulate free of competition. Some seek it by outdistancing their rivals in production and consumer preference, and others by exploiting advantages in technology, location, or possession of natural resources. More commonly than we think, businesses and industries obtain government privilege, regulations for their own advantage, licensing newcomers to a market, health and safety rules to limit competition, protection against foreign imports. Union collective bargaining is no less a means of reducing competition among workers for jobs and pay. Only consumers find it difficult to organize collective action and must rely upon their individual veto power of refusing to buy.

Viewed from above the economy appears chaotic. All things considered, gain-seeking and competition are inadequate by themselves to channel this unruly effort toward socially beneficial results. There is a role for state control over the economy. Indeed, even in *laissez faire* theory, maintaining justice in exchange was always accepted as requisite. Now the emphasis is on social justice, not in our sense of a personal virtue but as a social condition. This is the source of confusion, there being as many understandings of social justice as there are advocates of and resisters against it. The problem is much like restlessness in a classroom of youngsters. There is a restlessness which prevents learning and there is a restlessness natural to children trying to learn. The disciplinarian whose class is anesthetized by fear or boredom no less fails as educator than the teacher whose class is in constant tumult. Social justice ideally results from that kind of intervention into the competitive gain-seeking process where benefits would be so distributed to encourage the dispossessed and disadvantaged few but not to destroy the incentive of the many. It is a neat trick if you can pull it off.

The perceptive student will at this point surmise that, although this section set out to explore the inter-relationship between state and economy, its drift is toward analyzing the relation of government to business and not the reverse. Indeed most economic and political comment goes in the same direction.

There are good reasons. Economic activity is more spontaneous, individual and closer to people's primal needs -- one must live first before living well. Political action is more deliberative, collective, and responding to new conditions. Second, in examining what is the proper planning and directive role of the state over the economy, we are implicitly defining the limits to its authority over the economy. In recommending methods of influence which respects the nature and purpose of the economy, we are at the same time condemning methods which violate them. Finally, the many suggestions for inducing business social responsibility can be applied, _pari passu_, to government agencies which supply the plethora of public goods the state provides.

Controlling the Economy

As with the individual, the first rule of government is "Know thyself." When people in government forget the primary duties of government and its instrumental role in caring for the social common good, government goes off in all directions, assuming burdens and providing services it was not designed for. Certainly, this the message of George Cabot Lodge, even while arguing for a more communitarian and less individualistic ideology:

> "If the role of government were more precisely and consciously defined, the government could be smaller in size. To a great extent, the plethora of bureaucracies results from a lack of focus and comprehension -- an ironic bit of fallout from the old notion of the limited state. With greater awareness of what needs to be done it will be possible to consider more fruitfully which issues are best left to local action, to regional planning, to centralized coordination, and which transcends the nation-state to require a more global approach."[9]

In addressing business, politicians, judges and bureaucrats should exercise the same discernment, leaving to business what it can do better and assuming only those tasks which the state can perform. There are obviously some economic goods and services only government can provide. But these will vary from nation to nation and from period to period. Space exploration, for example, could well become more accessible to private enterprise. The government's present postal monopoly does not foreclose advancing reasonable arguments against it.

Here we limit discussion to two roles vis-a-vis business: the government's role in policing business and its role in setting national priorities.

The overall policing principle is well established. It is largely founded on the moral code: Thou shalt not kill; thou shalt not maim; thou shalt not steal, especially from the poor; thou shalt not defraud, etc. These apply whether the perpetrator is a moral person or a legal fiction. With rapidly changing production techniques and the flood of new products, whose noxiousness is not fully known, the scope of government's regulatory duties stretches to the horizon. Reason, however, should prevail, for everything is dangerous to others and remaining in bed will eventually kill.

To these morally based mandates, democracies have added a pragmatic one: Thou shalt not monopolize (unless the state allows it). The irony of this mandate is that in its name almost as much competition has been squelched as has been encouraged. It is a dangerous power to put in the hands of regulators who regulate in the interest of the regulated. This is not an argument for doing away with the power but does argue that this power, as well as the other police powers of the state, need constant review and updating. Employee compensation awards, for example, are so low relative to current wages that in some instances they encourage rather than penalize employer carelessness.

In setting national priorities, political authority must keep two things in mind. First, the process should be truly open, inviting debate from all groups, interests, and view-points concerned, and national policy should be formulated by known and/or elected officials with enough specificity that faceless bureaucrats down the line cannot change it to suit their ideas. Second, national policy should enunciate overall goals and, as much as possible, avoid specifying economic means. For national policies can never be absolutes. They are always limited because they inevitably conflict with each other, as an energy policy conflicts with a clean-air policy. Specifying means, like the catalytic converter, just makes the inevitable compromise harder to achieve. Every new piece of legislation, furthermore, imposes costs. Government acts wisely in leaving business flexibility in balancing these costs with concern for market preferences. The hybris of politicians that passing a law achieves a result is, as we saw, bound for frustration.

This is not to deny to the state the right to forbid certain conduct and to mandate other. But always there is a fine line between socially intolerable and reasonably tolerated conduct. Safe working conditions is a universally accepted desideratum but removing all potential physical risks is an impossibility. The minutiae which regulatory agencies get into become irrational and almost seems spiteful.

Such irrational exercise of the power to forbid or to mandate also deflects agencies from using procedures of persuasion which, though less clear-cut and specific, may in the long-run, because they allow greater business flexibility, be more effective. Use of taxes and tax rebates immediately come to mind. Jonathan Boswell advances the idea of 'induced social responsibility' as a way of eliciting voluntary business compliance to national policies. "The essence of the voluntary method," writes Boswell, "is to design a framework of information, contact and concern so that decision makers (a) feel it is important to do the socially right thing as a matter of conscience, (b) clearly see how their resource decisions do in fact affect others and (c) expect unpleasant social criticisms if they err, social approbation if they conform."[10]

Steering a beat between free-market and government coercive solutions, Boswell argues that these neglect a large arsenal of social pressures which can be marshalled to persuade businesses to act in a socially responsible manner. He, in fact, finds nothing new or unusual in his suggestions. For business history is replete with instances of corporate policy decisions motivated by social approbation even against short-run monetary interests. Executives also, who in theory supposedly make bloodless, cost-calculating decisions, do fall in love, adore their children, love their dogs, and root for the Green Bay Packers. They may be more insulated from social pressures and public opinion than politicians but they are not immune from them. Boswell urges that this moral suasion be sharpened and systematically employed.

For a program of social prescription to be effective, Boswell suggests seven pre-conditions. 1) Executives should have absorbed in their childhood and education the prevailing socio-ethical Values, including some influence from religion. 2) Responsibility for decisions should be clearly located and individuals and groups bearing responsibility pin-pointed. 3) Decision makers should have personal contact sometime in their careers with the people, individuals or groups, affected by their decisions. 4) Similarly, corporate decision-making should be transparent not only to government agencies but to the wider public. 5) Business organizations should not be of such size that they overwhelm the political agency monitoring their conduct. 6) There should exist social counterpoises to business, not just labor unions but a critical press and television and groups representing consumers, minorities, environmentalists, academia and the rest who will not hesitate to reprobate business conduct but also to praise it. 7) Finally, government should have at hand its own arsenal of guide-lines, moral suasion, procedures to grant or withhold honors, as well as its own economic power to bring weight to bear on recalcitrance without resorting to legislation.

Certainly, the list is not complete but, on the other hand, none of the pre-conditions is non-existant. What gives the argument cogency is the call to marshall these pressures systematically. While not denying the validity and usefulness of legislation, taxation, and sanctions to control business, they imply that government should devote more of its resources to gathering and disseminating information and marshalling public opinion than in promulgating rules and regulations and inspecting for violations. Such shift in government control procedures will prove less costly, and by allowing greater freedom more effective.

In all this, the individual person seems merely a spectator at a game which he hopes ends in a stand-off between the contestants and not a clear-cut victory for either. But just as he has a vital interest in the outcome, so he has an important input into the contest.

Democracy like the market is so unwieldy and slow-moving that whether we vote by ballot or purse or whether we do not makes little difference. Yet both democracy and the market is premised on the assurance that each vote does count, or at least, is counted. Beyond this minimum we can raise our little voices in praise or protest. Intelligent discussion of issues will have some influence on acquaintances. Letters to senators or corporate officers usually elicit some response. One may air his views at public hearings and in letters-to-the-editors columns. None of these, of course, will have discernible impact without a national organization to give these views visibility. But all such started small, friends meeting over coffee and cookies.

Failing to persuade, moreover, does not relieve a person of his moral obligation. We can sharpen our understanding of the social Values of liberty, equality and fraternity and, at least, in the small pools of people our conduct affects try to implement these Values in our dealings with them.

CHAPTER TWELVE

ETHICS AND META-ECONOMICS

For eleven chapters we have climbed a long and perhaps tortuous way together. We studied affluence, the attitude born of abundance, as it blends with other principles of action, mutually modifying and being modified by them. In particular, we saw the paths of our moral and economic aspirations criss-cross many times. From this new moral perspective we viewed the distinguishing features of highly industrialized and abundant economies, catching vistas of hope that economic abundance is not in itself dehumanizing and that affluence can be informed by higher aspirations.

But the end is not in sight. Indeed, the task of directing affluence toward higher purposes than material well-being can have no surcease until we are ready to lay down the burdens of life. The book has widely missed its mark if the reader is not convinced that affluence can be a lethal impulse unless it is devoted to achieving Values which yield a fuller life and a more compassionate concern for others.

This chapter, therefore, is more a valedictory, an epilogue, rather than a conclusion. Its purpose is to present a few general guides to conduct in the pell-mell of living, signs to watch in riding the rapids of choosing and deciding, when only instinct and not reflection is possible. From analysis of both the ethical and economic enterprise, it will develop two sets of simple guide-lines, one ethical and the other economic. Then it will show how they mutually constrain and support each other, especially in their most important contacts at the beginning and end of action.

For readers who have captured the intent of the book, this chapter will perhaps add little new, except the distillation of its insights into a more handy compendium, a hand-compass for personal decision-making. For those for whom the preceding chapters have not left this clear impression, this chapter may bring into sharper focus the seeming conflict between moral and economic principles and suggest an operational resolution. This chapter hopefully will form a capstone, not just a bridge between, but a wedge which locks the two endeavors into place in a dynamic tension, simultaneously conflicting and supporting.

THE CONFLICT

While we do proceed in the hope that mutuality exists between ethics and economics, we first take a hard look at how they conflict. For the moral and economic endeavors are two persistent and divergent aspirations, which together spell conflict. The question, therefore, is not whether they conflict, they do, but whether this conflict is divisive or integrative of the human personality. For conflict need not destroy but may result in a higher dynamic. For example, the pull of gravitation conflicts with the forward thrust of a jet-engine, but together they cause an airplane to fly. Indeed both are necessary: without gravitation, the airplane would fly off into space and without the thrust of the engine the craft would sit on the ground. So the conflict between ethics and economics results, in neither the contradiction nor the negation of the one by the other, but rather forces a resolution on a higher place where both are not only saved but complement each other.

The Divergence

The ethical and economic aspirations diverge precisely in seeking different levels of human well-being. Ethics proposes that a person be good; economics that he be materially well-off. Applying to different levels of well-being, they do not exclude each other, and suggest the possibility of complementarity. This easy way out, however, will miss the very message of this chapter, which is that there is, or should be, an interplay between the ethical and economic endeavors which is salvific especially for affluent people. For it is easy to slide away from the issue because some actions are more apparently moral and others more apparently economic, the temptation being to pocket moral principles in certain contexts and to assuage conscience by neglecting economic principles in others. For Americans, the least philosophical of people, need to look squarely at the questions: Can we consistently act morally without violating economic principles and -- more frequently -- can we follow economic principles and not neglect moral principles? This is really the stuff of the American moral dilemma.

Ethics, in proposing that people seek the good and to be good, sets people on a transcendent vector of aspirations. The word transcendent need not frighten. It simply means here a becoming what one is not at present. It may have a religious sense, to achieve a state of being far superior to the present in union with an absolute or infinite Good. Such an other-worldly meaning does not contradict the present usage -- many ethicians will say that without such an other-worldly aspiration the ethical enterprise here is doomed to failure and is meaningless -- but the term can have a purely secular meaning, a going beyond what I am, here and now, toward becoming what I should be.

The ethical effort is not divorced from reality, what I am now. It is not merely wishful thinking. It starts with myself as I am, with my present circumstance of physical abilities, emotional make-up, intellectual and moral capacities, my circumstances of family, friends, and economic well-being. Ethics does propose that I do the best that I can in those circumstances, not to fight against but to accept what I am. But it goes beyond this to propose that in and by means of these circumstances I can become a better me. Ethical aspirations are not content with the moral status quo but urges to patterns of acting and living which express progressively higher ideals.

The essence, therefore, of the moral endeavor is intention, a freeing of aspirations from what is to what can be. Moral growth is organic: it is both conditioned by and draws sustenance from what is. But whereas a tree, rooted in its particular soil and experiencing its particular climate and cultivation, grows from an inherent dynamic, the moral person grows intentionally. A tree cannot be other than what it is in embryo, but a person proposes goals beyond himself, dreams which he strives to fulfill, espousing Values which motivate his action and conduct. In this sense, the moral endeavor is transcendent, a breaking free of the integument of what is. Thus ethics deals with human aspirations, of what one should be more so than what one is. In addition to good intention, however, one must decide what is right in concrete decisions, where the many rights of all affected by the decision may seem to conflict. This, a more complex and difficult phase of acting, demands a special science to sort out rights according to a hierarchy of priorities. This science is Ethics.

Economic aspirations, on the other hand, are not only secular but bound to the here and now. Economics is a this-worldly wisdom, for the problem it addresses is a this-worldly condition, scarcity, the persistent difficulty that human wants as a whole outpace the means to satisfy them. Most prophets of heaven, of another higher stage of human existence, preclude the possibility of scarcity -- and, hence, the need for economists. Whatever that may be, economics proposes a concern for the efficient use of material and scarce goods to achieve the best level of want-satisfaction here and now. That is, the economic enterprise is to optimize the use of material goods presently available. But like ethical aspirations it is not satisfied with the status quo but would strive for more material goods to satisfy more wants. This drive to maximize total satisfaction seems to place economic aspiration on the same level of transcending the present as the ethical aspiration. Indeed here lies the danger of substituting economics as an ersatz ethics.

But economics differs from ethics in its thrust in two important respects. Economics always involves a trade-off, a giving up something in order to get something. That which yields lesser satisfaction is exchanged for that which yields greater, now or in the future. Thus the techniques radically differ: ethics is a moral (that is, intentional) growth, involving an excelling beyond, not a sacrifice of, prior aspirations; economics always demands giving up amounts of one thing in order to get more of another. More importantly, they differ in what they propose. Ethics proposes an absolute, that I become a good human being and in the Christian sense that I reflect the goodness of the Absolute Good. Economics deals only with instrumental good. It does propose the perfect satisfaction of wants, but 'wants' in economic analysis has no content. Because a want can be a desire for any good, physical or spiritual, moral or immoral, the content of the want is specified by the good sought. Further, economics is not about the wants themselves but about the means to their fulfillment. As means, human skill and effort, material resources, capital goods, and money, can take on as many aspects of usefulness as the wants seeking satisfaction. It is clear, therefore, that economic and ethical aspirations diverge, ethics being on the level of intentions, ends, and purposes, while economics is on the level of means to those ends. Here lies both the source of the conflict and the possibility of reconciliation.

Their Persistence

Since economics and ethics set the individual on divergent vectors of conduct, they will inevitably conflict, if each is a continuing concern of people. To validate that inevitable conflict, it is not necessary to establish empirically that ethical and economic aspirations are operative in all people in all their actions. It is only necessary to demonstrate that being concerned both about being good and about being well-off makes sense for the individual. More particularly, I need but to be convinced that it is rational for me so to strive. Each person must work out the degree to which he will bring economic and ethical principles to bear upon his life and behavior.

Since the ethical enterprise, as we shall see, participates in the philosophical enterprise, it may be sufficient to our purpose to show from the history of philosophical thought that, in Gilson's words, "Philosophy always buries its undertakers".[1] That is, philosophical inquiry and questioning always begins again as soon as men have pronounced that philosophy is dead or its final statement been made.

But our interest lies more in ethics as guiding conduct than in moral philosophy, that is, analysis of what is goodness, and what is the good life. Obviously, people are not consistently ethical in their conduct. Ethical concern and ethical perception differ. Courses in ethics imply that the teacher's ethical keenness is superior to that of the student. (Note: this does not say that ethical principles are more operative in the life of the professor than in the lives of his students.) We can also agree that ethical concern differs from culture to culture. Americans today are more concerned about the ethics of discrimination while reducing sexual ethics to the simple rule that sexual congress be voluntary and mutually satisfying. We need but appeal to common experience that people do wonder about the meaning of life, what is a good life, whether life is worth living. Persistently ethical questions are asked about conduct; questions about fairness, justice, moderation, loyalty, respect for others and for one's self. All of these manifest a general concern for ethics, and asking these questions about my own conduct, demonstrates an operative concern for ethics in my own life.

Whether the morally calloused can absolutely still this ethical concern in themselves is another empirical issue which can be set aside. The facts we are well aware of are that even people, hardened in their crime and injustice to others, cherish the appearance of virtue, social acceptance, and respectability. When caught they rationalize their misdeeds. Not at all surprisingly, even the convicted criminal will have a truncated code of ethics or never trespass some cherished Value. The question whether all people, who have lived lives of crime or, worse, moral hypocrisy, can be morally rehabilitated, may well be left to psychologists, penologists, and religious counselors. The fact is that such have proclaimed their conversion. Watergate bunglers and Manson-murderers announce that they are born-again in Christ.

More to the understanding of ourselves is the experience that moral concern is a dynamic, that neither virtue nor vice can be compartmentalized in our lives. An irrational anger can produce hate, injustice, and even violence against others. Ruthlessness in business life will spill into domestic and private life. Conversely, truly to love another requires loving what and whom the beloved loves, that is, true love is diffusive, not exclusive. Even when the moral effort only contains vice, it may compensate by enriching other virtues. Thus the reformed alcoholic may always fear that his alcoholism threatens his family, his job, and his self-respect, but the very struggle for sobriety may be rewarded by a keener joy in family life, a greater sense of self-respect, a more profound pride in being socially functional. In this sense, no virtue and no vice, can be compartmentalized but potentially can transform any life. That most of us simply contain our bad and do just enough to maintain our good habits is in itself testimony of the persistence of the ethical impulse.

So common experience testifies sufficiently for a person's own acceptance that the ethical aspiration is a persistent thrust in one's life and that it is entirely reasonable to sharpen one's perceptions and to bring these perceptions to bear upon one's life.

That economics is a more apparently pervasive dimension in our aspirations needs little proof. The every day experiences of worrying about meeting bills, getting a raise, complaining about taxes, trimming budgets, meeting a payroll and making sales are responses to the problem of scarcity, that we want more than we can afford. In Adam Smith's often-quoted words:

> "In the whole interval which separates those two moments/birth and death/, there is scarce perhaps a single instant in which any man is so perfectly and completely satisfied with his situation, as to be without any wish of alteration or improvement of any kind."[2]

One need not ascribe to the psychological overtones of Smith's comment to agree with their basic import. We do not have to agree that everybody all the time is on tenterhooks to wring economic gain out of every action. In view of scarcity it is obviously rational to expect to be better off after an exchange of goods for money, money for goods, services for money, or money for services. A moment's reflection on how exchange is involved even in the most sacred and intimate relations yields assent to the basic proposition that the economic motive is a persistent and universal aspect of human action, that the economic thrust cannot be compartmentalized, some actions having an economic dimension and others not. All externalized actions are economic because all are placed in a context of scarcity.

There are some seeming exceptions to the rule. There is the wastrel who throws his property away and there is the generous person who gives it away. Even here there is a trade-off; the wastrel seeks esteem, the generous person freedom from the cares of property in order to help others. Neither can dispossess himself completely from property, for the wastrel is ultimately reduced to begging, borrowing, stealing, or, worse, working, and the generous person must maintain a minimal for survival lest he becomes a burden on and not a help to others. The history of dedicated religious poverty is largely a struggle to maintain that delicate balance between religious aspiration and the demands of charity and the administration of property necessary to sustain those purposes.[3]

So much does the problem of scarcity form the context of action that we act without adverting to it. It is part of the human condition as we know it here. Consequently, one need not dramatize the psychology of bettering one's material conditions, as Smith did, still to agree that scarcity must be taken into account in everything one does. In this sense, the economic endeavor is a persistent aspect of human action. While more overt in some acts than others, while more strongly felt under some circumstances than others, while a more conscious motive for some people than others, it is an element in every act and no more so than in the life and action of the affluent.

Thus we have set the scenario: two abiding concerns set on differing vectors of human aspirations. The most idealistic can founder on the economic realities of making ends meet. The most calloused materialist wants his gain-seeking draped in respectability or rationalized as virtue. For the vast majority in between who, each in his own way, wants both to live decently and to make out economically, the two aspirations will clash. When the conflict can be neither accommodated nor resolved, the individual may be suspended in indecision. More frequently, a hypocritical accommodation will result, economic rationality suppressed in the name of ethical ideals, or, more likely, ethical ideals eroded for the sake of economic realities. The resolution lies in seeing clearly the validity of both aspirations, each with its own principles and criteria of behavior and in examining the possibility how they, though conflicting, mutually inform each other.

To these two tasks we now turn: delineating the ethical and economic aspirations, each with its own principles and criteria; and identifying the points of conflict and support.

THE ETHICAL ENTERPRISE

Ethics has traditionally been treated as a branch of philosophy. Moral philosophy is a speculative wisdom concerned with ultimate questions about the good and the good life, while ethics is a practical wisdom concerned about codes and criteria of conduct. Since the ultimate criterion of action is whether it is good or bad, ethical questions form part of the philosophic enterprise. A general look-see, therefore, at this vast human effort will throw light on the ethical enterprise by positioning it within this broader concern.

The Philosophical Enterprise

Philosophy is the perennial quest for wisdom. It is not knowledge, but the desire to know, especially the answer to the fundamental question, What is life all about? In no respect do we differ more from animals. In Daniel Villey's words, philosophy represents our "meta-animal strivings".[4] At the same time, it addresses the most basic questions, as Karl Jasper says, the questions of children.[5] In other words we philosophize because we are human. We seek ultimate answers about ourselves, about life, and about the world in which we live. Even though no answer is, or can be fully satisfying, we philosophize because we have to.

Philosophers pose three fundamental questions: What is it to be? What is it to be true? and What is it to be good? Philosophy, therefore, takes as subject for inquiry, being itself and, of course, ultimate being, God, whose very nature is to exist; the reality about us, what is it and do I really know it; and finally, our own reality, not only what we are but what we should be. These three thrusts are called ontology, the study of existence, epistemology, the study of knowledge and knowing, and axiology, the study of Values. Ethics is a part of axiology because what we should be is measured against the Values we espouse and realize in our lives.

While each of the questions is specific, thus differentiating philosophic effort, they are not separate and distinct. They so interpenetrate each other, that none can be answered in isolation from the others. For I can know being only by knowing myself and knowing that I know. Finally, to know what I should be implies knowing myself as existing and as capable of having true knowledge of myself. For our purposes, consequently, Axiology or Ethics will always have a metaphysical, that is, an ontological and epistemological, premise. Ethical colorations do arise from implicit or explicit metaphysical presuppositions.

In the beginning, man's entire intellectual quest was called philosophy. A relic of that state remains in the Doctor of Philosophy degree which is granted by Universities as evidence of the highest level of intellectual preparation not only in philosophy but in fields far removed from it. This is not entirely anachronistic because even the least philosophical science, let us say, astronomy, has a metascientific base which is philosophical. Questions about the meaning and reality of what is studied, whether the scientist can truly know, and what are the implications for human conduct are often the burning issues in scientific debate. Nevertheless, the splitting off from Philosophy of all the different fields of knowledge testified not only to insatiable human curiosity but to the fertility of the basic philosophical questions.

The first differentiation occurred in Ontology. Religion always claimed a special insight into the reality and mind of an ultimate being or beings. This is true of primitive religions. It is all the more so of the great religions like Judaeism, Christianity, Mohammedanism, Buddhism whose special knowledge of the Divine rests on an act of faith in the word of a prophet. Thus Revealed Theology became a separately organized body of knowledge, seeking answers to the same philosophical questions but proceeding not from natural reason but revealed knowledge. In so doing revealed religion developed its own conception of ultimate reality, its own justification for faith and its own code of Values. From this total vision of man, theologians inevitably re-interpreted history, explored God's working in the world, man's new relations to other men, and consequent new criteria for conduct. While variously open or closed to philosophical and scientific inquiry, Theology always jealously guarded these prerogatives.

In the knowledge explosion which began in the Renaissance and continues unabated to the present, other bodies of knowledge about the physical and social universe broke out of the philosophical integument. First, the physical sciences and later the social sciences and psychology. Each followed its own principles, mapped out its area of inquiry, developed its own methodology, and reported its implications for human activity. Even in these disparate pursuits each betrayed its filiation to Philosophy, asking the same questions: What is real? What is the validity of this knowledge? What are the implications for human living and Values?

Since economics is one of the social sciences, a word about their special development from Philosophy is called for. Two comments can be made. The principles of the various social sciences can be found in embryo in formal philosophizing almost from the beginning, and one of the social sciences, Political Science, with its handmaiden Law, began almost contemporaneously with Philosophy as an independent field of study. Secondly, the empirical revolution of the 17th and 19th Century did not cause as much trauma in the social as it did in the physical sciences for several reasons. There was a longer tradition of empirical interest; no new and radically different methodologies were introduced, and finally there were fewer myths to dispel and superstitions to overcome. Consequently, their development into independent disciplines took longer and their births were less violent. More so, therefore, than the physical sciences, they betray their philosophic forebears and are more consciously concerned about the philosophic issues of Being, Truth, and especially Values.

It is easy to conclude that the role of Philosophy in the quest for understanding has diminished. Certainly, philosophers no longer receive top billing in the intellectual drama. But the role of Philosophy is more necessary than ever before. It is also more complex. Villey suggests a useful analogy in proposing that Philosophy needs both a Ministry of the Interior and a Ministry of Foreign Affairs: it must manage both its own internal affairs and maintain liaison with the social and physical sciences.[6] When Philosophy encompassed all knowledge, human curiosity was constrained within philosophic forms with some rather egregious, even puerile, results. But now that every science is independent, each proceeding on its own principles, developing its own methodology, forming cross-disciplinary alliances, philosophers must have some understanding of the general content and methodology of other sciences to participate usefully in discussions arising within the sciences of questions which touch upon ultimately philosophic issues.

Thus the knowledge explosion requires a greater differentiation of function among philosophers. Where previously ontologists, epistemologists and axiologists -- and these were not distinct -- divided up the work, now another tier of specialties has developed. Natural Theology maintains liaison with Revealed Theology, Philosophy of Science with mathematics and the physical sciences, Philosophy of Man with Anthropology and Psychology, Philosophy of History, Philosophy of Politics, Philosophy of Art and Aesthetics, and the list is almost endless. Surprisingly, in view of Economics' obvious philosophic lineage, a Philosophy of Economics is hardly on the scene, somewhat in Europe, all but non-existent in the States. In a very inchoate and provisional form it is implied here in the term 'meta-economics', the basic principles, insight and purposes which form the premises of formal economic analysis. Much of the present work wanders through this largely unmapped land.

Should a Philosophy of Economics come into being, it will examine the reality of scarcity and debate the validity of the mathematical method in economic analysis, but its principal concern will be in the area of Values and the relation between Value espousal and economic choice. Consequently, Economics relates to Philosophy by way of the ethical and moral enterprise.

The Moral Enterprise

Ethics participates in the philosophical enterprise, though the two are not necessarily equally and simultaneously lively. Metaphysics, for example, is seemingly moribund today while Ethics is a hot topic, discussions overall generating more heat than light. This is particularly true of Ethics as opposed to Moral Philosophy. In other words, the current discussion is about practical issues of what to do and what to forbid, leaving the more speculative issues of what is goodness and the good life to languish. Yet pragmatic solutions to ethical issues at least assume as criteria some vision of what the good life and the good person should be. What Keynes said of economic policy decisions applies: current ethical decisions are justified by the ideas of some past and forgotten academic scribbler.

Remembering the analysis of the Value experience will help here. For a Value is the perception of the good of another person or thing, which perception is simultaneously a preference. Thus a Value is both a criterion, a benchmark for estimating the worth of myself, of others, and of things about me, and a motive for action, directing not only the pursuit of Values but choice of the means to realize them.

Ethics, therefore, is about the good and the right: the good, what I do and should desire; and the right, what are the means to lead to the good? This implies a metaphysics, an ontological and an epistemological understanding of what is real and what is true. For what-is for me is only what I can know in some way. And if it is and I do know it, then it is good. To say otherwise, that what-is is evil, is bad for me, would simply make a mockery of life, that I am evil and whatever I do or want is evil. This does not resolve the problem of evil, nor denies that I do experience people and things, indeed, myself, as in some respects evil. But it does start with the affirmation that what is is both true and good.

There is, therefore, a metaphysical foundation to moral philosophy and a moral purpose in philosophizing itself. For in seeking ultimate meaning, I seek my ultimate meaning. In seeking to know the other, I know myself better in the knowing. In seeking to know what I should be, I know myself as better relating to God, to other people and to the world about me. Moral Philosophy, therefore, is clearly premised on an ontology and epistemology. Ethics as a praxis, including both a code of conduct and habits of behavior, similarly draws sustenance from a moral philosophy. It is precisely this dialectic between moral ideals and practice we explore next.

Ethics as a Practical Wisdom

The ethical enterprise, however, is not simply speculative knowledge of what is good but a putting of that ideal into practice. Ethics is not just an ideal but a praxis. We do ethics. Thus the ethical enterprise is better viewed not as an achievement but as a <u>quest</u> whose goals are progressively spelt out for us in the movement toward them. It is a pilgrimage, attended by mistakes, ambiguities and failures, in which our failures, perhaps more so than our successes, clarify the goal. Thus, like walking, the ethical enterprise is a dialectic, ideals guiding conduct and conduct revealing new dimensions of the ideal.

This view can be tied to our earlier discussion of Values. Recall, first, the emphasis on Values not only as criteria for judging conduct but motives for action. Secondly, in analyzing the dynamics of Valuation, we saw that the espousal of one Value disposed us toward deeper penetration into the goodness of another and thus to espousing progressively higher Values raising our sights from the lower sensual Values to the highest sacral or absolute Values. The dynamics of Valuing is but one way of viewing the dynamics of the moral enterprise.

This dialectic furthermore is a human effort. I act morally. Though I begin life imitating others and grow relating to and being influenced by them, my persistent drive in these dealings with others should be to know myself. Thus self-knowledge is necessary: what and who I am, my strengths and weaknesses, my physical abilities and emotional make-up, my intellectual and moral background, my circumstances of family, friends, economic status and the like, and above all my openness to others. The ideal I set myself must also be practicable, achievable by present capabilities. Differing in all these respects, we each follow a different course in our moral development.

Thus whatever practical judgment one may be required to pass on another -- this man is a danger to others or that woman has a bad moral influence on me -- one can never issue a final moral judgment about another, because no one knows either another's starting point or his progress from that point. This consideration should teach us tolerance and sympathy for others, but more importantly it should teach us patience with ourselves if our level of moral achievement seems lower than that of others.

This inescapable subjectivity is not, however, moral relativism. While each person will perceive the moral good differently and translate it differently into his life, models abound which are instinctively attractive of what a good man or woman should be. An example might help. A friend was associated with the international team of Russians,

French, English and Americans who administered Berlin after its surrender. When *frauleins* were available for nylons or chocolate bars, my friend remained faithful to his wife. Once he overheard a Russian soldier comment that my friend had no *fraulein*, to which the other replied, "Yes, Mike is a good man." However much these models may differ in emphases and details, they possess a familiar likeness responding to our almost instinctive conviction that the good person is just, is moderate in his appetites, is prudent in conduct, and courageous in action.

The most powerful such models are people we know and admire. In addition a vast amount of intellectual effort from the beginning of human discourse has been devoted to depicting models of moral probity. The two principal sources are literature and moral philosophy. The former is concrete, the latter analytic.

Biography is an obvious source of moral ideals, men and women who exemplified in their lives the qualities we would realize or avoid in our own. Indeed, the purpose to edify frequently distorts biography into secular or religious hagiography, portraying caricatures not real life. Literature from *Gilgamesh* to Harold Robbins (using the term comprehensively) fascinate as portrayals of men and women struggling with their implicit or explicit ethical ideals. Even contemporary American literature with its anti-heroes and heroines broken on the wheel of life, celebrating the depressing themes of fine Jewish boys castrated by possessive mothers, Catholic girls repressed by an obscurantist religion, ghetto youths trapped in vice and crime, empty people lost in a maze of moral, political and social ambiguities, present ideals at least in the negative. For a moral statement of what people should be lurks under the depressing details of defeat, of aloneness, of individuals at cross-purposes with themselves and with others. Moral statements lurk there, often deeper than the author's conscious intention.

Formal analysis of the qualities of a good person and of good conduct is found in the vast literature on moral philosophy. However, philosophers from Plato to the present differ in defining the ultimate meaning of life and the end of action, their portraits of the good person betray familiar likenesses. A good person is above all just in his conduct toward others; he controls and is not controlled by his appetites; he acts reasonably within the context of circumstances; and acts firmly on principle whatever the results. The virtuous man Adam Smith pictures in his *Moral Sentiments* would have been called a good man by Aristotle and Bertrand Russell. Where philosophers principally differ and thus highlight one aspect of the moral quest at the expense of others is in their analysis of the moral imperative. By this is meant the underlying 'should' which explains the ultimate purpose of acting and consequently becomes the basic criterion of conduct.

The Moral Imperative

The moral imperative is milder in form than the simply imperative. MacIntyre[7] differentiates them in that the simple imperative presents no reason for the command while the moral imperative does. But this distinction does not get to the crucial difference, for even the bluntest command implies a reason. Firemen, for example, commanding a woman on a third-floor window-ledge to jump, certainly imply a reason, to avoid death by fire, no less than does the marriage counsellor, urging a husband to be more considerate if he wishes to keep his wife's affection. The simple imperative is stronger, not because it presents or implies no reason, but because it presents no alternative. Only a Jack Benny would treat as an alternative the mugger's brusque, "Your money or your life". But the inconsiderate husband has a choice; change his manner and keep his wife, or continue as is and lose her.

But MacIntyre's emphasis is correct in that the moral imperative, expressed in the auxiliary verb 'ought', implies as reason for acting an obligation which the one making choice should perceive. "You ought to be considerate because you owe it to your wife." So obligation implies a bond, 'ligo, ligere' which arises from a debt. Indeed, 'ought' was originally the past participle of 'to owe'. Debt, in turn is from the Latin 'de-habere', to have something from another and, consequently, to be under obligation to return it. Our word 'duty' through the Old French 'duette' has the same root. Thus I ought to be considerate of my wife because she has been and is a good wife to me. But I am under no physical restraint to do so. I have a choice. "I owe all my success to my good wife but I will not cherish her but divorce her." I am not constrained because I can keep the success and reject the cause.

The moral imperative, in brief, always implies an original grant or gift, and, consequently, someone to whom a debt is owed, which debt imposes a moral bond. For this reason, many moral philosophers insist that the moral imperative implies some ultimate Good from whose graciousness I take my being and to whom, therefore, I am obligated in some way. Acknowledging this debt is always described as a conversion, a turning toward a good, not an inversion, a turning into myself. For this reason, also, the religious person usually, and even when misguided, has a stronger sense of moral obligation than the irreligious.

But moral obligation can arise from different sources, and this differentiation goes back to the beginnings of Western Civilization. Latin, for example, has four words, 'mos', 'fas', 'jus', and 'lex', each with Indo-European roots, which express various kinds of moral obligation. 'Mos' is a measure or guide which arise from social custom. 'Fas' is stronger, indeed for people of religious sense, the strongest, for it is a divine utterance. From it comes the word 'fatum', fate, that which, no matter how men resist it, will be fulfilled. 'Jus' implies an obligation arising from the nature of a thing or person. It is 'jus' to use a bat to hit a baseball but not to eat spaghetti. It is 'jus' to treat children as persons but not adult persons because that is what they are. Finally, 'lex' is a formal obligation proclaimed as law with sanctions attached.

Thus deep in western consciousness, at least, lies the recognition that moral obligation arise from the many facets of the human condition, from man's mysterious origin, from his relation to other people, from what things and people are in themselves, and from civil authority who can impose obligations and duties upon us.

There are three other terms, good, right and Value, which are very much a part of moral discourse and whose examination will shed additional light on the moral imperative. The Latin 'bonum' in its original form 'duenum' reveals its Indo-European beginnings. Good does not specify any particular quality but rather a state of being, that a thing or person is sufficient for its purpose. A good ball can be used in the game; a good man realizes in a general way what a man should be. What is good, therefore, is always with reference to its own perfection, and all goods are relative except that which is complete and perfect unto itself, the absolute Good whose very purpose is to be. The good, therefore, is first and foremost a point of reference, a benchmark and a standard. But because a thing is good it is desired and, more importantly for the moral imperative, it should be desired to the extent of its goodness.

Rights are the hot topic of current ethical discourse, human rights, constitutional rights, and above all, my rights. The original meaning of right, 'riht' in German and 'reg' in Latin, is preserved in mathematics 'right angle', meaning a complete turn as opposed to angling off, and in the popular phrase 'right on', to the point as opposed to off the mark. Something is right if it leads to the desired good. Rights arise because of an obligation, a duty, or because of a good which should be desired. To claim a right is to acknowledge a duty. Civil rights are necessary to fulfill the duties of citizenship. To defend rights is to imply a moral imperative. Rights, therefore, are means to ends, not ends in themselves.

Finally, there is Value, upon which we have, following Scheler[8], expended considerable effort in analyzing. That Value from 'valere', to be strong, to prevail, is the key to our particular concern is revealed in the almost contradictory derivations from it. 'Valour' means pursuing a good with little concern for personal cost, while economic value means precisely estimating the opportunity costs of obtaining a good. They are not contradictory because they are both encompassed in, though at the extremes of, Scheler's hierarchy of Values. Valour is the preference for one good above all other goods; exchange value arises from the estimation of the utility of one good over that of another.

Value is also key by linking what is good to what ought to be done. When what is perceived as good is preferred, then it ought to be espoused, then it becomes a purpose or goal. Moral obligation follows perception and not the other way around. It is right, consequently, to pursue the means to achieve the Value.

Scheler's analysis of the dynamics of valuing is also helpful in showing that the moral enterprise is a growing up and a growing into. For valuing is not achieved all at once but it is a deepening insight into the goodness of another. It is a dynamic growth in appreciation of another. A man may love a woman because she is beautiful, sexually stimulating, a career asset, an intelligent confidant, a loyal wife and mother, and ultimately a good person. But this last deepest insight into her goodness does not preclude the others. Indeed they may all be encompassed in the last. That such love is rare, either because it is the rare woman who bears all these Values or more likely the rare man who could love so truly, does not deny the inherent dynamism of valuing. For, in fact, any great love is a blending of lesser Values into more absolute Values. Thus analysis of Value adds another rich dimension to the concept of the moral imperative. The simple word 'should' implies a debt and obligation which may arise from the many facets of human existence. It implies turning to a good and respecting rights leading to the good, but above all it implies Values which a person should espouse as purposes of action and goals for life.

The Moral Imperative in Moral Philosophy

Another rich lode of meaning comes from the literature of moral philosophy. Even a summary and superficial survey such as the following will repay handsomely in understanding the facets of meaning which professional philosophers have mined from the concept of the moral imperative.[9]

Plato is always a convenient beginning. For Plato the Socratic "Know thyself" led to the imperative to seek the Good which for Plato was an immutable and transcendant Form illuminating all the other eternal Forms. Plato saw the life of virtue as a spiritualizing struggle past the appearances of things toward an insight into the Good in all its naked glory, as if peering unblinking into the furnace of the sun. By implication, therefore, the State must so order the affairs of men that all are set on this path of striving, though only the elite, the souls purified of their own and life's evils, can achieve the goal.

For Aristotle the good was what all men seek in all things, persons, and states of being. For possessing the good yields happiness, the goal of human striving. But happiness for Aristotle is multi-faceted, not only possessing moral goodness but faring well in all aspects of life. The happy man, therefore, is the complete man, walking the path of virtue carefully between the extremes of vice and enjoying in moderation the good things of life and society. But the ultimate happiness consists in exercising one's highest faculty, contemplation, upon the absolute good. Thus Aristotle, though more cosmopolitan and comprehensive in his tastes, defines the happy man as not unlike Plato's philosopher-kings. Their different styles provide the foundations for the differing codes of conduct of Stoicism and Epicurianism which were the most extensive practical ethics of the classical world. Their reconcilability is evidenced in the practical, worldly wisdom of someone like Cicero.

At the hands of a Christian philosopher like Thomas

Aquinas, Plato and Aristotle are reconciled on a higher plane where the absolute Good of Plato as well as its contingent manifestations according to Aristotle are incorporated in the Christian God who is Goodness itself and the source of goodness of all created things. Thus the law, the nature given to each and every thing by God, becomes the criterion for treating all things. The natural law of man, informed by the Christian law of love, and its reasoned specifications, determine what man should be and how he should act.

This accord between the Divine Will and human reason -- faith seeking understanding -- was dissolved when Western Civilization entered its modern phase. Luther, who distrusted that "whore reason" restricted the moral imperative to the individual's faith-inspired understanding of God's literal word, denying that any human authority could interpret that for another. Renaissance individualism, on the other hand, widened the split by relegating religion to private and personal morality, relying on reason alone to devise rules of morality in secular matters. Further fragmentation occurred from the wedge Descartes drove between speculative and empirical reason.

What emerges from the ethical discourse of the 17th Century is the doctrine of natural right. Formulated by philosophers as diverse as Hobbes, Spinoza, Rousseau, Locke and Henry Moore against a general acceptance of Judaeo-Christian ethics, man's natural rights of self-preservation, property, association, expression and the like were perceived as the original endowment of every individual and the foundation of personal freedom. They are unlimited except in explicit or tacit contract to respect the natural rights of others. From them are derived the basic and universal moral propositions which now possess the clarity and cogency of mathermatical propositions.

The Sentimentalists, Shaftesbury, Hutcheson, Smith and particularly Hume, sought a more radically empirical foundation of natural rights and conduct respecting them than the _a priori_ and rationalist assumptions of the earlier natural right philosophers. For the Sentimentalists asserted that people can sense what is morally good and bad conduct in specific situations, and from such experiences develop an empirically founded moral code. Thus our basic instincts and wants are best served by following this moral code and, consequently, we ought to follow it. In this manner they preserved social benefit and efficiency of action which was radically individualistic. Sentimentalism, consequently, often shaded into Utilitarianism which, elevated to a social ethics by Bentham and the Philosophic Radicals, formed the agenda for many needed social reforms.

Immanuel Kant stands at the watershed of modern ethical theory. In his search to find a fixed center of reference in the chaotic Humean world of sense experiences, Kant discovered a 'should' deeper than the conditional imperative. He calls it a categorical imperative, a non-rational, absolute, and universal imperative: This I must and can do, not for pleasure, nor for happiness, nor even for love of God, but because it is the right thing to do, it is my duty. Thus, duty in this unspecified sense becomes for some a moral individualism which is impervious to influences from the social order. On the other hand, for others the very content of duty is defined by the demands of a particular social, political or moral system. The Kantian categorical imperative, therefore, justifies both absolute moral relativism and moral totalitarianism.

The way out of this ambiguity was as varied as the philosophers who tried it. Hegel affirms that the individual finds his moral imperative "in the norms of the free and rational society."[10] For Marx, individual man finds fulfillment in species man but only through and after a total transformation of the economic and social order. On the other hand, the absolute moral autonomy of the individual, according to Kierkegaard, can be fulfilled only in a blind and irrational "leap" into Christianity. In the same vein but completely atheistically, Nietzchean moral individualism is an overriding "will to power".

In the less Kantian Anglo-Saxon thought of the early 20th Century, Intuitionism in England and Pragmatism in the States tended to hold sway. The former reflected the Sentimentalist tradition. C.E. Moore's dictum that those actions should be performed which cause more good to exist than any alternative summarizes this position. To this the question "What is good?" Moore can only respond that one cannot define the good but can infallibly intuit it, that one feels what is good. Dewey's Pragmatism, by contrast, invests intention of the good in the very purpose for acting. Thus good is achieved in realizing one's purpose. Like Intuitionism, however, Pragmatism lacks an ultimate standard by which to judge purpose.

While contemporary moral theory seems to end in a babel of opinions about the ethical 'ought' and any explanation seems up for grabs, nevertheless, even a superficial review such as this reveals the many facets of the moral imperative, all of which add to and can be blended into one's own perception of the imperative. Overall is the search for some summum bonum which is reflected in the good of actions, of other people and of other things. Their good, in turn, is grasped in insight of their nature and of my own, which nature in turn define what is right for me and for others. The search for this good is a duty, what I owe as a moral being, and my fulfilling this duty is corroborated by the results, in the happiness I realize in using my human abilities to their fullest, in perceiving that my conduct sets well with others, in fulfilling my purposes, in doing something useful and good in the social order.

Like the blind men describing an elephant, the great minds who wrestled with the concept of the moral imperative have given us bits and pieces of the whole. But from these shards of insight we can fashion a conception of the moral 'ought' to judge our lives and conduct in a reasonably consistent way.

The Moral Dialectic

The process of formulating moral ideals, it should be clear by now, is no task for whiling away a Sunday afternoon. The formal study of Values, the Value experience, and the moral imperative, must be fleshed out by sensitive observance of our own and others' conduct, by reading literature and biography, and by contemplation and above all by tolerance, respect and compassion for fellow human beings. This life-long effort justifies calling it the ethical enterprise.

But this enterprise is more than an aspiration. It is a realization, an imperceptible becoming, a dialectic between what I am and what I am not to what I would be. The change it proposes is growth, an information not a transformation, a growing up and a growing into what I should be without growing out of what I am. Ethics, it is said, is not for children for the simple reason that it is a life-long endeavor. Ultimately, ethics is a doing, and a being, not simply a knowing.

The outline of this dialectic presented here can only be sketchy and summarize points already made. First, the ideals we aspire to must be realistic in terms of what I am and what my circumstances in life are. But these ideals are never static or given once and for all. Rather the very effort to realize them in our behavior opens up new dimensions. Much like the maturation and acculturation process of children in the painful passage from infancy through adolescence to adulthood, moral ideals are always a receding horizon, beckoning gently another step, another mile, another goal. But whereas maturation is largely biological and conditioned, moral growth is intentional, self-conscious, and never-ending.

Failure, secondly, is very much an element in this dialectic, not the total failure of moral indifference or despair, but the litany of little failings to live up to one's aspirations. Once again, St. Paul's lament, "I do what I would not do and do not do what I would." The fomes peccati are always with us. Such failings, however, are not defeat. To the contrary, since every failure is different, each, when acknowledged, in revealing what I am not, suggests what I should be, reveals another, though only microscopic, aspect of the ideal. Thus failures, by being seen as failures, testify to moral growth. By contrast the morally defeated are not failures. For either they never seriously aspire to live at a level higher than the sensate and thus never fail their aspirations, or, become weary of and callous to failures, they no longer acknowledge that they can fail. Such people, the morally callous and those impervious to self- or any other criticism, often possess an equanimity which those striving for moral growth do not. It is the difference between the living and the dead: the dead always seem more at peace.

Patience with one's own stumblings is required -- and its companion virtue, tolerance of others. In addition, one needs some sense and conviction of success. Chartering one's moral growth against some scheme like Maslow's stages of psychological and moral development, provided moral growth is not perceived as an elevator ride to a higher floor, one can obtain a sense that one has indeed changed. While recognizing that passing into the stage of fulfilling social and self-actualization needs never preclude satisfying physical and ego-centric needs, a comparison on a Maslowian scale can testify that one has grown in aspiration, in Values, and in moral conviction.

From such assessment of both success and failure comes the appreciation that the essence and real value of the moral enterprise consists neither in successes or failures but in the struggle itself. Moral endeavor is judged not so much by how well we carry off an action but by our purposing and intending it. Further, the very persistence of this effort points to an ultimate goodness, an ultimate completion, and an ultimate happiness. In brief, an ultimate what-I-should-be. The very root of the word, virtue, connoting manliness--and now, also, womanliness--emphasizes the persistence in aspiration and consistence in action which radically differentiates the person of moral convictions from the morally indifferent, the morally calloused, or the morally defeated.

From this lengthy description of the moral enterprise, we can distill at least these five thoughts as a compendium in the give and take of life:

1. The moral enterprise is personal. I do ethics and I start with myself. But the "I" with which and upon which I work exists at a particular time and in a particular setting of political and economic circumstance. Above all I am social, I exist relating to other people, some by birth, others by preference, most by accident. Since I can never undo what I am, how I am circumstanced, or to whom related, my moral endeavor consists in acting well within these circumstances and in dealing well with everyone I contact.

2. Yet the enterprise entails a vision, a turning toward an ideal, a conversion not an introversion into myself. I am required to be open to and sensitive to others for the light they shed on the ideal. Above all the ideal must be desirable, not impossible fantasy, but concrete improvements I can realize in my life and acts.

3. Making this effort, therefore, becomes an obligation, a duty. There is an ultimate good which I should strive for--an ultimate Value I should espouse. All the better, if I can identify this good with the source of my being and can find this good reflected in everyone and everything about me, which reflections reveal their rights as well as my own. Finally, honoring these rights sets me well with other people, contributes to social order and brings happiness.

4. Both the vision and the obligation inspires my doing, my putting into practice. My resolve will produce no dramatic transformation but rather a day-by-day

realization, an informing of my conduct, especially toward others, by moral ideals.

5. Finally, failure is endemic, but failure is not defeat. Indeed moral growth is fashioned from failure. Thus the element in moral growth is persistence, patience with one's self, tolerance of and, beyond this, compassion for others, and most importantly joy and rejuvenation in the effort itself.

META-ECONOMICS

Meta-economics relates to economics as Aristotle's Metaphysics relates to his Physics. Just as Aristotle in his metaphysics dealt with the principles of being which are prior and common to all natures, so meta-economics addresses the very assumptions of economic analysis, the reality of its subject, the validity of its formulations and laws, and the efficacy of its principles as guides to human behavior. These questions, of course, are the same ontological, epistemological and axiological questions philosophy asks. So meta-economics is a first step toward a Philosophy of Economics.

Our interest will lie mainly in the Value questions but, recalling how the three are intertwined, a word about the ontological and epistemological aspects of meta-economics.

Ontology and Epistemology

The subject of economics, man in relation to his physical environment, lies between the physical and social sciences, drawing upon both. For economics views people, both individually and socially, as studying, organizing and exploiting natural forces in order to fulfill their needs as persons. For the human person, while like Anteaus bound to and drawing strength from the material world, has purposes which transcend his physical boundaries. Most people would agree on two observations about man's dependence upon his physical environment. First, nature yields its bounty with reluctance. Man is frequently and well described as conquering, as taming the powers of nature to his use, as hacking out a lebensraum of relative freedom from the, if not hostile, wild and reluctant world of nature. Second, transcendence implies needs which surpass the limited capability of the material world to fulfill. No matter how bounteous man's state, his wanting surpasses his having. These two facts of reluctant physical forces and needs without limit form the essence of the problem which economics calls scarcity and takes as its special concern. Thus economics is commonly defined as the study of the allocation (sharing) of scarce material means toward satisfying unlimited human wants.

Scarcity, therefore, is always relative, a ratio between what is available and what is wanted, the latter generally surpassing the former. Particular material goods may be more plentiful for a particular want -- a quart of tutti-frutti may satiate Johnny's love for ice cream -- but the sum total of material goods, and, more so, human time, energy, livable space and the rest are in short supply relative to wants. Thus scarcity is a universal problem, a problem experienced not only by individuals but by all people collectively. And this problem will not go away, not only because nature is reluctant and its dowry is wrested away with effort, but because people always want more. Indeed, the two are related. For the very wages of productive labor, the rewards for risk-taking in uncertain ventures, and the returns for investing resources rather than consuming them grant rights to share in the economy's output and thus to satisfy more wants. Scarcity is inevitable because the effort to resolve it generates more.

Economists draw three implications from the universal and inevitable condition of scarcity. First, it necessitates choice. If everything taken together is scarce, having more of one thing requires giving up some amount of something else. Note: this is seldom an all-or-nothing but rather a more-or-less decision. It is a balancing act. As one want approaches fulfillment, having more of the same becomes less important than satisfying another want less fulfilled. At the same time it points up the real cost of anything, as not the past surrender of money, materials or other good, or time, labor and the like, but the sacrifice of the future opportunity to fulfill some other want. Secondly, scarcity implies competition. Since all people experience scarcity, an individual can fulfill a particular want only by outbidding others for the means to satisfy the want. But just as necessarily and finally, scarcity demands cooperation, indeed that highest form called complementarity. That is, one person cannot achieve his goals without assisting others to achieve theirs. The obvious example is buying and selling, the good of each is the sacrifice of the other. In addition, production and exchange requires cooperation in the usual sense of playing the agreed-upon rules of the game. This is no less true in traditional, in market, and even in command economies.

Economics has been called the dismal science. In truth, scarcity belongs to the harsher side of human existence. It constrains and imposes discipline upon all actions and every aspiration. Many people frustrate their lives in attempting just to overcome scarcity. Utopians dream of such abundance that no one will suffer scarcity. Most people bear with it here in hopes of another existence not subject to scarcity. The view here is that since scarcity cannot be avoided nor ignored it adds a quality, indeed a virtue, to human existence which is salvific.

Epistemologically in analyzing scarcity, economists implicitly affirm that they say something about reality. Thousands of them spend their time gathering, collating, and analyzing data on the exchange of goods, money, titles to income and the like. These thousands of statistical series and their analyses and cross-analyses preserve the historical record of how economies and people have behaved. Some empirical formulations like the Cobb-Douglas function achieve relative predictability; others like the Phillips Curve are of limited or passing validity. All such empirical analysis suffers the inherent defect for prediction that their very enunciation becomes input for future decisions and thus changes them. Analysis of current high interest rates, for example, may cause savings to increase, or borrowing to decrease, or may introduce an entirely new investment instrument so that no one knows how the rates will change. Prediction is not a strong point of empirical economic research. On the other hand, it does not invalidate it as historical record.

A more abstract type of analysis works toward formulating general rules of behavior in response to scarcity. The history of this analysis is replete with dead-ends, controversy, and self-doubt. Amazingly all this ambiguity has not prevented the profession from growing from a handful of amateurs two hundred years ago to hundreds of thousands of professionals, teaching, writing, advising business and government here and around the globe, some becoming relatively wealthy in the process. Despite the debate, perhaps because of it, a hardy residue of economic principles have been hammered out, the two most fundamental being the principle of substitution and the principle of complementarity.

Substitution says that in view of scarcity people act rationally in choosing alternative goods and wants, when having more of a particular good or satisfying more of a particular want entails a greater and greater sacrifice. Applied in a variety of circumstances -- in decisions to consume, to produce and what to produce, and to hire resources, in decisions to save or to invest, to work or to take leisure, in decisions over time, to borrow or to lend, present value versus future value -- the principle of substitution is involved in all economic choice. Less obtrusive but no less pervasive, the principle of complementarity reminds that satisfying one want mandates attending to others, that increasing one's own well-being requires enhancing others. The interplay between the, in essence, competitive and cooperative elements in economic choice, like the interplay between the sexes, makes economic analysis frustratingly complex. Add to that the need to feed in a flood of changing empirical data and one sees the difficulty of saying something both verifiable and up-to-the-minute about the economy.

Yet positive economics presents clear seas in contrast to the swamp of normative economics. First, most economists will deny any normative aspirations. This, of course, is belied by their assumption of the rationality of substitution and complementarity. Either they are engaged in nonsense or they affirm that what is rational to do <u>should</u> be done. Hence, economic efficiency is a goal in all of life and <u>economizing</u> a norm for every act. <u>Optimizing</u> economic well-being in view of scarcity, therefore, requires both <u>maximizing gain</u> and <u>minimizing costs</u>. The logic of economic choice is irrefutable.

But now comes the parting of the way. The economic purist will stop here. Economic logic, he insists, holds in every and all decisions, to build a church, to rape your neighbor's daughter, to rob a bank, or to manage a business, and it does hold because that logic is a set of purely formal relations in which neither gain nor loss, and, least of all, <u>their desirability</u> are specified. The purist stops at the edge of the Value swamp, offering only a technique for decision making or policy formation, but a technique devoid of content.

Most economists, however, boldly plunge in, following a well-trod path marked 'revealed preferences'. This is the positivist position that economic choices can be called neither right nor wrong, but simply accepted as given. Underlying, however, is the assumption that a collective hedonistic pleasure-pain calculus, or, that failing, the wisdom of benevolent laws will achieve a Paretian optimality which accords with <u>desired</u> social and individual Values. Note: 'desired' easily slides into 'desirable'. The hope of substituting an economic for a moral calculus is made more inviting by the quantitative possibilities.[11] The positivist, however, quickly loses direction in contact with the real world of Value-formation, where sense pleasures overcome reason, greed overpowers altruism, and bureaucracy serves itself. Extrication is possible only if the economist returns to the sterile shores of pure analysis, or admits that there is a world of Values beyond his ken.

The axiological path this chapter, indeed the entire book, follows lies in recognizing this world of purposes, goods, rights, virtues and Values to which economics must be alert and attentive if it is to subserve them. Thus this approach maintains both the autonomy of economics as a science, and disciplines it to its role as handmaiden to a Value-hierarchy derived from psychology, political science and especially the moral disciplines. The distinction is neatly captured in the French terms, justesse and justice, both derived from the same Latin root. 'Justesse' means efficacy, efficiency, a valid norm applicable to all action. 'Justice', broadly defined, means righteousness, placing proper means to worthy ends. To the point here, this distinction prevents economics from parading as an ersatz ethics and warns ethics against ignoring economic realities. We turn then to a fuller presentation of economics as a Value-laden science.

Economics as Axiology

Given the interpenetration of ontology, epistemology and axiology, it should come as no surprise that most of the ideas already encountered will be run through again, but now from their axiological purport.

Economics is an axiology because, as we have seen, it studies the Value, utility, that is, the perception of the usefulness of things for which reason people desire and prefer them as means to higher purposes, goals or Values. Even economists, like Smith or Ricardo, who failed to see the analytic importance of utility, took for granted that economics was about useful things, the 'necessities, conveniences and comforts' of life. Where economics differs as an axiology is in studying useful things as scarce and drawing the implications of that scarcity.

The condition of scarcity -- here we go again -- has two interrelated sources: the niggardliness of nature and the insatiability of human wants. The physical universe is not lacking in what sustains human life. To the contrary, it is bountiful even according to our meager knowledge of what this tiny speck of dust in the galaxies of stars contains. But Mother Earth yields her bounty with reluctance. No less reluctant is the human planning, effort and skill which is necessary to unlock that bounty.

Considered in itself, however, human husbandry could conceivably overcome scarcity. Certainly the productive capacity of the Sumerian Cities of 2500 B.C. could satisfy the wants of Cro-Magnon men and women and that of modern economies could satiate the wanting of the people in the Roman Empire. It is no less indisputable that today's economic abundance experiences greater scarcity than yesterday's dearth. World population, of course, has increased from millions to billions, but even on a per capita basis wealth and the possession of material goods have vastly increased. History reveals an inexorable increase in man's wanting for more material goods, and no government and no ascetic motivation has stopped it. Indeed in someone like Mother Theresa of Calcutta one finds combined the most exalted religious motive with a ravenous hunger for material goods. Why? needs some explication.

The answer is given in the view of the human person as a union, in some way or other about which philosophers will differ, of a material sub-stratum and non-material aspirations. Man, though bound to, is not limited to a physical here and now. A person, that is to say, is a creature of insatiable needs. Contemporary psychology -- Maslow, Fromm, Allport come to mind[12]-- in updating Aristotle's picture of the happy man, have detailed human needs for nutrition, protection, creating and procreating, self-esteem, knowledge, responsibility, love and the like. These needs are ordered hierarchically, but all by definition must be fulfilled in some sense for rounded human development. Some of these needs are repetitive but temporarily satiable; others, like knowing and loving, experience no surcease. Taken together the needs of man are boundless.

Here the economist's distinction between needs and wants is most serviceable, needs referring to human purpose and fulfillment, wants to the materials goods, time, energy and the like which are means to achieving needs. They are, given man's materiality, the only way to satisfy his unlimited needs and are at the same time universally and inevitably scarce. Even contemplation, while requiring less material means than three sets of tennis or building a home, uses at minimum scarce shelter, time and energy. Indeed in its most dramatic form of glorifying the deity -- Angkor Wat or St. Peter's -- it has consumed enormous amounts of material wealth, human skills, and artistic talent. Whatever one's hierarchy of needs and however one balances their fulfillment, he must utilize and want scarce material means.

But if means are scarce relative to needs, then no particular material good, or time, energy, space and the like and the want for it is necessary to realize a particular need. I need to shelter my family, and I may want this house as best meeting my need, but I do not need this house. Others could also service my need. Obviously, one can object, the need is not being serviced as well as it might have been by this house. This objection is well taken and exposes the hard fact of the human condition: all needs cannot be fulfilled completely and no need can be fulfilled perfectly. The fact is, as economics points out, every want has alternatives.

This fact produces the fundamental economic rationality, that, given needs, alternative wants, and scarcity, a person will change his wants from one good to another as their relative costs change. This logic becomes locked into conviction when all sacrifices of money, goods, time, energy, status and the rest are included in costs. As we have seen, this rationality is implicit in every economic decision. It may not be so apparent in consumer demand where a given price may motivate one customer to buy more than he or she intended, another less, and another not at all. But it shouts loud and clear in the complaint "We can't afford it." For this seldom pleads lack of money but rather that buying this commodity entails too much sacrifice of others yielding greater satisfaction.

Consumer choice, as we saw earlier, is seldom an all-or-nothing but most often a more-or-less decision. The usual explanation, that successive amounts of anything yields diminishing satisfaction, while a satisfactory rationale for substitution in most cases, does not apply as well to addiction. For the addict wants increasing dosages in order to maintain the same or to increase the level of satisfaction. Here complementarity provides a more telling rationale. For man is a creature of many needs and many wants, whose fulfillment must be kept in balance. A hungry student studies poorly; a sumptious repast aggravates a toothache; a hypochondriac worries about every pleasure. Experience testifies that satisfactions complement each other. This fact is the basis for most product differentiation, which is really packaging complementary satisfactions in different ways. Consequently, the basic irrationality of addiction, whether of drugs, alcohol, skiing or anything, is that the addict spends his substance on the one satisfaction, sacrificing not only those wants necessary for his full development as a person but even those which would enhance the pleasures of his addiction. Beyond this complementarity plays a more objective role. Like substitution it is of the essence of exchange, for buyers cannot buy unless sellers will sell and sellers cannot achieve their purposes unless buyers achieve theirs.

On the side of supply the substitution principle is called _comparative advantage_: the simple criterion that between two jobs, two product lines, two industrial outputs one chooses that yielding the higher net return. While simple, the choice may not be obvious. A woman, who is indifferent between being a top-notch legal secretary or a run-of-the-mill lawyer, would in following comparative advantage choose the latter because even mediocre lawyers make more than outstanding secretaries. Even less obvious is that in choosing according to one's own comparative advantage a person creates a comparative advantage for someone else. In abandoning typing for writing briefs, the lady lawyer creates another secretarial position. So, too, the efficiency of one firm in handling the more profitable large orders creates opportunities for less efficient firms to handle smaller orders. As General Motors increased its efficiency in producing automobiles it spun off their retailing to other firms.

Like demand, comparative advantage follows gain maximizing and cost minimizing rationales, gain being the higher revenue of the one endeavor against the sacrifice of the lower revenue from the other. Like demand, too, it has a time dimension. Serviceable machinery will often be replaced by more productive, and profitable lines phased out in favor of lines expected to be more profitable. In such decisions, of course, risk-taking and waiting for a return enter as considerations. Finally, like demand comparative advantage is not fixed once and for all, but is affected by changing supply conditions, changing technology, changing customer preferences. It suffers erosion from diminishing returns. As output increases, productive facilities become crowded, management encounters more red tape, less efficient labor is hired and selling costs increase. Thus increasing output becomes more costly and the initial advantage diminished.

Complementarity is even more apparent on the supply side. Supplying product requires hiring labor skills, raw materials, tools and machinery, and energy. The demand for productive resources is derived from the demand for product. A firm will hire more labor -- substitute labor for money -- provided the additional output promises to bring in revenue greater than the additional labor costs. Complementarity is obvious: no labor, no product; no product, no sales. Complementarity extends to the productive mix itself, the proportions with which various inputs are combined in production. While labor can replace machinery and more frequently machinery labor, neither can be eliminated entirely. Indeed the reverse is often the case. New machines, for example, can make labor so much more productive that actually more labor is hired. Finally, complementarity extends beyond production. For the very income generated as wages, interests and profits in production increases the overall demand for goods. Thus the circle of interdependence is closed: production generates demand; demand motivates production.

Substitution and complementarity not only cause economic change but they are the cohesive factors which holds the system together. More importantly, mutual gain is the very condition for individual gain. Indeed every exchange is premised on the anticipation of both exchangers' being better off after than before the exchange. Thus economic Value is created, and both parties can gain and neither necessarily loses. Besides this universal way, economists recognize three particular avenues by which gain is distributed throughout the economy. We have seen them several times. Consumers can realize a surplus when the price they actually pay is less than they would have paid for a commodity. People call this a bargain, and for many bargain-hunting is their favorite sport. Profits are well known but not generally understood. This is a gain a business realizes above all its opportunity costs, including most importantly the opportunity costs of money invested in the business. Finally, the least known is economic rent, the gain suppliers of space, land, natural resources and especially human skills realize when they are paid more than they would be willing to take. Thus gain can be realized not only generally through exchange but in whatever role one plays in the economy.

Against this somewhat roseate picture must be placed a somewhat harsher reality. Not only does the economy support my aspirations but it constrains them. For I realize my Values by choosing economic goods whose price is set by an objective exchange process in which my influence is microscopic. Choice imposes a trade-off, not according to what I would like or what I consider right or just, but according to the market's mandates. Such mandates seem harsher when the market caters more to mass than my particular tastes, and, even worse, when firms, unions and government agencies, possessing market power, can influence prices to their advantage and against mine. Resorting to substituting, in pursuit of my self-interest, seems more a response of frustration than of gain-seeking, unless and until a measurable minority of like-minded customers begin to affect the market.

While substitution is a form of competition among goods, it is ultimately competition among people, each trying to outbid others for what is wanted. It is reflected in the point and counter-point between buyers and sellers, and among buyers for commodities and among sellers for money. Substitution in the macro-sense sets the demands of government against that of the private sector and in the private sector investment in future output against present consumption. Substitution is basic to the intergenerational conflict between the present and future values of natural resources and the environment.

Competition, therefore, sets the tone of the economy. Where its tension diminishes, the economy becomes slack and change slows down. For competition motivates shifting from lower-valued to higher-valued uses, from higher costs to lower costs, from lesser advantage to greater, from present value to future value. Competition and the resulting change are perhaps the most distressful features of an abundant economy. Its concomitant requirement constantly to calculate gains against costs is wearisome and for many distasteful.

Complementarity is no less a hard task-master, and no less an organizational principle of the economy. Trade cannot exist long on the basis of force but will flourish only on the mutual surrender of goods to gain. Exchange requires consulting another's interest. Buyers create sellers and sellers must service buyers. Profitable enterprise requires a willing work force and employability is premised on profitability. Exploiting one's comparative advantage necessitates creating a comparative advantage for someone else. In order to gain one must allow others to gain. Complementarity, cooperation and mutuality are obvious operational principles in traditional societies which could not survive unless these principles are active in the community. But they are no less necessary, though perhaps not so apparent, in market and command economies. In the harsh world of scarcity, substitution and complementarity are hard masters. But without them the lot of men would be worse.

An Economics Compendium

Before proceeding to examine how economic and ethical principles interact, we can, as we did with the ethics, summarize the preceeding in a compendium of principles for economic action.

1. As with ethics economic rationality begins with myself, my talents training and education, opportunities, ambitions, my leisure-work preferences and my willingness to undertake risk, not in isolation from but in relation to others with comparable abilities and aspirations.

2. Whatever my vision of the good life, I must act within a context of constraint. My unlimited needs are confined within the limits of available material means. No aspiration can be perfectly fulfilled; every want must be kept in balance with all other wants.

3. Thus scarcity imposes sacrifice, a trade-off of what is less for what is more wanted, the less for the more profitable. Economic choice implies competition, choosing within constraints imposed not only by limited resources but by others' wants and desires. I can obtain what I want only by outbidding others in what they want.

4. Economic rationality is not just an intellectual exercise but a hard practical wisdom of substituting what will entail lesser sacrifice for what entails greater, of preserving the complementarity of wants, not satisfying one to the exclusion of others, and of recognizing the complementarity of gain, that I gain only by allowing others to gain.

5. Finally, economic choice is fraught with failure. No getting is had without giving up something. No aspiration is fully achieved. No wanting fully satisfied. Since choice is of an uncertain future, the risk of failure is always present. Yet it is precisely in submitting to this discipline that values are created, gain realized, and wealth and income generated not only for myself but for others as well.

ETHICS AND ECONOMICS: THEIR INTERACTION

Even a cursory comparison of the two compendia reveals their intermeshing. Both deal with the same context of action, myself with my needs, capabilities, circumstances and opportunities, and most importantly the network of human relations within which I am immersed. Both, that is, deal with reality. Both on the other hand, imply a vision, a turning toward an ideal, the one of fulfilling economic wants, the other of achieving human needs. Each proposes a rationality: economics that of choosing the more for the less preferred; ethics that of preferring the more over the less absolute Value. Each is a praxis, not just an intellectual exercise but a doing. Each implies acting within a context of social restraints and supports, in one the market context of supply and demand, in the other in the context of the rights and goods of others. Each is fraught with failure: every economic good is achieved by sacrificing something else, the ethical ideal progressively reveals itself in our acknowledging our very failures to live up to it. Each, in sum, is a dialectic between what I am and what I am not but aspire to become.

While economic and ethical principles interact throughout the course of acting, the two moments of initiation and end or purpose of action deserve special scrutiny.

At the beginning of action, the constraints of scarcity are more apparent. For every human act and aspiration can be realized only by using material means which are never sufficient, generally or for the task at hand. Every human dream begins with inadequate capital funding. Moreover and consequently, every aspiration requires sacrifice, seldom a total sacrifice but always a scaling down of other hopes and expectations. The ethical ideal, however pictured, Aristotelian happiness, the Pauline vision of putting on Christ, or any other conception of the ideal human, requires facing the hard fact of scarcity as an universal and inevitable element in the human condition.

Scarcity, therefore, provides the first test of Value espousal. Setting one's steps toward a goal, knowing that the goal will never be fully realized and not foreseeing all the sacrifices entailed, requires both a faith and a courageous hope. Yet the sincerity of so aspiring is supported by economic rationality which insists that means leading to a more desired end are, thereby, more to be valued. Any goal worth aspiring to is worth choosing the means to realize it.

Even more so, economic rationality, though morally neutral, is a kind of pedagogue of virtue. (Pedagogue is here taken in its original meaning not as the schoolmaster but the slave who conducts the reluctant youth to school.)

Certainly, economic rationality is a kind of prudence, balancing the good one must forego for the good gained. Economic choice requires assuming responsibility for a present decision about an uncertain future. There is a courage in assuming risk that this purchase will fulfill its promised satisfaction, that this job will be better than the last, that this production decision will be profitable. Every exchange is a sharing. My realizing my economic goals necessitates my considering others' goals and hopes, and the more equitable the sharing the more likely the exchange relation will last. Finally, economic rationality requires moderation. Rational choice is set within a complex of wanting, and satisfying one want or set of wants must be balanced against satisfying others.

The compatibility of economic rationality with ethical rationality expressed above differs sharply with contemporary views. The Marcusan Great Refusal, for example, affirms that economic rationality, at least in its capitalist context, has no other meaning than to enslave people to material goods. Contemporary Mandevillians recognize only an economic rationality inspired by self-interest so that economic abundance can be sustained only by sensual satisfaction and self-aggrandizement. Positivists parade economic rationality as an *ersatz* ethics in that, given a context in which no one has advantage over others, the free play of economic choice will produce, if not just men, a socially just society. Our personalist view, perhaps, is matched closest by the Puritan Ethics, the only other ethic specifically formulated to address the problem of increasing economic abundance. Indeed hard work, prudent expenditure, a strict exchange justice, and conservation of gain are elements in each. Where the Personalist sharply differs from the Puritan Ethics is in denying the assumption that economic success in itself demonstrates moral probity, that acquisitiveness is its own justification.

The Puritan Ethic and, more so, the other "economic ethics" all lack a teleology, a purpose or final cause for economic action. All fail in some respect and some totally in providing a vision of what the human person should be or become. Thus, if ethics is muted somewhat in the beginning of action, it becomes the dominant theme in considering the purpose of acting. Only a vision of the ideal human being and how human needs and wants are blended into this ideal can give meaning to the often frenetic pace of economic activity. To gain is meaningless unless one specifies what is to be gained, what goal or purpose is to be realized.

This specification must be specified in turn. The problem is not that people have no goals. They do seek some change in themselves or in their condition which they perceive as betterment. The real problem consists in establishing a hierarchy of goals and aspirations among my many nutritional, environmental, social, intellectual, creative, and spiritual needs, which completes me, given my native talents, physical and social circumstances, and opportunities, as a human person. It is the same problem of developing a hierarchy of Values, not as some abstract ideal but as operational in directing both my daily intercourse with others as well as my economic choosing. This is the specific and unique field for the ethical enterprise. It simply exists on a higher plane of intentionality than economic rationality. Indeed, the latter is meaningless, or worse, destructive without it.

The obvious danger to social order of an economic rationality without social and ethical norms is detailed in Tawney's classic, The Acquisitive Society.[13]

o On a more personal plane, the peddler principles of calculating gain against costs, estimating risks, and weighing advantage can dessicate the spirit of generosity, of love,
o of giving without getting. But a greater personal danger lies in playing the game of gain and loss for its own sake. Rightly philosophers, Marxist no less than Classical and
o Christian, have condemned the infinite appetite for wealth, not so much as an appetite, nor, strictly speaking, as infinite. But the gain-motivation is condemned when
o and because it proposes no purpose beyond accumulating wealth for its own sake. It makes a means an end. "Men will always confuse means with ends," writes Tawney, "if
o they are without any clear conception that it is the ends, not the means, which matter."[14] The personalist slant of this book stressed the moral danger, resulting from the
o affluent psyche, of dissipating increasing income and material abundance in satisfying sensual and trivial wants, and in vain displays of material superiority.

Fare Well: Fare Thee Well

Countering this danger is the dominant theme of the book, played in many variations: the value of value-thinking over price-thinking; the importance for personality growth of refining one's Value hierarchy; moderation as an internal control on the wealth-appetite, what is enough being defined by one's Value aspirations; social justice as a virtue recognizing the right of others as social beings to benefit from the general economic well-being; and, finally, discovering in affluence a manifestation of God's bounty, bringing the obligation both to share it with others and to be detached from it, using it as means to, not the end of living.

This theme was then played out in the real world of mammoth productive, commercial and financial institutions, in the struggle to match contributions to with distributing the benefits from economic productions, in a financial system where an evanescent credit-debt effects exchanges, and where, finally, the individual person must act within a net of economic power centers and is caught in the inter-meshing of the economic and political order. Throughout was stressed the need for and the possibility of moderating one's economic hopes, maintaining a sense of community, and the integrity of one's personal aspirations.

In all this ethical intentionality has primacy. It should play a role, though perhaps sotto voce, in the daily litany of preferences and choices which make up ordinary living. Kenneth Boulding has an appropriate passage in which he suggests, paralleling the idea that economic rationality is the pedagogue of virtue, that disordered affections can foul up economic rationality:

> "It would be interesting to go through the seven deadly sins and to see them as critique of unhealthy preferences; pride preventing learning and feed-back, anger preventing cool and rational judgment, lust involving inordinate desire which destroys rational choice, envy involving malevolence at the welfare of another, greed or covetousness involving not only inordinate desire but lack of benevolence and a crippling of identity, gluttony likewise involving a loss of restraint and rational choice, and sloth involving the decay of the decision-making power itself."[15]

In the broader sense of the overall direction of our life, the ethical effort is paramount. In every conscious act we commit our selves, risking our selves in realizing or in failing to realize our ideals. Where this vision lacks specificity or is blurred in the flux of events, the ordinary good person with ordinary good intentions dissipates income, time, and energy haphazardly pursuing goals at cross-purposes with each other, all his effort summing up to frustration and disillusionment. This, more than the moral shipwreck of the willfully evil, the materialism of the indifferent milking affluence for whatever pleasure it offers, the moral bitterness of the self-righteous or of the dispossessed at "society's" moral bankruptcy, this, the failure of the vast majority of ordinarily good people to keep their Value sights high and in focus, is the real tragedy of affluence.

As the famous husband and wife chemists, Pierre and Marie Curie, got nothing from months of toil boiling tons and tons of pitchblende, but a tiny stain of radium glowing in the dark, so we may find the last paragraph a final distillation of our efforts. If so, it is a farewell which is really a "Fare thee well!"

FOOTNOTES

CHAPTER ONE

[1]Adam Smith, Wealth of Nations, ed. Edward Canaan, New York: The Modern Library, 1937, pp. 78-9.

[2]George Katona, Psychological Economics, New York: Elsevier, 1975, p. 26. This distillation of over a quarter-century experience in monitoring changes in consumer behavior and attitudes cannot be recommended too highly.

[3]Sir Josiah Child, A New Discourse of Trade, printed at John Everingham: London, 1693; Preface.

[4]Z.J. Lipowski, "Sensory and Information Inputs Overload: Behavioral Effects", Comprehensive Psychiatry, Vol. 16, No. 3, pp. 199-221.

[5]Louis-Joseph Lebret, O.P., The Last Revolution: The Destiny of Over- and Underdeveloped Nations, New York: Sheed and Ward, 1965.

[6]Norman Macrae, The Neurotic Trillionaire, New York: Harcourt, Brace & World, 1970, p. 8.

[7]For a good, though somewhat jaundiced, description, see Robert Nisbet, The Degradation of the Academic Dogma: The University in America, 1945-70, New York: Basic Books, 1971, esp. Part II.

CHAPTER TWO

[1]Aristotle, Nicomachean Ethics, trans. W.D. Ross, Oxford: Clarendon Press, 1905; Bk. V, chs. 4-5.

[2]Augustine, The City of God, trans. M. Dods, Chicago: Encyclopedia Brittanica, 1952; Bk. XI, ch. 16.

[3]Thomas Aquinas, Summa Theologica, trans. Fathers of the English Dominican Province, New York: Benziger, 1911-20; II-II, Q 77.

[4]Joseph A. Schumpeter, History of Economic Analysis, New York: Oxford Press, 1954, p. 97.

[5]The best short presentation of the intellectual filiation among Petty, Cantillon, and Quesnay can be found in Schumpeter, Ibid., Part II, ch. 4.

[6]David Hume, Writings on Economics, ed. E. Rotwein, Madison: University of Wisconsin Press, 1959.

[7]Adam Smith, Wealth of Nations, op. cit.; Bks. 1 and 2.

[8]David Ricardo, The Principles of Political Economy and Taxation, New York: Everyman's Library, 1912; esp. ch. 1-8.

[9]John Stuart Mill, Principles of Political Economy, Boston: Little, Brown, 1848.

[10]Karl Marx, Capital, ed. F. Engels, trans. S. Moore and E. Aveling, Chicago: Encyclopedia Brittanica, 1952.

[11]Again Schumpeter, op. cit., is the most convenient short account, pp. 825-9.

[12]Alfred Marshall, Principles of Economics, New York: Macmillan, 1890.

[13]See Tibor Scitovsky, The Joyless Economy, New York: Oxford University Press, 1977; ch. 5.

[14]Helen H. Lamale, "Poverty: The Word and the Reality", Monthly Labor Review, Vol. 88, July 1965, pp. 822-27.

[15]Adam Smith, The Theory of Moral Sentiments, New York: Published by Evert Duyrinck et. al., 1822, p. 46 and p. 153.

[16]Thorstein Veblen, The Theory of the Leisure Class, New York: Macmillan, 1912.

CHAPTER THREE

[1]See, for example, Lewis Mumford, The Transformations of Man, New York: Harper & Row, 1956.

[2]Pierre Teilhard de Chardin, The Phenomenon of Man, New York: Harper & Row, 1965, and The Divine Milieu, New York: Harper, 1960.

[3]Eduard Spranger, Types of Men, trans. P. Pijors, Hulle: Niemeyer Verlag, 1928, pp. 88-106.

[4]Nicholas Rescher, Introduction to Value Theory, Englewood Cliffs: Prentice-Hall, 1960, pp. 2-3.

[5]Robert C. Angell, Free Society and Moral Crisis, Ann Arbor: University of Michigan Press, 1965, p. 18.

[6]Gordon W. Allport, Pattern and Growth in Personality, New York: Holt, Rinehart, and Winston, 1965, p. 454 and pp. 126-7.

[7]Rescher, op. cit., p. 60.

[8]This section is almost totally owing to Max Scheler, Formalism in Ethics and Non-formal Ethics of Values, trans. M. Frings and R. Funk, Evanston: Northwestern University Press, 1973.

[9]Ibid., p. 99.

[10]Ibid., pp. 105-110.

[11]Gunnar Myrdal, An American Dilemma, New York: Harper & Row, 1944, is a classic chronicle of how contradictory Social Values can be held simultaneously for centuries.

[12]John Locke, Some Considerations on the Consequences of the Lowering of Interest, 1691, in Works, London, 1777, Vol. II, p. 28.

[13]David Ricardo, The Principles of Political Economy and Taxation, Homewood: Irwin, 1963, p. 161.

[14]Karl Marx, Capital, op. cit., p. 13.

[15]W. Stanley Jevons, The Theory of Political Economy, 2nd ed. from Classics of Economic Theory, ed. G.W. Wilson, Bloomington: Indiana University Press, 1964, p. 545.

[16]Friedrich von Wieser, Social Economics, trans. A.F. Hinrichs, New York: Adelphi, 1927, pp. 144-5.

[17]Ibid., p. 39.

[18]Alfred Marshall, Economics of Industry, London: Macmillan, 1958, pp. 61-2.

[19]Scheler, op. cit., p. 104.

[20]Rescher, op. cit., p. 134.

[21]Eugene Böhm-Bawerk, Positive Theory of Capital, New York: Speckert & Co., 1930, p. 159.

[22]Thorstein Veblen, op. cit.

[23]H.R. Trevor-Roper, The Crisis of the 17th Century, New York: Harper & Row, 1956, pp. 80-89.

[24]For Ayn Rand's individualism her essays For the New Intellectual, New York: Random House, 1961, and The Virtue of Selfishness, New York: New American Library, 1961 are recommended; for B.F. Skinner, his Beyond Freedom and Dignity, New York: Knopf, 1971, and for Herbert Marcuse, his One-Dimensional Man, Boston: Beacon Press, 1964, are suggested.

[25]Marcuse, op. cit., passim.

CHAPTER FOUR

[1]Aquinas, op. cit., I-II, q. 84 al, a2.

[2]Aristotle, Politics, trans. B. Jowett, The Works of Aristotle, ed. W.D. Ross, London: Oxford University Press, Bk. I, ch. 9.

[3]Plato, Republic, from The Dialogues of Plato, trans. B. Jowett, London: Oxford University Press, 1953, IV, 430-443.

[4]Plato, Laws, op. cit., V, 740-6.

[5]Aristotle, Ethics, op. cit., Bk II, ch. 7.

[6]Aristotle, Politics, op. cit., Bk 1, ch. 9.

[7]Augustine, On Christian Doctrine, op. cit., Bk I, chs. 3-4.

[8]Aquinas, op. cit., I-II, q. 84 al.

[9]Ibid., II-II, q. 77 a4.

[10]John Calvin, Institutes of the Christian Religion, ed. J.T. McNeill, trans. F.L. Battles, in The Library of Christian Classics, vol. 20, Philadelphia: The Westminster Press, p. 798.

[11]Ibid., pp. 719-725.

[12]Montesquieu, The Spirit of the Laws, trans. T. Nugent, rev. J.V. Prichard, London: G. Bell & Sons, Bk V, Ch. 7 sec. 6.

[13]Bernard Mandeville, Fable of the Bees, 2nd Edition, London, 1723.

[14]David Hume, A Treatise on Human Nature, p. 452 and Of Interest, p. 53, op. cit.

[15]For a fuller treatment see Peter Danner, "Sympathy and Exchangeable Value", Review of Social Economy, Dec. 1976.

[16]Richard Hofstadter, Social Darwinism in American Thought, Boston: The Beacon Press, 1955.

[17]R.H. Tawney, The Acquisitive Society, London: G. Bell & Sons, 1921.

[18]G.W.F. Hegel, The Philosophy of Right, trans. T.M. Knox, London: Oxford University Press, 1967, III, par. 240.

[19]J.S. Mill, On Liberty, Chicago: Encyclopedia Brittanica, Vol. 43, pp. 304-12, 1955.

[20]Albert Einstein, "Why Socialism?", Monthly Review, May 1949.

[21]George Katona, Psychological Economics, op. cit., p. 400.

[22]For a fuller treatment, see Tibor Scitovsky, The Joyless Economy, op. cit., Chapter Three.

CHAPTER FIVE

[1]Aristotle, Ethics, op. cit., V, p. 1129.

[2]Josef Pieper, Justice, trans. L.E. Lynch, New York: Pantheon Books, 1955.

[3]Plato, Republic, op. cit., pp. 357-366.

[4]Ibid., pp. 587-8.

[5]Augustine, City of God, op. cit., ch. 21.

[6]Aquinas, op. cit., I, p. 95 al, ans.

[7]Aristotle, op. cit., bk V, ch. 1.

[8]Ibid., ch. 2-4.

[9]Aquinas, op. cit., II-II, q. 58 a. 9 res. 2.

[10]Ibid., al, ans.

[11]Ibid., a6.

[12]Thomas Hobbes, Leviathan, Everyman, New York: E.P. Dutton, 1950, p. 120.

[13]Baruch Spinoza, Ethics, trans. W.H. White, Cambridge: Oxford Press, Part IV, Prop. 37, Schol. 2.

[14]Immanuel Kant, The Metaphysics of Morals, trans. T.K. Abbott, Great Books, Chicago: Encyclopedia Brittanica, 1952, Vol. 42, p. 275.

[15]Immanuel Kant, Science of Right, trans. W. Hastie, ibid., p. 400.

[16]G.W.F. Hegel, Philosophy of Right, op. cit., Introd. para 31. The student will find the Additions the most helpful.

[17]G.W.F. Hegel, The Philosophy of History, trans. J. Sibree, op. cit., pp. 364-5.

[18]J.S. Mill, Utilitarianism, Great Books, Chicago: Encyclopedia Brittanica, 1952, Vol. 43, p. 468.

[19]Pieper, op. cit., p. 26.

[20]This follows the thought of J. Th. Delos, O.P. in La Justice, ed. M.S. Gillet, O.P. and J. Th. Delos, O.P., Paris: Desclee et Cie, 1948, Vol. 1, p. 193.

[21]Alfred Marshall, Principles of Economics, 8th ed., New York: Macmillan, 1961, p. 103.

CHAPTER SIX

[1]Karl Rahner, S.J., *Christian in the Market Place*, trans. Hastings, New York: Sheed & Ward, 1966, p. 21.

[2]*Ibid.*, pp. 22-3.

[3]*Ibid.*, pp. 23-6.

[4]*Ibid.*, p. 26.

[5]Betty Bock, *Statistical Games and the "200 Largest" Industrials: 1954 and 1968*, New York: The Conference Board, 1970.

[6]Helen H. Lamale, "Poverty: The Word and the Reality", *op. cit.*

[7]C. Delisle Burns, *The First Europe*, London: Allen & Unwin, 1947, pp. 389-91.

[8]See in particular Marx's contrasting descriptions of the poverty-wealth dialectic in socialist man and capitalist man. *Economic and Philosophic Manuscripts of 1844*, trans. M. Milligan, ed. E. Struick, New York, International Publishers, 1964, pp. 143-7.

[9]See Philip Mulhern, O.P., *Dedicated Poverty*, New York: Alba House, 1970. Most particularly his interpretation of spiritual poverty in the light of Vatican II, ch. VI.

[10]Albert Gelin, *Les Pauvres de Yahve*, Paris: Les Editions du Cerf, 1955, p. 13-28.

[11]*Ibid.*, p. 10.

[12]Pierre Grelot, "La Pauvrete' Dans L'Ecriture Sainte", *Christus*, 8, 1961.

[13]Alphonse Humbert, C.SS.R., "L'Attitude des Premiers Chretiens Devant Les Biens Temporels" in *Studia Moralia* IV, 1966.

[14]Christopher Dawson, *The Formation of Christendom*, New York: Sheed & Ward, 1967, p. 132.

[15]Burns, *op. cit.*, pp. 407-8.

[16]Stephen A. Yonick O.F.M., introductory chapters to Covenant with God's Poor by Auspicius van Corstanji, O.F.M., tr. G. Reidy, Chicago: Franciscan Herald Press, 1966, pp. 51-2.

[17]Pierre Teilhard de Chardin, The Divine Milieu, op. cit., p. 85.

CHAPTER SEVEN

[1]Neil H. Jacoby, "The Myth of the Corporate Economy", The Conference Board Record, June 1971, p. 49.

[2]Information supplied by Public Relations Department, Allis-Chalmers Corporation, including an address by David C. Scott, its President, "Managerial Vision and Craftsmanship: To Meet Human Needs", at the "1979 Wisconsin Dinner" of the Newcomen Society, February 20, 1979.

[3]Cf. George Cawston and A.H. Keane, The Early Chartered Companies, New York: Burt Franklin, 1968, esp. pp. 4-9.

[4]Cf. A. Merryn Davies, Clive of Plassey, New York: Scribner's, 1939, esp. pp. 64-66.

[5]F.J. Scherer, Industrial Market Structure and Economic Performance, New York: Rand McNally, 1971, pp. 49-50.

[6]These arguments are the familiar Aristotelian defenses of the right to private property, Politics, op. cit., 1261-64.

[7]Adolph Berle, The Twentieth Century Capitalist Revolution, New York: Harcourt, Brace, 1954, ch. III.

[8]See for example, Eugene L. Cox, The Eagles of Savoy, Princeton: Princeton Univ. Press, 1974, esp. pp. 452-60.

[9]Beardsley Ruml, Tomorrow's Business, New York: Rinehart & Company, 1945, p. 99.

[10]William H. Whyte, Jr., The Organization Man, New York: Doubleday Anchor Books, 1956.

CHAPTER EIGHT

[1]The financial dealings recounted here were pieced out from articles, appearing in *The Wall Street Journal*, over the period from October 8, 1963 to January 30, 1967.

[2]U.S. Department of Commerce, Bureau of the Census, *Statistical Abstract of the United States, 1978*, Table 881.

[3]The two major federal legislations, the Truth in Lending Act, 1968 and the Fair Credit Reporting Act, 1971 set off a flurry of comparable legislation in state capitals and aroused the interest of Ralph Nader's Center for Responsive Law (*New York Times*, July 30, 1971, p. 37, col. 2).

[4]Raymond de Roover, *The Rise and Decline of the Medici Bank*, Cambridge, Mass.: Harvard University Press, 1963, pp. 17-19 and Ch. VI, "Banking and the Money Market at the Time of the Medici Bank", pp. 108-141, *passim*.

[5]*Statistical Abstract*, *op. cit.*, tables 525, 528, 538, 540, 542, 727, 728, 866, 870, 871, 895, 898, 899, 902 and 905.

[6]John T. Noonan, Jr., *The Scholastic Analysis of Usury*, Cambridge, Mass.: Harvard University Press, 1957, pp. 1-7.

[7]Lien-Sheng Yang, *Money and Credit in China*, Cambridge, Mass.: Harvard University Press, 1952, p. 9 and pp. 93-98. Henri Pirenne, *Medieval Cities*, Princeton, N.J.: Princeton University Press, 1925, p. 126.

[8]Noonan, *op. cit.*, pp. 295-300.

[9]*Ibid.*, pp. 202-203.

[10]Joseph A. Schumpeter, *The History of Economic Analysis*, *op. cit.*, pp. 104-106.

[11]Georges Oudard, *The Amazing Life of John Law: The Man Behind the Mississippi Bubble*, trans. by G.E.C. Masse, New York: Payson & Clarke, Ltd., 1928.

[12]This de-materialization of money is described, though not specifically named, in Norman Angell, *The Story of Money*, Garden City, New York: Garden City Publishing Co., Inc., 1929, chs. III, IV and X.

[13]Lawrence A. Welsch, "A Proposal to Automatic Money", Business Topics, Autumn 1966, pp. 59-68.

[14]Published monthly by Board of Governors, Federal Reserve System, Washington, D.C.

[15]Noonan, op. cit., pp. 312-13. Also Bernard W. Dempsey, Interest and Usury, American Council on Public Affairs, Washington, D.C., 1943, p. 124, pp. 154-5 and pp. 159-63.

[16]Franklin D. Jones, "Historical Development of the Law of Business Competition", Yale Law Journal, Vol. 35, No. 8 (June 1926) pp. 905-38; and Vol. 36, No. 3 (January 1927) pp. 367-72.

[17]Oudard, op. cit., pp. 220-33.

CHAPTER NINE

[1]U. Viglino, "Metaphysical Dimensions of Work", Philosophy, 1961, 5, pp. 121-136.

[2]J.S. Warmath, Toward a Theology of Work in a Technological Society, unpublished doctoral dissertation, The Southern Baptist Theological Seminary, 1968, p. 14.

[3]Cicero, On Moral Obligation, tr. J. Higginbotham, Berkeley: University of California Press, 1967; Bk. I, ch. 42, pp. 92-3.

[4]Warmath, ibid., p. 81.

[5]Walter M. Abbott, S.J., The Documents of Vatican II, New York: American Press, 1966, p. 262.

[6]Bernard W. Dempsey, S.J., The Functional Economy, Englewood Cliffs: Prentice-Hall, 1958, pp. 137-145.

[7]U.S. Department of Labor, Handbook of Labor Statistics, 1977, Washington, D.C.: Bureau of Labor Statistics, p. 272 and U.S. Department of Labor, Three Standards of Living for an Urban Family of Four Persons, Washington, D.C.: Bureau of Labor Statistics, 1967, p. 3.

[8]Handbook of Labor Statistics, 1975 and 1977, op. cit., Table 6.

[9]See Theodore Purcell, S.J., Blue Collar Man: Patterns of Dual Allegiance in Industry, Harvard University Press, 1960, esp. pp. 248-62.

[10]Handbook of Labor Statistics, 1975 and 1977, op. cit., Tables 1, 86 and 113 of 75 edition; and Tables 1, 76 and 105 of 1977 edition.

[11]William F. Glueck, Personnel: A Diagnostic Approach, Dallas: Business Publications, Inc., 1978, pp. 556-7.

[12]Handbook of Labor Statistics, op. cit., Table 162 from 1975 edition and Table 141 from 1977 edition.

[13]Karl Marx, Capital I, ed. F. Engels, op. cit., V. 50, 1952, Chs. VII and XXV will give the basic elements of this theme which runs through the entire Marxian corpus.

[14]Bert L. Metzger, Profit Sharing in 38 Large Corporations, Evanston: Profit Sharing Research Foundation, 1978, passim.

[15]Joseph Schumpeter, History of Economic Analysis, op. cit., pp. 465-467.

[16]John Bates Clark, The Philosophy of Wealth, Boston: Ginn & Co., 1892, pp. 196-7.

CHAPTER TEN

[1]Adolph A. Berle, Power, New York: Harcourt, Brace & World, 1967, p. 60. Berle's work cannot be recommended too highly, for he writes from a background of a vast erudition as well as from experience in the exercise of power.

[2]The thought of these two paragraphs was suggested by an article of Kenneth W. Stikkers, "Max Scheler: Toward a Sociology of Space", Journal of the British Society for Phenomenology, October 1978.

[3]Robert A. Nisbet, Community and Power, New York: Galaxy, 1962, p. 49.

[4]Berle, op. cit., p. 216.

[5]Ibid., pp. 99-100.

[6]Robert J. Larner demonstrates that the overwhelming majority of the 500 largest industrial corporations are controlled by management groups. Management Control and the Large Corporation, Cambridge: Dunellen, 1970, pp. 69-117.

[7]Berle, op. cit., p. 19.

[8]Noonan, The Scholastic Analysis of Usury, op. cit., pp. 13-17.

[9]Nisbet, op. cit., pp. xiv-xv.

[10]Peter F. Drucker, Delbert C. Miller and Robert A. Dahl, Power and Democracy in America, ed. W. D'Antonio and H. Ehrlich, University of Notre Dame Press, 1961, p. 21.

[11]Berle, op. cit., p. 541.

[12]"Religious Rights Suppressed", Catholic League Newsletter, March, 1976.

[13]Nisbet, op. cit., p. 30.

[14]The Milwaukee Journal, September 7, 1978, p. 1, Col. 2-8.

[15]Nisbet, op. cit., p. 54.

[16]Saul Alinsky, Reveille for Radicals, Chicago: University of Chicago Press, 1946, p. 111.

[17]Nisbet, op. cit., p. 73.

[18]Berle, op. cit., p. 88.

CHAPTER ELEVEN

[1]Clarence Walton, The Ethics of Corporate Conduct, Prentice-Hall: Englewood Cliffs, 1977, p. 28.

[2]Alexis de Tocqueville, Democracy in America, ed. P. Bradley, New York: Vintage Books, pp. 336-7.

[3]Ibid.

[4]Alfred M. Skolnik and Sophie R. Dales, "Social Welfare Expenditures, Fiscal Year 1976", Social Security Bulletin, January 1977.

[5]Ibid.

[6]F.A. Hayek, "The New Confusion About 'Planning'", The Morgan Guarantee Survey, January 1976.

[7]Opinion Research Corporation, Public Opinion Index, End December, 1975, 8.

[8]Gabriel Hauge, The Economy: Private Initiative and Public Responsibility, School of Business Administration, University of Minnesota, 1969.

[9]George Cabot Lodge, "Managerial Implications of Ideological Change", in Ethics of Corporate Conduct, op. cit., p. 95.

[10]Jonathan Boswell, Social and Business Enterprise, London: George Allen & Unwin, Ltd., 1976, p. 200. The next few paragraphs are in debt to Boswell's thought here and in an as yet unpublished manuscript.

CHAPTER TWELVE

[1]Etienne Gilson, The Unity of Philosophic Experience, New York: C. Scribner's Sons, 1937, pp. 301-6.

[2]Adam Smith, The Wealth of Nations, op. cit., pp. 24-25.

[3]Philip F. Mulhern, Dedicated Poverty: Its History and Theology, op. cit.

[4]Daniel Villey, "Prolegomenes a L'Enseignment de la Philosophie Economique," Revue d'Economie Politique, V. 59, p. 377.

[5]Karl Jaspers, Introduction a la Philosophie, Paris: Aubier, 1951, p. 4.

[6]Villey, op. cit., p. 390.

[7]Alasdair MacIntyre, A Short History of Ethics, New York: Macmillan, 1966, p. 173.

[8] Max Scheler, Formalism in Ethics and Non-formal Ethics of Value, op. cit. Cf. Chapter III - "Affluence and Personality".

[9] MacIntyre, op. cit. This following section is largely owing to MacIntyre's treatment.

[10] Ibid., p. 209.

[11] For a good discussion of the 'arithmomorphic' vice and social engineering, see Nicolas Georgescu-Roegen, The Entropy Law and the Economic Process, Cambridge: Harvard Univ. Press, 1971, p. 141.

[12] Cf. Gordon W. Allport, Pattern and Growth in Personality, op. cit.; Eric Fromm, Man For Himself, New York: Holt, Rinehart and Winston, 1947, esp. ch. III; Abraham Maslow, Motivation and Personality, New York: Harper and Brothers, 1954.

[13] R.H. Tawney, The Acquisitive Society, op. cit.

[14] Ibid., p. 46.

[15] Kenneth Boulding, "Ethics of the Critique of Preferences", in Limited Resources and Social Policy, eds. W.M. Finnin, Jr., and G.A. Smith, Baton Rouge: Louisiana State Univ. Press, 1979, pp. 9-10.

INDEX